The Secrets of Money
A Guide for Everyone on
Practical Financial Literacy

Braun Mincher

Braun Media, LLC

Copies of the book are available at special quantity discounts for sales promotions, training, fundraising or educational use. The author is also available for speaking engagements, seminars and other multimedia presentations.

Published by:
Braun Media, LLC
P.O. Box 1079
Fort Collins, Colorado 80549-1079
www.BraunMincher.com

Printed in the United States of America

First Edition, First Printing (November 2007)

The Secrets of Money: A Guide for Everyone on Practical Financial Literacy
Braun Mincher
1. Title 2. Author 3. Personal Finance

Library of Congress Control Number: 2007904067

ISBN-10: 0-9797003-0-2
ISBN-13: 978-0-9797003-0-9

Acknowledgements

To my parents, who instilled in me the value of hard work, perseverance and taking the time to do the job right, I appreciate all of that you have done and continue to do for me.

To Angela—
You mean the world to me, I love you.

There are numerous additional people to thank and recognize who lent their assistance, guidance and support throughout this project, and without whom this book would have not been possible:

Andrew & Pam Bantham, Mark Bower, Rose Brinks, Kevin Brock, Jimmy Buffett, Chad Carden, Adam Carroll, Chuck Decker, Allen Dye, Barry Eastman, Brandy Ferner, Oliver Frascona, Jessica Gorham, Steve Harrison, Mary Hasl, Joel Hochman, Kevin Houchin, Michael Jensen, Doug Johnson, J. Michael Johnson, Rob Koellner, Mark Kross, Scoo Leary, Ian McBride, Randy Pfizenmaier, R. Bruce Potter, Ray Reeves, Ryan Smith, Jason Sullivan and Kerry Zukus

Disclaimer

This book contains the subjective opinions and ideas of the author. It is intended to provide helpful and informative material of a general nature on the subject matter covered. Although the author has researched the sources of information contained in this book, neither the author nor the publisher assume any responsibility for errors, inaccuracies, omissions or any other inconsistency herein. If you use the materials in this book, we hope you succeed, yet this book discusses financial management where each person is ultimately responsible for one's own success and failure. Accordingly, use of this publication shall be at your own risk. THERE ARE NO WARRANTIES, EXPRESS OR IMPLIED, INCLUDING FITNESS FOR A PARTICULAR PURPOSE MADE WITH RESPECT TO THIS MATERIAL. Although the author has used the names of friends and associates, such usage should not be interpreted as an endorsement or disparagement. In some cases, names have been changed; any perceived slights against people or organizations are unintentional. Reference to gender (masculine, feminine or neuter) shall include reference to the other gender.

Although the author is a licensed real estate broker, neither the publisher nor the author are engaged in rendering any type of legal, accounting, tax or other professional advice to the reader through this book or through the author's lectures or through any other media format derived from the content of this book. Nothing contained in this book creates any legal duty, fiduciary duty, or agency relationship.

The advice and strategies contained herein may not be suitable for your situation. Tax codes and other laws change frequently. The reader is instructed to seek independent advice from a competent attorney, tax advisor, real estate professional and/or other qualified advisor for his or her specific situation. These professionals are invaluable even to the author, but it is important to establish relationships with them before the need arises. (It always costs less to stay out of trouble than it does to get out of trouble). Laws and local customs are different from area to area, so the readers should work with their professional team to verify how important tax and legal matters are handled in their part of the country.

The author and the publisher expressly disclaim any duty, responsibility, liability, loss, or risk, personal or otherwise, that may be incurred as a direct or indirect consequence of the use or application of any of the contents of this book, lectures, or other media-based derivatives of this work.

Many designations of products and services referenced in this work are used by manufacturers and sellers to distinguish their products, and are claimed as trademarks by those companies. Where those designations appear in this book and the author or publisher was aware of a trademark claim, the designations have been printed with capital letters or ®. All trademarks are the property of their respective owners.

TABLE OF CONTENTS

Why I Wrote This Book

First, let me thank you for buying this book—you have made an important investment in your financial future by doing so. I hope that you will find the information to be useful to your specific situation and that you in turn will share it with those you care about. Second, you are encouraged to keep this book as a reference manual, referring back to specific chapters as you need them again in the future. Finally, this book is a compilation of multiple years of work and true passion; I hope that you enjoy reading it as much as I enjoyed writing it.

You've all probably heard the doom and gloom reports: The average American savings rate is now a *negative* number. American children are falling behind in math and reading scores. And don't even *think* about geography—we have young men and women fighting and dying in countries most of us can't even locate on a world map.

Personally, I have my own pet peeve: **financial literacy.**

Back in my day, my own normal, basic, public high school had 6 teachers of business. Today it has two. You're probably imagining that I'm some old coot rhapsodizing about the good old days and grousing about this new-fangled era of electric lights and hoochie-coochie music. Guess again. I'm still in my early 30s. The "old days" for me were only about fifteen years ago. We actually had computers, video games, and rap music way back then.

But I don't want you to think I've got an ax to grind against my old alma mater. Even today, my old school has it better than a lot of other schools in this country. They have elective classes in economics, accounting, and numerous other valuable life skills. Many other high schools have none of that. What they do have are three levels of calculus, AP courses in every type of hard science, and foreign language study from grammar school on up through the senior year of high school. Now, don't get on me for being a charlatan. View me as a lobbyist, and not for my own personal self-interest, either. I'm a modern, American capitalist and businessman. One could argue that I make most of my money off of the ignorance of others. So why should I care? Because I have a moral center. Anyone who tells you that the only way to make money in this world is to screw over someone else is lying to you. It is possible to be healthy, wealthy and wise without stealing another person's savings. I sleep well at night, and this book will only make me sleep better.

So my issue is this: why can't we have Hemingway and *The Wall Street Journal* in our schools? For while a handful of kids will really need those three levels of calculus (our nation's future engineers), I shall guarantee you from life experience that at least 99% of them will:

- Use a bank
- Have a check book
- Own a credit card
- Buy a car
- Own or rent a home
- Need a mortgage
- Have running water, electricity, and other utilities in said domicile
- Need health insurance
- Marry or have some sort of domestic partnership
- Want to retire someday
- Pay taxes
- Die

(Personally, I hope to be able to avoid the last one.)

I won't fool you into thinking this is a dumbed down, super-easy read. It's not. At the same time, you won't need a PhD to get through it, either. Although I dropped out during my 3rd year of college to grow my first business, I have more than the equivalent of an MBA from the school of hard knocks. But let me get on my soapbox again: Why must we keep lowering the bar and downsizing expectations? What you're about to read is the **minimum level of financial literacy every American should know in order to survive, period.**

Personally, I'm not the most voracious reader. I never pick up fiction—I find no time for it and it is, in the end, purely for entertainment purposes, and when I find time for entertainment I seek it elsewhere. But I do read a lot of what I expect to be constructive non-fiction— how-to books, industry journals, technical manuals and the like. Much of what is out there in the marketplace leaves me feeling wanting as a consumer. The bar has been lowered, lowered so close to the ground that many other so-called financial literacy books do nothing more than say—at a 2nd grade reading level—"Work hard; have a dream." The reader comes away with little in the way of actual constructive lessons he can really use or apply to his own situation.

Not this book.

This is not a "get rich quick" book or "you, yes you, can be an overnight millionaire." I happen to be a millionaire, actually a multi-millionaire, and I did it all on my own. Perhaps someday you will be, too. But this book isn't really about that. You can take the lessons from it and build wealth and yes, perhaps, if millions are your goal, you may be lucky enough to achieve that goal. But if you are a schoolteacher, a social worker, a caregiver—someone who has made a conscious decision to follow a dream of good works that is spiritually, but not necessarily economically, fulfilling—you, too, will find that almost every single topic in this book will still be germane to your life and your lifestyle.

I might also add that while I have been talking about schools and kids, this is not just a book for young people. It should only be a book for young people, but the need is so great and so vast that it stretches across the entire American landscape of age, race, gender, and even economic status. Would you believe there are doctors and lawyers out there who make the same financial mistakes that homeless people do? And why? Sure, sometimes it is simple recklessness, a quirk of personality that causes some people, no matter how well educated, to have a sort of "financial death wish." But often times it is the doctor who knows everything about brain surgery, but has been taught nothing about leasing an office or equipment for his practice. Or an engineer who designs systems to run extraordinary factories, yet tosses a mish-mashed pile of receipts at his accountant at the end of the year and says, "Whatever." This book is for you as well.

Like any good entrepreneur, I saw a need that was not being met. Without even realizing it, numerous friends, family members and others would frequently contact me whenever they had questions about any of the types of transactions explained in this book. They thought as a "been there, done that, got the T-shirt to prove it" entrepreneur that I would have the explanations they desired, and in cases where I did, I freely gave of my advice. (Unfortunately, my publisher and lawyer now limit this "free" consulting for legal and contractual reasons, but most of what I know about the topics is contained in this book anyway). After noticing this opportunity, I started asking just about everyone I came in contact with what their personal knowledge was of "basic" personal finance, and I overwhelmingly discovered that the vast majority of people I spoke with were naive and intimidated by much of this and would greatly welcome some type of medium to give them the answers they so desired. (If you want to test your own knowledge of financial literacy, give the quiz on my website at www.BraunMincher.com a try). The only exceptions to this were people who already had a lot of *experience* in these fields (i.e. experienced real estate agents, CPAs, financial planners, etc.) For the rest of us, however, how many times in our lives do we plan to buy a house? Even though this is likely the largest asset most people will ever own, many people feel intimidated by the process and consequently end up making some mistakes along the way. I am here to give you my "two cents worth," based upon my experience as a successful entrepreneur and a person who has put great amounts of research into all of the topics presented. Consider this book to be the "Reader's Digest" version of Practical Financial Literacy 101.

Some of the best lessons I have learned in the business world have come from the mistakes that I have made—in most cases these "learning experiences" cost me substantial money and I knew that I would not be in business very long if I did not do something different the next time around. I am very fortunate that none of these experiences were devastating enough to bankrupt me, but I have certainly had my share of bad transactions that put a dent in my net worth. You are probably familiar with the saying "that which does not kill you only makes you stronger." I agree wholeheartedly with this. The point that I am trying to make here is that you need to LEARN something from each and every deal you do—successful or not. This will make you better equipped to handle that same situation, or one similar, when it comes up in the future.

Although there is obviously some commercial benefit intended by me writing this book, my true desire in doing so is to inform others of some very basic, but still very important, practical financial principals that I was fortunate enough to learn over time. There are a lot of other businesses that I could invest my time into versus publishing this book and make a much better return on my time; I already made my money from being financially successful in a variety of business ventures, not from writing this book. Compare this to some of the other "experts" in the field. Understand that I am doing this as a way to give back some of the good fortune I have been lucky enough to have enjoyed. Please read and then re-read this book as many times as you need to thoroughly understand the concepts presented and tell your friends about this book as well—they likely have the same questions.

My Story

My name is Braun Mincher and I am a self-made multi-millionaire. I am in my early thirties and was born, raised, and continue to live in Colorado. I did not win the lottery, inherit a fortune, have an on-going successful business handed to me, marry a ninety-six-year-old "billionairess" on her deathbed, or win American Idol or the Super Bowl. I did not even finish college.

But as I've said before, this book isn't about how to become a millionaire, nor is it necessarily about me. But like most people, I don't tend to take financial advice from a guy living in a van down by the river, wearing ragged clothes and stinking of cheap malt liquor. I'm humble and thankful to say that I am a classic American success story, a kid who bootstrapped himself up and now lives a life he can be proud of. I've been able to do things I've always dreamed of doing and given back to my community and to the people I've been associated with.

The thing is, none of this could have been possible without the financial knowledge I feel is so basic to adult life. I did not fear going into business because the thought of walking into a bank sent shivers down my spine. I did not remain living under my parents' roof because I had no idea how to rent or buy a home. And one of the most important lessons we must face in today's society: I did not think I could have it all without working for it, simply because someone had sent me an application for a credit card.

My personal background was not particularly affluent, although I would never describe us as poor. My mother and father are natives of St. Louis and met there. He had always been in the construction business, working his way up first as a draftsman, but eventually allowing his intellectual curiosity to branch him out into learning each and every aspect of construction. **Knowledge is power**—I know I didn't make that one up. But as a society, we somehow seem to mix up classic school learning with knowledge. My father did not earn a college degree. My mother received an associates degree from a community college. But what they both craved and eventually possessed was knowledge.

My father loved the mountains and was quite the outdoorsman—hunting, four wheeling, and camping, so the mountains of Colorado beckoned. I was born and three years later my sister joined me, but shortly after her birth in the late seventies, the Colorado construction scene hit a lull and my father made a decision to relocate the family to Ohio. Our Ohio experience lasted less than two years and Colorado was looking good again, so we returned. By now, my father had climbed his way up to the vice-presidency of a large commercial construction company that built hospitals, office buildings, and large condo projects up in the ski resort areas.

In 1983, my father took a major risk, which for him was quite the departure. He was a Depression baby, weaned on caution and conservative thought and living. He continued to play things carefully and prudently, but he and my mother formed their own general contracting firm, the fulfillment of a lifelong dream of financial independence and self-sufficiency. It was a success, and my parents were suddenly dealing with millions of dollars in gross revenue. But it was still a classic mom and pop business. Dad oversaw the construction; Mom did the books and the billing. They worked long, hard hours, but placed a strong value on family life, spending quality weekend time with my sister and me, as well as exposing us to the family business during the work week.

The hard work paid off. Mom and Dad's company was a success, and suddenly we were living the good life. This didn't mean caviar for breakfast while sunning on our yacht, but it did mean that my birthday presents became a little plusher. I was immediately able to see the correlation between hard work and comfortable living. These good things in our lives were earned, not handed out. And if my parents could do it, I felt I could, too.

My father became very involved in state and national trade associations for contractors, and he would bring me along on business trips. I can still recall being only about six or seven years old and sitting in conference rooms while my father negotiated multi-million-dollar deals as I sat with a yellow legal pad, doodling or taking notes, but always staying respectfully quiet, taking it all in. Shockingly enough, I enjoyed it. I felt close to my parents and loved that they included me in their life's work. It also allowed me an up-close look at cause and effect—putting into action the platitudes that most parents recite to their children. My sister and I would go to these trade shows and business conferences, and we made quite the impression on others. No one had ever seen children so young in situations such as these. You hear about derelict parents doing drugs or drinking with their kids; ours were out buying heavy equipment with us.

You might imagine this sort of thing might bore the average kid and I admit, from what I've seen, it probably would. But this became part of my personality. When other kids wanted to play sports or video games, I preferred working. Crazy, right? But crazy often pays off in life. Many of the world's most successful people were a little off-center in their interests as children. My family always had projects going on around the house and I loved it. During the time I lived at home, we probably rebuilt or remodeled every single part of our house by ourselves. I loved playing with tools. It's a skill that comes in mighty handy in life, no matter what you do.

I'm not going to tell you that I was being primed for any particular occupation in life, nor did I have a specific vocation in mind. But the ethics of hard work and mental curiosity prepare a young person for absolutely anything they may desire to do when they grow up. That being said, there was a lingering assumption that someday I would eventually take over my father's construction business. I didn't feel badly about such a prospect, but it just seemed like the unspoken plan. No pressure, no attempt on my parents' part to dissuade me from other dreams, but if I wanted it, it was mine for the taking (and probably a payout plan to the "former" owners). I must admit, that was a nice security blanket to wrap myself up in, but I felt it was better kept as just that—a fall-back option, and one I liked, too. However, the commercial construction industry continued to change before my eyes; things like new government regulations, a lack of qualified workers and insurmountable liability followed by litigation all gave me pause about pursuing this business. As goals began to form in my young mind, I dreamed more of doing not what my father did—running his construction company—but what he had done—taken a risk and become a successful, hands-on entrepreneur.

Along the way, despite how successful my parents were becoming, if I wanted something, I had to work for it. "Allowance" was not a word that was used in my house. You were simply expected to do things around the house. That was the price you paid for living there. It wasn't malicious, it was simply understood. These were our values. If I really wanted something between my birthday and Christmas, I had to work for it, independent of my household chores. I shoveled snow (very lucrative in Colorado), mowed lawns, and even had the classic all-American lemonade stand. With these I saved up my money and bought what my little heart yearned for. There was no false sense of "entitlement." You earned what you wanted.

While I did those typical "kid" jobs in my younger days, that eventually evolved into my working for my parents' construction company over a summer. That was great, but I had wanderlust for something more independent, something I could call my own, without any help from them. I found it in the first "real" job I ever had and one I loved to death. I got a job at America's Store—our local Sears.

My passion was hardware and soon I was selling Craftsman tools to old men. I was in heaven. The job taught me salesmanship and customer service, skills that are invaluable in any field of endeavor. I started at minimum wage ($3.35 per hour at that time), but after a while I worked my way up to a guarantee of slightly below minimum plus a 3% sales commission. That had to have been the worst deal Sears ever made. I wiped them out. With commission, I was pulling down about $14 to $15 an hour. I was out-selling adult veteran employees who had been there for over twenty years. I saved a lot of it—being a high school kid still living at home, I had no expenses or financial responsibilities—but I also had money for fun and frolic. I went to school full-time and squeezed in about twenty to twenty-five hours of work per week at Sears.

My first manager at Sears was also my first mentor outside of my father and mother. He was tough, but encouraging, and was always teaching, teaching, teaching; his continuous motto was to do whatever was necessary to keep the customer happy, and I still practice that belief today in my various businesses. No matter what the job, you can sleep-walk through it or you can excel at it. Lots of people sleepwalk through sales jobs, whether they work at Sears or at the New York Stock Exchange. Those people never really make it. I believe there is no such thing as "unskilled labor." To do any job well, you have to get schooled properly by showing personal initiative and drive. At Sears, we were offered free correspondence training from their corporate headquarters. I lapped it up. Other employees would say, "You're just a part-timer. What do you care? Besides, we don't get paid extra to read that stuff." No, we did not get paid extra to read it. But we got these golden nuggets for free. They were leaving valuable information on the table. I was picking it up. **Leaving knowledge on the table is as bad as leaving money on the table.**

A major profit center at any store that sells equipment or hard goods is extended warranties or maintenance agreements. We received bonuses and recognition for selling them. I outsold everybody. How? Drive. But also, I used what I was learning from those free courses Sears was offering me. While other salespeople would mention the extended warranty just as the customer was checking out, I would talk about it right from the start, the same as I would any other aspect of the item the customer was interested in purchasing. The extended warranty was just another value-added feature. By the time we reached the checkout, I'd been talking about that maintenance agreement so much that the customer would have felt like a fool for not picking it up.

While still at Sears, I also tried my first entrepreneurial venture—an "honor box" vending system. I'd read about it and it sounded like something simple even a teenage kid like me could do and do well in my spare time. I took $500 of my savings and sent away for fifty cardboard boxes, then went down to my local discount warehouse to fill them up with candy and snacks. From there, I went around trying to place the boxes in offices and small businesses. Well, like many people, I found out that things were not always as easy as they might at first appear. I hoofed my way all over creation and I could only place two boxes. This was a disaster. But instead of throwing in the towel, I called up the company and told them my plight. They informed me that there was this guy in New Mexico who had a consulting business. For about another $500—predicated mostly on his ability to perform—he would come up and help me get those snack boxes placed. This was a crossroads. Do I double-down and go for broke? Or do I toss in my cards and write it up to experience? I took a deep breath and forked over the extra money.

This fellow came up from New Mexico and he was a dynamo. He had turned every mundane aspect of this job into a science. "When you go into an office building, start at the top and work your way down. That way if you get thrown out of someone's office, you can hit some more places on your way out." He thought of everything. My first month alone, I placed only two boxes. One day with him, we placed the other forty-eight. Holy cow! But I was no "gentleman farmer." I didn't just hand him the money and have him do the job for me. I stayed with him step-by-step, learning every little nuance to selling this product and service. By doing so, I learned lessons I would transfer to every business I would ever be involved in. **Selling is selling.** Learn it, and you've learned something invaluable. It's all about listening and truly learning the needs of your customer.

Things were so good, I sent away for another fifty boxes and placed them in no time flat. Once a week, I would go around making my collections, picking up those little handfuls of pocket change that added up to some real money.

Eventually, though, I got bored and wanted to try something new. But you can't just walk away from a business. I took out an ad in the local paper offering to sell my sales route. I got a respondent, a married couple who had failed at a few other types of franchises and wanted to try something else again, but with as low a buy-in as possible. I offered to sell my snack route for $5,000. We agreed on them paying me $1,000 up front, and then paying the balance over time. Well, it was soon apparent that these people had a lot of reasons for their past failures. They were not honorable and after the first down payment, disappeared on me. I tracked them down and confronted them. Someone once told me, **"Never be bashful about asking for money people owe you."** It was a good lesson. I was persistent and firm, but ended up getting most of the balance owed to me in barter—I think I got a gun and a few other garage-sale items from them until I felt satisfied that they had gotten close to paying me what had originally been agreed upon. That was another lesson I learned: **Don't renegotiate. A deal is a deal.** Not that I'm not flexible—we never agreed on me being paid for items in trade, but I always perform what is expected of me, so I expect others to do the same. These are the basic rules of civilization.

But this was all the lead-up to my first really big business venture. When I was a senior in high school, Colorado voted in limited stakes gambling in three small mountain towns outside of Denver. These were rather remote mining towns with winding mountain roads leading up to casinos with very limited parking—overall, not the greatest business plan. But I wasn't in the casino business.

A distant family acquaintance began a transportation business running hourly bus shuttles to the casinos for the casino personnel, as well as charter bus tours for the general public to the casinos, emanating out of Denver. I took a job with him doing group sales. My job was to call on fraternal organizations, senior citizen groups, literally any organized group that might want to schedule a day or night of gambling. We owned no busses, nor did we employ any drivers. We were no different than your basic travel agency. We'd book groups, then call up a bus company and hire the bus and driver. Simple. And lucrative. We would charge the casino bus patrons $10. To get their businesses off the ground, the casinos would greet the bus passengers with $10 worth of money to gamble with—essentially making their trip free. Then, the casinos would give us a $10 commission for every customer we brought in. Incredible! Our profit margin was astronomical. This experience taught me another financial gold nugget: **The best time to enter a business is at the beginning.**

But all was not well in casino bus paradise. The very day I started, everyone else there quit. No, it wasn't me—I checked my breath before I walked in. But the boss was a jerk. Sometimes there's no easier way to say it. The world is made up of lots of different types of people and among them are some jerks. I've heard the religious explanation that jerks are the irritants God sends to test the rest of us. If so, God knew what he was doing when he made this guy. **Rude, arrogant, and surly—when your entire staff walks out en masse, you must be the problem, not your staff.**

Anyway, I spent the next month working my tail off, learning the business. It was cool. Of course, I also learned that a boss's toxic personality is often only the tip of the iceberg. Jerks fail far more often than they thrive, and as simple as it was for this business to soar given the circumstances, he wasn't doing anywhere near the volume and profitability of business he could have been doing. Even a high school kid like me could see that.

My high school still had lots of business classes that I soaked up. They taught me how to write a business plan—an invaluable life skill. So I took the ideas I'd culled from a month on the job and wrote up a very impressive-looking business plan for my boss. A good boss would have welcomed this, especially from an ambitious kid. Mine was not a good boss. He tossed it in the trash and said, "This is my business. I am in charge. No one knows this business better than me. Sit down, shut up, and if I want your opinion, I'll give it to you."

I left in tears. I was just a kid and I wasn't used to this level of virulent abuse from an adult for having done nothing wrong. If I'd quit then, no one would have blamed me. But I don't give up that easily. Maybe it was me; maybe my business plan really wouldn't work. I had to find out.

One of my business classes in high school frequently invited in a local banker as a guest speaker. He really impressed me and he knew all about business plans—he had to look them over every day while deciding whether or not to lend money to business start-ups or expansions. If anyone would be able to neutrally judge my plan, it would be this banker.

I made an appointment to see him and he graciously agreed. He looked over my plan and asked for a copy in order to re-read it at his leisure. Next thing I knew, I got a call from him.

"I'll back you on it."

"What?"

"This plan is great and I see the potential. I'd like to invest my own money in your company."

I nearly fainted. When I got back on my feet, he offered me $7,500 of his own money—not the bank's money, but his own money out of his own pocket—that's how much he believed in me and my plan. Was he a family friend, a rich uncle who was doing me a favor? No way. He hardly knew me at all. What he discovered, though, was my ambition, my drive, my work ethic, my vision, and my ideas, and he liked the total package.

Needless to say, I had to protect myself from flying objects when I came in to see my soon-to-be former employer to give my notice and clear out my desk. He threatened me with everything in the book—lawsuits, the works. Scary stuff for a teenager. But I knew I had gone about things in an honorable way. I worked hard for him and I had given him first dibs on my plan. He tossed it back in my face. His loss. I took nothing proprietary with me, nothing that belonged to him. All I left with was my own plan, my self, and my knowledge, all the things he could have had if he had wanted them.

Spring break of my senior year of high school, Western Starr Charters, Inc., was born. My banker mentor had extra space in the upper floors of his bank building and he gave it to me so that I had my own first office from which to conduct business. I was really on my way.

I printed up business cards, designed brochures, started calling up potential clients, basically doing everything I discussed in my business plan. I was working it. What a feeling! But then spring break was over and I had another few months of high school to go until graduation. Luckily, I had just about all the credits I needed to graduate, so I discussed my time-management dilemma with my high school principal and guidance counselor. They saw the value in what I was doing and arranged for me to go to classes in the early morning and be out by eleven-thirty am. From there, I went to my office and accounted for what I was doing there. My high school accepted my little enterprise as a sort of work-study program and gave me educational credit for it. What a great idea on their part! How better to teach a high school kid real life skills?

Things took off. I met with the casinos; I met with bus companies. I worked my plan. I also began to make my first mistakes. Looking back, this was a good thing. **The only people who don't make mistakes are people who don't do anything.** I did advertising; I printed fliers; I took out Yellow Page ads; I worked trade shows. Some things worked, others didn't. Some things appeared to work, but when I did a cost/benefit analysis, they took me into the red. Most of these lessons I was able to learn from—albeit the hard way. In other cases, no one really knows all the answers. The world is ever changing and what was a good idea on Monday may not work by Thursday. But the successful businessman tracks it all and forges on.

Things got so good, I was named an Ernst & Young / Inc. Magazine "Entrepreneur of the Year" at the state level in 1994. Basking in the glow of recognition at such a young age was heady stuff. I was starting to make money and making a name for myself, which definitely helps you make more money. I even made it onto *The Today Show* in New York.

I hired sales people. They wanted a guaranteed base salary. Some I gave it to, some I did not. Some took the base and gave me nothing in return. Some, whether they got a base or not, simply never produced. They either left on their own or I had to let them go.

I started hitting hotels in Denver, trying to wrangle deals where they could offer casino bus trips to tour groups and conventions. At one of the hotels, I met a lady in her fifties who did group sales. Wow, a professional! That's what I thought I needed. Looking back, I know it was insecurity on my part. I saw how some people were looking at me when I went to visit them. "Kid," they thought. "Just a kid." I wanted to be taken seriously. Perhaps I needed an older person to act as a "front."

She smoked like a chimney and drank like a fish. A real wheeler-dealer, I thought. I had to have her on my team. Bad move. Her first day of work, I get a collect call—from jail. "I took my son's car and he had all these unpaid tickets, so they stopped me and impounded my car and…" I should have seen the writing on the wall, but I only wanted to see what I wanted to see, so I let it go. Things went downhill from there.

I paid her practically nothing and she gladly accepted it. Another bad sign. But I was naïve and trusting. By now I was ready to start college. Despite how I've typified my feelings about higher education, it never quite occurred to me not to try college at all. I was registered to attend Colorado State University, not too far away. I would go to class and live in the dorm during the week, then return to run my business on the weekend. I felt with this smart, experienced lady in charge, what could go wrong? Answer: everything!

The business's numbers stayed stagnant, despite her rambling tales of "big deals" she had in the works and tons of meetings with "big shots" she bragged of being tied in with. Truth was, all she did was answer the phone, taking orders from clients I had already cultivated. She brought in no new business herself. She had me so snowed; she even suggested I hire her best girlfriend to handle the "overflow." I bit—another mistake.

Thank God for my mother. I asked her to do my books and in fact, I still do. If you're going to put your trust in someone, let it be your mother. Well, Mom gave me a call at college.

"Are you sitting down?"

This is not a good way to start a conversation.

It seems Mom discovered that my two older ladies had formed a partnership named Western Transportation—quite similar to my Western Starr Charters. Using this empty name, they were diverting checks written out to my company and depositing them into their own bank account. By Mom's estimation, they had stolen at least $10,000 from me.

I literally flew back from school. I called my banker/investor; I called the sheriff's office. I dragged everyone to the homes of the two women while I banged on their doors, demanding that they answer me and face the music—not that it could ever be that easy. I ended up filing my case in small claims court and winning. But winning and collecting are two different things. I was emotionally crushed and nearly financially ruined. What an embarrassment as I had to face both my parents and the banker who mentored me. All this, while I tried to be a successful college student both academically as well as socially. But the lesson I learned stayed with me: **Absentee ownership is an invitation to be robbed.**

The experience also taught me a very valuable lesson regarding the hiring of professionals. I know a lot of people are loathe to buy a book like this because, "Oh heck, I can just hire an accountant or a lawyer or a real estate agent or a (fill in the blank). What do I need to learn any of this stuff for?" Well, once I tracked down the two ladies who robbed me, I was advised to get myself a lawyer to help me file and win the claim in court. I was still in my teens and what did I know about stepping into a courtroom? The truth was, as soon as someone mentioned the phrase "small claims court" to me, I began researching the daylights out of it. It didn't seem so hard. Then I paid a visit to the attorney my banker had recommended to me.

"No problem. Easy as pie. Just give me a $5,000 retainer and your problems are over."

I'd just been robbed of $10,000. Why did I need to be robbed of $5,000 more? As I read it, small claims court was the common man's court. You don't need a law degree to get satisfaction there. Just have your proof and your facts and be prepared. And so I decided to represent myself. It worked. I won the full amount I was owed and it didn't cost me anything more than the nominal filing fee. I'd saved $5,000. You can, too. **Don't underestimate yourself. Most things can be learned.**

Soon after, though, luck shined on me. I kept selling and selling and just then, I managed to land a very big, steady account. That account guaranteed me about $70,000 to $80,000 per year, every year. Whew! Boy, I needed that right about then.

But by this time, the handwriting was on the wall. I either had to dedicate myself to running a business or get out and start up again once I was out of college. A person cannot serve two masters. I counted off the days until I finished spring semester at CSU so I could come home and throw myself completely into my bus business, and I made the decision to not look back.

With my one big contract under my belt, I shot off into the fray and began writing all the business I could. Things were looking up again. I even bought out my banker, the mentor who so believed in me that he reached into his own pocket to back me. All he asked for from me was his original investment back—no profit, no interest, just what he had put in. Great story, right? Well, there eventually came a dark side.

He later sold his bank and retired a wealthy man. Shortly thereafter, he got the entrepreneurial urge again and threw in his lot with some real estate developers. Despite his vast experience, he did not do his due diligence and they turned out to be crooks. They cooked the books and my friend ended up being stuck for $10 million dollars on a loan he had co-signed. It broke him. A lifetime of wise investments, all gone in an instant.

Flash forward a few years. I hadn't heard from him in a while and did not know anything about this bad fortune that had befallen him. When he told me, he accompanied it with the typical request: could I loan him some money? How could I refuse? This was karma and I had no other choice. He asked for $20,000 and I couldn't give it to him fast enough. He said he was going to use it to build and sell a house or two, which he was more than capable of doing.

Time went on and I did not hear from him. We had arranged a formal payback schedule, but nothing was happening. I looked for him—couldn't find him. Oh no, not him! Here was a man I respected greatly and look what he does to me. When I found him, he wouldn't return my calls. He had turned into the same sort of deadbeat he had chased down himself so very many times over the years as a commercial banker, a sad twist of fate. Eventually, I got him on the phone and he confessed to me that he never used that money to build anything, but used it to live on. Had he told me that in the first place, I probably still would have helped him out. He had taken a risk on me with no collateral, and now I was being asked to do the same for him. But I had been honest and he had not. That part I can never forgive. By being dishonest, he took away my ability to be gracious and charitable. Essentially, he stole from me. Even when I think about it today, it makes me physically ill.

But back to buses. I recovered by landing my big deal and had a nice base from which to grow. I hustled and sold, but always kept my eye out for the next big opportunity. In 1994, the new Denver International Airport opened to much fanfare. It also had cost a bundle to build and that cost had to be recouped. United Airlines was the primary airline running out of DIA, accounting for about 85% of their business. Due to lack of competition and high overhead, United was charging astronomical airfares. I can recall paying around $500 for a trip to Los Angeles.

A year later, a small operation by the name of Western Pacific Airlines decided to enter the Colorado marketplace as a discount airliner. Still, getting to use DIA would be price prohibitive. On the other hand, just one hour south of Denver was Colorado Springs, which also had an airport. Western Pacific swung a deal to use Colorado Springs and was greeted there with open arms. Western Pacific began charging around $79 to Los Angeles at the same time it cost $500 to fly there from Denver. It didn't take a genius to figure that every savvy traveler would be making a mass exodus from Denver to Colorado Springs. Are you thinking what I was thinking?

If I could run a shuttle from Denver to Colorado Springs airport, I'd make a bundle. But I needed consistency of service. That required me to work much closer with a bus company than I ever had before.

Enter Ed Conlon into my life. Ed was a transplanted New Jersey guy who became one of my finest mentors. Ed owned two companies: Airport Express and Express Charter. Ed had been running shuttles for fifteen years from Ft. Collins, Colorado, which is an hour north of Denver, to DIA. He owned buses and I had been using him for charters for a while already. Ed was the ultimate hands-on guy. Every time I went to see him, he'd be underneath a bus, getting grease all over himself. There was nothing about his business Ed couldn't do himself. That's the mark of a successful businessman.

Ed had something I had to have in order to make my plan work: a license. There were state and federal regulatory agencies that oversaw airport shuttles. You had to have a certain kind of license to run them. Getting one of those was like trying to get your own key to Ft. Knox. You had to almost have been born with one. I knew if I had to buy one it would take me years and hundreds of thousands of dollars. Those licenses were worth their weight in gold.

I made my pitch to Ed. I described my plan to run shuttles from Denver to Colorado Springs. Ed would technically be the operator and would subcontract the route to me for a 5% royalty. Ed and I shook on it. Was it a great deal for Ed? Probably not, but I wasn't screwing him. I had no idea whether this venture would get off the ground or not. Neither did Ed. He even said, "Tell you what. For the first three months, forget the 5%."

It was the last quarter of 1995. We started running six-passenger vans every two hours. Within five days, we had to move up to eleven-passenger vans. A week later, we were using twenty-one-person people movers. I had sent out press releases to every newspaper, radio station, and local TV affiliate in the state. They all thought it was a great story and my face, name, and company name were plastered everywhere—free media worth tens of thousands of dollars. My office phones were ringing off the hook. I was keeping twenty-two drivers busy. It was the Christmas season when everyone traveled. What a perfect launch time! That first season, I was clearing $20,000 to $30,000 per month in pure taxable profit after expenses. I couldn't spend all the money I was taking in.

A few months later, I suggested to Ed that we merge our companies. He agreed. Ed had a call center in Ft. Collins; I had one in Denver. I did casino marketing; Ed did not. I had customers; Ed had busses. Plus, we liked, trusted, and respected each other. These are the reasons people should consider mergers.

I became the new company president. Ed was still the head honcho and oversaw operations, while I ran marketing and sales. I worked the phones and ran around meeting hotels, casinos, groups, what-have-you, while Ed kept the busses running like clockwork. We became one of the biggest ground transportation companies in Colorado. We even began running trips from adjoining states to Colorado casinos, ski areas, professional football, hockey, and baseball games, as well as our bread and butter airport business. We were as self-sufficient as possible. We had our own in-house towing service, maintenance service, leasing company; eventually we even had our own fuel trucks. We hardly ever even had to use other people's gas stations!

From Ed, I learned more about financing and leasing. I got more and more comfortable going into banks to get money to buy new busses, heavy equipment, all the way down to copy machines. This was hands-on education. I was building relationships, asking questions, and gaining confidence.

Like me, Ed didn't have an extensive formal education, but he had street smarts. And such lessons he taught me! I remember one time some bus driver was running behind schedule. Ed got on the radio with him, and the driver, instead of taking responsibility and apologizing, started giving Ed some lip. Next thing you know, the driver gets to his next stop and Ed is standing there. Ed boots the guy off the bus and drives the rest of the route himself, leaving the guy stranded. Now that's old school people management!

For about a year and a half, I learned from Ed and continued my pursuit of world domination from a business standpoint. But, for a variety of reasons, by May of 1997, Ed and I agreed for him to buy me out. I thought it through and saw what I liked and what I didn't like about the business. By then we had seventy plus vehicles and one hundred twenty-five drivers, some of whom were high maintenance—the drivers more than the vehicles. Ed offered me a very fair price, and I asked that he allow me to keep my original Denver to Colorado Springs route. To me, that was still the cash cow. Well, I was about to learn from another mistake. Shortly thereafter, Western Pacific Airlines went belly up after moving operations to DIA and trying to compete with the dominant carriers. I had assumed that such a thing could never happen. But **when your entire business depends on one other business that you don't own, you are in peril.** To keep that route, I left a substantial amount of money on the table in my negotiations with Ed. Dumb, dumb, dumb in hindsight.

Around 1998, I shut down my route and liquidated my assets. I was still very nicely in the black, but had no real plan for the future. I was up in Ft. Collins a lot by now—the home of my semi-alma mater, Colorado State University—and couldn't help but notice that there was a significant need for college housing. Now, this would be different from the bus business. I mean, an entire college wasn't going to up and leave me high and dry. They had over twenty thousand students. That was a nice, captive audience.

I started buying up houses, condominiums and apartment buildings near the campus, fixing them up and renting them. By now I knew how to work with a bank, understood mortgages and real estate, was handy with tools, and I had loads of customers.

But it wasn't enough. I had been working ninety hours a week since I could drive, and my whole life revolved around doing business in one form or another. I was heading for burn-out if I didn't find a way to have fun. I had a friend who was a professional automobile racer. He invited me to see him in a race, and I got hooked. By the end of the weekend I had acquired a car, a truck, and a trailer, and we had formed a professional racing team.

Do you want to know how to make a small fortune in auto racing? Start with a large fortune. Laugh, go ahead, laugh. But everyone in racing knows it to be true. Racing is fun (even when you do it as a profit seeking business, as we did), but it's no way to get rich. But for the first time in years, I didn't care. I needed an outlet. But that didn't mean I still didn't keep my eyes and ears open for opportunity.

Since racing is such a money pit, everyone in it always is looking for sponsorships—all those garish decals you find slapped all over those beautiful vehicles. In our quest to get us some sponsorships, my partner and I met with a telecom company that had approached us at a race. What did I know about telecommunications? Uh, I knew how to use a phone, that's about it. Well, this company, which I had never heard of before, was selling what they called a "sponsor package." They knew that racing teams were more than drivers and mechanics—they usually also had a businessman or two involved. This company was soliciting race teams to sell their long distance services—sort of like a franchise or a sales force—and the race team could keep a percentage from the residual spending of its customers. It wasn't very creative, but it struck me as interesting.

I talked with them and while we didn't really hit it off, I still liked the idea. So, instead of signing with them, I searched out all the other telecom companies I could find to ask if they'd do the same deal with us. Remember: A good idea is usually portable—and non-proprietary.

Eventually, I found a company named UniDial in Louisville, Kentucky, who thought it sounded like a good idea and who I had a good feeling about. They gave us a $2,500 cash sponsorship and an agency arrangement to sell their long distance service and collect 10% of whatever the customers we signed up paid for long distance. So we signed up our friends and family. I called up all the businesses I knew, knowing that their usage would far exceed any individual's. The first month we got a check for $500; the next month, $1,000. Compared to the kind of money I had made in transportation, this was chump change, but I had a conservative cushion in the bank and this seemed like a new frontier.

Then the frontier got larger. Federal deregulation broke up all the "Baby Bells" and allowed open competition for local telephone service. Boom! We were in the right place at the right time with a service to sell.

The thing was, I knew that the racing team would always be a drain on our finances. My partner really had no passion for the telecom business— his love was racing, so he and I went our own ways but remained friends. He got the racing team; I got the telecom business. Sometimes a business divorce can be a win-win. Along the way, I met some other guys who were selling this telecom stuff like mad—top producers for UniDial (which later renamed itself "Lightyear"). I took them out for breakfast and put it to them straight: "What do you do and how do you do it?" You'd be surprised at how easily many successful people will open up if you just ask them that point- blank. That's how I learned to place snack boxes; that's how I learned to run a charter bus company.

They told me that they set themselves up as telecommunications *consultants*. They did not simply sell for UniDial—they sold for lots of companies. So in 1998, I did the same. I created a new company, PCG

Consulting Group, Inc. I got agency agreements for about half a dozen long distance companies and half a dozen local carriers. I would go into businesses as a consultant. I'd analyze their phone bills and their operation and fix them up with the carrier or carriers I thought would best meet their needs. In return, I not only got the 10% agency commission for their usage, I also charged the customer a consulting fee of whatever they saved over the first two months of new service. That savings in only two months time alone could run as high as $15,000. Bingo!

Again, it was great to get in on the game at the start. As businesses mature, profitability drops. Telecom companies were dying to get customers, so price wars were rampant. This made my job easy, as every business I went to visit showed me a phone bill I knew I could practically cut in half. Tell someone they can have something for half price with no compromise on quality and just stand back while they write you out the check. The telecom companies I represented got so rabid for expansion and raw numbers that they started giving me bonuses—an additional $50 per phone line for every new phone line I brought them. Mo' money, mo' money, mo' money.

For about two years, I signed up customer after customer and the money kept rolling in. Today, years later, I still get residual checks every month from many of these customers. As long as they stay with the carrier I hooked them up with, I get my 10%. It's the gift that keeps on giving, known as a residual income. I know, I wrote up the agency contracts that way.

Well, phone service is a soft good. But what about the hard goods, the telephone hardware itself? I was getting asked about that all of the time. I did not feel comfortable going into yet another business at that time, so I looked around for some hardware companies that I could refer my customers to. One company, I must have sent a quarter of a million dollars worth of business in one year. All I asked of them was not to make me look bad and to treat my customers well.

Two things happened. One, I did not ask them for money, and despite how much I enriched them, they did not give me any (**never rely on the charity of strangers**). Two, they did not treat my customers right and they did make me look bad; to this day, they are the sole cause of me ever losing a customer.

Kicking and screaming, in early 2000, I was dragged into another business venture. By now I had learned enough about the hardware end of telecom and had seen every conceivable mistake that could be made. I began trolling around for some good equipment manufacturers to form a like-minded relationship with. I finally found one, a company that was smart and had some very interesting new products. I liked their management and felt I could put my trust in them. They were experimenting with a new concept, something known today as VoIP, or Voice over Internet Protocol. We shook hands and I formed my newest company, CTI Communications, LLC. I continued to own and run PCG at the same time. Both companies had their own customers, but many customers used both companies. I made money both ways. PCG was already established, and what better time to discuss upgrading a telephone system than when you are working with a consultant to lower your phone bills? Each company helped the other grow. **Internal synergy—become a turn-key operation and the only person you have to depend upon is yourself.**

Because of the wonders of the Internet, CTI Communication was able to sell phone systems all over the country. We could do everything remotely, including customer support. We even offered twenty-four-hour a day technical support. Then I saw another wrinkle. A lot of our customers were suffering from "future shock." They wanted the new high-tech equipment, but they didn't know how to use it. The manufacturer we were working with didn't have any kind of training program for customers. So…I negotiated to set up a training center in Ft. Collins. We would have exclusivity in this regard. We charged $1,500 per person for a two-day training session at our state-of-the-art facility. We drew from not only our own customers, but customers from every other vendor there was. Our training sessions were packed, proving that the business concept was sound.

I was back up to ninety-hour work weeks again, but at the end of the day it was paying off. Like most business owners, I got the occasional call from a business broker spouting off about how he or she had "pre-qualified investors who were interested in buying my business." Yeah, right. After fending off hundreds of these calls over the years, one actually sounded legit. I gave them an hour of my time and I still thought they were legit, which shocked me. I wasn't looking to sell, but I was asked a price and I came up with one, and a high one at that, being that I really wasn't dying to sell my business. This broker not only came back to me with a sincere customer for my business—he came back with three! Then, they started a bidding war. When the smoke cleared, I had sold my telecom business for more than I had hoped for after just four short years.

If you are keeping score, I had become a self-made millionaire before the age of twenty-five and a multi-millionaire before the age of thirty. It was time to "retire."

I built my dream house. I traveled. I recharged my batteries. I did some real estate deals and learned more about that business. I invested in some new businesses and spent more time managing my other business ventures. I searched out lots of new business opportunities both locally and around the world. I continued to draw residuals from some of my businesses, and I let my money work for me instead of the other way around. I am still looking for the next big venture to put my time, experience and capital into.

And now I'm writing this book. None of what I did could I have done without basic financial literacy. No house can stand without a foundation. Everyone wants to soar like a jet airplane, but first you have to understand how the parts work. That's what this book is about. Will it make you a millionaire? Maybe, maybe not. Can you become a millionaire without the knowledge in the coming pages? Maybe, but you'll never hang onto it. So come along, class is now in session.

CHAPTER 1
CONSUMER CREDIT

Credit Reports

Whether we like it or not, each of us will have a *permanent* record of our credit history associated with us for the rest of our lives. This starts with the very first credit transaction we ever enter into, which for most of us is either during high school or college upon turning eighteen. Maintained properly, this record will be a big benefit, but neglected, its content becomes available data to cause us substantial setbacks in our pursuit of success. Not only does our **credit score** affect our ability to borrow money and get the best interest rate, but it has progressed to being a determining factor for many employment offers and even insurance rates. Yet, only a small fraction of Americans know what their credit score is.

We constantly see ads from car dealers, mortgage companies and others which say "Bad Credit OK" or "We Finance Everyone." The reason this "B-Paper" ("Bad Paper," or potential borrowers with sub-par credit and higher risk to the lender) is so attractive to them is that there are **big** profits to be made from the group of people who are in most cases the least able to repay and will do **anything** to get a loan. With bad credit, your loan rates will usually be higher and your terms will be less favorable. It is not uncommon for a person with bad credit to pay double the amount of interest paid by

1

somebody with good credit, in addition to thousands of dollars in unnecessary junk fees.

While some of the "get rich quick" schemes profess that you do not need perfect credit to become wealthy using whatever program they promote, and although I agree that this still is possible with some creative financing, I have personally found it much easier to become wealthy by maintaining excellent credit. Does this mean that I do not believe in debt or leverage? No, it just means that I believe in evaluating your ability to repay before taking the loan, not overextending yourself, and making all payments on time as agreed.

While it is certainly easier to start out with good credit and continue to maintain that path for a lifetime, those who already have some blemishes on their credit reports can still take action to have their credit repaired over time. My feeling is that it is *never* too late to improve your credit; taking such action now will only help you when borrowing in the future.

Credit Bureaus

There are three main credit reporting bureaus, each of which maintains an independent credit history for consumers. They are **Equifax, Experian** and **TransUnion.** These are giant companies which each have an entire business that revolves around collecting and analyzing data to determine credit risk for lenders. These companies are funded by your creditors who all pay fees for access to consumer credit reports. While it would be ideal for the information in such an important report to be completely accurate, the reality is that 29% of credit reports contain serious errors and another 41% contain other mistakes (70% total containing inaccuracies), according to a survey commissioned by the U.S. Public Interest Research Group (1998). This revelation can obviously pose a big problem and is why it is vitally important that you understand how credit reports work and frequently monitor the information that is being reported about you, even if you pay all your bills on time and do not apply for credit often.

Almost all consumer credit issuers will analyze a copy of your credit report in making a decision about whether to loan you money. These credit issuers may include credit card companies, retail stores, car financing companies, mortgage lenders and bank loans. In recent years, even car insurance companies have been analyzing customers' credit reports, not so much to determine whether you are going to be able to pay your premiums (which are generally paid in advance anyway), but more as a means of analyzing your risk as a driver. It is their premise that if you handle your financial affairs properly, this will also translate into how well you drive. Some people (and even some state governments) consider this approach to be controversial, but it is accepted practice in business, and therefore, reality for the time being.

When people attempt to get their financial houses in order, they generally focus on fixing up bad mistakes of the past. The length of time that information remains in your credit report varies:

Credit and collection accounts will be reported for seven years from the date of the last activity with the original creditor.

If you've filed a Chapter seven or Chapter eleven bankruptcy this information will be reported for ten years from the date filed.

All other courthouse records will be reported for seven years from date filed.

Reading Your Credit Report

To see a Sample Credit Report and for a color-coded explanation of how to read your own credit report, please visit the "Links & Resources" section of my website at www.BraunMincher.com and look under the "Chapter 1" heading.

Credit Scores

To save each lender from having to come up with its own subjective formula to analyze all of the information and from weighing the various factors in your credit file, back in the 1950s the industry devised a standardized formula that summarizes everything in your credit history, translating the data into a numerical score known generically as your "**credit score.**" This saves humans at the lender's office from having to manually interpret all of the information on your credit report to make an approval decision.

Sometimes, you may see the term "**FICO Score.**" FICO is the acronym for the "Fair Isaac Corporation," which is the industry trade association that pioneered the scoring system. FICO scores range from 350 to 850 (the higher the better), and although it is no longer the only credit scoring system, it is still the most popular model.

A higher credit score means lower interest and significantly less cost over time. Check out these sample home mortgage rates from a national lender for a $250,000 loan sorted by credit score:

Credit Score	Interest Rate	Monthly Payment	Monthly Difference	Yearly Difference	30Yr Term Difference
720-850	6.25%	$1,539	-0-	-0-	-0-
700-719	6.37%	$1,559	$ 20	$ 240	$ 7,200
675-699	6.91%	$1,648	$ 109	$ 1,308	$ 39,240
620-674	8.06%	$1,845	$ 306	$ 3,672	$110,160
560-619	12.04%	$2,579	$1,040	$12,480	$374,400
500-559	13.09%	$2,783	$1,244	$14,928	$447,840

Believe it or not, your credit score is probably one of the biggest determinations of your future financial success. By carrying the burden of bad credit (by making late payments or having too much debt), all your dreams and aspirations become that much more encumbered.

Here is a chart from MyFico.com showing the National Distribution of FICO Scores:

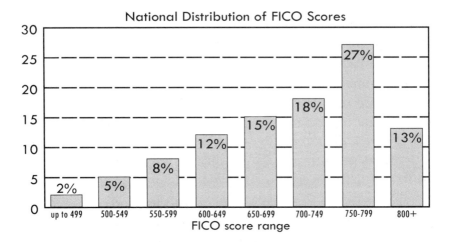

The very complex algorithms used to calculate your credit score take into account such things as your tendency to pay on time, the length of time the credit has been established, your overall available credit, the percentage of your available credit that is currently utilized, public records, the number of inquires made on your credit report and other information. While some have fairly good speculations as to the exact formula used to derive a credit score, the exact calculation is probably one of the most guarded secrets in the country.

Although the traditional credit report is still considered to be the "gold standard" used by consumer credit issuers, and I still foresee this to continue indefinitely, the reports have two fundamental problems:

- The reports and the accompanying credit score computation are **completely oblivious** to your income.
- Your assets and any other borrowings you have with a private lender who does not report to the bureaus are never considered.

Because of this, you could make $1,000,000 per year, have $10,000,000 in the bank, have an excellent history of paying back your loans from family members (or others that do not report to the credit bureaus), and just because you have still failed to pay a $500 credit card balance from back in college, your credit score could be severely tarnished and you could actually be denied for a loan—although the numbers were certainly not this big, I have seen it happen. Understand that most big lenders are not very creative or flexible in looking at all aspects of a credit situation, but rely *solely* on the credit score provided to them by the bureau(s); they depend on the credit report to summarize and predict the credit risk so that they do not have to.

While a credit report is probably a good predictor for most consumers, it is not well suited to assessing those with unique situations such as entrepreneurs, small business owners, trust fund babies and others. For these reasons, I consider consumer credit reports to be nothing more than a game. I personally do not believe in them, but you should still avoid decisions and actions that would saddle you with anything less than perfect credit. Every bank and commercial lender I work with continues to check my credit report periodically throughout the year to insure that I properly maintain my finances.

What Affects Your Credit Score?

The largest factor in determining your credit score is your **payment history**. If you have a proven track record of paying your past creditors on time, then you will likely be considered a good credit risk because others will think that you will do the same for them. However, if you have a spotty payment history, you may either get a lesser credit limit, a higher interest rate, or be denied completely. This is where the three months during college when you decided to "check out" and ignore your creditors can come back to haunt you later, as that information remains in your credit file for years to come. It is possible for a single delinquent payment to lower your credit score by more than fifty points. It is estimated that your payment history alone accounts for approximately one third of your credit score.

A friend of mine in college worked part-time in the electronics department of a large department store. The day he turned eighteen, he applied for and received one of the store's credit cards, which he immediately used to purchase an expensive top-of-the line TV and stereo system for his dorm room. Although he was the envy of his friends and most dorm social gatherings occurred in his room, there were several times throughout his college career when he did not work and thus, was unable to make the monthly payments on his department store credit card, which he did not think was a big deal at the time. Several years after graduating from college, he found a good job and climbed up the corporate ladder very quickly. Within a couple of years and now making a good salary, he had saved up enough money to make a 20% down payment on his first house. The only problem was that his credit score was so low that he could not qualify for a mortgage due to his poor credit habits five years previously in college. Do not let this happen to you!

Another negative effect on your credit score is your **use of revolving credit**. This includes unsecured credit cards, which are characterized as "short-term" lending, with the balance varying from month-to-month. How much this affects your score primarily depends on your balance ratio to the maximum limit, but generally lenders frown on large credit card balances or having a high debt-to-limit ratio. For example, if you have a credit limit of $9,000 on one of your cards and your balance is $8,900, this can lower your credit rating because it is a signal that you are near the over-extension of your finances. **Ideally, you should not have a balance greater than one-third of your credit limit**, or $3,000 in this case. Or better yet, live within your means and pay your balances in full on a monthly basis. It is estimated that your use of revolving credit accounts for approximately one-third of your credit score.

Another factor is the **length in years of your overall credit history**. The longer you can demonstrate responsible credit management, the higher your credit score. Some of my research has indicated that twenty-eight years is the "ideal" length of credit history for the best possible score. Assuming that you first established credit when you were eighteen, this means that you will be forty-six before the credit bureaus stop penalizing you for your age. This is even more of a reason to properly maintain the other factors affecting your credit score. It is estimated that this factor accounts for approximately 15% of your credit score.

Newly acquired credit and application **inquiries** into your credit also have a negative effect on your credit score. Multiple new accounts create additional risk for lenders because they know that you have a lot of borrowing power and can easily get yourself overextended. For this reason, **do not apply for every credit card advertised** just to get a one time discount or a free T-shirt! The moral of the story is to **severely limit any inquires to your credit report.** Make sure they are only for necessary purchases and as a rule, you should avoid letting people run your credit until you are ready to buy. It is estimated that "new credit" accounts for approximately 10% of your credit score. While it is certainly not scientific, my personal experience is that each inquiry deducts less than five points from your credit score for a year.

Obtaining Your Credit Report

A recent amendment to the Federal Fair Credit Reporting Act requires each of the three nationwide consumer reporting companies to provide you with a free copy of your credit report, at your request, once every twelve months. I strongly recommend that people take advantage of this great free service. Consider it part of your yearly health regimen— your *financial* health regimen.

Quick note: there is presently one flaw to this free yearly report system: your free report will *not* give you your credit *score*. **To get the three-digit credit score, you have to pay.**

To find out where to obtain instantly both free and paid copies of your credit reports (which contain your three-digit scores), please visit my website at www.BraunMincher.com for the most current information and links. Be wary of websites and TV advertisements that offer supposedly "free" credit reports, but only with the purchase of other products or ongoing subscriptions.

Correcting Errors

So, do the credit bureaus ever make mistakes? Anybody who maintains hundreds of pieces of information on millions of consumers is bound to do so. Let me give you some real life examples of mistakes. This material alone could fill an entire book.

A client of mine once missed an installment loan payment due to a bookkeeping error. He amended the situation as quickly as possible and even sent in his next payment early. He continued to make all of his payments right on time. Except for that one boo-boo, everything should have been fine, right? Wrong. He checked his credit report and found out that not only did they report that one payment as being late, they then continued to record every single payment he made thereafter as being one month late. Every single month, thirty days late, thirty days late. Consequently, he had to send multiple letters and call several times in order to get the situation corrected.

I'll give you one more scenario. This happened to me personally. I wanted to make a large purchase. I wanted to use a particular credit card of mine that did not have a high enough limit. So, I called up the credit card company and was instantly approved for a higher credit limit. Then I did my quarterly credit check. Lo and behold, while the bank happily gave me the higher limit, the credit bureau did not get that information, only that I used the card for two times what my limit had *previously* been. I mentioned that you should always try to keep your credit balances below one-third of your total credit limit. The credit bureau said I was at 200% of my limit. Holy cow! Had I not checked my own credit, I would have been in big trouble and since I was also getting ready to apply for a mortgage, I would either have gotten an exorbitant rate or not been approved at all.

As mentioned previously, don't be surprised if you find errors on your credit report. All of the credit bureaus have processes set up for you to formally fix any incorrect information—say an account that isn't yours, or a disputed amount. Sometimes you can do this easily on their website, but for more complex issues it might require a formal letter like the samples available from the "Links & Resources" section of my website at www.BraunMincher.com. You also have the right to have a formal statement appear on your permanent credit report.

Maintaining Good Credit

The best way to maintain *good* credit is to never have *bad* credit in the first place. That's a no-brainer. **Pay your bills and pay them on time.** As mentioned previously, don't simply accept that by doing so you can be sure it has been recorded as such. Check from time to time to make certain that your sterling record is reflected on your credit report.

Get and establish your own credit as early on in your adult life as possible and manage it prudently.

If you can't pay a bill on time, use pre-emptive action. Call the creditor immediately and apprise them of the situation. The biggest key here is...*you* call *them.* **Don't wait for them to call you.** By then it's too late. Maybe you can make a partial payment. Believe me, they would rather get something than nothing, and get it right away rather than next month. Be specific in your discussions with a creditor. Say exactly what you can and will do and when exactly you can and will do it. Then don't make yourself out to be a liar—follow through. Most creditors are more reasonable than you think, but you have to give them a chance. I see this all the time in my role as a landlord and a private lender.

My next piece of advice is crucial. **If a creditor agrees to accept a partial payment or a reduced payment, ask if they will be reporting you as "late."** Do not assume one way or the other. Always ask for what you want. The worst they can say is no. You can even counter that by putting it in their lap: What can I possibly do, short of making the full and expected payment right on time, to make you *not* report me as being late? Maybe there's an additional option you hadn't thought of offering them that you might find palatable.

This is key. Just because you arranged a payment plan with a creditor does not mean they will not report you as having paid late. These are *two separate issues*. Therefore, you must address them both. Customer service representatives are sometimes very sweet and will say, "Okay, everything will be all right now." Get them to tell you exactly what that means. You want it to mean that you will not be reported to the bureaus as having paid late. If I sound like I'm repeating myself it's because this is *so* important. Once you have already been reported—accurately—as having paid late, getting them to reverse it is almost impossible.

It should go without saying, but be sure to document in writing any agreements the creditor makes with you. If they do not provide you with something, send them a letter summarizing your conversation.

But then you get your next bill and there's a large "late fee" on it, whether or not they reported your delinquency to the credit bureau. Late fees are just one tack-on fee lenders can legally get away with. So, be careful—be aware of how they use it. But they still can hit you with a $35 late fee they refuse to waive no matter how much you beg.

Another concern is over-limit penalties. Go $1 over your credit limit and watch them hit you with a $39 fee. Again, you call them, they agree not to contact the bureaus; but you still get stuck paying $40 to borrow $1. Several credit card issuers are coming under scrutiny by consumer groups who say that they are intentionally providing multiple accounts to customers, rather than just increasing the credit limit on one of them. This way, they can charge a separate over-the-limit fee for *each* account rather than just one.

Big lenders are like casinos and "the house" never goes broke. In their defense, they also have high administration costs and get stuck with any defaults, so they need to make money where they can. It never hurts to ask them to waive such fees, and the worst they can say is no. Watch your balances and limits carefully to avoid even being put in this position.

Another gotcha is moving. So many otherwise responsible people move and forget to contact all the proper people. Sure, your mail will eventually get forwarded, but that can take weeks. That's another reason that paying bills online is great, as is automatic bill-pay. You can move all over the world, but your e-mail address can stay the same. Either way, though, bear in mind what bills you have and when they are usually due. Even when contacting a creditor with a change of address, it may take them a few weeks to process your new data in their own system. Stay on top of it. Call up your mortgage company or your auto leasing company or whomever and ask them when your next bill is due, for how much, and where you should send it. **Not getting a bill is never an excuse.**

Here's a question I get a lot. What if there was a time when you got a ton of credit cards and ran all their balances up so you could have lots of nice toys you really couldn't afford? Now you've been a good boy or girl and you've paid them all off and now live within your means and no longer borrow money at exorbitant credit card interest rates. Should you cut all those cards in half and close the accounts?

Generally speaking…no. Those cards are your credit history. Remember what we said about "time" as being a factor in your credit profile? Close all those old accounts (which are now in good shape with no "lates" and are not over their limits) and you toss your credit history away. There may be other areas in your life where you wish you were years younger, but your credit profile isn't one of them.

Another wrinkle on this: what if you have multiple cards with varying interest rates? You aggressively pay off the highest interest cards so that all your action is on the one with the lowest interest rate. Good, smart move. So should you cut up those other cards and close them down? The answer now even goes beyond the issue of time and history. When we talked about how much of your available credit you are using, that was an aggregate number. Watch this:

Credit card A:	$ 10,000 limit	$ -0- balance
Credit card B:	$ 10,000 limit	$ -0- balance
Credit card C:	$ 10,000 limit	$ -0- balance
Credit card D:	$ 10,000 limit	$9,000 balance

You are using 22.5% of your total available credit. This is good. Now, if you cut up cards A, B, and C and close them down, you are using *90%* of your available credit. Whoa! Not good; not good at all. By closing accounts, you lower your "total available credit" and thus, increase your debt ratio with any balances that you have on the accounts that remain open.

On occasion, when applying for a large loan such as a home mortgage, a lender may be forthcoming enough to tell you that you are not a good candidate for a loan at a decent rate because you have too much "potential" credit (i.e. revolving credit that you *can* use, even though you have not *been* using it). If that ever becomes the situation, deal with it on a case by case basis. Shop around and if it appears to have validity, then you may need to close some of those accounts to get into your dream house. If you do cancel cards, start with department store or gas station charge cards that can only be used at designated places. But like the old tailor says: measure twice and cut once. Don't get rid of credit unless you have to.

Credit Cards

As the years go by, we become less reliant on cash and more reliant on our plastic cards. Used properly, credit cards can be a good tool for consumers, but without knowledge and discipline, credit cards can be the start of financial ruin. Some cards, such as Visa, MasterCard, American Express and Discover, have almost universal merchant acceptance, while others are restricted to use at certain department stores, gas stations or the like. Credit cards are considered to be "revolving credit lines" and the average American consumer has eight such open accounts at any given time.

Credit cards offer us a convenience that can be used to buy goods and services online, at the corner store, or in almost any country of the world. Certain credit card issuers also have "rewards" programs that provide lucrative cash-back, merchandise credits or travel. When paid in full each month, credit cards also offer us the ability to use the interest free capital of somebody else for a period of time. Finally, credit cards give us the organization of an itemized monthly statement along with a host of advanced chargeback rights and fraud protections.

The major fundamental problem with credit cards is the temptation to obtain immediate gratification with minimal thought being given to the future payment obligations. They say the greatest invention in gambling was the chip, creating the illusion that real money was not in play. Credit cards are chips for the world outside the gambling casino.

When a credit card balance is not paid in full each month, interest begins to accrue (usually back from the date of purchase) and then compounds on a daily or monthly basis. Also, since credit cards are an unsecured debt, unlike a mortgage or car loan which has collateral, there is more risk for the lender because there is nothing to recover if you default. Next to owing a loan shark (yes, like you see on TV), credit card debt and its associated interest is probably the least favorable debt that consumers can carry. Improper use of credit cards is a MAJOR reason for the decline of the US savings rate over the past fifteen years.

How Credit Card Issuers Make Money

So, if some people pay off their credit cards in full each month, how do the card issuers make any money? Well, there are several ways.

Interest and Fees Paid by Consumers

Obviously, a major source of income for the credit card issuers is the monthly interest they collect from consumers who do not pay their bill in full. In essence, credit card issuers provide a "revolving loan" to the consumer each month and may even add interest charges on top of past interest charges (known as compounding interest) and even extend more credit as the consumer uses the credit card throughout the month to purchase more goods and services. This can become a vicious cycle, and most consumers are already in deep before they even know it.

Some credit card companies also profit by charging annual fees, over the credit limit fees, late fees and the like. This may sound like small change, but it has added billions of dollars to their bottom lines. However, all of these costs are avoidable.

Merchant Fees (1 to 5%)

First, merchants pay card issuers for the privilege of accepting their cards. While accepting credit cards certainly exposes merchants to more consumers who will likely spend more money, it does not come without a significant cost to the merchant, which is indirectly passed back to the consumer. The typical merchant pays the card issuer a fee of 1% to 5% of the gross transaction. Here is an example from the standpoint of a merchant:

Daily Credit Card Sales:	$1,000
Less: 3% Merchant Fee:	$ <30>
Total Net Daily Sales:	$ 970

There is a great difference in the percentage of merchant fees charged by the card issuers. Notoriously, whereas Visa, MasterCard, and Discover are comparatively priced, American Express generally charges a significant premium that can sometimes be as much as double the others. However, American Express tends to attract a more affluent consumer, and that may translate into more business for the merchant.

The exact rate a merchant pays is determined by a variety of factors, including the overall annual volume of the merchant, whether the purchases are made in person or online, the average transaction amount and the quantity of chargeback disputes received from consumers.

The reason that it is important to understand how merchant fees are assessed is because this cost is generally built into the overall pricing of the product, even if you pay by cash or check and the merchant does not have to absorb this business cost. While you will certainly not be able to negotiate a discount with large companies or chains, many merchants may provide you with an incentive to pay by some other means than a credit card. Unfortunately, the reverse of this can also sometimes be true—merchants may try to charge a premium percentage to the consumer (usually 3%) who wants to use a credit card. While this may technically violate the agreement the merchant has with the credit card issuer, the net effect is that the purchase ends up costing the consumer more than the face value of the item.

Sale of Customer Demographic Information

Finally, credit card issuers also make money by selling the demographic and contact information of their customers. Sometimes this information is just used internally or among their affiliated entities, but many times this information is sold to third parties. Who knows your spending habits better than your credit card company? Whether you are into traveling, food and wine, or simply buying books, your credit card company knows this and then sells that information to companies who want to market to you, generally in the form of direct mail and catalogs, but depending upon their privacy policy, they may even be permitted to have telemarketers contact you!

But it does not just stop with your demographic information— companies may want to market to you based upon your credit score, good or bad. Local car dealers will purchase mailing lists of customers with good credit scores to send direct mail about their vehicles and special financing programs. Catalog companies will buy mailing lists of consumers who spend frequently on a certain type of product. By doing this, they already know that they have reached their target audience and that the consumer has the means of a credit card to make purchases of their products and merchandise.

Credit Cards vs. Debit Cards

Credit cards have been around a lot longer than debit cards have. Most places which take credit cards also accept debit cards, and debit and credit cards have fairly similar formats and appearances. When you present your plastic card for payment, the retailer sends data to the bank which processes card transactions on its behalf. This data then passes to the card company (such as MasterCard or Visa), which then electronically contacts your card issuer to gain approval for the transaction. The relevant information will then be sent back down the line, and your card issuer will debit your bank account or credit-card account and pass it down the chain. Today, all this communication is literally instantaneous.

There are big differences, though, between credit cards and debit cards. When you use a credit card, you are billed for the amount you charge and you usually have a grace period of between twenty to forty-five days (depending upon the time of the month and your issuer's policies) to pay that amount before interest is charged. When you use a debit card, however, the money comes directly from your checking account and *no interest* is charged. In other words, **a debit card is just like writing a check**, because you will be overdrawn if you spend more than what you have in your account at that very moment. And whatever you do, do *not* let your account become overdrawn. Keep extra-careful track of the running balance in the checking account that your debit card is associated with. Otherwise, the penalty fees will kill you.

Debit cards usually double as ATM cards. Because of bank competition, many do not charge annual fees and also waive ATM fees at their network of branches. However, you may incur an ATM fee, as much as $2 per transaction, if you use an out-of-network ATM. Again, shop around, be an educated consumer, and read the fine print. It may also behoove you to verify how many ATMs the company has and where they are. What's the benefit if they only have one machine in your state and it is two hundred miles away?

Actually, many people still call debit cards "ATM cards," and appropriately so. **Credit cards**, on the other hand, **should NEVER be used for cash withdrawals**. Why not? Simply because credit-card issuers usually charge withdrawal fees, oftentimes 2.5% to 3% of the amount withdrawn. In addition, most credit cards don't provide any interest-free period for cash transactions, so you start paying interest at ultra-high cash advance rates (usually 20% annual percentage rate or more) from day one. Oh yes, check all that fine print on your credit card information. Cash advances are usually at a much higher rate than regular purchases. Credit cards and ATM machines don't mix, so be careful which card you stick in when it's late at night and your wallet is empty.

The Credit Card Application Process

Literally, everyone receives pre-approved credit card applications in the mail these days. Mind you, the "pre-approved" part is a fuzzy-wuzzy phrase. People have been known to fill out the application and still get turned down, depending upon what information is gathered about them. Another marketing tactic of some credit card companies is to tease you with a low interest rate, but then to approve you with one that is much higher by citing that your credit score did not meet their criteria to receive the lower interest rate.

You are certainly not limited to only the card offers you receive in the mail. You can also initiate the relationship yourself. Some online research may turn up some very good credit card deals that may be worth exploring. There are some links to these on my website as well at www.BraunMincher.com. Remember, you are allowed to be a shopper in this process, even if it is your very first credit card. Most of these leads will direct you to websites where you can apply right online for an immediate approval, although hard copy applications are still quite common.

Lenders use a wide range of information to assess your credit card application. This includes information you provide on your application form as well as data from credit bureaus. I have never heard of a credit card application asking for financial statements or income verification. You are asked what you earn and they take it from there. Still, I would not recommend lying—who knows where your data goes? Add a few zeros to your income to get a credit card with a high limit and you may find Mr. IRS knocking on your door asking what's up.

Lenders use a system known as Risk Based Pricing. This means that their customers pay different APRs (Annual Percentage Rates) depending on their risk profile. The less they know about you from your application and credit reference file, the lower your credit limit is likely to be in the first instance. Once you have become an established customer, you can look into increasing your credit limit, usually after a minimum "seasoning" period of six months.

Consumer Protection for Cardholders

The most common worry regarding credit cards is theft of the card. Such a theft could occur as the result of the innocent loss of your wallet, being the victim of a mugger or a pickpocket, or less direct methods such as thieves going through your trash.

If you ever receive pre-approved credit card offers (and most of us do all the time), **make sure you shred them if you are not interested**; do not simply toss these offers in the trash. This is especially important **if they send you an actual card**, which is also quite common. **Cut the card up.**

True story: Back when I was working at Sears during high school, a guy approached me and said, "Hey, I have a whole bunch of Visa cards that I stole out of people's mailboxes. If you allow me to make a bunch of purchases with them, I'll sell the stuff and split the money with you."

I knew this spelled trouble and wanted nothing to do with it. So, I told my supervisor and we called the police. They suggested setting up a sting. When the fraud came into the store and made a bunch of large purchases, I (*wink, wink*) ran his card through and got the charges approved. Since these were, in fact, large purchases, I instructed him to go down to the loading dock to pick them up. He walked in and the cops put badges and a gun in his face. Sometimes, crime does not pay. Now, do you want to know how much more foolish this whole episode was on the part of the fraud guy? This happened back in the days when Sears did not even *take* Visa cards!

I hear a lot of people saying, "I would never make a purchase over that new-fangled Internet thing. You have to give them your credit card number." Well, yes you do. You also do so every time you go to a restaurant and pay by credit card. 50% of all credit card fraud is perpetrated in face-to-face transactions, such as handing your card to a waitress or a clerk. And yes, the other 50% occurs over the Internet. Let's face it—the moment that card is out of your hand, it is in someone else's. There are machines that can copy the magnetic strip from your card in seconds. Even more low-tech is simply the ability for someone to copy down the number, even the little "secret" three-digit number on the back of the card. This is called *skimming*.

Credit card fraud costs hundreds of millions of dollars a year and most of that burden is placed upon the merchant, which is why my Visa card thief at Sears wanted my cooperation. Merchants have to protect themselves in order not to be stuck holding the bag. Of course, the more that merchants get victimized, the higher consumer prices go in order to compensate. Thus, we all bear the brunt of crime.

Always keep your account numbers and card issuer's phone numbers in a safe place. Keeping them in your wallet—*with your cards*—is not a safe place. Can you say "redundancy?" As a backup, you can also just look at your most recent statement, which probably has that information as well.

Don't carry *all* your credit cards with you. If you have eight credit cards, you don't need all eight with you at the same time, just for this reason. I mean, if your wallet *is* stolen, you *will* have to cancel your cards and it will take a few days to get new ones. That could leave you without *any* credit cards, which is not a comfortable position to be in.

If you left three of them back home in your safe, at least you can use those in the meantime.

Another thing to think about: some cards can be used as either a debit *or* a credit card. **If you are doing a face-to-face transaction and are asked whether you want to use your card as debit or credit *always* request credit.** Reason? With debit, you have to key in your PIN (Personal Identification Number). That gives people around you, such as the clerk or even that guy a few feet away with the camera cell phone a chance to not only get your account number, but your PIN as well.

Reconcile Your Monthly Bill

How can you possibly know if you've been ripped-off if you don't reconcile your transaction slips with your monthly credit card bill? Always keep all of your transaction slips. If necessary, demand one. If you are making an online purchase, print out a receipt. If for some reason it is a recurring charge, such as a subscription of some sort that does not provide you with transaction slips, keep a log of each charge somewhere so that it, too, can be checked off of your statement.

Sometimes people go into a panic unnecessarily. When reviewing their statement they see a charge from a company they never heard of. It happens all the time, but it's not always fraud or theft. Many companies you do business with are D/B/A's—"Doing Business As." This means that you may be in Joe's Men's Shop, but Joe's business banking and merchant card set-up are listed as "Smith Enterprises, LLC." You buy your suit at Joe's, but you get a charge from this Smith Enterprises place and you freak out.

Now, if you kept all your receipts in order to match them up with your monthly statements, you would notice that on March 12th you made a $799 purchase at Joe's, which turns out to be the exact date and amount of this charge from Smith Enterprises. Mystery most likely solved.

Something else along these lines is that sometimes a business name is too long to fit entirely on a credit card statement. Thus, the partial representation looks odd and unfamiliar. Again, check your receipts.

Limits of Liability

Once you report a lost or stolen card, you are no longer responsible for any unauthorized charges. Even if you *don't* report it, by federal law, your maximum liability is $50 per card. This is an amazing consumer protection and further buttresses the argument that credit cards are a good thing for smart consumers.

Credit card fraud is actually investigated by the US Secret Service, but they will only get involved if it exceeds $2,000. For this reason, smart criminals will actually keep fraudulent purchases at any single merchant under $2,000 in order to avoid prosecution.

Bear in mind, all of this is germane only to credit cards, not debit cards. If you have your debit card stolen, it is game over. They can clear out that bank account and that's that. For that reason, I advise only keeping a limited amount of money in an account for which you have a debit card. But let's say that limit is $1,000. Do you really want to part with $1,000 when instead you could be liable for just $50?

Merchant Disputes and Chargeback Rights

Chargeback rights became popular in the 1970s under Federal Banking Regulation Z, better known as the Truth in Lending Act. Essentially, **chargeback rights is the money a merchant refunds a customer after the customer successfully disputes an item on his or her credit card statement.** Customers usually dispute charges to their credit cards when goods or services are not delivered within the specified time frame, goods are received damaged, or the purchase was not authorized by the credit card holder. These rights are upheld by both federal and state laws.

Chargeback rights pertain *ONLY* to credit cards, not debit cards. Thus, consumers have much greater protections with credit cards versus debit cards, or even cash or checks. Now, while I endorse the use of debit cards for ATM usage, I do not agree with some people who believe in using their debit cards for all purchases because they "don't want to pay interest charges." True, there is no interest on a debit card—it's merely a bank withdrawal. On the other hand, **if you don't want to pay interest, pay your credit cards in full and on time.** And yes, I know the argument against this one: "But with a debit card, I won't ever have the temptation to spend what I don't have." True. But **self-discipline is the key to wealth creation.**

There are two major types of chargeback rights. One is *billing error rights*. This is the dispute of a charge. You must do this within sixty days. Sometimes you can get this extended up to a year, but you then have to jump through of the following hoops:

- The purchase must be over $50.
- It must be within 100 miles of your home address.
- You must first make a good-faith effort to resolve the dispute with the merchant.
- You must *not* have paid for the disputed item. **If you act within the sixty day period, you do *not* have these particular restrictions.**

Now, as much as we've been talking about pure fraud where someone, say, steals your credit card, let's delve into simple merchant disputes.

True story: I recently went on a long business trip that started with an early morning flight. Upon arrival at the airport, I was informed that there were upgrades to first-class available for only an additional $100. This sounded good to me, but what I really wanted was a hot breakfast, which the counter agent assured me would be served on this trip in first class. When I got on the plane, they only served peanuts and I felt ripped off.

The moment I got home, I called the airline and told them that the promise of breakfast was the only reason I bought the $100 upgrade and that they had not delivered on the service that they had expressly represented. Tough luck, Mr. Mincher. They weren't going to refund my money.

I called up my credit card company, told them my story, and they sent me a simple form to fill out and sign. In the end, I got my $100 back. This is a chargeback. If I had paid with check, debit card, or cash, I would be out $100.

If you do a chargeback, the entity that is responsible in the end is the merchant—fine for you; not so fine for the merchant.

Shopping for Credit Cards

These days, it seems as though credit cards come in all sizes, shapes, and colors. What may be the right card for someone else is not necessarily the right card for you, and the right card for you today may not be the right card for you in the future. Thanks to the Internet, it is actually very easy to shop for credit cards and compare them on equal points.

First, pick the type of credit card that you want. Both **Visa and MasterCard** are almost universally accepted anywhere in the world that accepts credit cards. **Discover** has a great annual "cash back" incentive, but is slightly less commonly accepted. **American Express** has many advantages such as prestige and no pre-set spending limit, but again, not all merchants accept it, and even when they do, they sometimes try to surcharge the purchase because the merchant fees are so high. Note that both Visa and MasterCard are issued by a multitude of companies such as banks, credit unions, credit providers and other affinity programs, so it is in your best interest to shop around for the best deal. American Express is simply American Express—no comparison shopping allowed. Also, most American Express cards traditionally require consumers to pay the balance in full each month.

I would recommend staying away from obscure cards such as Carte Blanche and Diner's Club. Maybe there was a place for these cards in the disco '70s, but I have no clue as to how or why these cards even exist today. This also includes gas station or department store credit cards, as they offer limited usage, generally charge higher interest rates, and affect your credit score just like a traditional credit card.

Second, find out if there is an **annual fee**. The majority of the major credit cards are available without an annual fee, but be sure to check if this is just a first year promotion or a permanent policy. Most of the cards with some type of "reward" program *do* charge an annual fee to help offset the cost of providing such a service. These range from about $60 per year for the United Mileage Plus Visa, to $395 for the American Express Platinum. **Do not pay an annual fee just to have a credit card**; only do so if the benefit they offer you more than outweighs this cost.

Next, research whether the card offers any special "**rewards programs**" or "affinity programs." In these cases, you may receive airline miles for every dollar you spend, free gasoline, merchant discounts, or even have part of your purchases support a cause that you believe in.

Airline miles are by far the most popular credit card rewards program. In most cases, consumers earn one mile for every dollar they spend, but the exact formulas vary widely and some even cap the number of miles you can earn per year. If you like to travel, using one of these cards to make your everyday purchases might make sense.

When I built a new house several years ago, I used some of my credit cards to make the purchases of everything from lumber to appliances. In the end, I had accumulated enough miles for several airline tickets. Although they are a regionalized carrier based out of Denver, I personally think that Frontier Airlines has one of the best values with their credit card. They offer one mile per dollar spent, and it only takes 15,000 miles for a round trip ticket (35,000 for an international destination).

"**Cash Back**" is another great selling point for a card. It allows shoppers to receive cash along with their goods when paying by card.

Other credit card programs co-market with national merchants or causes. For example, Starbucks has their own credit card where consumers earn points that can be used for free lattes. This might be a sizeable savings for somebody who frequents the store often. Even the Hooters restaurant chain has their own credit card; I can only imagine what their reward is. Some credit cards offer additional perks to lure customers and help justify their annual fee. My American Express Platinum card gets me free access to several airline lounges when I travel, and they have an international airline travel program that provides a free companion ticket on certain trips that recently saved me about $2,000. Some cards also donate a percentage of your spending to a variety of causes such as the American Cancer Society, the Red Cross, and others.

Take a look at the **grace period** offered by the card. At the worst end are cards that may have no grace period at all. Interest begins accruing the moment you make a purchase. Read your fine print and find out. More typically, a competitive grace period may be twenty to forty-five days from date of purchase, depending upon the billing cycle your card uses.

You are probably going to use a credit card in some manner anyway, so you should get whatever card best matches your particular needs. I cannot emphasize enough, though, the importance of maintaining good credit and paying off your balances monthly to save you from excessive interest charges. We have become a society conditioned on immediate gratification and keeping at pace with our neighbors with little regard for the long-term consequences.

Credit Card Interest Rates

The most important thing for people who carry credit card balances is to compare interest rates. Some cards may offer low 1.9% promotional rates, but you need to be aware that these are probably for a temporary period of time and then may increase substantially if you have not either paid off the card or transferred the balance somewhere else. **Beware of introductory "teaser" rates**. The best ones may last for a year or more, but some of them only last a matter of days. **As always, read the fine print**. A simple web search will show you multiple comparisons of credit card interest rates. The best permanent (non-variable) rates available as of this writing are about 6.9%, with the high being as much as 25%; the average is probably around 13% on an annual basis, making it one of the most expensive forms of debt. Remember that interest, especially compounding interest, adds up fast and even a couple of percentage points can have a big impact if you carry any type of significant balance. Unlike mortgage interest, credit card interest is *not* tax deductible.

It is important for consumers to know whether they are getting a card with a fixed or a variable interest rate. Variable is going to be tied to some market like the Prime Rate Index in some way. A common example may be 10% over Prime. If Prime is 5%, your rate is 15%. If Prime rises to 7%, you rise to 17% and so on. It is interesting to note that the Prime Rate has more than doubled over the past three years prior to this writing and currently sits just below 8%.

Credit card issuers generally have different interest rates that they charge to different classes of consumers and for different types of transactions. Ironically, the people who are least likely to be able to pay are charged the highest rates. This is because these people pose the highest risk for credit card issuers, and also the most profit potential. People with bad credit and limited finances, even if they perform well, get stuck paying for others in their same situation who default. If you handle your finances professionally and maintain good credit, you will generally get more credit and lower interest rates in the future.

The credit card business is very competitive and you can generally negotiate better rates with your issuer simply by calling them up—assuming that you have good credit, are not overextended, and have made all of your payments on time.

I generally do not carry credit card balances, but recently one of my businesses wanted to use one of its credit cards to carry a small balance for a short period of time. When I saw that I would be charged almost 19% interest, I called the credit card company and told them that I would use their card for an upcoming purchase if they could offer me a better interest rate. They lowered the rate by almost half to 12%, simply by my asking! In my case, this probably resulted in a nominal savings of twenty or thirty dollars, but think about the savings for someone who has thousands of dollars in credit card debt for a period of time.

Credit card issuers also classify transaction types differently. Generally, you receive the lowest interest rates on balances associated with regular purchases. Other transactions, such as **cash advances, have much higher interest charges** that are generally just under the limits to be considered *usury* (illegally excessive), depending upon which state you live in (18 to 29%). Both balance transfers and convenience checks (next subchapter) are sometimes classified as cash advances after their promotional rate period ends.

So at the end of the day, what are you looking for in a credit card?

- Low or no annual fee
- Some sort of rewards program
- A long grace period
- A low interest rate (if you carry balances)

Convenience Checks and Balance Transfers

Many credit card issuers offer consumers the ability to "write a check" for purchases, rather than having to present the credit card to be charged. These are generally known as "*convenience checks*," blank copies of which are provided to consumers either when the account is opened, periodically in conjunction with special interest rate offers, or even included with the monthly statement.

You should **beware of these convenience checks** for several different reasons. First, they can generally be spent just like any other check, even with merchants who do not accept credit cards. The major problem comes when consumers deposit these checks into their own checking accounts to pay other bills and in essence, borrow from Peter to pay Paul. Second, the **convenience checks generally have some type of fee associated with them**; since there is technically no merchant to pay this, the burden then falls upon the consumer. Generally, these fees equal an additional charge of 3% added to the transaction, but sometimes have a maximum limit of $50 per check. Finally, the interest charged on convenience checks is generally considered to be a *"cash advance"* which means that it is at a much greater rate than normal purchases, because the credit card issuer perceives more risk and the opportunity to charge more interest. Be sure to read and understand the fine print of any convenience check offer before using this method.

Most credit card issuers entice new business by offering consumers the ability to transfer their balances at a special low rate for a temporary period of time. This offers the credit card issuer the ability to take business away from their competitors. **If you do carry credit card balances, transfers to other cards with low promotional rates can be a good strategy** so long as you keep aware of how long the rate is good for and either pay it off or transfer it to another card before the interest rate rises. Again, it is very important that you read and understand the fine print contained in any balance transfer offers.

Another one of the tricks to this come-on is a fee charged for the actual transfer of balances from one card to another. It may be, say, 3% of the amount transferred, up to $50. This may seem negligible, but just be aware and insert this into your calculations.

Now, this whole thing is quite the game, and yes, although the odds are stacked against you, you *can* win if you're smart. Let's say you lost your job and had to live on your credit cards for a few months. Now you've gotten a good new job. You still have new expenses every day, but the way you figure it, if you could cap that backlog of expenses you rang up on your credit cards, and then lock that in at an incredibly low interest rate—say 1.99%—you might be able to pay it all off in, perhaps, six months and the 1.99% deal is for twelve months. Bada-bing! You just did some credit card gymnastics and saved yourself some serious money.

But then there's the other side, the side where the house wins. You transfer to that 1.99% rate card. You fail to notice that transfer fee. Okay, so you eat that, but that wasn't that bad, was it? Just another $50. Then you make those payments. But you fail to read the part where all your new purchases are at 18% interest. Pretty high. But you use that card anyway and you ring up some new purchases. You also don't notice that **often times the credit card company applies your payments to the balance carrying the lowest interest**. You're paying down that transfer balance at 1.99% but you're not making a dent on those new purchases you made at 18% and that just keeps compounding and compounding.

There was also another thing you forgot to investigate. The fine print said that all unpaid balance transfers still in place at the end of twelve months would convert to *21%* interest! Between those new purchases you made, their high compounding interest, and some other extraneous spending in your life, suddenly, at the end of the twelve-month cycle, you're actually in worse shape than when you started this whole juggling act!

Strategic balance transfers are not for the sloppy or disorganized. They are for the plodding, plotting, anal retentive, disciplined fiscal warrior. Is that you? I hope so.

Credit Card Universal Default Clauses

There's a new game in town, and it will bite you hard if you're not aware of it. By this point in the book, you probably know that if you pay a credit card bill late, you will get a late fee, it will hurt your credit score, and the card you were late on is likely to raise its interest rate on you.

Well, it appears that's no longer punishment enough. Nearly 40% of all credit cards now carry a *Universal Default Clause*. **With a universal default clause, not only will your credit card company raise your interest rate if you are ever late paying *them*, they will also raise your interest rate if you are late to *other companies*!** And this may happen not only if you pay another company's credit card bill late, but also if you pay your car loan, mortgage, or even your phone bill late!

It's all in the fine print of your credit card agreement—that paper that no one ever reads but should. The credit card issuers' theory is that, while you may never have been late paying *them*, you are, in fact, a late payer, and late payers are bad. They think, why wait to get burned by one tomorrow if you can start charging them for their inherent risk right now? This, of course, has always been the case when initially applying for credit, but the idea of doing it mid-stream, and when you have never made any late payments to the issuer in question, is rather new.

Credit cards with universal default clauses keep a tight check on your credit report—which you should ALSO do. And if they see something they don't like…BAM! They can and will up your interest rate overnight without warning. The average "default rate" in 2005 was 24%.. As the prime lending rate has increased, that figure is likely to be even higher today.

Always be aware if you have a card with this feature. If you do, consider switching out of it via a balance transfer. Also, look at your statements every month. Don't just look at your balance; look at your interest rate as well. It may have gone up and you didn't even know it.

Identity Theft

Simply put, identity theft is someone trying to use your good name and credit to consummate financial transactions. If you feel this has happened to you, there are four important steps to take:

1. Call the fraud department at the credit bureaus. They will put a fraud alert on your credit account. Technically, you only need contact one of the major bureaus and they are supposed to contact the others on your behalf. **Contacting the credit bureaus first is the best way to prevent a thief from opening up *new* credit accounts in your name.** People usually only think about what lines of credit they have open *now*. That's the easy stuff. Imagine someone stealing your identity and successfully applying for ten new credit cards. Yikes! With a fraud alert on your name and personal data, anyone attempting this will be put through the wringer— asked to produce all sorts of additional documentation proving identity.

There are two different kinds of fraud alerts. An *initial fraud report* will last for ninety days. That's a good way to go if you've been the victim of a scam or perhaps had your wallet stolen.

An *extended fraud alert* will stay on for seven years. Among other things, this will remove your name from all pre-screened credit offers (you may know this as "junk mail") for five years. The extended fraud alert will basically stay on until you take it off. This is a good route to go if you feel that there are still outstanding issues after ninety days. You are not married to it for the full seven years.

When either of these actions are taken, the credit bureau will usually assign you a PIN for you to use when you, yes YOU, want to open up a legitimate credit account. You would be asked for this number before you could open up any new accounts.

2. Call the actual credit card companies. Call them up and close the accounts you feel have been tampered with or which have stolen cards associated with them.

Once you have had a particular credit issue resolved, you will want to ask for something *in writing* from the credit card company stating that they have *closed* the violated account and *discharged* the fraudulent debt. This is your best proof if errors regarding your accounts show up later on your credit report.

3. File a complaint with the Federal Trade Commission. This is most pertinent if your loss has exceeded $2,000. But even if it is less, they will put your issue in their data base and share it with other law enforcement agencies across the nation. This is a "good citizen" action for you to help put away big-time identity thieves, and yes, there are some major ones out there. Identity theft has become a major industry.

4. File a complaint with your local police department. You may need this in order to deal with your creditors. Some may require that you report your identity theft as a crime...because it is one. Creditors have become wary of people making extravagant purchases, then claiming someone else stole their wallet and did it. Meanwhile, they're sitting in their living room, looking at the ball game on their new (free) big screen TV.

Phishing

"Phishing" is the number one scam on the Internet right now. By definition, phishing is attempting to fraudulently acquire sensitive information, such as passwords and credit details, by masquerading as a trustworthy person or business in an electronic communication. One of the most common methodologies is for you to receive what looks like a legitimate e-mail from a company you already deal with (say, America Online, PayPal, American Express, etc...). Once you open it, there is often a request for you to update your personal information with them, usually via an Internet link they want you to click on. Scare tactics are common, such as saying, "Someone has recently tried hacking into your personal account. To protect yourself, click here and re-answer your personal questions so that we can prevent further violations of your account in the future." This may be accompanied by a request for your existing passwords or data and then a request that you now "change" them. The scare is often further heightened by telling you that your account has actually been "shut down" because of attacks by frauds. Imagine how scary it is to receive an e-mail telling you that your only credit card has now been closed for such a reason the night before you are to leave on a long vacation. Frightening stuff.

Do you have any idea of how successful this scam is? A few years ago, I recall a test being done where a college full of students was all "phished" to see how many "phishes" the ruse would catch. Would you believe 80%? Eighty percent of all the students scammed willingly gave out their personal information over the Internet. Social Security numbers, account numbers for banks and credit cards, passwords, you name it. We are such cooperative people!

Armed with this information, someone can make another \person's life a living hell. Your credit cards can all get run up, new accounts can be started, purchases can be made, and cash withdrawn. The possibilities are endless, and it can take you hundreds of man-hours to amend the situation, if you can at all. Even under the best scenarios, you could still be held responsible for certain minimum "threshold" amounts (often $50 per credit card).

The thing to look out for is that they run this scam by using an e-mail account name that looks for all the world like a legitimate one. Example: you have an account with onlineauctions.*com* (I'm making this one up). You get an e-mail from onlineauctions.*net*. Close, but no cigar. But at a quick glance, you're convinced this is the real deal.

Once you open the e-mail, you are told to click a link. NO, NO, NO, NO, NO! Have I made myself clear? If you want to communicate with this company for real, type their real web address DIRECTLY into your browser and go from there. **Do NOT click on a link from an e-mail.**

This is called *link manipulation*. What they send you to is called a *spoofed website*. It looks legit, but it's not. Another method is via a *subdomain*, which is when you are in one website and see what looks like a familiar name, perhaps in an ad, as a link, such as your bank or mortgage company, and think, "Oh, I know them. That's safe," but it isn't, much like if someone changed the names on the doors of the men's room and the ladies' room in a restaurant. A bad joke indeed.

Once gained, this information may be used by the thief himself or may be sold on the black market. The going rate for each stolen profile is between $1 and $50.

Always be suspicious if an e-mail from a company you do business with does not contain at least one piece of private information. If the e-mail simply says, "Dear Customer," and does not at least have your user name or the last four digits of your Social Security number or your credit card ...be on alert.

In light of the rash of phishing expeditions, some companies are fighting on your behalf by creating what is called "two factor user authentication." Here is how it works: instead of being asked for your user name and password at the same time on the same screen, it only asks for your user name. Once you type it in, the screen changes and you see a picture or a phrase that you have previously chosen. If what flashes up on the screen is not what you expected, you know you're in a bad place. Get out now. A method that has been out longer is where, when you are setting up your online account, you are asked to put in one or two personal questions for you to answer later. Typically, this may be something on the order of, "What was the name of your first grade teacher?" or, "Name your favorite childhood pet." This all occurs before you are asked to put in that very important password of yours.

Are these safety features foolproof? No. But they're a step in the right direction.

Credit Repair

Repairing your credit score from either negative information or errors can sometimes be a long and painstaking process since there are multiple credit bureaus, and possibly even creditors, to deal with in making the necessary corrections. Just like you would see a specialist for a medical condition or a mechanic to fix your car, there are experienced companies who specialize in helping you to repair and/or improve your credit, which ultimately translates into significant cost savings due to lower interest rates. I have seen multiple people, with both good and bad credit alike, improve their credit score substantially by enlisting the assistance of one of the *legitimate* credit repair services. Please see the "links" section of my website at www.BraunMincher.com for a listing.

Unfortunately, many people wait until they apply for a loan to learn they have blemishes on their credit report. Knowledge is power, and as a good consumer, you should know of any adverse information on your credit report at least six months prior to applying for credit so that you have the opportunity for improvement. This equally applies to somebody who already has "good" credit and wants "great credit" to save even more.

The strategy of legitimate credit repair consultants is to analyze your credit report and advise you what can be done to improve your credit score. This can be as simple as transferring your balance from one credit card to another to reduce the balance ratio, or by spotting incorrect information and getting it corrected by a creditor. They then contact the credit bureaus on your behalf and literally hound them to death until the corrections are made. A friend of mine even got a letter from one of the credit bureaus advising that his credit repair consultant was overwhelming them with paperwork and offered to make the requested correction if he would ask them to stop sending letters. The credit bureaus may not like this, but that is what I call action with resolution!

Unfortunately, the FTC (Federal Trade Commission) has found that some companies in both the credit repair and credit counseling (next subchapter) business are less than scrupulous, preying upon the desperate among us. They have passed the Credit Repair Organizations Act (CROA) for our protection. Under CROA, **it is illegal for consumers to be charged money for promised credit repair services before they have been performed**. Also, some companies claim that they can remove *legitimate* negative credit information about you for your benefit. This is also patently illegal. Credit repair and counseling companies must also give you written statements telling you that everything they do, you can, quite frankly, do for yourself.

Disputing negative, inaccurate and/or misleading items on your credit report is your right as a consumer. The right to use a legitimate credit repair agency is also legal and encouraged if you have multiple errors or a complex credit reporting situation.

Credit Counseling Services

There is a significant difference between credit repair and credit counseling services. **Credit counseling is a type of debt negotiation.** While credit repair is something that even people with very good credit may try to make it even better, credit counseling is for critical situations just prior to declaration of bankruptcy. Serious stuff. Contacting creditors on your own, negotiating payment arrangements, asking permission to skip a payment, or asking for a lower interest rate are simple measures you can take to manage your debt. Don't consider any other course of action until you've tried these options.

Debt negotiation by a credit counseling service usually involves that company calling your creditors and telling them that you are on the brink of bankruptcy and would they consider accepting less money than what you actually owe them. A lender has little motivation to accept a pay off for less than the full amount you owe unless you are already several months behind on your bills.

If you have a substantial amount of debt, a qualified credit counseling service may be able to help you reduce payments and prevent further damage to your credit report. Although credit counseling can provide consumers with valuable assistance, some firms exist only to cheat their vulnerable clients. These companies use their non-profit status to attract customers who are then tricked into paying large fees to them. Those fees are sometimes funneled to for-profit companies. Along with CROA (see last subchapter), recently the FTC and the IRS issued the following tips for choosing a credit counseling organization:

- Pay careful attention to the fees an agency charges, the nature of the services it offers, and the terms of the contract.

- Make sure that creditors are willing to work with the agency you plan to use.
- Consider using agencies that offer actual counseling and education instead of simply enrolling all clients in a debt management program.

Another option for consumers overwhelmed by debt is to consolidate debt by establishing a new loan with lower monthly payments. A **debt consolidation loan** helps manage your debt because the loan is usually over a longer period of time and possibly at lower interest than your existing debt. Consolidation should be used when debts are mostly current.

As a general safety precaution, anyone who plans on using a third party to handle their finances should remember to check them out with the Better Business Bureau and the state Attorney General's Office of Consumer Protection. These agencies keep records of credit repair and credit counseling services that have misled their customers about the impact the service would have on their credit rating, the fees involved, and the possibility of legal action from the creditors. As always, I also suggest getting referrals and references from other satisfied customers.

Banks versus Credit Unions

A bank is a for-profit entity that holds deposits, makes loans, cashes checks and provides other related services for the public. **A credit union is a not-for-profit** financial cooperative that offers many of the same services to individuals who share a common affiliation. This can be as specific as the same employer (i.e. State Employees Credit Union, ACME Corporation Credit Union, Teachers Credit Union, etc.) or be as general as being open to all residents of a particular city or county. Because of their non-profit status, credit unions are exempt from both local and federal taxes, which as you can imagine has caused some controversy with banks in recent years who are claiming that this structure is unfair to their industry. Credit unions are owned by their members (customers) and even pay them back a dividend out of their earnings. Because of these reasons, **credit unions generally have lower operating costs and can charge below-market rates on loans while paying savers higher rates.**

Businesses are generally prohibited from being members of a credit union, but they are still a great option for individual consumers. In my experience, **credit unions are the best place to go for auto loans** as they seem always to have some of the lowest rates.

Service Fees

Over the past few years, banks and credit unions have added billions of dollars of profit to their bottom lines by charging consumers service fees for things that they previously did for free. This includes monthly account maintenance fees, overdraft fees, check copy fees, and some have even tried to charge customers for using a live teller to complete a transaction. The good news is that with all of the competition now in the industry, you should be able to locate a financial institution to fit your needs that does not nickel-and-dime you in fees, which all add up over the course of time. Even a $6 per month account maintenance fee is $72 per year. Now imagine if you have several different accounts all being charged these fees—you can do the math.

Whether I am opening an account for my personal or business needs, I always negotiate with the bank to make sure that it will be free of any unnecessary fees. My theory is that the bank should earn its money off me in the form of the interest that it charges on any loans I might have with them, or from their having the use of my deposits to loan out to their other customers. I should not also be charged a fee for the privilege of keeping my money at their institution. It is also interesting to note that most business checking accounts are not able to earn interest.

From a business account standpoint, some banks try to charge a fee (usually $.20 to $.30) for each and every deposit or check that passes through the account. This is ridiculous and you should either ask them to waive this fee or find another bank—there are many these days that offer free checking for both business as well as individual customers.

Direct Deposit

If you are not already using direct deposit for your paycheck or other income, sign up today. I cannot believe the number of people who still waste all that time standing in line at the bank each week to deposit their check. Worse, some people end up using check cashing outlets with exorbitant fees that chew up a good chunk of their income.

Just about every type of payment you receive for services can be deposited directly into the bank, even your IRS refund check if you give them your checking account information on the tax return. Personally, I have both my tenants and the borrowers that I lend money to go to the bank to deposit their monthly payments directly into my checking account so I do not have to.

Your time is valuable and you should think about automating routine tasks whenever possible.

Automatic Bill Pay

Just as setting up direct deposits adds efficiency, so does automating your routine payments. With most recurring payments such as utilities, your mortgage, car payment and the like, you can set up ACH (Automated Clearing House) payments with your creditors wherein they will deduct the payment from your checking account.

For occasional bills, you can also set up online "Bill Pay" services from your bank. You simply log-on to your account, enter the payee name, address and amount, and like magic they print and mail the check for you from their central processing facility. In many cases banks find this to be such an efficient process for them that they do not even charge you for the cost of the stamp.

Get Organized

Although it may seem like overkill, I **save every receipt** in case I ever need to return something, get reimbursement, or justify it to the IRS at some point in the future. I use separate credit cards for both my personal and business purchases, and I empty the receipts out of my wallet every few days into a box that I have in one of my desk drawers. When the monthly credit card bills arrive, I match up all of the receipts and staple them to the bill. At the end of the year, I scan all of the bills and receipts into my computer, make a CD for backup, and then shred it all. This process has worked extremely well and I am amazed about two to three times per year how easy it is when I need to locate some detail on a past purchase. There are also some professional systems on the market that help you to organize your personal financial papers.

This same kind of organizational process can be applied to statements from your bank, mortgage company, retirement account, etc. I have a separate folder or three-ring binder for each one of these that I file the statement in each month after reading it. At the end of the year, I scan all of the documents, make a CD for backup, and then shred them.

Another way to get organized is to **cut down on the quantity of solicitations received by mail, e-mail, and the telephone.** I specifically request vendors, credit card companies, and online companies not to place me on their mailing lists and "**opt-out**" whenever given the option. I use a separate e-mail address for all online purchases, as they inevitably sell your name to others even if they do not inundate you with their own marketing. Finally, I have a separate phone number that goes directly to my voice mail that I give out to all of the credit card companies, airlines, online vendors, and the like. The time I save by doing these simple things probably saves me two to three hours per week that I can then spend doing productive and income-generating activities.

Collections and Public Records

When a customer does not pay as agreed, many creditors may turn them over to either their internal collections department or an outside collection agency. This scenario is not good for either the consumer or the creditor, as unnecessary resources are expended and expenses are involved. Collection action may become a public record and in turn get reported to the credit bureaus. Public information is also now posted on many websites, which means that people you deal with may have access to it either now or in the future, and this may put you in an uncomfortable situation.

We typically think of credit card companies as the ones who turn deadbeats over to collection, but this can also be done by banks and other lenders, insurance companies, hospitals and medical practices, and even landlords.

My best advice to avoid collections is to make sure that all of your creditors always have your current address and telephone number so that they can contact you. This is especially important for people who move around frequently, which tends to happen both during or shortly after college for most people, as well as before they get married and have children; (families tend to be more stable address-wise). As mentioned previously, it is also smart to be aware of what payments you are obligated to pay and to contact the creditor if you do not receive a statement for some reason. So, too, you should obtain a copy of your credit report at least annually to make sure that none of your creditors have reported you as late or taken collection or legal action against you. Finally, **if you do find yourself faced with having to deal with a collector for a valid debt, it is generally best to acknowledge their contact (rather than try to avoid them) and work out some type of reasonable repayment plan that you can both live with.** You will find that most people are willing to work with you if you make an effort, but I will tell you from experience that most creditors such as myself will go through great effort and expense to hold deadbeat debtors fully responsible for their contractual obligations if they are not cooperative or try to completely avoid responsibility.

Case Story: As a landlord and private lender myself, I usually have to pursue several collection issues each year, mostly from residential tenants. Recently, I had to seek collection against a college student (we will call her Molly) who defaulted on the payment of her lease after she broke up with her boyfriend and he moved out of state. Because the lease was "joint and several" (see the upcoming "Leases" chapter), we could collect the full amount from either of the tenants, and since Molly was the most accessible with roots in the community, she was the easiest for us to reach. However, Molly would not answer any of my phone calls or respond to my letters requesting that we work out a reasonable payment plan. She instead avoided the situation completely, hoping that it would go away. We had no other choice but to file a small claims action against Molly, and when we went to court she not only had to pay the original amount, but interest and court costs. Because this is now a public record, it will likely show up on her credit report and may prevent her from getting future credit, housing, a job, or even car insurance at some point in the future. The moral of this story is that it would have been much easier and less costly for everyone involved if Molly had just made the effort to work with us before we had to undertake legal action.

I would like to mention one last thing about collections. When faced with multiple collection matters (and pray this never happens to you), some experts recommend paying the *newest one first*. Yes, I realize that this flies in the face of all conventional wisdom of paying your oldest debts first, your newest debts last. But here is the logic: the moment a collection debt is paid, it gets listed on your credit reports as a new activity. Thus, to someone considering whether or not to extend you credit, they may look at your credit profile and say, "Well, she was put to collection for something five years ago, but since then she has had a sterling record." But pay that five-year-old collection issue off, and it literally looks like it just happened yesterday, is nullifying the "oh, that's old news" benefit-of-the-doubt you might have received from a new application for credit. It's tricky, yes, and very controversial. But it is worth thinking about if this particular tragedy should ever befall you.

Bankruptcy

In most cases, declaring bankruptcy should be a last resort for consumers, but sometimes it is the best choice. Almost 1.5 million people in the United States file for bankruptcy on an annual basis. **Bankruptcy allows debtors to get a fresh start by having most of their debts discharged**, such as credit card debt or medical bills. Generally, people who file for bankruptcy have gone through a life-changing event such as unemployment, a serious illness, or divorce. Many filers also started amassing credit card debt during college and then let it get out of control. Obviously, the best way to stop this from happening is not to let it start in the first place.

Contrary to popular belief, you do not lose everything and become homeless when you declare bankruptcy. Exemptions vary by state, but in most cases you are able to keep your house, your vehicle, insurance benefits, pensions, 401k or other retirement accounts, tools of your trade, and your personal property such as clothes, pictures, and books.

There are two main types of bankruptcy for individuals: Chapter 7 and Chapter 13. The first is a complete liquidation without the requirement for the debtor to repay their creditors. The second is a reorganization plan wherein a payment plan is worked out with the creditors. You can also file for Chapter 7 bankruptcy again after eight years and can file again for Chapter 13 at anytime.

Bankruptcy is probably one of the worst things that can affect your credit score and it can remain on your credit report for up to ten years. Some people think that they will not be able to get credit at all after filing for bankruptcy, and while this is incorrect, you will pay significantly higher interest rates.

In October of 2005, a new and more restrictive bankruptcy reform bill became effective to reduce abuse and encourage people who have some means of paying back some debt to do so rather than using the system as a financial planning tool. Among the requirements is a new "means test" to determine whether a debtor deserves to have some or all of their debts discharged, based upon their income as it compares to other families of the same size. The new law also requires debtors to complete courses in financial management before their debts are discharged in bankruptcy.

Payday Loans

Payday loans have become a vicious cycle for many working consumers who are already living paycheck to paycheck. Intended to provide short term cash until your next payday, many people find themselves with no other option but to rollover the payday loan and pay even more interest in the form of fees. **Payday loans are an extremely expensive way to borrow money** with effective APR's ranging from 300% to over 1,000%. Before taking out a payday loan, you should clearly understand what you will pay in the form of interest, be sure that you will be able to pay the loan off in full with your next paycheck, and first see if there are any other alternatives.

Payday loans, which are generally small, short-term and high-rate loans, are now made by a variety of check cashers, finance companies, and others, usually out of a small retail storefront or online. After verifying the existence of a checking account and steady income of at least $1,000 per month, the borrower writes a personal check payable to the lender for the amount he or she wishes to borrow, plus a fee. The company then gives the borrower cash for the amount of the check minus their fee.

Fees charged for payday loans are usually a percentage of the face value of the check or a flat fee charged per amount borrowed (e.g. $15 for every $100 borrowed) and repayment is due in two weeks (when you get your next paycheck). If you extend or "roll-over" the loan for another two weeks, you will pay the fees for each extension.

A payday advance loan is generally secured by your personal check. For example, you would write a personal check for $115 to borrow $100 for up to fourteen days. The payday lender agrees to hold the check until your next payday. At that time, depending on the particular plan, either the lender deposits the check, you redeem the check by paying the $115 in cash, or you roll-over the check by paying another fee to extend the loan for two weeks. Under this last scenario, the cost of the initial loan is a seemingly nominal $15 fee, yet this translates into an exorbitant 390% when expressed on an annual basis.

You can probably find other places to borrow for less than what payday lenders charge. Consider a small loan from your bank, credit union, small loan company, an advance on pay from your employer or a loan from family or friends. Even a credit card cash advance or accessing your overdraft protection would likely cost you much less in interest than a payday loan.

CHAPTER 2
REAL ESTATE MORTGAGES

In exchange for a real estate loan, borrowers provide their lender with a "*mortgage interest*" in a piece of real property. In other words, they use the property as **collateral** (something real and perceived to be of equal or greater value than the amount of money being borrowed). Unlike a credit card, this is considered a "**secured loan**," meaning that the lender can take the property instead of money if the borrower defaults by not paying the money back. For this reason, mortgage interest rates are usually far lower than credit card rates or the rates on any loan that is not accompanied by stable, tangible, and valuable collateral. Real estate is considered, on the whole, to appreciate or at least relatively hold its value, unlike, say, a car, which begins to lose its value the moment it is driven off the lot.

Mortgages can be used to purchase properties, **refinance** existing loans; (if one has a mortgage that is no longer at the best rate possible, there is the ability to recast the loan at newer, better terms), or to take **equity** (value above what has been borrowed and what is still owed to a lender) out of a property (known as a "*cash-out*" *refinance*). An example might be a home that has a value of $500,000 and has an unpaid mortgage of $200,000. The owner of that property is said to have $300,000 of equity in that home.

A **cash-out refinance** may sometimes be more difficult to obtain or may not have rates as favorable as a mortgage for the purchase of a property or the refinance of an existing loan amount. This is because the lender is concerned about the financial stability of somebody who is borrowing against his home and what he plans to use the cash for. On the other hand, putting the equity in your home to work for you can be prudent financial planning, depending upon how you manage it. If you foresee the need to pull equity out of your house in the form of cash and want to avoid your refinance being classified as a "cash-out," there are alternatives that we will explore in other subchapters.

Historically, mortgages required a 20% down payment so that the borrower was not offering 100% of the equity in the property as collateral. Were a 100% financed property to drop in value due to market conditions, or just considering the costs involved with a forced sale, the lender would be in peril. But in recent years a variety of new mortgage programs, ultra-low interest rates, and competition among lenders have enabled borrowers with good credit to purchase homes with little or nothing down. While this may sound good on the surface and may have worked well when property values across the country were rapidly appreciating, times are changing and I would argue that these types of mortgages are setting consumers up for failure, not to mention the lenders. Those with little equity in their homes do not have much to lose from *foreclosure* (the taking of the real estate collateral because the borrower failed to pay back the lender). Because of these reasons, and due to increased mortgage fraud, lenders across the country are rapidly becoming more restrictive.

TRADITIONAL MORTGAGE PROGRAMS
Conventional 15 & 30-Year Mortgages

A *fully amortized loan* is one where the periodic payments cover both interest *and* principal. There is no outstanding loan balance following the last payment. With this traditional type of a mortgage,

your payment generally stays the same over the entire term, and a portion of your payment each month is applied to principal and a portion is applied to interest. Please see the *"amortization schedule"* and the examples below for greater detail.

A. 30-Year (360 Month) Term – This is the most common term for new residential mortgages. Under this scenario, your interest rate and monthly payment amount are fixed for the entire term of the mortgage.

B. 15-Year (180 Month) Term – This is a very popular option for those who re-finance their mortgage at some point during the term. However, as you will see below, there are significant cost savings if you can purchase your home using this type of a mortgage. Not only do you pay the mortgage off fifteen years earlier and avoid fifteen more years of payments, but this option also generally offers rates that are about ½% less than a 30-year term.

I feel compelled to mention at this point another reason why I feel strongly that a shorter mortgage term is better than a longer one. Most of you have probably heard that mortgage debt is "good debt," much as health professionals refer to "good" versus "bad" cholesterol. While it is true that mortgage interest payments are tax deductible, there is still a limit to how "good" this is for you.

If you gross $50,000 in a year and spend $5,000 of it on mortgage interest, you will only be taxed on $45,000 of income. This is the good part. The less good part is that you are still out $5,000. You could have invested that money and earned more money with it, or you could have simply saved it or spent it. Either way, it would have been yours. But now it is gone. **Always have something to show for your money. Paying interest to someone else benefits them, not you.**

In common practical terms, if you were to take my advice and get yourself a 15-year mortgage, that extra few hundred dollars per month that it costs you might preclude you from buying that dream house you've had your eye on. Still, I ask that you look at the big picture of your financial life. Do you really need that big, big house and need it right now, or can you go with something a bit smaller and cheaper and be in overall better financial shape?

C. Other Terms – While the 30-year term and 15-year term are certainly the most popular for residential mortgages, your mortgage lender may offer almost any other term. Some lenders are now offering **40 and 50 year terms**, but in practice I have only seen 40-year terms for large apartment projects, while a slightly more volatile purchase (such as a mobile home) may only offer financing on a **10-year term**.

D. Balloon – Be VERY careful when committing to this type of a mortgage. Although the loan may be "amortized" (monthly payments kept constant) as if it were a 30-year term or a 15-year term, the "balloon" means that the balance will automatically become due at some point. In most cases, I have seen the balloons "burst" in either three, five or ten years. This does not mean that the payments are divided up evenly so that the loan is paid in full at the end of only three, five, or ten years, but that the payments are divided up as if it were a 15 or 30-year mortgage. Then, at that three, five, or ten-year point, whatever principal balance remained would need to be paid off in one lump sum. You just need to make sure that you are prepared to pay off or re-finance your mortgage when the balloon happens, or you run the risk of having your property foreclosed on and losing all of the past payments that you made. In general, I would only advise balloon-type mortgages for those who already have the resources to deal with the balloon payment when it comes due.

The come-on with balloon mortgages is that the interest rate you lock in for three, five, or ten years is usually rather attractive. On the other hand, even if you accept that you are going to refinance again at the end of that period, you are probably assuming that the economy will be at least as good as it is today or perhaps even better. That's a BIG assumption. By the end of that period, the nation's economy could make people yearn for the good old days of the Great Depression. I say, don't gamble with money you don't have. Understand how the product works and look at it with a jaundiced eye to decide whether or not this is for you.

We refer to all of these variations as "conventional" or "conforming" loans. We also frequently refer to a mortgage loan as either a loan or a mortgage. Either term will do for simplicity.

It is also important for me to mention that **you are generally free to pay down more of your mortgage principal if you suddenly begin to earn more or are the recipient of an unexpected financial windfall.** However, do be aware that some mortgages contain a "pre-payment penalty" that may prevent this. Some people get into a mortgage with the lowest possible mandatory monthly payment. This is good. Far too many people are suckered into the salesman's philosophy that, "Oh, you're young. You'll be making double what you're making now in only a few short years." From his lips to God's ears. But what if you don't? Better to go conservative. Perhaps you've calculated that you can afford mortgage payments of $1,000 per month. If you can send more sometimes, do it; it will allow you to pay off the note that much quicker. Make sure, though, to indicate on your payment what you are doing so that it gets properly credited to principal. I know lots of people who go with a 30-year mortgage, but through financial discipline pay it off in 15 years, sometimes even less.

Loan Amortization Schedules

In an amortized loan, a portion of your monthly payment is applied to principal and a portion is applied to interest. In the industry, this is called "**P&I**" which obviously stands for "principal" and "interest" and is the total of your mortgage payment before factoring in an estimate for taxes and insurance (more about that later). However, how do you know how much the monthly P&I is? This is something that most people probably could not calculate on their own without the use of a computer program, but it is actually very simple.

First, you need to understand that **initially the vast majority of your P&I payment will be allocated to interest.** As time goes on and you pay down the principal balance, more and more of your monthly payment gets allocated to principal reduction. This is because your monthly payment remains the same over the term (30 years, for example), but you pay less interest each month because the principal balance continues to decrease (albeit very slowly).

Here is an example: Assume that you purchase the home on January 1st, have a $250,000 mortgage for 30 years (360 months) with an interest rate of 6.0%. With most mortgages, interest is paid in "arrears," which means at the "end" of the month (or other period). Here is an "amortization schedule" for the first year of the mortgage:

	Date	Payment	Interest	Principal	Balance
Loan	01/01				250,000
1	02/01	1,498.88	1,250.00	248.88	249,751
2	03/01	1,498.88	1,248.76	250.12	249,501
3	04/01	1,498.88	1,247.51	251.37	249,249
4	05/01	1,498.88	1,246.25	252.63	248,997
5	06/01	1,498.88	1,244.99	253.89	248,743
6	07/01	1,498.88	1,243.72	255.16	248,487
7	08/01	1,498.88	1,242.44	256.44	248,231
8	09/01	1,498.88	1,241.16	257.72	247,973
9	10/01	1,498.88	1,239.87	259.01	247,714
10	11/01	1,498.88	1,238.57	260.31	247,454
11	12/01	1,498.88	1,237.27	261.61	247,192
12	01/01	1,498.88	1,235.96	262.92	246,929
Totals		17,986.56	14,916.50	3,070.06	

In most cases, it is easiest to calculate loan amortization using a computer program. Personally, I use a software program called "TValue 5" because it is very flexible with advanced loan calculations (i.e. adjustable rate mortgages, balloon payments, etc.), but you can also find some simple loan amortization calculators online or from the links on my website at www.BraunMincher.com.

In the above example, the P&I remains constant at $1,498.88 per month, but as time goes on you *slowly* pay down the principal balance, and when this happens more and more of your payments each month are allocated to principal.

30 Year Versus 15 Year Mortgages

While "compounding interest" works in your favor when you are investing money, it equally works against you when you are borrowing money as in the case of a mortgage. **Compound interest** is the measurement of interest in which interest that becomes payable is added to the original principal. When new interest is calculated, it is based not only on the original principal, but also on the interest that has been added to the principal. The more frequently interest is compounded, the faster the principal grows.

Probably the most common mortgage uses a 30 year (360 month) term, but **you can save SIGNIFICANTLY on interest and only increase your payment slightly by reducing the mortgage term to 15 years** (180 months). In most cases, 15 year mortgages are very common with those re-financing, but I would encourage you to consider this option if you want to pay your house off in HALF the time when purchasing one as well. Unless your promissory note has a "pre-payment" penalty (read the fine print!), you can actually "self amortize" a 30-year mortgage as if it were a 15-year mortgage by simply sending in more money every month or at times when you have extra cash on hand. Most lenders require you to notify them if you do this so that they apply your additional payment to the principal.

Here is an example of the differences between 30 year (360 month) and 15-year (180 month) mortgages assuming a 6% interest rate:

30 Year Mortgage

Event	Date	Amount	Number	Period	End Date
1 Loan	01/01/2008	250,000	1		
2 Payment	02/01/2008	1,498.88	360	Monthly	01/01/2038

	Payment	Interest	Principal	Balance
Grand Totals	539,596.80	289,596.80	250,000.00	-0-

15 Year Mortgage

Event	Date	Amount	Number	Period	End Date
1 Loan	01/01/2008	250,000.00	1		
2 Payment	02/01/2008	2,109.64	180	Monthly	01/01/2023

	Payment	Interest	Principal	Balance
Grand Totals	379,735.20	129,735.20	250,000.00	-0-

Monthly Payment for a 30-Year Term:	$ 1,498.88
Monthly Payment for a 15-Year Term:	$ 2,109.64
Difference in Monthly Payments:	$ 610.76
Total Interest Paid for a 30-Year Term:	$ 289,596.80
Total Interest Paid for a 15-Year Term:	$ 129,735.20
Total Interest Savings:	$ 159,861.60

Note: In reality, mortgage lenders may actually offer a discount of up to 1/2% for a 15-year mortgage versus a 30-year mortgage; (this is because they get their money back more quickly). Here is an example:

Nominal Annual Rate: 5.50%

	Event	Date	Amount	Number	Period	End Date
1	Loan	01/01/2008	250,000.00	1		
2	Payment	02/01/2008	2,042.71	180	Monthly	01/01/2023

	Payment	Interest	Principal	Balance
Grand Totals	367,687.80	117,687.80	250,000.00	-0-

Monthly Payment for a 30-Year Term:	$ 1,498.88
Monthly Payment for a 15-Year Term:	$ 2,042.71
Difference in Monthly Payments:	$ 543.83
Total Interest Paid for a 30-Year Term:	$ 289,596.80
Total Interest Paid for a 15-Year Term:	$ 117,687.80
Total Interest Savings:	$ 171,909.00

Summary: By being able to make a monthly payment that is $543.83 larger, you will save $171,909 over the term of the mortgage AND pay off your property in HALF the time!!! While it may take some sacrifice to make this happen (i.e. purchasing a smaller or less expensive house or foregoing some other luxury such as a new car), the benefit will be significant.

Here is an example of a $250,000 mortgage at 6% interest with a 30-year amortization and a 5-year balloon payment:

Compound Period: Monthly
Nominal Annual Rate: 6.0%

	Event	Date	Amount	Number	Period	End Date
1	Loan	01/01/2008	250,000.00	1		
2	Payment	02/01/2008	1,498.88	60	Monthly	01/01/2013
3	Balloon	02/01/2013	233,798.84	1		

Note: Even though you will have made payments of $1,498.88 per month for five years, the principal balance that will be due in full on 2/1/2013 is still $233,798.84. You've hardly paid much principal off at all! Know in advance what you are getting yourself into with a balloon mortgage.

P&I vs. PITI (Escrow Impounds)

All of the amortization samples so far have only encompassed principal and interest (P&I). However, in practice, mortgage lenders generally require their customers to maintain an **escrow impound account** (non-interest-bearing account) and make monthly deposits for the estimated taxes and insurance payments that the lender will then make on your behalf. Your payment then consists of **PITI**, which stands for **Principal, Interest, Taxes, and Insurance.** PITI mortgages are sometimes also referred to as "**budget mortgages**," as they help keep you living within your household budget.

Here is an example of a mortgage payment which contains PITI:

Principal & Interest:	$ 1,498.88
Taxes (estimate):	$ 150.00
Insurance (estimate):	$ 40.00
TOTAL PAYMENT (PITI):	$ 1,688.80

As you can see, you need to add your P&I (the actual note payment) to the estimates that the lender collects each month for taxes and insurance to determine your total mortgage payment (PITI).

Lenders love a PITI set-up because they know for sure that property taxes and insurance are being paid regularly. Without property insurance, if the property were to be destroyed, say, by a fire, the lender would no longer have any collateral. And even though first mortgages are, as the name infers, in the "first position" (no other mortgages can collect on the collateral before they do), **the taxman** *always* **comes first, before** *anyone* **else.**

The escrow account itself also benefits the lender. Although you will still be making tax and insurance payments every month, what is the lender supposed to do if you fall behind? They would rather have some of your own money in reserve and use that, rather than allow your property to either go uninsured or be sold at a tax sale. Furthermore, and more commonly, property taxes and insurance rates often go up. When they do, again, the lender can reach into your own escrow account and use that money that they already have on hand first. Then what they will do is bill you to build up that escrow account again and refigure your monthly PITI mortgage payments to reflect the new, higher costs.

It's funny, but sometimes in PITI situations, borrowers will get mad at their banks when their property taxes go up, raising their monthly mortgage payments. Banks don't raise taxes, politicians and voters do!

Spinning off of this, bear in mind that while your monthly P&I payments may be fixed, your property taxes and property insurance are not, at least not permanently—perhaps only annually. Again, some borrowers express initial dismay when their PITI bill comes in one month and it has changed. Sometimes, it actually changes for the better, but more often it rises. Take this into account when doing your household budgeting. Also, some people who engage in automatic payment withdrawals do not take the time to analyze each month's invoice. Thus, if a change occurs, they are oblivious to the change and they may bounce a check. Always remember that the "TI" in PITI is *always* subject to change, and it is no fault of your lender.

A PITI situation may also be good for the consumer from a budgeting standpoint, since estimates are collected on a monthly basis. Depending upon where you live, property taxes may be billed quarterly or yearly, and property insurance is usually billed once yearly, so this spreads your burden around more evenly without there being any interest charges, which is usually what happens when you are offered the opportunity to spread out your payments for something.

Some lenders actually charge a higher interest rate (typically ½%) for customers who do *not* want the lender to hold their escrows in an impound account. Other lenders are indifferent or can be easily negotiated out of this requirement, especially for customers with 20% or more equity in the property. If you choose not to have the lender escrow estimates for your property taxes and insurance, just be very aware that you will have to come up with a significant amount of cash when it comes time to pay these annual expenses.

In general, lenders will conduct a yearly analysis of your escrow impound account to analyze what payments they have made on your behalf, as compared to what they are collecting from you each month. If they have more funds than they need (as defined by law), they will send you a refund. If you have a shortage, or if they foresee one in the future, they will give you the option to either provide a lump-sum payment or increase your monthly escrow impound amount.

360/365 Basis

Although it is generally incidental, lenders sometimes use a different basis of days per year for calculating the amount of interest charged. The two common practices are "365 Actual" and "360Days."

In the first, the lender charges interest based upon the actual number of days per year. In the latter, interest is charged as though there were only 360 days in the year, or 30 days per month, which is easier to calculate and more consistent.

Rate vs. APR

You pay an interest rate, right? *Or do you?*

What you really pay is an **Annual Percentage Rate** (APR). The difference between an interest rate and the APR is that the APR is the *real* interest rate. Confused? I'll use another phrase. **The APR is your real cost of borrowing** calculated over a year's time (thus the "annual" part). Still confused? That's understandable.

The APR takes into consideration all the costs and fees associated with you getting your mortgage. I mean, you paid all those closing costs and fees, right? (If you don't know what I'm talking about, the answer is, "Yes, right!") That money came from somewhere. If you paid an additional $7,000 in various fees to borrow your money, there must be a way to track or designate that somewhere, somehow.

Luckily, the federal government mandates that your APR, your *true* interest rate, your *true* cost of borrowing per year, be included in consumer loan disclosure documents. In fact, they consider it *so* important that you must get this information *prior* to the closing. *Significantly* prior, via something called the **"Good Faith Estimate."** Additionally, it is not buried somewhere in fine, fine print, but stands out like a neon sign on a form called the **"Truth In Lending"** **disclosure, or "TIL."**

Since there are almost always some costs associated with having a real estate closing, your APR will almost always be higher than your advertised interest rate. Do not panic. The issue is *how much higher*. This is where you can compare apples to apples. Do not listen to any hype or be bewildered by any smoke and mirrors. If Mortgage Lender A shows you a TIL with an APR of 11.27% (yes, they will express it that specifically), and Mortgage Lender B shows you a TIL with an APR of 9.22%, then Lender B is the better choice.

Of course, remember to always be comparing apples to apples. We've discussed that different loan products serve different purposes and are designed for different types of borrowers and situations. The higher APR on a 30-year fixed mortgage versus the lower APR on a 15-year fixed mortgage does not mean that one company is ripping you off and the other is wonderful. They are two totally different loan products.

Now, perhaps you do not want to get so far into the relationship with a mortgage lender that you are only finding out the APR (and possibly canceling the transaction) a few days before closing. You may have already gone out of pocket for some application fees that are non-refundable. **Any advertisement that mentions an interest rate must generally also advertise the accompanying APR.** Get the information early so you can shop wisely and not waste your valuable time. ***The moral of the story here is that shopping the APR is prudent; simply comparing on interest "rate" is not.***

Mortgage Bankers, Brokers, and Underwriters

You've now been introduced to the most basic of basics concerning mortgages, and by the end of this chapter you will know far more than that. But before we go further,

- **Where exactly do you get a mortgage?**
- **Who are the players involved?**
- **How does this industry work?**

Traditionally, **a MORTGAGE BANKER lends you the money. It is** *their money* **to lend.**

A MORTGAGE BROKER is *not* **a bank. They arrange a mortgage for you, but it is** *not* **their money being lent to you.**

An **UNDERWRITER** is similar to a bank or banker, and sometimes those two terms are used interchangeably, but technically, there is a slight difference. Residential mortgages are most often funded, in the end, by large national lenders. You may walk into your local bank—not necessarily the local office of a national bank, but an actual local bank—and get a residential mortgage through them, but they are not actually lending you the money that they have on deposit.

- **Fannie Mae** (FNMA) The Federal National Mortgage Association and
- **Freddie Mac** (FHLMC) The Federal Home Loan Mortgage Corporation

The above are large agencies that purchase the bulk of residential mortgages in the U.S. We also have another name for them: Wall Street. The people in the end who are "holding your mortgage" (who *really* own your home until your mortgage is paid off) are these people. That bank, mortgage office, or savings and loan you started with only has the ability to absorb so much risk. Fannie Mae and Freddie Mac are mortgage loan aggregators that are built to handle the risk of holding onto the bulk of

America's homes. Even large national banks bundle millions and millions of dollars worth of mortgages and sell them off to Freddie Mac, Fannie Mae, and other large investment entities.

So why bother? If these mortgage companies and banks don't actually lend you their money, what's in it for them?

Where they continue to make money is in the "*servicing*." Although they have sold the mortgage to some larger entity, you still get your monthly mortgage bills from that same bank and for doing this clerical work, that bank gets in the neighborhood of ½% of your payments. Sure, it doesn't sound like much, but it's a cash cow and all the real risk is now on someone else.

This is not to say that you are guaranteed that you will always be making that monthly payment to the same bank or company. Sometimes even the *servicing* is sold from bank to bank. At your real estate closing, it will often be explained to you that every bank has the right to sell a mortgage to any other bank. You have no say in this and frankly, it should be fairly irrelevant to you. No matter how many times your mortgage changes hands, your terms remain the same.

Two other phrases that you'll commonly hear are "*loan officer*" and "*loan underwriter*."

Mortgage loan officers are salespersons. They may have all types of education or training, or they may have none at all. The term "loan officer" may be applied to mortgage brokers *or* mortgage bankers. Their primary concern is selling you a mortgage. They get paid for closing the deal.

A loan officer generally only has limited authority to make credit decisions. He may lead you to believe he has full authority; he may use phrases like, "Let me see what I can do," but in reality someone else is deciding what can or cannot be done. That person is the **underwriter.**

So what was I talking about when I mentioned them "closing the deal?" The underwriter tells the loan officer what deal *can* be made, and then the loan officer tries to close *that* deal with you.

If you live to be one hundred years old, if you get your picture on the cover of *Time* magazine, you may still never in your life actually meet an underwriter. They are the wizards behind the curtain. Do not look at the man behind the curtain! For some reason, the magical underwriters do not get to communicate directly with the borrower, or vice versa. Think of them like as the "banker" on the TV show "Deal or No Deal."

Because of this, do not rely on your loan officer to be your advocate. If there is a blemish on your credit, make sure you have documentation to properly explain it. Take responsibility to make enough materials available so that your loan officer can bring your best case forth to the person who makes the real decisions. Don't rely on him doing it orally because you did such a good job of explaining it and you and the loan officer became such good friends while talking over your deal. **Unfortunately, most every loan officer makes more money the worse the deal is that he gets you to accept.** Not exactly an alignment of interest, but this is how it works. So go in prepared and be prepared to walk if you don't get what you think you deserve. Shop around. Be ruthless. Find somebody to work with that you like and trust, but still advocate for yourself.

Pre-Qualification/Pre-Approval

A pre-qualification means absolutely nothing. Even though loan officers make no loan decisions, they are "qualified" to pre-qualify you. Why? Because my Labrador can pre-qualify you for a loan and it would carry just as much weight.

A pre-qualification is the product of your initial, short discussion with a loan officer. You've told her what you want, what you make, etc., and in return for listening to you, she says, "Well, if all that is true, you will most likely be able to get a mortgage." That is a pre-qualification.

Pre-approval, on the other hand, **means they have taken an application, verified information, and made a commitment to you to loan**—subject to the property and possibly some other underwriting requirements.

A lot of real estate agents will not work with you unless you are pre-approved. It wastes their time. So if you are serious about buying property, it is best to figure out financing before picking out a house. And as far as figuring out financing, it is best to get yourself a pre-approval. If you have a mortgage pre-approval in place when you submit an offer, it gives you far more credibility. In many cases, it makes sense even to attach your pre-approval letter to the actual offer.

Commercial Mortgages

What I've been referring to here are residential mortgages. In the case of *commercial mortgages*, **your best source, indeed, will be a local bank.** Mind you, I am not talking about building a skyscraper; but, rather, a small office building, industrial unit, or retail store.

The **Small Business Administration (SBA)** also has some great programs (such as their **504 Plan**) for these sorts of ventures. If you qualify, they will sometimes finance up to 90% of an owner-occupied commercial property, although their rates may be just slightly higher than a local bank. On the plus side, they will do a 20-year fixed term on a commercial property. Most local banks will not give you a fixed rate on a commercial property for more than five years.

You actually get these SBA loans through your local banks and other lenders. Depending on the SBA program, there is often a cost-sharing between the local bank and the SBA. If you are borrowing $100,000, you get half of it from the local bank and the other 40% directly from the SBA (the remaining 10% is from your down payment), although you could arrange all this at your local bank.

How Do Mortgage Companies Make Money?

1. The "*origination,*" also known as the "*discount point(s).*" This is known as a "*front end*" *charge* and will generally range from 0 to 3%. Essentially, this is how the mortgage broker gets paid for his efforts. Remember that a broker is not an actual lender; he may have agency relationships with numerous *actual* lenders. Just like any other kind of broker, once you fill out an application with him, he is supposed to shop around on your behalf in order to get you the best possible rate and terms.

Now, origination, even if expressed as a percentage, is not to be confused with your interest rate. It is more like a type of up-front fee that you pay only once. If you are taking out a $100,000 mortgage, one "point" is $1,000. Yes, this amount adds to your APR, but it is basically paid up front, which is why we call it a front-end fee. Your mortgage broker gets this $1,000 right away in a lump sum. He himself, if he is a sole practitioner, puts this right into his pocket. If the broker works for an agency, he splits some of it with "the house."

2. Junk Fees. Just as the word infers, these are utter pieces of garbage that are primarily tacked onto deals given to people with bad credit. They may have names like **document preparation fees, underwriting fees, processing fees, courier fees**, etc. In some states, these are regulated and often capped at a certain dollar or percentage amount. But a person savvy in the ways of finance, particularly one with excellent credit, will throw these back in the face of a mortgage broker and say, "Do better." Junk is junk. Keep that garbage out of *my* house.

3. The Back End. The actual money lender generally pays these points to the mortgage broker. In some cases, these fees simply represent additional incentive from the lender to the broker to make a particular loan. In other cases, it represents a payment from the lender to the broker as a reward for obtaining a loan with a higher interest rate. For example, a borrower may potentially be able to obtain a loan at a 10% interest rate, yet the broker will only offer you an 11% interest rate in order to receive two extra back end points from the lender. In cases where a lender is merely trying to promote a certain product and offering brokers a small reward through back end points, there may be no harm to the consumer.

Problems with back end points predominately take two forms.

First, as with front end points, unscrupulous brokers may attempt to charge far in excess of market practices. These problems are compounded by the second issue: some states do not require disclosure of back end points, leaving the consumers no way to even realize what is happening to them unless they have a very, very clear understanding of market interest rates that allow them to discover a discrepancy resulting from back end points. Where mandated reporting exists or has been undertaken by a responsible loan broker, look for back end points on the closing statement form. Since the broker gets paid directly by the lender, it may be called a *"yield spread premium"* or they may simply list the fee as an amount paid from the lender to the broker *paid outside closing (POC).*

I must remind you that **the only bright light to all this is the APR.** All of these fees factor into the calculation of the APR; thus, once you are looking at that figure, you are looking at *reality.*

Bottom line time again. The mortgage industry is incredibly lucrative. If I had it to do over again, I would have gone into this industry. I know hardly anyone good in this business earning less than $100,000 per year, and the best at it are making in excess of $500,000 a year. They are working with incredible profit margins if they can produce a large quantity of loans. When you go to get a mortgage, be ruthless; be *far* more ruthless than when buying a car. Let them make their big profits off someone else, not you.

Applying for a Mortgage: Income Requirements

A really quick and dirty rule for deciding upon how much house you can afford is that your mortgage amount should not exceed three times your gross salary. Note, I started with the word "house," then switched to the word "mortgage." If you happen to have inherited a lump of $500,000 that you can use as a down payment and you make $100,000 a year, you should theoretically be able to afford an $800,000 house, rather than a $300,000 house.

Again, regarding most preferable situations, lenders would like to see an amount equal to six months' worth of mortgage payments sitting in your bank checking or savings accounts. This is not mandatory, but it would qualify you for their best rates possible.

Loan to Value Ratios (LTV)

Also, when shopping for a house and plugging house prices together with your income and your cash on hand for down payment, you must also look at **Loan to Value ratios (LTV)**. Example: You want to buy a $500,000 house. You have $50,000 available for use as a down payment. That's only 10% of the home's value. You have an LTV of 90%. You will see throughout this chapter that the traditional rule of thumb is that the best mortgage rates come from having at least a 20% down payment. In this example, your down payment is less.. As you read on, you shall see that there are still ways around that and ways to get you into that $500,000 house. But I can guarantee you they will cost you more.

LTV does not stay the same forever. The longer you live in the house, the more you pay down your mortgage, the more it potentially appreciates, the more the LTV tips in your favor. What you want is a low LTV.

Example One: Your house has a value of $300,000. Your loan is $50,000. You have an LTV of 16.66%. This is good.

Example Two: Your house has a value of $300,000. Your loan is $275,000. You have an LTV of 91.66%. This is not good at all.

Paying off your mortgage and lowering the actual amount you owe on it is not the only way to change your LTV. If your property rises in value, your LTV also changes.

Example: Using the numbers from Example Two again, your $300,000 house has drastically jumped in value in a short time; so short, in fact, that you haven't even paid off enough of your loan principal to even make it worth mentioning (it still remains at about $275,000). Despite that, your house now has a value of $350,000. Your LTV improves to 78.57%. And you haven't done a darn thing!

Full Doc/No Doc/NIV

"*Full Doc*" stands for "*full documentation*," as in, you turn over to the loan officer all of your personal financial information for his consideration. **Full doc should get you the best interest rate.** We are talking two years of W-2s, 1099s, tax returns, employment verification and your last three bank statements. There is also a caveat that you can become subject to this information being compared to similar information acquired directly from the IRS. If either version does not agree, you can be charged with mortgage fraud and sent to jail.

Full doc usually does not work well with the self-employed or people in unique situations.

NIV stands for "*No Income Verification.*" An entrepreneur who does not wish to disclose his income, but has a credit rating to be proud of, might go this way. Again, the less information provided, the more the interest rate will probably rise. Mind you, this is not to say that this person will not answer the question, "How much do you make?" It simply means that the party will not provide documentation to back it up.

Lastly, there is **No Doc**. No Doc is exactly what it sounds like. You provide no verification of anything. You will also most likely get a higher interest rate. Due to the recent mortgage crisis, these types of loans are becoming much more rare.

OTHER TYPES OF MORTGAGES

Adjustable Rate Mortgages (ARMs)

Here in America, we take fixed rate mortgages for granted. But in other countries in the world, adjustable rate mortgages are the norm. We have a stable enough economy and a money market that make fixed rates sensible to lenders.

The idea of an adjustable rate mortgage is rather simple. It begins with a set interest rate, usually a rather low and attractive one. That rate is locked in for a certain period of time. After that time period elapses, the rate is subject to change, usually by a factor above an index such as the Prime Lending Rate or the LIBOR Average (more on this to come).

The most common *adjustable* rate mortgage products on the market today usually involve the rate being locked in for three, five, or seven years. But the amount of time in which the initial interest rate is set is not the only thing you should be concerned with. That tells you *when* the interest rate is subject to adjustment. There is also the issue of *how often*. Most commonly, after the initial period, the rate is immediately adjusted and then the index is checked once every year or six months. In actuality, the rates are changing sporadically whenever and as often as they please, but if you are set to have it adjusted once per year, it's like a birthday—if your anniversary date is, say, July 29, then every July 29 the index is checked, the margin added to that index, and that is your new rate for the next twelve months until the next July 29th.

Common mortgage terminology is to call an ARM a 3/1 ARM, or a 5/1 ARM or something to that effect. The first number indicates the length of time (in years) until the first change. The second number is the frequency (in years) of change. A 3/1 ARM is initially locked in at one rate for three years, then changes and shall change again every year thereafter.

Please do not be misled into thinking that all ARMs change annually. Some change as often as monthly. Some even change as frequently as the index does. Be vigilant and take notice. This is crucial.

ARMs are most attractive and practical for someone who knows they are not going to stay living in or owning a property for very long. The initial ARM rate is often significantly lower than any fixed rate commonly available, because lenders figure they will make their money from the lazier borrowers who will not keep up on checking the rate changes and will eventually net them some seriously high interest rate payments.

Now, APRs on variable rate mortgages are a bit more challenging to pin down. If your initial rate is locked in for over a year, though, you should get a fairly accurate APR quote. Still, be vigilant when comparing one ARM to another before committing.

Interest Rates and More on ARMs

In the credit card section, we talked a lot about interest rates, yet spoke very little about what on earth they are and how they are arrived at. For credit cards, it is often simply enough to know that the lower the better. Frankly, that still holds true for mortgages as well. On the other hand, when talking about any type of ARM, it is good to know what mortgage lenders are talking about when they discuss *interest rates, indexes, margins*, and the like.

An interest rate is based upon many factors. It is not simply a number plucked from the sky, but it is based upon some institutionally accepted "*index.*"

Ready for some vocabulary? Some of the more popular indexes are:

- **Prime Rate** – also known as *The Wall Street Journal Prime Rate*, is traditionally 3 points above the *federal funds target rate*. Although over-simplified, the prime rate generally changes in tandem with the Federal Open Market Committee meetings—up to eight times per year. This does not guarantee it *will* change, but it *can* change. Over the past ten years, it has been as low as 4% and as high as 9.5%.
- **Federal Funds Rate** – is set by the governors of the Federal Reserve, which they enforce primarily by open market operations (the buying and selling of bonds). When the media refers to the Federal Reserve "changing interest rates," this is what they mean. The *target rate* is generally a range, as the Federal Reserve cannot set an exact value through open market operations.

Thus, to bring these two terms together, when 75% of the United States' largest banks change their prime rate, *The Wall Street Journal* prints a composite prime rate change.

- **LIBOR** – (pronounced LIE-bore) the London Interbank Overnight Rate, is a daily reference rate based on the interest rates at which banks offer to lend unsecured funds to other banks in the London wholesale money market (or interbank market). LIBOR is published shortly after eleven am each day, London time.
- **COFI** – the Eleventh District Cost of Funds Index, reflects the actual interest expense incurred during a given month by all savings institution members of the Federal Home Loan Bank of San Francisco. Consumers like the COFI because it does not move up or down as rapidly as market interest rates— such as the prime rate or Treasury bill rates.
- **Treasury Bills** – These indexes are the weekly or monthly average yields on U.S. Treasury securities adjusted to constant maturities. Treasury bill indexes are volatile and move with the market. They reflect the state of the economy, and respond quickly to economic changes. These indexes react more quickly than the COFI.

Now, we do not simply tend to deal with indexes, but with *margins added to indexes*. In other words, an interest rate may be expressed as "2.75% over LIBOR." If LIBOR is expressed on a given day as 6.25%, then the interest rate you would be subject to in this case would be 9.0% (LIBOR: 6.25%, plus the 2.75% margin over LIBOR that was part of your agreed upon interest rate).

- When discussing an ARM, ask the questions:
- What is the initial lock-in term?
- What is the initial interest rate?
- What index is used to calculate the adjustment to the rate?
- What is the margin above the index that will be charged?
- How often will rates be scheduled to change?
  And finally,
- What is the "*cap*?"

A cap is the highest possible amount that your interest on an ARM can go. This is also often referred to as the "*lifetime cap.*" This is important if a catastrophic national economical situation was to occur. What if your ARM was tied to the Treasury bill rate and that rate went up to 20%? It could happen. Could you imagine paying credit card-level interest rates on your home mortgage? Unfortunately, things like this have happened historically, so a wise person is always ready to make course adjustments as they sail their financial boat through the storms of life. This particular example, of course, is a neon-bright advertisement for conventional fixed-rate mortgages that are solid as a rock. Outside of that, though, if you are in the midst of an ARM and the time is coming upon you for a rate change and the new rate looks to be horrendous, it's time to refinance (more on this later) and get yourself into a better deal. With any mortgage, there is the ability to get out and get into something else, just like buying a new car, a new house, or getting a divorce (ouch). That is not to say that it is easy as pie, but I'll show you how and what restrictions are on your movement. But initially, a lifetime cap in this case of, say, 12%, would give you some protections. **Make sure you *have* caps.** These are usually not automatic.

Caps are also used to limit the amount of change that occurs on each of your change dates. This is a benefit to the borrower. If the initial lock-in was, say, 6% and the LIBOR (which was the agreed-upon index) on the change date is 8.5% with a 2% margin, it is a large burden to go from paying 6% to 10.5%. Thus, another cap is often set so that the amount of any single change can only be, say, a maximum of 2%. Now, although you should be jumping to 10.5%, you only jump to 8% this time. But if the next time your anniversary date comes and the index is still that high, you will jump another 2%, getting you up to 10%, and so on.

Sometimes the cap is a hybrid, where if the initial term is rather long—say, five years—the cap on that first change may be, perhaps 5%, but all subsequent changes that occur annually from there on will be capped at, maybe, 1%.

It is also not unusual for there to be caps on the bottom end as well, for the benefit of the lender. What if the Prime or LIBOR goes down? Your lender may write up the loan to indicate that you cannot participate in this event that is beneficial to you. Your mortgage may be written so that your rate can only either stay the same or go up. Be on the look-out.

Rate Lock

You shop around for a mortgage. You get the deal you want. But bear in mind, with many of the indexes, mortgage rates change on a daily basis. What to do?

When you apply for a mortgage, they will usually "lock" the then current rate for you. If the indexes change and rise tomorrow, you will be spared. You've locked in your rate. That lock will usually last anywhere from thirty to ninety days.

Putting aside the possibility of daily rate fluctuation, realistically, you get yourself approved for a mortgage, then make an offer on the house you want to buy. The offer gets accepted and you and the seller arrange a closing date—the date upon which the two of you sit and sign a stack of papers and he moves out and you move in. Rarely does that ever happen the very next day. Both of you have a lot of things to take care of. That's why you need a rate lock when you get your *mortgage commitment.*

While thirty to ninety days is the norm for a rate lock, you can sometimes get your lender to extend it to as much as a year, but they will usually require a 1% premium. To clarify, that is not another full percentage point on your interest rate; it is 1% of the total amount you are borrowing. Example: You are getting a $200,000 mortgage. You want to lock in today's good interest rate, but you can't arrange to close on the house for another nine months (maybe because it is under construction). You get the bank to lock in that rate, but because the closing is so far away, they charge you 1% of the $200,000—$2,000. You pull that out of your pocket and you never see it again—unless you finance that as well by increasing your mortgage amount.

But what if you lock in and the rates go down? Usually the answer is "too bad; so sad." Your only recourse is to either suck it up and pay or else threaten to bolt for another mortgage company. Some lenders will not want to lose you and will bend their own rules in order to keep your business.

FHA

A Federal Housing Authority (FHA) mortgage allows for a purchase of a home with a low down payment (3%) while the lender is insured against loss from the borrower. These loans are insured by the Federal Department of Housing and Urban Development (HUD). FHA insured loans have several restrictions, but are generally a great tool for first time buyers or those with limited resources for a down payment. To get one, shop around for mortgage specialists and ask specifically if they handle FHA loans. Either they do or they don't. These mortgages can only be used for owner-occupied properties.

FHA insured loans have maximum lending limits depending upon where in the country that the property is located. As of this writing, the base amount is $200,160 for a single family residence, but this is increased in some counties depending upon the local housing costs. For example, the maximum in Maui is $544,185 and in Los Angeles it is $362,790.

In order to prevent consumers from purchasing a home that they cannot afford, the FHA has specific guidelines relating to *Debt to Income Ratios*. First, the amount of your new mortgage payment (*including* property taxes and insurance—PITI) cannot exceed 29% of your gross monthly income. Second, your *total* monthly debt obligations (mortgage, credit cards, student loans, car loan, etc.) cannot exceed 41% of your gross monthly income.

Private Mortgage Insurance (PMI)

FHA insured loans generally require a variation of Private Mortgage Insurance (PMI) to protect the lender against losses that result from defaults on home mortgages. With a larger down payment, the property itself will almost certainly cover the lender's losses. But if you only put down a small amount and default fairly early into the process, the lender could really be stuck. Thus, they want an insurance policy taken out to protect them against such an occurrence. In this world, we have insurance policies for just about everything.

The premiums for this insurance are passed on to the borrower, making the total monthly mortgage payment greater. The FHA charges an upfront MMI (Mutual Mortgage Insurance) premium (similar to a PMI premium) of 1.5% in addition to an annual rate of 0.5% of the loan amount. For a $100,000 loan, this can amount to $1,500 upfront in addition to $500 per year. Once a certain amount of equity is achieved in the property (10 to 22%), the MMI/PMI requirements can sometimes be removed.

MMI/PMI is an issue that comes up not only in FHA loans, but in many mortgage situations, typically when there is formula involved that allows the borrower not to have to have a significant down payment or have little to no equity in the property. **This insurance does not benefit you—it benefits the lender, but *you pay for it.***

Whether it is an FHA loan or any other mortgage that requires MMI/PMI, make sure that you monitor the situation carefully as time passes. It's a fool's game to wait for your lender to inform you that you have enough equity in your home so that you no longer need to make those additional monthly PMI payments that strain your personal budget. You're paying the premium; it's your problem. Your lender will only refer to your amortization table to determine when you've attained enough equity in your home. But if your home rises in value, the time is significantly shortened.

I have a subchapter further on detailing the difference between *appraisals and assessments,* but let me get into it a little now as it pertains to MMI/PMI.

You live in a neighborhood. Most of the houses are similar in size, style, age, and condition. You buy your house for $150,000. Six months earlier, the house next to yours sold for the same price. See?

A year later, the house behind yours sells for $200,000. It seems fairly indistinguishable from your house or the house next to yours. Most likely, your house is now actually worth $200,000, too. If you tried to sell it, that is probably what your asking price would be. This also means that the equity in your house is now $50,000 more.

So you started out buying a $150,000 home with an FHA loan that allowed you to put only 3% down ($4,500). Let's say that after a year, you've paid off $2,000 in principal (running total: $6,500). And now, due to a market change, you have another $50,000 in equity in your home (running total: $56,500). Now you have home equity of 28.25%! That should get you out of those onerous, additional monthly MMI/PMI payments.

Now, you will have to *prove* this, though, to your lender. That means hiring an appraiser. Some lenders will even force you to use *their* appraiser, or an approved appraiser on a list that they provide. We'll talk more about that later, too. But if you think you will come out with a result such as this, it will be money well worth spending.

Get out of having to pay MMI/PMI as quickly as you can. Don't depend on anyone else—do it for yourself.

In the old days, every mortgage seemed to require a 20% down payment. Today, there is a whole cottage industry that has been created around specialized mortgages, or "*mortgage products*" as they often are called, involving little to no down payments. If you can't do things any other way, this is a good way to go...EXCEPT...I can almost certainly guarantee that you will have to pay MMI/PMI. This may raise your monthly mortgage payments $50, $75, $100, or more, depending on the size of the mortgage. Again, an appreciating market will help you get out of this burden faster, but again, don't think there's a free lunch.

There is also the possibility of taking out a second mortgage to pay your down payment. This would replace PMI. Look at all the numbers, though, to make sure this scenario benefits you. But yes, **some people**

borrow their down payment. Most primary lenders require that this be stated in their mortgage documents and yes, it may affect your primary mortgage rate. Some also prohibit any portion of the down payment from being borrowed. On the other hand, **sometimes your primary lender will be more than happy to do two loans with you—your first mortgage (primary mortgage) for 80% of the value of your property, and a second mortgage for a portion of your 20% down payment.** If you do not have money to put down on a house, this is worth asking about.

Prior to 2007, another problem with PMI was that it was not tax deductible, but that is now a thing of the past. Congress has just passed a law stating that borrowers who have annual household incomes of $100,000 or less will be able to get a low down payment mortgage and deduct the full cost of their mortgage insurance premiums on their federal tax returns.

Lastly, APRs don't take into consideration PMI. If you are paying another $75 or so per month due to PMI, your *true* APR shoots up even more, although this will *not be reflected on your TIL.* Bottom line: You have to factor PMI in yourself to see what your real monthly mortgage payments are and your true APR is.

VA

A VA mortgage is guaranteed by the Federal Veterans Administration. The loan may be issued by qualified lenders. The VA mortgage was designed to offer long-term financing to American veterans or their surviving spouses (provided they do not remarry).

A VA mortgage loan allows veterans 100% financing *without private mortgage insurance (PMI).* A VA funding fee of 0 to 3.3% of the loan amount is paid to the VA, although you may also finance this as well. In a purchase, veterans may borrow up to 100% of the sales price or reasonable value of the home, whichever is less. In a refinance, veterans may borrow up to 90% of reasonable value, where allowed by state laws.

The maximum size VA loan you can presently get is $417,000, lent to you at a fixed rate over fifteen, twenty, twenty-five, or thirty years.

VA loans can often times be assumable, meaning that as an incentive to get someone to buy your home, you can offer them the ability to simply pick up the payments where you left off, provided they are credit-worthy. This person who assumes the VA loan need not be a veteran.

Home Equity Line of Credit (HELOC)

I am a great believer in home equity lines of credit. Some people use them for the wrong reasons; I like to think I use them wisely.

Example of the wrong way or the wrong reason to use a HELOC: You put 20% down and bought a big house you could ill afford. Now you need to furnish it, so you take out a HELOC on half (10%) of the remaining 20% equity (i.e. your down payment) in the home. For example, if you purchased a $200,000 home, your 20% down payment would have been $40,000. You get a HELOC for half of that ($20,000). You are now in debt up to your eyeballs, you have little real equity left in your home, and if you go bust, not only will you lose your home, you may lose your home and *still* owe money. Bad, bad, bad.

You can get a HELOC most anywhere you can get a regular mortgage, but I've found some of the most competitive rates at local bank branches. A HELOC is almost always a variable interest rate rather than a fixed one. At best, I've found rates to be anywhere from Prime minus one point to Prime plus one point. Lenders of HELOCs will usually allow you to borrow an aggregate of up to 90% of your home's value. Example: $200,000 home. You put down $100,000, you get a first mortgage for the remaining $100,000, you can then take out a HELOC for $80,000.

Now, there is another product called an **Equity Loan**. With an equity loan, you are borrowing a specific amount of money, getting that money all at once, and using your home as collateral. In this case, you can often qualify for a fixed rate. A perfect situation in which to do this is when you are planning home improvements. You are doing it all at once, and you know what you are doing and how much it will cost.

The beauty of a HELOC is that it is more like a credit card than a mortgage loan. Using the example from the previous paragraph, you can take out an $80,000 HELOC, yet not actually draw out a single penny if you do not need it right now. As the name infers, it is a *line of credit*, not a loan. **It does not become a loan until you use it.**

I absolutely love the flexibility of a HELOC. Almost everyone should consider one. Why? Here is the very best reason: What is better, using a credit card at 12% interest for a large purchase that you will not be able to pay off in one payment, or using a HELOC at 12% interest? Answer: The HELOC. Why? Credit card interest is not tax deductible; but mortgage interest is. And a HELOC is considered a type of mortgage. **HELOC interest is usually tax deductible.**

When people talk about savings and liquidity (large amounts of money you can reach on a moment's notice), there is little that can compare to the ease and benefits of a HELOC. If the greatest business opportunity of a lifetime comes along and you have a nice-sized HELOC in place…boom! You're ready to go immediately, while someone else is shifting things around, agonizing over early-withdrawal penalties, etc. If you get sick and can't work for six months, there again, you have equity from your home that you can draw on until you get back on your feet. **With a HELOC, your home becomes your savings.**

When it comes to borrowing, the cheapest interest you can ever get is the first mortgage on your house. It is secured and collateralized. The second cheapest interest you can get is a HELOC, for the same reason.

Want to buy a car? That interest you pay on your standard car loan is not tax deductible. But if you use a HELOC to buy your car? Yep, it's usually tax deductible.

Is there *anything* bad about a HELOC, I mean other than overextending yourself after already overextending yourself? Yes. You are gambling your residence. If everything goes bad for you, you can declare bankruptcy and still manage to have a place to live, that's true. But bankruptcy is an ugly, ugly thing and it will ruin the next number of years of your life. Furthermore, while you can keep a roof over your head once you've declared bankruptcy, you cannot keep a mansion's roof over your head. I've seen people try it; the bankruptcy courts do not like seeing people living in butlered estates while not paying their bills, hiding behind the safe walls of bankruptcy. So just because a HELOC is great, it is not an excuse to go crazy and bury yourself in debt. You still have to pay that money back—it's a loan, not a gift from heaven.

If you have excess cash and a HELOC balance, I recommend using those funds to pay down the balance. You can always get the cash back as an advance off your HELOC, but you are probably making only a nominal interest rate on your cash, and will save yourself significant interest on the HELOC for placing your cash there. For some people, it is probably not a bad thing to be cash poor and HELOC rich.

Second or Third Mortgages

A **second mortgage**, sometimes also known as a second or even a third *deed of trust* (more on the true difference between mortgages and deeds of trust later on in this chapter), is a secured loan (or mortgage) that is subordinate to another loan against the same property. More specifically, it is the second loan in sequence.

In real estate, a property can have multiple loans against it. The loan that is registered with the county or city registry first is called the **first mortgage**. The loan registered second is called the second mortgage (simple enough, right?). A property can have a third or even fourth mortgage, for that matter. I once even saw a property with twelve mortgage liens against it.

Second mortgages are called subordinate because if the loan goes into default, the first mortgage gets paid off first before the second mortgage gets any money. Thus, second mortgages are riskier for the lenders, who generally charge a higher interest rate for them.

Examples: You have a $500,000 home. You have a $100,000 first mortgage. You want to buy a pizza franchise. The buy-in is $50,000. You don't have that much money sitting around. *Or do you?* You can take out a second mortgage for another $50,000 and buy that pizza place. You will make two mortgage payments per month. Further more, the interest you pay on the second mortgage is usually tax deductible, just like the first mortgage interest. Pretty good way to borrow money and start a business.

Also, you don't have to stop at two. See a burger joint you want to buy next door to the pizza parlor? Take out a third mortgage and buy that, too! All of this, all because you're a homeowner with equity in his property.

The risks? Obvious. Each time, you are risking the roof over your head, bankruptcy protections or no bankruptcy protections. There is still risk involved. Don't go crazy and purchase geological rights on the planet Mars just because you're a homeowner. And yes, each time you do this, your interest rate will most likely be higher, as each lender takes a significantly higher risk than the previous one.

A HELOC is a secondary mortgage. It may be in second position or third or fourth, depending upon how many loans you have out. Most major HELOC lenders will not go out past second position.

For as good as all this sounds, though, I am not a debt junkie. I still believe that you should have more assets than debt, and luxury vacations and helicopters are not really assets. They are pleasure and they are toys. The money you spend on interest, even if it is tax deductible, is still money you don't have and is enriching someone else and giving you nothing tangible in return. Remember this: When you make a mortgage payment—whether it is a first, a second, or a third—if it is $1,000, and $500 of that is principal and $500 is interest, you just threw $500 down the drain. How smart is that? Think before you borrow.

Interest Only Mortgages (IO)

It sounds too good to be true. Imagine only having to pay the interest on your mortgage. What an incredibly big house you could afford! And what a dumb idea, too, for most people.

This sort of program now exists and it is exactly what it sounds like: You just pay the interest. You pay down no part of your principal. The only equity you may get in the property is through appreciation—the possible increased value of the property over time. IF it appreciates in value over time. Talk about a gamble.

Who can afford to make such a gamble? The wealthy. Who tends to apply for these types of mortgages? The un-wealthy! And people wonder why the rich get richer and the poor get poorer. Poor decision making, in this case.

But I'm not here to insult the poor. While most people are honest and trying to do the right thing for their customers, there are vultures out there in mortgage land (and in every other industry as well). An ethical mortgage lender will dissuade anyone with unsteady means and slender savings from taking out a mortgage such as this. The unscrupulous flock after the wealthy, too, but if someone worth $4 million dollars loses half his savings, he still has $2 million dollars. If someone worth $30,000 loses half his savings…ouch.

An interest-only loan is like renting. Think about it. When you rent, you create no equity in the property. You pay, you live there, you leave, and you're in the same situation you were when you moved in, only you had a place to live for x number of years and you paid for it. Zero sum math. This is the same deal, except for the gamble on the overall housing market in the area where you live. The value can go down, stay the same, or go up. So, three things can happen and two of them are bad. That's poor casino odds. Picture this: You can do a 30-year interest-only mortgage, pay out your hard-earned money for thirty years just like all of your neighbors, but while they are all retiring with no housing debt because they had conventional mortgages, you still owe EXACTLY the same on that house as the day you moved in thirty years earlier. If that sounds frightening…good. It should.

So let's explore why I think this even has a glimmer of benefit for the wealthy. Well, they can afford to gamble. A wealthy person sees a new residential development being planned in a high-growth area. He decides to get in on the ground floor as an investment. He gets the cheapest mortgage he can—such as an IO. Maybe he doesn't even live there, but rents it out, thus he cannot afford for the monthly mortgage payments to be too high or else he'll never find a renter to help him carry it. The rest of the development gets built, the units sell off, the new office park next door gets built, all these new workers come, dying for a nice place to live close to their jobs, and boom! Our hero's place has doubled in value and he sells it. Cha-ching! That's how you make money.

If you can afford the risk.

Jumbo Mortgages

Fannie Mae and Freddie Mac set a limit on the maximum dollar value of any mortgage they will purchase from an individual lender. As of 2007, the limit is $417,000, or $625,500 in Alaska, Hawaii, Guam, and the U.S. Virgin Islands.

The reason a limit is set is because it is perceived that homes valued above these figures are much more susceptible to market fluctuations. I mean, a $5 million dollar home could always lose its value and have to sell for $4 million dollars. That's only a 20% drop. But that's also a million dollars, which, the last time I looked, was real money. Fannie Mae and Freddie Mac don't take those kinds of gambles.

This leaves a portion of the market to look elsewhere for placement. A *jumbo mortgage* is a mortgage with a loan amount above those figures I mentioned in the first paragraph, also referred to as "*conforming limits.*" Now remember, we are only talking about the mortgage amount, not the price of the property. You can have a million-dollar property, but have only a $250,000 mortgage on it.

If your mortgage is above $417,000 in the "lower forty-eight states," you will need a jumbo mortgage…and the interest rate will most likely be higher.

Other large investors, such as insurance companies and banks, step in to fill the need for jumbo mortgages. Mortgages over $2 million dollars are sometimes particularly difficult to place. We should all have this problem.

Negative Amortization

Who would have ever dreamed it? A negative amortization loan, or "negative am" is the equivalent of running an endless bar tab—on your credit card. Essentially, **you are being loaned more money each month.**

Here is how it works: A principal is set—the amount you wish to mortgage. An interest rate is set. Then, *you are given the opportunity to pay less than* <u>even the interest</u> *per month!* This is not a misprint. Example: If interest-only on your mortgage is $1,000 per month in a given month, you can get away with sending only $500 if money is tight.

Is this heaven? No. For you have now added $500 to your mortgage principal. Remember our amortization tables from conventional mortgages? Remember how little principal you were paying off each month early on in the life of your mortgage? In the beginning, it may have taken you six months to pay off $500 in principal. Well, in this example, you just added half a year to your mortgage. Furthermore, since you just borrowed more money, you just added greater interest payments. Remember how compounding interest can work against you?

Not smart.

Now, in addition to people who believe in a free lunch, the other customers for these types of mortgages are, again, savvy, experienced and wealthy investors who are willing to make large bets that a property will appreciate significantly in value. Perhaps, again, they want to rent it for a few years while waiting for the price to rise and need to keep the rental price low enough not to have the place go vacant. For them, a negative am structures their risk.

Graduated Payment Mortgages and Option ARMs

These are interesting mortgage products. The payments may change, but the interest rate might remain the same over the entire term. It can work well for just about any borrower, but particularly a younger person who may have significant income fluctuations as they bound from job to job, career to career.

Most commonly, **Graduated Payment Mortgages** (**GPMs**) are set up so that the borrower is "sort of" locked in with a fixed rate, but that rate is really an average starting out small and growing. Example: You have a 15-year mortgage. You pay 5% interest for the first five years, 10% for the second five, and 15% for the last five years. Your *average* interest is 10%, so with a GPM, you are considered to have a 10% (sorta) fixed rate. Often times that initial rate is actually a negative am.

With a GPM, all of this is figured out in advance with great precision by your lender. This type of loan product is marketed primarily to young professionals who are reasonably certain they will earn more money each year, for example a doctor just starting out in practice. It is not as dangerous as purely going into a mortgage that is too large to carry, based on rosy future income projections. It is a bit more conservative.

An **Option ARM** is the height of versatility. Perhaps you work on commission. You don't do so well this month. You want to pay the bare minimum, which is interest-only, or maybe even *less* than interest-only. The following month, you break all kinds of sales records. You send in a very large payment, covering last month's principal as well as this month's principal and interest and maybe even some more. The following month, things level off and you make your basic P&I payment. See, the beauty is in your ability to send in just about anything and have the lender prepared to deal with it. As long as you don't take advantage of it and think this is license to never pay off your mortgage, it is a very attractive loan product.

Another dark side to an Option ARM is to never forget that it is an ARM. If you decide to play around with low payments just so you can have extra money to party with your friends, you may be wasting away times when the indexes are low. Then, when you sober up, you look around and see that the indexes have risen and your interest payments per month are astronomical…and an astronomical waste. Self-discipline is still required.

Teaser Rates

A well educated friend of mine came up to me and asked, "Braun, what do you think of this? It's a mortgage at only 1.99% interest."

Okay, so I figured it was a negative am. Those I understand. But I also know not to jump to conclusions. "Well, let's read the fine print," I said.

Turns out it was not a true negative am. It was an offer for a 1.99% interest rate…for one month. After that, the interest rate jumped to a fixed rate that was, conservatively, one full percentage point higher than any other lender around was currently offering. The "one month only" part slipped right past my friend and indeed, it was buried in the fine print.

This is called a *"teaser rate."* They are like any other come-on in business. Caveat emptor. Now, obviously, a deal like this *could* be a come-on for a graduated payment mortgage or a negative am. The only way to find out is to read the fine print and ask a lot of questions. But imagine thinking you were buying a negative am and you were only getting that 1.99% rate for just one month. Ouch! And is something like this illegal? No, not at all. If you look through that big pile of papers you will get at the closing (more on closings in Chapter Four), you would see that everything was legally disclosed (technically). But what's the point of disclosing things if you're not aware of what's going on and what is being disclosed? It's a dirty business sometimes.

Furthermore, if your initial rate lock is for less than one year— such as the aforementioned 1.99% one-month-only interest rate—and that rate then jumps to an adjustable rate that is tied to an index, you could really be in for a guessing game if you are trying to compare deals by looking at the APR. Be educated and beware.

Construction Loans

So you want to buy a piece of land and build your dream home on it from scratch. Custom everything all the way. Wonderful. So how do you do it?

First off, in the mortgage loan department—and we are still in the mortgage loan department of this book—you will be dealing with two separate loans. The *construction loan* covers funds throughout the construction process. That is then refinanced upon completion with a traditional mortgage from a traditional mortgage company. Thus, you will usually have two separate closings. You'll have your first one just before you break ground.

You can get construction loans from a variety of sources. I have found that local banks are the best source for this. They like short-term lending (you don't want those workmen on the property forever). Mortgage companies like long-term loan products such as traditional mortgages that they can bundle up and sell off to Wall Street. It's what they do and they like staying within their comfort zone.

With a construction loan, once you have had your closing, you will be advanced money as you need it—usually on a monthly basis.

Before I go any further, let me mention **land loans**. Often times with construction, you first have to acquire a building lot. This may involve a *third loan*, one that happens before the other two. Land loans are a little trickier because people sometimes buy a lot and then sit on it for a long time before building. Also, undeveloped land itself does not produce income. For this reason, lenders will give you a land loan, but the amount they will loan you is often more on the order of 70% or less of the value of the lot. Once you get into construction, though, the lender knows things will be moving along rapidly (or at least they hope so). Construction loans are usually for a maximum of one year.

With a construction loan, the lender will want to know who your builder is. This is another reason that small local lenders are more interested and better suited for these types of loans. The lender does not want an unscrupulous contractor leaving you (and in turn, them) high and dry with a half-finished structure that cannot produce income and thus cannot pay back the loan. So your lender will actually want to approve your builder. The lender will also monitor the building along the way. They will ask to see invoices, they will inspect the property; they will do whatever they need to do in order to make sure they are not being ripped off by your builder. This is a big help to you.

Along these same lines, construction loan lenders will rarely approve you to be your own builder, unless you are already a professional builder with a proven track record. The whole "the neighbors will pitch in and Mom will make lemonade" scene may look idyllic in old time movies, but modern-day lenders won't touch it with a ten-foot pole.

Your lender will usually not give you a construction loan until they know you have been approved for a regular "take-out" mortgage once the construction has been completed. Now, this is important in order to avoid confusion: The construction loan is for one year. Payments on a construction loan are usually interest-only payments on a monthly basis. Let's say your cost to build that home is $250,000. The lender does NOT expect that you will pay back $250,000 to them in one year's time, based on your monthly payments. They are loaning you that money. You in turn give it to the contractor. The contractor uses it for workers, materials, and profit. Then at the end of the twelve months (hopefully), you have a house that cost $250,000 to build, but has a value of $350,000 or more. You now take out a traditional mortgage for that $250,000. The bank that gives you that traditional $250,000 home mortgage pays off your construction loan and you are in this new house, paying your normal, basic home mortgage.

Construction loans are usually for 80% of the appraised value of the finished product or 100% of the costs. This is also why prior ownership of the lot is looked upon favorably by the lender. Let's say you inherited a piece of land. You own it free and clear. It has a value of $100,000. Now you want to build a $400,000 home on it. The bank sees that you already have $100,000 worth of equity, or 20% of the appraised value of the finished product ($400,000 worth of building on $100,000 worth of land = $500,000 total value of property). This gives them much greater security than if you needed money to buy the land, needed money to build the house, etc.

Notice that I have used the term **appraisal**, or **appraised value**. With new construction, you would first draw up plans for the house, then you would have that "theoretical" house appraised prior to building. This is what the bank calls a **pre-construction appraisal** wherein the appraiser uses the building plans, specifications and construction costs to determine the value of the finished product.

If you ever can find a larger national lender who is willing to do a construction loan, the benefit to you is that you might get them to agree to one closing as opposed to two or more closings, since you would also use them for your regular mortgage once construction was completed. This saves you money, as you will see in Chapter Four when we get into the costs of real estate closings.

There is another reason that some lenders are leery of construction loans: **mechanic's liens**. If you stiff a contractor, that contractor can put a lien against your property and that lien, by law, actually comes *before* the first position mortgage. **In most states, the only thing that trumps a mechanic's lien is a tax lien.** Lenders know that it is far more likely that this sort of conflict might occur during construction than at any other time during the life of the home, and if it does, it imperils their legal standing to collect on their collateral—your home.

One way of protecting yourself against a mechanic's lien is once you make a payment to your general contractor for a specific task to be completed, you get from them a **lien waiver**. You should also have your general contractor get these from his subcontractors and material suppliers. Essentially, this is a document that states that you paid for, say, the driveway. If the general contractor pockets the money and stiffs the blacktop guy who *he* hired to put in the driveway, you've got a "get out of jail free" card (or at least a good defense) that says you're not the scofflaw, someone else is. This can block the lien against your property and put the onus on the person you gave the money to. I have several horror stories about mechanic's liens and custom construction and cannot stress enough the importance of engaging a good attorney if you find yourself in trouble.

Assignment Options—Mortgages, Deeds of Trust, and Due on Sale Clauses

With most mortgages, there are two documents: a mortgage and a deed of trust. The *mortgage* is your promissory note, your agreement to pay the money back. The second document is usually filed with the county and it is the *deed of trust*, a securing interest in whatever the collateral is, usually the property in question.

Note here: With many of these issues, there are states' rights (i.e. what is true in Colorado may not be true in Wyoming, and so forth). While most states have deeds of trust—meaning you are entrusting a public trustee (the county, in the example I have used) to administer foreclosure actions—other states may not have this procedure and the lender must use private legal means to get redress of their grievance against a bad borrower.

Deeds of trust can sometimes have a strict *"due on sale"* clause. In such a case, if you change title on that house, the lender can immediately call that note as due. Despite this, people still try to get around it. In other words, they will not pay off their note when they sell their house. Example: You have a $100,000 balance due on your mortgage. You sell your house for $350,000. You put all $350,000 in your pocket and run like hell. Your lender still has a collateral interest in the property. This can happen if the new buyer did not have the title company search outstanding liens. Also read the upcoming subchapter on "mortgage wraps." Protection against this sort of problem, if you are a home buyer, is what title insurance is about, which we will cover in Chapter Four.

There are times (albeit rare) when a seller shows up at a real estate closing and actually tries to get away with not officially transferring the property's title to the buyer. They will instead substitute a worthless piece of paper that says, "You are now the owner of this house." This is a way of hiding the existence of a deed of trust with a due on sale clause.

But what happens if you want to get into the real estate investment game? You have a home to live in, but you also want to buy other properties to, perhaps rent, or maybe fix up and "flip" (sell once you've renovated it). Many professional financial advisors—your lawyer, your accountant—may suggest that you would be best protected by not owning the property in your own name, but by creating some type of legal entity. This idea has many advantages, but one problem it creates is that many lenders will shy away from lending to a corporate entity unless it is a very large project like a high rise or a shopping mall. Some of the legal protections you want to put in place actually protect *you* against *them*, and why on earth would they want to help you do that?

Sometimes a lender may still play ball with you, but if they are lending money to your corporation (I am using the word "corporation" generically. There are many different types, but what I am saying here holds true for all of them.) instead of you, they will charge you a much higher interest rate. Not good.

But why am I mentioning this here in the subchapter concerning "due on sale" clauses? Because what many savvy real estate investors do, or try to do, is apply for a mortgage in their own name (in order to get the best mortgage deal), then immediately transfer ownership to their corporation. Fine if you can get away with it, but if someone advises you to do this, there is always the risk that if your lender catches wind of it and they have a strict due on sale clause, they may call your loan. Again, not good. Be careful and get good legal advice if you are considering this.

Some lenders get so wrapped up in this that they even give some borrowers a hard time when they become married. Picture it: You buy a house when you're single. You get a mortgage. You get married. You show your love for your spouse by putting his or her name on the title. Then your lender shoots cupid with a crossbow by calling your loan because according to them, you technically "sold" the property. You "sold" it to *you and your spouse*, by adding that additional name. Again, not a bad thing to do, but be careful. You may need written pre-approval from your lender, particularly if your spouse has bad credit.

Assumable Mortgages

Some deeds of trust are actually *assumable*, as are mortgages in general (see "VA loans"). This, though, is becoming rarer and rarer as risk, scams, volatile markets, and temptations to develop bad credit increase. To be assumable means that a mortgage can be passed intact from one party to another, rather than starting up from scratch.

Something that is starting to gain traction is the concept of assuming your *own* mortgage. Allow me to explain.

People move more often now than they used to. You live in a house for a few years, then you sell it and move into another one. You probably still have an outstanding balance on the mortgage you had on your first house, so you pay that off with the proceeds of the home sale, then take out a whole new mortgage on your new house.

Well, mortgage lenders want to hold onto your business. Once you pay off mortgage lender number one, you may go to another lender the next time around. So…maybe, in order to keep your business, mortgage company number one says, "How about we offer you this: You can just move your mortgage over to that new house you just bought." As long as you are happy with the terms, this could be a win/win for you as well, since it most likely will cut down on your closing costs, and the interest rate may be more favorable.

If you are selling one home and buying another, try asking your mortgage lender about something like this. It may work; it may not, but it's worth a try.

Assumable mortgages are referred to as "*qualifying*" or "*non-qualifying*." Non-qualifying means that anyone with a heartbeat can assume it. Qualifying means you must get the lender's consent, which cannot be unreasonably withheld (for bias, etc.). The days of non-qualifying mortgages are long gone since the federal government stopped allowing them on new FHA loans back in 1989.

Owner Carry

This is also known as a private mortgage. You, the seller of the property, lend the money to the buyer (or you just collect your sale proceeds over time). The buyer pays you every month instead of a bank or financial institution. The risks involved in this are readily apparent, although what is more common is for the owner to "carry" a *part* of the mortgage.

Example: You're selling your house. You get a buyer. The buyer can get approved for a $100,000 mortgage. The only problem is that he needs a *$125,000* mortgage to meet your asking price. *He* feels he can pay the additional amount, *you* feel he can pay the additional amount, so what can you do? Well, you can have him take out that $100,000 mortgage and then you "lend" him the additional $25,000 yourself. Now, you are not actually giving him $25,000 cash; you are simply selling him your house and drawing up paperwork indicating that he owes you $25,000. The two parties agree to a payback schedule and boom! You're a private mortgage lender and your loan is secured by the property (albeit in second lien position).

As a buyer, some of the benefits of being involved in an owner-carry mortgage are:

- It does not show up in your credit report.
- You might get a little bit better interest rate, due to a motivated seller.
- You might actually get a *bad* interest rate, but at least you'll get a mortgage, period.

As a seller, one of the benefits of being involved in an owner-carry mortgage is:

- Delaying capital gains taxes, such as in the case of an investment or rental property. Example: If you own a property free and clear of any mortgages and you sell it for $200,000 and your buyer gets a traditional mortgage, he brings you a check for $200,000 and you will be socked with a large tax bill. On the other hand, if *you* lend him the money, you get that $200,000 apportioned out to you over x number of years, possibly creating better tax-planning for you.

One major thing to beware of, though, as a buyer, is not to be talked into a "*payment for deed structure*." What this means is that the owner, seeking to maximize his own personal protection, says to you, "Look, here's our agreement for you to pay me x amount of dollars per month for x amount of years and once you have done that, I will *then* give you the deed to the house." Does this help him? Of course. But it is terrible for you, the buyer. Technically, you do not own the house. You have no real equity. You cannot use the equity you have put into the house and collateralize it for any other purpose. You are literally a renter. And like a renter, the interest you pay is not tax-deductible. Ouch!

Bottom line: If you are the buyer, you must insist on taking title to the property.

Yes, a seller takes a huge risk by carrying the note, but he is not without recourse if the buyer defaults. A private mortgage lender (you) follows exactly the same protocols of foreclosure as a big mega-bank. And yes, those protocols are a pain in the neck, but they serve to create a fair and level playing field for both the buyer and the seller. Notices must be filed; timetables are put in place, etc. You just can't simply run in there the day the buyer is two days late on one mortgage payment and toss him to the curb. He has rights, too. And yes, by law, in the end you should either get all of your money or you will get the property back.

Private "Hard Money" Lenders

The phrase "hard money" is not a political term, like "soft money." Hard money, in the case of real estate, is money that is *hard* to come by because a person's credit profile, or some other issues, makes it difficult for him to get approved for a mortgage. Banks (which is the word I will use generically here to describe most traditional mortgage lenders) are not well known for their creativity and flexibility. They build a metaphorical box and everything either fits into that box or falls outside of it. The box is not elastic nor can it change shape. Banks cannot shoulder *all* the blame for this, because the loans they write eventually get bundled up and sold on Wall Street. Picture a "bundle." A bundle of *unlike* objects is hard to carry. But a bundle of, say, perfectly identical four-foot long broomstick handles is *very* easy to carry. Banks look at mortgages the same way.

Private money lenders are perfect for people who fall just outside that metaphorical box. These lenders are people or entities that are small and personal enough to be able to take the time to really analyze an individual situation to properly determine whether a loan will be successful (the payments will all be made and made on time) or not.

Most private hard money lenders are nothing more than individuals. If you are in a good enough financial situation, you can become one yourself. However, please recognize that there are lots of laws and disclosures required if you want to loan to consumers on their primary residences.

A private hard money lender will usually charge a *much* higher interest rate, in addition to up-front origination points (1 to 8%). But if you, as a borrower, are in desperate straits, this is an option that is available. Now, this is not to say that you can have no job, tons of debt, and no prospects whatsoever and get people like this to loan you money. These lenders did not get into a position to lend money by being utterly stupid. But they will at least listen to your tale and think outside the box.

There are even websites now set up that are like auction sites, only for the lending of money. Check out my website at www.BraunMincher.com for current links. On these sites, people post their credit profiles, how much money they need, what they need it for, why they are in need of private money lending (read: their tale of woe), and what terms they are looking for. In turn, people like me who might want to *legally* play shylock, can peruse the situation and decide whether it is a match.

Of course, the very best method of finding reputable private money lenders is the same as I'd advise you to find anything: trust-worthy personal recommendation. And as to my using the word "shylock" in the previous paragraph, always remember that no house is worth going to the leg-breakers for. What I'm talking about here are legitimate, law-abiding private citizens who have money to lend—not organized crime figures.

Mortgage "Wrap"

No, mortgage wrap is not a new type of hip-hop music. But it is an interesting scenario. Let me give you an example of how this works:

You want to buy a house. The asking price is $100,000. You can't get approved for a mortgage for one reason or another. But the owner believes in you and is willing to work with you. Sounds like an owner carry, right? Almost. Here's where it begins to differ. The seller still has a mortgage. Starting to sound like an assumable, right? You're getting warmer. But what if the bank will not let it *be* assumed?

Welcome to the mortgage wrap. It is technically *legal*, but not necessarily *allowable* by the seller's bank. In other words, no one is looking at jail time over a wrap. The worst that can happen is that if the bank finds out, they will call the loan for immediate repayment (strict due on sale clause).

What happens is the seller gives you title (remember what I said before, that you must *insist* upon receiving title). The seller techni-cally carries the note for you. But…(here's the new twist) the seller must then pass through some of what you pay him to his bank where he still has an outstanding mortgage. This is where both buyer and seller are in dangerous cahoots together. If everyone does what they promised to do, it works out as a win for everyone. But if you, the buyer, make payments to the seller and then the seller fails to use it for his mortgage payments, all hell breaks loose.

I have been very successful in using mortgage wraps for a variety of purchases and sales, but this is where you definitely want to get a competent attorney involved to prepare the paperwork.

Reverse Mortgages

Reverse mortgages have been a godsend to senior citizens who are "house rich and cash poor." This is the kind of person who bought their home way back when for some little amount like $12,000. They've lived in it their entire adult life and carry no mortgage. But their home value has skyrocketed—they could sell today for $300,000. Wow! But they don't *want* to sell. Where would they live?

Furthermore, their property taxes are based on the value of their home, not what they paid for it back in the 1950s. They are paying property taxes on $300,000 and tax budgets are always going up.

They could always take out a HELOC, but they presently have little or no income to qualify—they're retired. How would they pay the money back? Rob Peter to pay Paul?

Along comes the reverse mortgage. If you own your house free and clear (no mortgage) and you are above sixty-two years of age, you may qualify. **A mortgage company, based on an actuarial table (read: your life expectancy) pays YOU every month.** Imagine—a mortgage that pays *you*.

You, or your surviving spouse, can stay in that house until the day that you die. If, for any reason, you are forced to leave the house—say, for example, you require an in-patient nursing facility—and do not live in the house for twelve straight months, you will then be forced to sell it. But for all intents, you can stay there as long as you wish. Furthermore, this arrangement can even help pay for in-home nursing care and the like, allowing you to not have to go into a residential facility. That means a lot to so many of our elderly.

A reverse mortgage allows a senior citizen to have their house, essentially, pay for its own property taxes. Their house also provides them with an income—a retirement fund. It is most common that these mortgages are set up based on the aforementioned actuarial table, but some people simply set a duration—say, 15 years—and work out the amortization from there.

The only downside to a reverse is that it leaves less of a legacy for one's heirs. But, without sounding too selfish, there is the philosophy that one should be able to enjoy one's earnings while they live, rather than leave them to spoil the work ethic of another generation. To put another positive spin on that, it lessens the chance for there to be extensive infighting over splitting up estates because there is less estate to divide amongst heirs.

The way a reverse mortgage is structured, you can never ever owe more than the house is worth when it is sold. In other words, you can outlive your actuarial, meaning that the lender may project that you will live another twenty years, but you end up living another thirty. Well, then, good for you. Example: It is projected that you will live another twenty years. The projected value of your house is $200,000. That amount is paid out to you in even increments over twenty years. But then you keep living. The lender has to keep paying you. You live another ten years. You receive another $100,000. You die. The house is sold by the lender on the open market for only $200,000, even though they paid *you* $300,000 for it. Does this mean the lender will chase after your heirs for the missing $100,000? No. They took the risk; they take the loss.

Now, if your heirs do not want to give away the family homestead to the lender when you die, they may refinance—take out another mortgage themselves in order to pay off the reverse lender. But what if you die only a year or two into your reverse? The lender is still only entitled to the amount of money you drew down from the arrangement. Thus, if you got a reverse for $200,000 but only received $20,000 before you died, either your heirs can take out a note to pay that amount back to the lender or they can sell the house and they will only owe the lender $20,000 and get to pocket the rest of the sales proceeds themselves.

Also, **the income from a reverse mortgage is generally considered to be the proceeds from a loan, thus it is not taxable.**

There's Money to be Made in this Game: A Quick Look at Mortgage Fraud

In some states, there is no educational or competency requirement needed to become a seller of mortgages. Here you are, an innocent lamb being led to the slaughter, being introduced to a "mortgage specialist," and this person before you may have absolutely no training whatsoever, nor be truly and properly overseen and licensed by the state. Frightening stuff, but the states are starting to crack down and impose new registration or licensing requirements. And some of these same states license people to file your fingernails or give you a back rub!

While I do not wish to disparage all of the scrupulous and ethical people in the industry, always remember: **A loan officer is a salesperson FIRST!** They may not be your buddy; you have completely different alignments of interest. Even if you meet them *through* a buddy, they may still not be your buddy. This is a relationship that requires vigilance on your part in order not to be ripped off so badly that it may take you half a lifetime to recover. I hope I now have your attention.

A possible form of semi-legal collusion is the relationship between your real estate agent and your mortgage person. Both of them benefit by getting you to buy the most expensive property possible. If you tell them both that you only want to spend $250,000, they could try to get you to spend $300,000. This is their job. This is how they make a living. Never forget it.

Mind you, this, in and of itself, is not criminal fraud. Unfortunately, by the time this book gets into your hand, there will probably be half a dozen new forms of criminal-level mortgage fraud invented. Mortgage fraud is like computer viruses. You get daily updates for your computer. You literally need daily mortgage updates to protect against mortgage fraud. Unfortunately, no such programs exist that I am aware of, but good common sense and healthy skepticism are your best allies.

Many mortgage scams involve how the sales price is listed or how the property is appraised. Again, I will bring up the word "collusion." If it is in a certain party's favor to have the property appraised high or low, a less-than-honorable real restate appraiser might be willing to literally ask, "How much do you *want* the property to be appraised for? $300,000? $325,000? Just put the number on a piece of paper and I'll do the rest." I don't have to tell you how illegal this is.

The FBI is now looking at certain neighborhoods, communities, counties, and states where home sales are selling, on average, for 3% to 5% *more* than they have been listed for. Now, to clarify: there are times when a property is in such demand that a bidding war ensues. If this is your property, bully for you. If this happens time and time again in an entire neighborhood, either there are a lot of incompetent real estate agents setting asking prices too low, or something smells fishy.

This brings up another issue called "*straw scams.*" Let's say that you're a younger person, you've just gotten engaged, and you and your fiancée find your dream house.   But since you're just getting started in life, you can't get a reasonably-priced mortgage.

Your parents have a pretty good credit score and a strong income, so you ask them to buy the house for you and then transfer ownership to you. You promise to pay them on the mortgage that you couldn't qualify for yourselves.

Your parents are acting as a "straw man"—a fake front—through which you are getting ownership of a house. This scenario seems relatively innocent, but it's illegal and leaves your parents on the hook for mortgage payment responsibilities on the house you now own. You are now a straw scammer.

There's another class of straw scammers that cause real estate bubbles all over the country. More sophisticated straw scams require a different kind of team work and at least one unknowing participant, maybe more.

Let's say you are selling your house on your own—what we call a "FSBO" (pronounced 'fiz-bo'): For Sale by Owner. Someone comes along and offers you waaaay above what you are asking. Sounds too good to be true, right? It is.

When you ask why they want to give you so much more than you are asking, they say that they want you to refund some of that "overage" to them in cash. Well geez, you're getting to sell your house, you're getting even more than you asked; why be greedy, right? At this point, though, you should ask yourself how the heck this all works.

First off, it is illegal, and secondly, with you agreeing to participate, this deal makes you an accomplice. This scenario requires an unethical team comprised, perhaps, of a real estate agent, a knowing straw buyer, a loan officer, and most especially, an appraiser. The difference between the market value of the property and the price agreed to is the bounty that you, the buyer's agent, the buyer, the loan officer, and the appraiser split. The straw buyer must have credit good enough to not look suspicious purchasing—or even applying for a mortgage on—a house of that value. The appraiser is critical because the appraisal report is what is used to get the deal past the lender's underwriting department. Once the risk management folks sign off on the deal, the mortgage can fund so that all parties get paid.

For-sale-by-owner properties are good targets for this type of scam because the seller's priority is more often maximizing the value of the property than being a student of the details of real estate transactions. An ethical listing agent would alert the seller about a possible scam.

Sounds like a win for all parties, though, right? Everyone in the deal gets paid and the only loser is the investor in the secondary market who bought the mortgage the straw scammer took on, and even *they* knew the risk in buying mortgage-backed securities. Unfortunately, the market comparables in your neighborhood are now skewed because of a house that sold for a much greater amount than the market would usually bear. Market values for houses rise artificially. And as people in the neighborhood refinance, they do so against inflated property values, often cashing-out this artificially built equity.

Being the straw buyer often works during up-markets because they can refinance against the appreciated value of the house and take cash out of the loan.   But if they can't refinance, the straw buyer often has to walk away from the mortgage, or flee, leaving the mortgage unpaid and the house in foreclosure.   Why? Because this entire enterprise has been built upon a quick hit and run. The straw buyer, despite having decent credit, usually has no intention of living in that house. This entire thing is pure real estate speculation.

The aforementioned example features a criminal straw buyer who knows what the deal is going in. Other times, the buyer is just a sucker and agrees to this deal voluntarily and may even agree to deed the house to a third party after the transaction is complete, similar to the parents in the earlier example.

But identity theft plays a critical role in this type of scam because it eliminates the need to meet and convince a straw buyer to take the risk of applying for and then leaving a mortgage.   It's not uncommon for mortgages to be done sight-unseen, and by the time an unknowing identity-theft victim finds out about their "application," the mortgage might already have been funded. These are the sorts of deals that we see profiled on investigative TV programs.

While most of these cases are eventually resolved so that the identity theft victim is not responsible for the mortgage, please don't underestimate the amount of time and inconvenience this causes. An event like this is a major life disruption.

Once again, you are advised to work with mortgage and real estate professionals that you know and trust. Get personal recommendations and references whenever possible. Unfortunately, a few bad apples in the industry have tarnished the image of the majority who are doing a good job. Be vigilant and do not become a victim.

Default and Foreclosure

Unlike credit cards and other unsecured debts, lenders do not like partial payments on mortgages. When times get tight, it is very easy to find yourself three or four months behind in your mortgage. When this occurs, you are considered in "*default*," and most lenders will serve you with a foreclosure notice. This is usually served by the sheriff of your county and issued by an attorney representing the mortgage company.

At this point you are required to pay all of the back payments, late charges, and the attorney fees (attorney fees can be as high as $2,000 to $4,000). If you do not bring your payment up to date within a reasonable amount of time (usually thirty to one hundred eighty days), your home will be sold at auction at the County Court House and you must vacate the premises or the sheriff will put your belongings out on the front lawn.

Foreclosure is a type of lawsuit in which a bank, mortgage company, or other creditor seeks to take an owner's property to satisfy a debt. The bank or lender may actually take the property, or have the property sold to pay off the debt. As a result of the foreclosure, the owner loses whatever rights he or she had in the property.

If a homeowner fails to pay his or her mortgage loan on time, the lender that holds the mortgage on the house can bring a foreclosure action against the homeowner. Similarly, if a homeowner borrows money from a bank using a house as collateral and fails to pay, the homeowner can lose the house to the bank in a foreclosure action.

Foreclosure is a court process, and you must follow the process carefully to protect your rights.   Foreclosure happens one of two ways: **Strict Foreclosure** or **Foreclosure by Sale**. The court process is mostly the same for both, although many of the specifics vary from state to state.

1. Strict Foreclosure

In a strict foreclosure, a judge will set a court date. After your court date, you lose all rights to the property. Court dates can be assigned as soon as three weeks after the date the case goes to judgment, or it may be as long as nine months or longer. That decision is up to the judge hearing the case.

Until your court date, you may avoid foreclosure by redeeming the mortgage or debt. In other words, you have until your court date to pay off what you owe to the bank or other party bringing the case. The amount due will also include attorney's fees and court costs. Redeeming can be done in a number of ways: you could sell the property yourself or borrow the money from another lender.

If you do not redeem the mortgage by your court date, then the person or company foreclosing gets title to the property.

2. Foreclosure by Sale

In a foreclosure by sale, a judge will set a sale date. On the sale date, an entity appointed by the court auctions off the property to the highest bidder. The court gives the appointed entity the power to carry out all aspects of the auction, including advertising in the newspaper and posting a sign on the property. The court issues an order permitting the appointee to enter the property on the day of sale; however, the appointee is instructed by the judge to enter only with the consent of the occupant. The money from the auction first goes to pay for the costs of setting up the auction, then to the lender and any other liens on the property. Then, if any money is left over, it goes to you.

If you pay the amount of the judgment plus any costs and fees incurred by the auctioneer prior to the date of sale, you can prevent the sale from occurring and protect your rights to the property. As with strict foreclosure, you can pay off the debt by either selling the property privately or by refinancing. **Unless you have a lot of equity in the property, you should NOT seek a foreclosure by sale.**

Defending against foreclosure is complex and can be expensive. You must consider your options carefully, keeping in mind that you may end up responsible for additional legal and other fees. In order to defend in a foreclosure, you will need to pay close attention to court proceedings and deadlines.

In a foreclosure, an important alternative for you is to sell your property. You can usually sell your property any time before your court date or sale date. Selling the property before foreclosure may save you legal and other costs while preserving the true value of the property, particularly if you sell your property in the early stages of the proceeding. Throughout the foreclosure proceedings, you should consider conducting your own sale. But remember, if you find a buyer for the property, you must be sure that the sale price is high enough to cover the total debt, or you will need to find some way to bring cash to the table. In some cases, the lender may also agree to a "short sale" where they will take less than you owe, but when this happens they usually look to the borrower to make up this loss at a later date.

If you believe you have little or no equity in your property and that refinancing or a private sale is not possible, you may want to consider offering title to your property to the lender instead of forcing it to go through the entire foreclosure process. If the bank chooses to accept the deed (known as a "deed in lieu of foreclosure"), your future credit rating may be helped, since you will not have a foreclosure in your credit history. You may also be able to negotiate giving a deed to the bank in return for its promise not to seek a deficiency judgment against you for any difference still owed. One thing to bear in mind is that you may have to pay conveyance taxes to the state and town if you give a deed in lieu of foreclosure. You should seek the help of a lawyer if you think the option of deed in lieu of foreclosure is available to you.

The Bursting Bubble— How Did You Get Here and How Do You Get Out?

As I write this, foreclosure rates are at an all-time high across the country. One of the primary reasons, in my opinion, is all these "designer mortgages" that encourage people to commit to debts in which they really should not be involved. Also, of equal or maybe even more weight, is ultimately the lack of financial literacy of the borrowers, but by reading this book you will know more than most others. I hate to sound old-fashioned, but **if you do not have a 20% down payment in hand for a certain property and you cannot make the monthly payments for a traditional 15 or 30-year fixed mortgage on said property, with taxes, insurance, and normal property maintenance, then you really shouldn't be in that property.** The old rules of thumb would have forced you into something smaller and more affordable and frankly, that is where you should be.

Bubbles are bursting. People who did not lock themselves in with good low fixed rates are finding that they simply cannot afford the new, higher rates of today. Furthermore, those who got themselves involved in no-money-down mortgage products are finding that they cannot even *find* refinancing. Picture this: Three years ago, you got yourself into that McMansion you wanted but couldn't afford. You got yourself some wacky designer mortgage that allowed you to put no money down. Maybe it even had some sort of negative am feature. The rate was, of course, adjustable. Today, you wake up and it's smell-the-coffee time. After a certain period of time, you were to become tied in to the Prime Rate or some other index, and that day is today. You expected to be making more money by now and your house was supposed to have increased in value. Furthermore, once you became tied in to that index, indexes were supposed to have remained at record historic lows. But now they're not. Nor are you earning twice what you made three years ago, as had been your career plan. Also, if you had to sell your house now, you'd have to take 25% *less than you paid for it*!

You are now in a situation where your monthly mortgage bill has skyrocketed and you simply do not have the money to pay it. Also, you have absolutely no equity in your home. You, in fact, have *negative* equity—you owe more than your house is worth! And now for the final blow—you, my friend, cannot refinance and get yourself a new mortgage ANYWHERE. No one in their right mind would lend to someone in this sort of situation. And all because of the lure of "designer mortgages" and the feeling of personal economic invincibility.

In previous subchapters, I mentioned the appeal of home ownership—how your house is an asset that can do many things for you. We talked about HELOCs, which turn your home into a credit card—with tax deductible interest. We talked about cash-out refinancing, which is when you pay off your old mortgage, then get a new one for more than what you owed on your old one. With that additional cash in hand, you could do a multitude of things—pay off credit cards, buy a boat, start a business, take a trip around the world, or put the kids through college. And again, your interest would be tax deductible.

These are all wonderful options, but *only if you can afford to pay your monthly mortgage!*

In upcoming chapters, we will talk more about real estate and real estate investment. It's an exciting field and can be very lucrative. But the most lucrative investments carry the greatest risk. Since home equity is something that people gain not through work, but through simply living in the right place (your home) at the right time (an "up" market), people are all too reckless with it. I've always believed that knowledge is power, but in this case, power can be dangerous when knowing about the benefits of home ownership empowers people to run their lives into the ground.

Take the popular real estate concept of *"fix and flip."* **"Fix and flip" means that you buy a property, fix it up, then sell it for a profit greater than what you paid for it and what the fix-ups cost.** There is a popular misconception that this is a dummy-proof way to make money and it *cannot fail.* Well, actually it can, and it can send you into not one, but two defaults and foreclosures.

Misconception 1: Undervalued properties are lying around all over the place. Wrong. Yes, sometimes you can find one, maybe many. But they are not like weeds—something you can find everywhere in every season in every place. Two things often happen: In their eagerness to get rich quick, people either buy a "fixer-upper" that is not really undervalued—it is truly being sold at a fair market rate, *or*—they will pay peanuts for a property that they think only needs a cheap coat of paint. In reality, the place is structurally unsound and needs major work that is so expensive that it explodes the buyer's meager budget or handyman abilities. And then what does the buyer do? He takes more equity out of his own domicile in order to put lipstick on this pig he just bought!

Misconception 2: The market always goes up. Yes, over almost unlimited time, property values do eventually rise. Real estate is finite. There is only so much land in the world. But the "fix and flipper" wants a quick hit and run. This requires the market to stay hot—*intensely* hot—over a short period of time so that something like this can happen:

You buy a property for $100,000. You slap a coat of paint on it and get a "designer mortgage" that allows you to pay as little per month as humanly possible. Maybe you manage no money down, or maybe you even take equity out of your own home to cobble together a down payment. But what the heck; you're going to get in and out of this fast and at a nice profit, so what could go wrong?

You either manage to rent this house for six months, or maybe you just let it sit empty. Either way, between the paint and the mortgage, tax, and insurance payments, you dole out, say, $5,000.

Then, after only six quick months, you put it on the market and within days you get an eager buyer for $150,000! Take away the $5,000 you put in, and you, my friend, just made a quick and easy $45,000 profit. Yay!

Notice I labeled both of these things "misconceptions." That's because they are. In reality, "fix and flip" often turns to "fix and flop." The above example is the exception more often than the rule. It is quick and easy pie-in-the sky. And because it has become so popular, it is another one of the leading causes of default and foreclosure because it most certainly involves the investment property itself, but sometimes it also involves the investor's own home.

So, are there other things you can do to stave off default and foreclosure? In addition to the bigger moves such as selling the property, **you can also call your private mortgage insurer if you have PMI on the property.** I mean, that's the definition of mortgage insurance—it is insurance against you defaulting. Get that company involved. See what they can do. They often times lend money to homeowners to prevent foreclosure.

Don't pay any other bills. I know this sounds drastic, but what is more important—your cell phone or your home? Your cable TV with its five hundred premium channels, or the roof over your head? Cut, cut, cut. Nothing is sacred. Quit that fancy health club. Stop eating out. This might be a great time to have that garage sale.

I know this hurts. Maybe you were the victim of terrible circumstances that were absolutely beyond your control. Or maybe you made some stupid mistakes that you will never, ever make again. Remember: For the most part, life is long. Get your priorities in order. Even if you destroy the rest of your credit profile for a while, if you can keep that house, you might be able to pull through and keep yourself together. **When facing foreclosure, your credit score should be down low on your priority list.** Sure, you won't be buying yourself any presents for a while. But certain things—health insurance, food, a job, a way to get to that job, a roof over your head—these are the most important things. It's like going on a diet. You won't lose fifty pounds overnight, but if you stick to it, in a few years of healthy living, you can show some wonderful progress. **Eventually, you can build your credit back up again.**

One last word on this topic: There's a terrible scam out there that preys on people facing foreclosure. It is the "*foreclosure rescuers.*" If you ever see an ad or a sign saying, "Foreclosure? We can help!" Run fast and run swiftly. **Many of these people are scam artists.**

One of the most typical aspects of the foreclosure rescue scam is the "give us your deed and we'll rent your home back to you and let you 'rent to buy.'" Here's how it works: First off, it sorta sounds like an owner carry. Except...it violates the cardinal rule of owner financing. The moment you allow the other guy to hold the deed, it is a bad deal. Foreclosure or no foreclosure, walk away from this deal.

If they manage to get a sucker to take this deal, there are many variations of what comes next. Often, the "rent" situation is a month-to-month deal. There is no "cap" provision, so after only a few months, they drastically raise your rent and you have no recourse. Another flavor is to give you a long-term lease, but write it so that the *term* stays with the house, but not the *rate*. So after a few months, Bob, the guy who offered you this deal, "sells" the house to his cousin Vinny (played by Joe Pesci) and Vinny doubles your rent. You are forced out and Joe and Vinny do a happy dance.

One last variation is that there is a clause that says that, since you are a very naughty person and a bad credit risk, if you are late so much as one day on one month's payment, you have invalidated your option to buy. The new owner figures this will only be a matter of time.

Home ownership is a wonderful thing, and like all wonderful things, treat it like a precious commodity, like life, liberty, and the pursuit of happiness. Be conservative, be smart, and if you get in trouble fix it fast and fix it well.

CHAPTER 3
PROPERTY LEASES

Renting vs. Owning

Before most of us end up *owning* a home, we usually rent somewhere. This may be during college when we are young and moving around frequently, or later in life for a variety of reasons. Furthermore, there are times in our lives when renting rather than owning makes financial sense. Generally, you want to buy property (if you can afford to) if you plan on living somewhere for at least five years, to cover the costs associated with selling.

Author and speaker Robert Kiyosaki has made a cottage industry out of his series of books entitled "Rich Dad, Poor Dad." Most of his advice is rather uncontroversial, although one area where he has gained many critics is his philosophy that home ownership is an overrated asset, if an asset at all. While I am not here to explain, defend, and then refute his theories, let it be said that on this topic, I side with the majority: On the whole, I am an advocate of home ownership rather than rental. As illustrated in other chapters, home equity is tangible and can be used in a multitude of ways with only your imagination as your limitation. Additionally, there are numerous tax benefits and the possibility of appreciation over time.

But let's say you're a young person who has just decided, with a good friend or two, to move out of your college dorm. Do you have enough cash on hand for both the down payment and then the monthly payment on a home mortgage? Probably not. Would I advise you to go for some exotic "designer mortgage" that enables you to get into home ownership with little to no money down? Not usually. For one thing, while you're still in college, or even for the few years thereafter, how steady is your income? Do you even *have* an income? Most college students are lucky to be able to scrape together beer and pizza money.

Slightly off topic, but I have known some financially savvy parents who have analyzed just such situations and have "bought" Junior his own condo near campus. They knew they were going to have to cough up housing money anyway, so why not make a real estate investment rather than just an expenditure? Junior lives in the condo for four years, and by then, the local housing market has gone up and Mom and Dad sell that condo for a profit. Worked right— and with the right market conditions—Junior may have been able to live away at college for free, while at the same time building his credit if he was on the title. Wow!

But this is usually predicated on Mom and Dad being pretty darn solid financially and not all of us are that lucky. So back to renting.

Even after college, or taking college out of the picture entirely, few of us get to move from under Mom and Dad's roof right into a home and a mortgage. Again, even though there are wild new mortgage products on the market that allow for little to no money down, I look at them warily, much like how credit cards are now so easy to acquire. T'was a time when young people had to beg and plead for store credit cards (Sears was a famous starting point for many, including me), giving them only a few hundred dollars credit, before earning a good credit history over time and eventually making the big leap up to a Visa or Mastercard. Today, teens *without jobs* are inundated with offers for all the major credit cards. **The quick and easy way is nothing more than the quick and easy way to financial ruin.** But again, I digress.

It is still a common American tradition for a couple to get married and pool their wedding money in order to put together a down payment on a home. But as more young people are waiting longer to get married, this, too, is becoming more a thing of the past. In some cases, that "rental period" of life is even longer today than in previous generations.

Finally, there is the American dream of owning one's own business. Unfortunately, the rule of thumb is that two out of thee businesses fail, most of them after less than five years. The most common reason for failure is undercapitalization—not having enough money to operate properly.

Undercapitalization is not always the pure lack of money, but that the money the entrepreneur had was spent in all the wrong places. There's the classic fable of the guy who opened up a new business and proudly showed his father his brand new, top-of-the-line electric pencil sharpener. "You haven't written up a single order yet, and here you are with this $50 pencil sharpener! Why don't you get a dollar's worth of pencils first, then when you've written up enough business to wear them all down, *then* you'll be able to afford such a fancy machine."

Purchasing commercial property is one of those potential traps young entrepreneurs fall into. Sure, owning your own building has innumerable positive aspects—it is a tangible asset if you do fail and must sell, you can lease out excess space to other businesses, etc. But still, it is often a luxury a start-up business can ill afford. Perhaps you should consider renting while you get your dream off the ground, and then expand into building ownership.

This all being said, let's talk about the proper way to rent and the pitfalls novice renters face.

Lease Agreements

Your first rental agreement or lease is usually not your *landlord's* first. This is good and bad. It is good because it helps if at least one party to an agreement has some knowledge and acumen. It's bad if that party is not you.

Rule number one is...make sure there *is* a lease. You would be surprised at how many people like to do things on a handshake. It's a wonderful, idyllic picture of human values at their best, but like most such pictures, it is unrealistic. **Get something in writing, whether the term is for a few months or even a few years. This is a business arrangement.**

This does not simply pertain to the original lease, but should also include any modifications or extensions that may occur along the way. Let's say your landlord uses some pro forma (standard— something he bought from a stationary store) lease and it says "no pets." You have a little, innocuous goldfish. Your landlord says, "Oh, heck, what harm can a goldfish be? Sure, you can keep it." GET THIS IN WRITING. Otherwise, it just provides an excuse for him to boot you out for some capricious reason—like if he finds out he can rent to someone else for twice what you agreed to pay.

Also, in most states, oral agreements that are for more than one year in term are unenforceable. That means if it is for less than a year, it is usually enforceable, but it still comes back to the basic premise: It's your word against his. Who can prove their point? Not good, not good at all.

Landlord/tenant disputes clog up a huge portion of small claims courts around the country. Some lawyers also make a good living just specializing in this sort of thing. One way to stay out of court— whether you are a tenant *or* a landlord—and save on legal bills and court costs is to write everything down as it comes up and have both parties sign it.

As previously inferred, the lease agreement will almost exclusively be provided by the landlord—unless you are Starbucks or an attorney, I have a hard time picturing a tenant handing his own lease to a landlord. That being said, everything in life is negotiable, and most state real estate commissions do not oversee lease forms or terms. Of course, the market rules every situation. If you are in an area where there are far more potential tenants than there are places to rent, the landlord holds all the cards and can say, "Either sign whatever I put in front of you or step out of line; there's one hundred people waiting behind you who will." In other situations, you have a greater ability, as the potential tenant, to really read over that lease agreement and mark it up, suggesting changes where things do not seem fair or equitable to you.

If you are a landlord, or desire to be one, large stationary stores and internet web sites have standard lease forms available. A better idea is to spend a few dollars with your attorney and have something drawn up that makes sense for you. Your attorney will still probably begin with pretty standard stuff, but unlike what you buy at a store, you can state right from the start certain issues that are of concern to you and get them put into the agreement properly.

Being a landlord myself, I have one of the most comprehensive rental agreements one could ever imagine. Every time an issue or a conflict with a tenant comes up, I'm off to my lawyer's office to make changes in my lease agreements so that I am covered for it if it happens again in the future. Furthermore, by taking affirmative action, I get to control the situation. You want to know my policy on goldfish? Here's my policy on goldfish. Pit Bulls? Here's how I feel about Pit Bulls in my houses. Every issue not addressed in a lease agreement is open season—open to interpretation. Thus, as a landlord, the less left uncovered, the less time I might have to spend in some sort of collection action or legal battle—each of which is a complete waste of time for everybody involved.

One last word before we move on: I have used the word "rent" and the word "lease." You will sometimes hear the phrase "rental agreement" as well as the phrase "lease agreement." In everyday life, laypeople may interchange them without defining them, but technically, they are two slightly different things.

A "**rental agreement**" is usually for a very short period of time, perhaps only thirty days. It is often renewable, sometimes even self-renewing (more on this later). A "**lease agreement**" usually refers to a longer period of time, usually six months or more. As you read along, you will usually see me using the phrase "lease agreement," but the person paying it pays "rent" (I've never heard of anyone paying "lease.").

For an idea of what sample lease agreements look like, go to the "Links" section of my website at www.BraunMincher.com.

Standard Lease Terms

The basics of a property lease are:

- WHO are the parties to the agreement?
- WHAT are the financial terms? Who pays what to whom—how much and how often?
- WHEN does the lease begin and end?
- WHERE is the property, and what defines the property for the sake of this agreement (Is it only within the four main interior walls, or is it the outside of those walls as well? Does it involve area outside the property, such as the front or back lawn or the sidewalk, or does it not?)?
- RULES of care and behavior. Are there any? And if so, what are they?
- HOW can the agreement be enforced, terminated, extended or modified?

Lease Terms—WHO?

"*Joint and several*" is a phrase that constantly crops up in landlord/tenant disputes. "**Joint and several**" **means that whoever is on the lease is liable for payment; not just for their "own," but for everyone else as well** .

Example: You, Squiggy, and Moe decide to rent a place together. Squiggy decides to join the Peace Corps and moves out. You and Moe are under the false impression that now you two only have to pay two thirds of the rent. Ha ha! Now how would that be fair to the landlord? Oh yes, but you and Moe get all indignant, saying, "Look, there are three signatures on the lease. But now there're only two of us!" To which any landlord with the standard (yes, it is standard) joint and several clause will say, "So what?" The landlord is not going to chase after Squiggy. Squiggy is no longer in the apartment and all a landlord cares about is who is in the apartment and who he can find *easily* for payment. How those of you who remain split the costs is *your* problem. If the rent is $900 per month, the landlord must get $900 per month, period.

Pick your roommates carefully. This is not only a college student issue. It is even more common when couples live together, and then break up. The one left behind not only has to deal with a broken heart, but a doubling of their rent. Ouch!

Some smart renters, knowing about joint and several provisions, write up an agreement between themselves in order to deal with the possibility of "breakups." Sometimes they will draw up a plan where if one person were to move out, that person would be responsible to find an acceptable replacement roommate or else pay the rent in absentia until one is found. Unmarried couples should also have a written cohabitation agreement as well.

This also comes up with guarantors. Sometimes landlords want a responsible adult to sign the lease, rather than three or four kids under age twenty-one. So Squiggy's daddy signs the lease, but then he squawks when Squiggy moves out to join the Peace Corps. Again, tough luck, Mr. Squiggy. Joint and several. If you're the guarantor, you're responsible for monthly rent payments, even if you or the individual you are acting as guarantor for, moves out.

Some other issues with the WHO (not the classic rock group, but the renters): Some leases state quite clearly how many people can live in a particular dwelling. If your lease says a maximum of three people and you move in ten to cut costs, better hope the landlord doesn't find out, because you are in breach and yes, he can get redress of his legal grievances. You are wrong and he will win—and it could cost you money, it could cost you a place to live, or both.

Another WHO issue is this switching around of roommates. Some leases state that this must be approved by the landlord. Read your lease carefully.

Damages—another WHO issue. You, Moe, and Squiggy signed the lease. At the end of the lease, the landlord comes in and finds that two windows are broken. You and Moe say, "Squiggy did it, but he's not here." Tough luck on you. You and Moe are there, you and Moe are on the lease, and you and Moe are going to cough up the money to fix those windows.

From the landlord's end, there can also be problems. This especially happens a lot in college towns. You, Moe, and Squiggy move in and out and switch around so much that by the end of the lease, *none of you* are still there. Now the landlord is looking at three total strangers who are *not* on the lease and who he doesn't know from Adam. How is he even going to *take* any of them to court? This is why I advise landlords to get unconditional guarantors for underage tenants and put in lease clauses regarding the approval of tenant changes. Without those, a landlord should be on the lookout for rent checks with strange and unfamiliar names on them.

Lease Terms—WHAT?

What do you think is the most common problem between renters and landlords? Money. The most common reason people rent is because they are not financially solvent enough to own. So take the massive mortgage foreclosure rate in this country and—although I have no exact data on this—most likely quadruple it when it comes to failure to pay rent in a full and timely fashion.

If you are a renter, your responsibilities are clear—pay what you agreed to pay and pay on time.

Now, as a landlord, I've heard it all: The classic "The check is in the mail," as well as a thousand variations. Being a landlord is no bed of roses on a day-to-day basis.

While residential rent is rarely if ever to be found on one's credit report, some landlords actually ask for permission to call up previous landlords to check to see if you were a good tenant, as in, "did you pay on time?" or "would you re-rent to her?" Some even do credit checks. So…be a good citizen.

I have my own remedy to make it astonishingly easy for my tenants to pay their rent. I have them set up to directly deposit their rent into my bank account. All my tenants are supplied with deposit slips to a bank that is right in their neighborhood. Furthermore, I assign every one of my rental units a two-digit number. That number is reflected in the rent I charge them. For example, if you are in my rental unit #28 , your rent will end in the digit "28," as in $990.28 per month, perhaps. That way, it is incredibly easy for me to track who has paid and who hasn't, and I never mix up crediting a payment to the wrong renter. It's so efficient, I feel I should patent it! Furthermore, the direct deposit cuts out all the malarkey about things getting lost in the mail.

One last thing regarding WHAT are the financial terms: **In most residential leases** (which is what we've primarily been discussing here), **the renter has what we generally refer to as a "*gross lease*,"** meaning, they pay an agreed-upon amount per month and the only other expense they have pertaining directly to the property is their own utilities: heat, electric, water, phone, cable, Internet, etc. This may also vary from lease to lease/property to property, so, as usual, read and know before moving in. For example, some residential properties do not have separate meters on the heat for each unit, so the landlord simply estimates how much it costs to heat each unit per year and factors that into his asking price for the rent. Your phone, of course, will be set up just for your unit and you will not be cost-sharing with the guy who lives in the unit next door and spends all day on the phone talking to Taiwan.

In a gross lease, the landlord pays things like insurance on the property, property taxes, association dues, and routine maintenance and repairs.

Lease Terms—WHEN?

Check your lease to see if there are any types of automatic renewals or rent increases. Some leases will say, "If not terminated by either party at least thirty days prior to the next renewal period, the lease will automatically renew for another year." This is called a ***minimum termination notice***. What is far more common is for a lease agreement (remember, a lease agreement tends to be for a longer period of time than a rental agreement) to state that if neither party terminates the agreement will continue on for another thirty days, and then another, and then another, or words to that effect. This is referred to as a *"month to month" lease*.

This is all fine and good, but remember: thirty days is thirty days, not twenty-seven or twenty-eight. In these situations, you cannot call the landlord on October 4th and say, "I'm moving out October 31st." Technically, you are now committed to paying him until November 30. Whether you actually live there until that date is your problem.

These sorts of lease clauses are not only legal, they are fair. Your landlord needs time to advertise and rent your apartment. It is also typical that they will want to, perhaps, touch up some of the paint, replace a light bulb here and there, etc. Furthermore, a vacant property pays no rent. The landlord continues to have costs—a mortgage perhaps, a property manager, real estate taxes, and property insurance, even though no one is living there.

Also be on the lookout for automatic rent increases. You may have a one-year lease, but it not only self-renews, it automatically renews at a higher rate per month. Be careful!

This is not to say that automatic renewals are in all leases. Some landlords can't *wait* to get you out of their place. The provision may even be written in a way that says it is a matter of *offer and acceptance*. *If* you continue to live there and continue to pay rent, and *if* the landlord accepts that rent, you shall be allowed to stay for a certain period of time, if not indefinitely, so long as you pay and they accept payment. Note in most cases, there is a lease provision that says that under this scenario the lease rate will be some percentage (15 to 25%) *higher* than it was previously.

Lease Terms—WHERE?

I cannot stress enough that you, the renter, **know exactly what it is you are renting.** As with everything in life, NEVER ASSUME. The roof leaks. Is it your problem or your landlord's? *There is no standardized answer,* although some state statutes and/or local housing regulations specify bare minimum habitability requirements for the landlord (trust me when I say that they are the absolute *bare* minimum). If your lease clearly indicates that you are only responsible for the upkeep and maintenance of the *interior four walls,* then a leaky roof is your landlord's problem. But this sort of delineation must be clearly indicated on your lease.

What about the exterior of the building? Do not assume patterns here. For example: While your lease may indicate that you are technically only renting the interior four walls, and that you are not responsible for exterior damage (such as a leaky roof) that you did not cause, there may still be clauses indicating that you are responsible for things such as shoveling snow or cutting grass. The lease may not indicate that you are actually *renting* the sidewalk, the hallway, or the grass, but you may have—knowingly or unknowingly—accepted certain responsibilities for their upkeep. This may even stretch into legal liability. If the lease states that you are responsible for shoveling snow within a certain period of time after snow begins (a good lease will always be this specific), what happens if you don't shovel and someone slips and falls? You ought to know the answers to these sorts of questions before signing a lease.

Let's also talk about something I just breezed by. Are you "renting" the hallway, the sidewalk, or a back or front yard? If so, what are your privileges? Who do you share these privileges with? Can you put a hammock in the yard? If so, can other people use it? Although many of these issues are RULES (another subchapter), they do creep into the WHERE area of questions worth asking and knowing the answers to.

I also flew by a phrase having to do with "damage you did not cause." But what if you *do* poke a hole in the roof accidentally? Even though the lease states that you are not responsible for the exterior, if guilt can be proven, you may, of course, have to compensate the landlord. This may be clearly discussed in the lease, or the landlord may simply rely upon normal legal recourse to adjudicate the issue. Again …and I will say this a million times in this chapter: DO NOT JUST READ, BUT UNDERSTAND THE LEASE *BEFORE* YOU SIGN IT!

Lease Terms—RULES

Some landlords may try to tell you, "It's just a standard lease." **There is no such thing as a standard lease.** Even if he bought it at the local office supply store, there is nothing standard about it. It may not be "unusual," but standard is in the eye of the beholder.

So long as the landlord does not violate any laws (discrimination based on race or religion, for example), most all else is up for grabs. Most landlords won't allow large pets, or may limit the number of pets, but unless the town the property is in has a law concerning such an issue, it is still between the individual landlord and individual tenant. If you own four German Shepherds, see what you can do to get a landlord to allow you to move them in with you—but don't hold your breath.

As I said before, as a landlord myself, I try to put every little thing into a lease that I can imagine or have ever experienced so that I am not at the mercy of an unwanted situation. If, as a landlord, your tenant does something you cannot abide and it does not fit under any of the provisions you had drawn up when you first signed the lease, the best you can do is try simple reasoning. If that doesn't work, you may have to resort to an *eviction without cause*, which takes a lot of time (and which I will talk about in the next subchapter).

As a tenant, if you want to put a hot tub in the middle of your living room and you can find no clause in your lease saying that you can't, just be careful that it does not violate the common-sense "standard" clause of causing property damage.

Lease Terms—HOW?

Many of the issues of HOW a lease agreement can be enforced, terminated, or modified are spread over some of the previous subchapters. In WHEN, we discussed minimum termination notices. Often times, this is a non-issue—you've signed a one-year lease; it ends in one year. Rather than discussing termination notices again, what you need to do in order to *stay*, if that is your desire, is to give *notice* you wish to renew (not terminate). Do not assume that if you stick around, you can continue to do so. No one likes a squatter. The landlord need not agree to renew with you. On the other hand, a bird in the hand…most landlords would rather keep a tenant on, unless the tenant has been a problem. A **notice of intent to renew** may be included in your lease; it may not. Even if it does exist, your landlord will most likely make sure he has the ability to renew you at *his* discretion.

Another HOW/WHEN hybrid issue is when you, the renter, want to break your lease and leave early. Some leases make it easy for you to do so: You give thirty days notice and the landlord lets you go. Sometimes, the landlord puts in a penalty for leaving before the end of the lease; if so, check your lease before trying to run out. Some leases state that you are absolutely, positively responsible for your rent until the end of your lease (see joint and several). This means that if you have to leave for some reason (job transfer to another city, perhaps), you may have to *sublet*. Call this a WHO/HOW/WHEN hybrid issue. **A sublet is where you sub-lease to another party, yet you are still responsible to the landlord** (sort of like a mortgage wrap for renters). Just like a mortgage wrap, be careful. Some landlords require that you inform them and that they approve of the new tenant. If you are still being held responsible as the guarantor for this new tenant, you should draw up agreements with that person so they do not burn you.

Sublets can be incredible win/wins for all involved, or they can be nightmares. Your best protections are to first check your original lease, and then draw up a good sublease document with the person you are subletting to. And one last thing: Some leases (and some landlords) do not allow subletting. If your lease does not allow subletting and also does not allow you to break the lease, even with notice, you are in BIG trouble.

On the flip side, what happens if your landlord sells your apartment out from under you? Two issues come to the fore: One—will your lease be honored at all by the new owner? Yes. **Leases are transferable. They run with the property. If the property is sold, this alone does not terminate the lease agreement.**

The other issue is if your current landlord (or even your new landlord, after a period of time) wants to evict a tenant *without cause* (you did nothing wrong). Sometimes a landlord will have the opportunity to sell their building for a nice profit, but only if it is vacant. They don't want to let this opportunity slip by because you and some other tenants have many months to go before your leases expire. Your landlord may put a clause in your lease that states he may evict you without cause if he gives you formal legal notice of ninety to one hundred twenty days (there is no strict formula for this). This is certainly not a favorable clause for the renter, but it may be hard to negotiate it away in some cases. Certainly, if the period of time you are given to vacate is reasonable (and ninety to one hundred twenty days is rather reasonable), this is pretty fair to all parties.

Regarding general enforceability of any lease provision, most landlords will include a "*cure period*" in their lease. Booting someone out into the street isn't the world's easiest thing. There are certain legal protections—notices to be given, etc. It is sometimes cheaper and easier for a landlord to set certain guidelines for correction of deficiencies (late rent, paying for a window you broke, etc.) rather than immediately resorting to serving a tenant with legal notices for eviction.

Commercial Leases

While some people may never come across a commercial lease, others will. You never know when you might be opening a store in the local mall, starting a new business needing office space or getting promoted to a management position where one of your responsibilities involves negotiating the lease agreement for your company. I have included this brief section to give you some of the basics should you ever find yourself in this situation.

One of the major differences between residential leases and commercial (business) leases is that, while most residential leases are gross leases, **many commercial leases are called "*net-net-net,*" "*triple-net,*" or "*NNN*" leases. ALL THREE TERMS MEAN THE SAME THING.**

A NNN lease is where, in addition to the agreed upon rent, the renter assumes payment of most expenses associated with the operation of the property. This includes both variable expenses— such as taxes and insurance—and all operating expenses, including costs of maintenance and repair (which could even include significant capital expenses like a new HVAC system). This is not to say that this sort of arrangement is mandatory. There are some gross commercial leases, but they are relatively rare except for retail spaces and some office buildings.

If anyone ever asks you, **the "3 nets" are: Real estate taxes (net), building insurance (net) and common area maintenance, including utilities (net).**

These add-ons are often charged through to the tenant on a monthly basis based on the landlord's estimate. If, at the end of the year, it is discovered that the estimate was too high, money should be refunded; if it was too low, the renter will most likely be billed (usually in a lump-sum). If the estimates were significantly off, the landlord should make adjustments for the upcoming year that are more accurate. A tenant must be aware of this situation and budget accordingly. They should always have cash flow sufficient to handle these fluctuations.

A smart tenant will try to get caps on the triple-nets, or caps on the increase on them, either in terms of a dollar figure or a percentage. Imagine rolling along in your business and then suddenly getting hit with a bill for thousands of dollars due to some unforeseen circumstance concerning the insurance on a building or its tax bill. Unfortunately, few commercial landlords will grant caps, but again, it is always about the market. If it's a renter's market, it's something you should ask for.

Triple nets can pose a problem similar to calculating the difference between interest and APR on a mortgage—comparing apples to apples when shopping for the best deal. You want to rent a storefront. The landlord tells you the rent is $14 per square foot (commercial rents are often represented this way. You take the rent per square foot, multiply that by the square footage, then divide by twelve months and that would be your monthly rent. Example: $14 per square foot rent. 2,000 square foot space = $28,000 *per year*. Divided by twelve months equals $2,333.33 per month.), triple net. The novice walks away thinking, "Oh, my rent is $2,333.33 per month, plus something about nets." Dumb, dumb, dumb.

Even if the renter is a bit smarter and asks what the net cost is, it may still be deceiving. Example: $16 per square foot rent, plus $4 per square foot NNN, for a total of $20 per square foot. Ah…but what if the landlord is low-balling the nets to get the unsuspecting tenant into his building? Look in the fine print and you will likely see that this is an "estimate" rather than a hard number. Had the potential tenant asked to see the previous years' figures, they would have found out that the average NNN was more like $6 per square foot, and due to several increases it may be even more next year. Without investigating, our hero ends the year being socked with a bill for $4,000 ($2 more NNN per square foot over one year's time). Triple net expenses can easily add 30% or more to the cost of the base rent!

The right to actually see the landlord's books, such as his exact property insurance bills, property tax bills, maintenance and repair bills, both from the current year as well as previous years for comparison's sake, is called "*audit rights.*" **Definitely try to negotiate for audit rights if you are a tenant under an NNN lease.**

And again, even the savvy renter has no control over market fluctuations that may drive an honestly estimated triple net well over predictions. Beware, beware, beware.

Another issue with commercial leases is that there is frequently a "management fee" or "common area maintenance fee," which becomes one of the "nets." Often, the company that provides this service is either the landlord himself, or a company owned by the landlord. Thus, this is a nice little cash cow for the landlord, who may charge whatever the market will bear to sweep the sidewalk, vacuum the hallway carpeting, etc. If you are looking for sympathy from some benevolent government agency, keep looking. **As long as the landlord does not directly violate the terms of the lease and carries through with his promises, he can charge whatever he wants …so long as you're willing to pay.**

A NNN lease is completely beneficial to the landlord. As the above example illustrates, there is generally no incentive for the landlord to keep costs down. The tenant pays for everything variable. Think of it like a mortgage company who simply expects a certain and definitive percentage of return on its asset from its borrower, while it shifts all responsibility for any variable costs to the occupant. This is not necessarily a bad thing, but this is how most of the commercial real estate market works under an NNN lease arrangement.

Here's another example of how the landlord and the tenant's interests do not align: *tax appeals.* **A tax appeal is a form of legal redress where the owner of a property makes a formal complaint to a government entity that his property is being disproportionately assessed for tax purposes.** Any property owner can avail themselves of this legal right. That being said, what is the motivation for a commercial landlord to appeal his tax assessment if all his tenants are in NNN leases? None whatsoever (unless he has vacant space in the building that *he* pays taxes on). Only if the market was to upend him and his tenants started moving out would there be any such motivation.

Try to negotiate your right to insist upon a property tax appeal if you deem one necessary or advisable. This would also require you to have access to your landlord's books.

Security Deposits

Whether residential or commercial, **many landlords require that a security deposit be put up when a tenant moves in**, although this is negotiable. The logic behind security deposits is simple: If the property is damaged, the landlord does not have to chase the tenant for reparations—the money is already on hand. Some landlords even use security deposits to avoid collections—if a tenant skips out and doesn't pay their last month's rent, the landlord actually has that amount already.

There are few if any laws regarding security deposit amounts. **Some landlords charge one month, some charge two.** If a landlord ever tries to tell you that either one is "the law," they are fooling you. It is whatever you and the landlord negotiate.

It would behoove a tenant to insist that the security deposit be held in a separate trust account, also known as an *escrow account*. This is generally a non-interest-bearing account that the landlord technically cannot simply dip into as he wishes ("I need a new suit. Hmmm…I think I'll use this security deposit and pay it back later."). In some states, if a landlord has a certain number of properties or is licensed, he must have a separate escrow account for security deposits. Depending upon state law, such accounts may be subject to state audit, thus no right-minded landlord would dare try to steal from it. However, this still happens all too frequently when unscrupulous landlords run into cash flow issues.

Another reason that you, the tenant, want your security deposit in an escrow account is that if your landlord gets sued or has some action taken against him that allows his assets to be garnished (seized), an account like this cannot be touched since, technically, it's not his money.

Because of legitimate anxieties about security deposits, some renters are right in feeling more comfortable with a large (licensed) property management company than an individual who is simply leasing out one or two properties, unless that individual appears well-organized and savvy regarding state laws and regulations regarding leases and trust accounts.

Of course, many tenants complain of having a hard time getting all their security deposits back at the end of the lease. It is typical for landlord and tenant to have a final "***walk-through***"—**a joint inspection of the property.** I would also suggest they have a joint *initial* walk-through—you and the landlord go through the place even before you start moving your things in. That way, if you see a hole in a wall, you can have it notated that it was there before you took control of the property.

At final walk-through, both parties should make a check-list, taking into consideration what had been noted at the initial walk-through. **Most leases state that the tenant is responsible for any damage *other than normal wear and tear.*** This is the magical, mystical catch phrase that sends so many landlords and tenants to court. Logically speaking, over a year's time, painted walls will show fingerprints and small marks. Hardwood floors will have some scuffs and signs of use. But this is logic. Not all people are logical. There is no way to put "logical" in writing. Even when it's there, it is open to interpretation, sometimes by illogical people. All you can do is give it your best effort. If a landlord is ridiculous, calls every little thing "damage," and refuses to refund your security deposit or takes a significant chunk of it, you may have to go to small claims court for resolution. I would of course suggest first sending a formal letter to the landlord explaining your situation and offering some type of a compromise.

Another good idea is photographic evidence. Especially with the ease and availability of digital cameras, you can take pictures on the initial walk-through, and then do it again at the final if your landlord is unreasonable. This will help you win in court if it comes to that.

This all works two ways, of course. Big holes in the wall are not "normal wear and tear." Neither are broken cornices, burn marks on carpeting, etc. Photos at both walk-throughs help you landlords, too.

Taxes and Other Benefits

While some people will always rent their homes for one reason or another, ownership of your home is probably one of the soundest financial decisions you will make in your lifetime. Historically, real estate has continued to appreciate, and after making mortgage payments for many years, your house is now really yours.

But, other than owning a piece of property that you can live in indefinitely, what are the current financial benefits of owning versus renting? Most people automatically think of the obvious—potential appreciation—which is the theory that you "buy" something in today's dollars that has the likelihood to be worth more in the future. If the home is your primary residence for at least two of the last five years before selling, then your "profit" (appreciation) is actually "tax free" up to $250,000 if you are single, and up to $500,000 if you are married.

Many people overlook two additional tax benefits that homeowners receive and renters do not. This is the ability to deduct both property taxes and mortgage interest from your taxable income at the end of the year. As a renter, you do not have this ability; you pay your rent and get absolutely no tax deductions.

Here is a simple example of a homeowner versus a renter when both make the same annual salary:

	OWNER	RENTER
Annual Salary	$ 60,000	$ 60,000
Tax Deduction: Property Taxes	$ 3,000	$ -0-
Tax Deduction: Mortgage Interest	$ 11,862	$ -0-
Adjusted Income for Tax Purposes	$ 45,138	$ 60,000
Combined Income Tax (30%):	$ 13,541	$ 18,000
Tax Savings:	$ 4,459	$ -0-

Assumptions:
Combined state/federal tax bracket of 30%
Annual property taxes of $3,000 (US average)
Traditional 30-year mortgage @ 6.5% for $200,000

Also, if the property is used as a commercial or residential rental, you will be able to "depreciate" the value on your books for tax purposes (and claim an additional deduction) even though the property is probably "appreciating" in value rather than "depreciating." This will be explained in more detail in the Taxes chapter.

Mortgage interest is generally deductible up to $1,000,000, and as previously stated, your property taxes are deductible. Things that are *not* deductible are your insurance and your repairs—unless it's a rental property and you are the landlord.

CHAPTER 4
BUYING AND SELLING REAL ESTATE

This is an important chapter for you, the reader, and because of its importance, it is rather voluminous. Allow me to first introduce you to the main points I wish to make:

1. If you choose not to represent yourself, use an experienced and qualified real estate agent.
2. Understand, at least in general terms, what happens at a real estate closing.
3. You will probably have to pay property taxes. Understand them, and how they are arrived at.
4. Real estate is historically an excellent investment over the long term.

I should end each of these four major points by calming you and saying, "…And I will show you how," because that is what this book is about: showing you how. Let's begin.

Real Estate Agents

If life is a battle, no one wants to leave their house unarmed. While I did not become who I am today by being a completely cynical, paranoid, defensive, distrusting person, I am far from a Pollyanna. I believe the middle road is that **knowledge is power** and we must also know *what we don't know*!

I am not a lawyer, but I know some law. I am not a doctor, but if I cut myself, I know the basics of how to stop the bleeding. A lot of what I cover in this book is about how and when to use professionals. There are most certainly times when we do not need them. There are plenty of professional chefs around, but I can make my own sandwich for lunch, thank you very much.

When it comes to real estate, I believe that more often than not, using a qualified real estate agent has more plusses than not using one. But once we've talked about it more, I'll let you decide.

I believe all analysis of professions begins with, "How does this person get paid?" and, "How are their interests aligned with mine?" Far from cynical, this is just basic realism. People do not work for free. I certainly don't. Whenever I step into a new arena, which most of us do from time to time, I try to figure out the answer to those two questions. Do my interests and the interests of the professional I have retained to advise me line up? Or are we thinly-veiled adversaries? Do I believe I am hiring someone to advocate for me when, once I put the relationship to the test, it is clear that they may have more to gain by selling me out? These are the questions always to ask. Furthermore, try not to let your glass half full/glass half empty world view color your goals. Although most people are honest, ethical and looking to do the best job they can for their client, there are unsavory, unscrupulous characters in every single profession. If someone tells you a story about a crooked dentist, should you let all your teeth rot and fall out of your mouth? Heck no! Just learn from their story and figure out how this person got taken and try to ask the right questions the next time you are sitting in a chair with a drill poised above your face.

Everyone seems to be in real estate today, in one form or another. There's a joke spreading around that goes like this: A cop pulls a motorist over in California and asks for her real estate license. The driver says, "You mean my *driver's* license, right?" The cop says, "No, see, not everybody in California HAS a *driver's* license."

That being said, on the selling end, can you sell your home *without* a real estate professional? Of course you can. Commonly known as a **For Sale By Owner (FSBO),** you put a sign on your lawn, perhaps put an ad in the local newspaper, and you're in business.

The downsides to this are that national studies have shown that FSBOs tend to stay on the market longer, sell for less, and the lack of professional acumen when it comes to the required paperwork can range from "annoying" to "problematic," all the way to "catastrophic," if one fails to follow all aspects of prevailing local, state, and federal laws or customs. Ignorance of the law is never an excuse.

So let's say you want to explore the pros and cons of selling property or buying property with a real estate agent. Here we go…

Commissions

First off, let's go to Braun's Acid Test: How do real estate agents get paid? More specifically, is there a direct alignment of interest?

No.

A real estate agent generally gets paid a commission based upon the sales price. Commissions are completely negotiable and are not set by law anywhere in the United States. Don't ever forget this because you will often be told otherwise. Some people will tell you commissions are 6%, period, end of issue. That is a lie. While 6% may be one of the most common figures, that's like saying that Coca Cola is the most common soft drink, so by law we must all drink Coke. The true standard throughout the nation is, indeed, that commissions are typically between 4 and 7% for what we call "full service agencies" (more on this later). But this is America and you can pay whatever you can negotiate. In fact, the larger the property, the more leverage you have to negotiate a lower commission percentage if it appears that they will be doing no more work than if it were a small, inexpensive property.

Back to the non-alignment of interests. If you are the seller, the higher your home sells for, the more your agent makes. You're probably scratching your head saying, "But wait; I *want* the highest possible price for my home. This *is* an alignment of interest."

Yes and no. As a seller, your agent can price you out of the market. Furthermore, your agent is human and can put their personal interests before yours. You may want to get your home sold very quickly, but your agent wants to wait for a higher bid and they feel that, given enough time, that can happen. Misalignment of interest. Reverse: You want the highest possible price and you're willing to wait until you get it. Your agent, for whatever reason, needs some money now, and so she tries to lowball your price and convinces you to accept a low bid. Misalignment of interest.

From the buyer's side, it's even worse. **There is absolutely no motivation for your real estate agent to negotiate the best possible price for you.** None whatsoever. Every thousand she knocks off the price is less money for her. She has no financial incentive at all to do this. Pure common sense.

Let's take an even closer look at the whole commission-based payment thing. The joke I quoted about the California traffic cop is funny because I did not say Kansas, or Nebraska, or Kentucky. Certain areas of the country—California is certainly one of them—are boom areas where real estate prices have skyrocketed. Modest homes that people bought for $150,000 have shot up to $450,000 in only a few years. In these markets, some real estate agents are making millions. Now, let's stop and analyze this: Are these agents doing anything different than they did before? Are they working harder? No. They are simply the beneficiaries of a marketplace. People want to live in California or similar coastal boom areas. Prices go up. *But commission percentages remain the same.*

Braun's future prediction: Ten years from now, there will be a great fallout of real estate wannabes. There are actually far too many people running around with licenses, "trying out" real estate (refer to the California joke). The really savvy ones will thrive, while the wannabes will fade. Then, these savvy professionals will be forced by many intelligent consumers (like you) to accept flat or hourly fees (like other professionals) rather than commissions, with those fees being tied, perhaps, to certain performance benchmarks—number of showings, length of time working with the client, price range of the property in question, etc. In my opinion, the good real estate agents have nothing to worry about with this forthcoming transition; they will always be in demand and successful. However, this change will weed out some of the people in the industry who should not have gotten involved in the first place.

Commissions are generally paid by the seller. This means, if you have a house for sale, you use a real estate agent, the house sells for $100,000, and you agreed to a 6% commission, you put $94,000 in your pocket and your real estate agent—in this case referred to as the "listing agent" because she "listed" (advertised on your behalf) your house—gets $6,000.

So…how does a real estate agent representing the *buyer* get paid? Or does she get paid at all?

Of course she gets paid. She gets paid via what we call a "split," sometimes also referred to as a "co-op." **A co-op or a split is where the listing agent agrees to split part of the sales commission with the agent bringing the buyer.** So, using the example above, the listing agent doesn't really put $6,000 in her pocket. Assuming a 50/50 split, she puts $3,000 in her pocket and gives $3,000 to the buyer's agent.

Just like there is no rule regarding commissions in general, there is also no rule regarding splits. While 50/50 may be somewhat of a norm, it can deviate based on the traditions and market-driven practices of a given state, county, or municipality. It is also subject to change, with that change frequently driven by the parties themselves—parties, meaning not the real estate agents, but the individual buyers and sellers.

Example: I own a house. I really, really want to sell it fast for one reason or another. I enlist the services of an agent who lists my property.

But it's not moving and I'm not happy. No one is coming to see it. It doesn't seem to be over-priced, but my agent and I discuss lowering the price to see if that works. It doesn't. Now I'm really upset. Maybe I can negotiate with my listing agent and convince her to lower her split from 50/50 to 60/40 in favor of the *buyer's agent*. This is a good idea for me, the seller, because, as I said before, I really want to move this house NOW. Agents representing buyers know all about the splits and so they would be more highly motivated to show their clients homes where they can receive a higher percentage commission. The only flaw to this plan is that my chances of getting my listing agent to cut her commission once I've already contracted with her is about as likely as my teaching a pig to fly. I could make sure that I had a short-term contract with her for the listing and, if that contract is nearing its end, I can negotiate a renewal of the contract conditioned upon making this change.

That leaves another variation. I tell my listing agent, "Okay, so we agreed to your getting the 3% (her 50% of the 50/50 split of a 6% commission). Here's what I want to do: You keep that 3%, but now I'm going to offer 4% to the buyer's agent." In other words, you, the seller, can choose, in this case, to increase the total real estate commission from 6% to 7%. Heck, if you think it'll get more potential buyers in to see your house, you can go to 8, 9, or 10% total commission! It's all a matter of what you want to do and what satisfies your personal agenda.

This is all perfectly legal and ethical. Except...let's talk about alignment of interests again. If I'm the *buyer*, how do I know I'm not being shown certain houses simply because they are the ones where my agent can make the most money for herself? I *don't* know. I'm just a lamb being led to slaughter. Maybe that's a bit dramatic, but the spirit of it is correct.

Isn't there a way for you, as the buyer, to know the splits and the commissions paid? Yes. It is disclosed at the real estate closing, the official legal sit-down where all parties have already agreed to transfer ownership of the property. By then, it's too late.

Referral Fees

Let's say I'm a real estate agent in Northern Ohio. Someone who knows and trusts me calls me up and says he wants to buy a new home in Southern Ohio. I could fake it, but in the end, I'm not really set up to travel hundreds of miles, day after day, showing this person homes in places I don't know from Adam. It's too much work, too much expense, and I'm not really able to give this customer good value for their dollar, since I truly don't know the area.

So what do I do? I could just say, "Sorry, can't help you," and hang up. Or...perhaps I happen to know a real estate agent *in* Southern Ohio. That's probably why I got the call in the first place. They want a *referral.* Fine, so now instead of hanging up, I spend some time getting some data from the potential buyer, then I call that agent I know in Southern Ohio, tell him all about it, and insure that he is qualified and will treat my referral professionally. For this, I get paid. How much? I know I'm sounding like a broken record, but it's all negotiable. I'd say that the going rate is for him to give me between 15 and 30% of his part of the commission. Were it not for me, he wouldn't have this new client, so I have definitely provided him a service. It may be years, if ever, when he can actually return the favor, so it's best that he and I settle up right then and there. If he ever does send me a referral, I would of course be happy to cut the same deal with him. One back scratches the other.

How does this affect you, the client? No harm, no foul. You don't have to pay any more or any less, and instead of just picking a name out of the Southern Ohio phone book, you've got a trusted advisor recommending a friend and that's always safer.

ABA—RESPA Disclosure

What we discussed in the "referrals" subchapter is something entirely legal and ethical. Unfortunately, it has many less legal and less ethical cousins.

ABA stands for Affiliated Business Arrangements (not the old American Basketball Association), and **RESPA stands for Real Estate Settlement Procedures Act.** These are legal and ethical protections put in place for the benefit of you, the consumer.

Without getting overly technical regarding the history of these documents and so on, they came about because many people wear multiple hats. Would it surprise you to know that your real estate agent might also be a mortgage broker? Or that the company your real estate agent works for might also own a bank, a mortgage company, and/or a title insurance company (more on title insurance coming up)? Is this legal? Most likely—with the proper disclosures. There are numerous regulations that such a person or company would have to go through, but in the end, most of these things are doable in most states. Furthermore, the concept is a popular one. One-stop shopping. Why just be a hat store when you can sell shoes, socks, pants, shirts, coats, you name it? Everyone's doing it in every sector of the marketplace.

The issue is actually one of the perceived convenience for the consumer versus the obvious conflicts of interest. If your real estate agent refers you to a mortgage company with which she is affiliated, is it the best mortgage company for you? Even if it is, if you were not told that she had an affiliation with it, that would just not be right.

In the "referrals" section, you can rest assured that when you go to one real estate agent and she refers you to someone else, she is getting paid...*and there's nothing wrong with that.* If you asked, she would disclose it. If you forgot to ask, I am telling you about it. Referrals from a person providing one product or service to a person providing a completely different product or service (mortgages, home inspections, title insurance, etc.) must be looked at more warily. **In some states, referral fees are completely illegal from one profession to another** (mortgage companies "kicking back" money to real estate agents, etc.). In any case, even if the real estate agent in question is simply "keeping the business in-house" and not actually receiving monetary compensation for referring you to another division of her employer's company, **there is a legal and ethical responsibility to disclose that relationship.**

ABA forms and RESPA forms are presented at real estate closings and reveal all such business relationships. But as I mentioned before, by closing time, it's almost too late to do much about it if such a thing bothers you. That being the case, it is a good idea for you to ask your real estate agent (who is often a key source of referrals for the other goods and services you will use further on down the line as you buy or sell property) if there is a business affiliation between her or her company and the person or company she is referring you to. If there is, she has to tell you.

If you are informed that there is a business affiliation of any sort, I would simply take it with a grain of salt. If it was for a termite inspector, for example, I would make a few calls and price out the competition. If the original price turns out to be fine, then no harm done. One-stop shopping does not automatically mean you are getting ripped off.

In any case, I would probably refrain from asking if she is getting a referral fee. It's a tacky question. Furthermore, as I said, in most of these examples, it is illegal for her to do so and thus you are asking someone if they broke the law. Not only will the person be offended, but even if it were true, they would never admit to it, so what's the point of asking? All you should care about in the end is your own bottom line—how much does it cost, and will they do a good job.

Salespeople, Real Estate Agents, Brokers, and Realtors®

You will hear these four job titles bantered about constantly; occasionally they will even be used correctly.

By and large, the major differences—and there ARE differences—between the four comes down to education, qualifications and experience. *Salespeople,* **also known as** *real estate agents,* **are generally those with the least amount of real estate education and experience.** Now, just to confuse you, a broker or a Realtor® may *also* allow you to refer to them as a real estate agent—just don't call a broker a salesperson or they *will* be offended.

The licensing or lack thereof varies from state to state. On average, a licensed salesperson needs between thirty and seventy-five hours of classroom training followed by a standardized test. As to experience, in most states no actual apprenticeship time is required, other than being supervised by a broker for a period of time. The salesperson who greets you at the door of XYZ Real Estate may have just passed her test yesterday, or may have been in the industry for many years.

By and large, **a *broker* requires more education**, again varying from state to state with the average being **about twice as many classroom hours as that same state requires for a salesperson.** Most states also require that someone with a broker's license have a certain amount of real life experience in the field, the average being about two years. Furthermore, **a broker generally may hire and supervise other salespeople or may open up their own agency. A salesperson cannot officially hire or supervise any other salespeople, nor can they go into business for themselves.**

Terminology also varies from state to state. Colorado, for example, calls everyone a broker, but has three, rather than two, levels of "brokers." What most other states call a salesperson, they call an *associate broker.* The next level is an *independent broker,* who has more education and at least two years experience, but can only function on their own. Finally, the third level is an *employing broker,* who can, as the title states, employ other brokers and thus open their own shop. This requires even more education in the field.

When you step into XYZ Real Estate, the staff may have varying ratios of brokers to salespeople. Some may boast of having literally nothing but brokers, while others may have only one or two brokers and a plethora of salespeople. Judging by the difference between a broker and a salesperson, you may conclude that you are better off with a broker. Ironically, both will cost you the same—they all work on commission and commissions do not usually vary within the same agency. For this reason, you may request a broker versus a salesperson, and perhaps you may get your wish. On the other hand, some agencies judge you by what you are looking to do. If you are buying or selling a large commercial building, they will probably put you with a broker. If you are buying or selling a $75,000 starter bungalow, you may be paired with a qualified salesperson. It doesn't hurt to ask, but don't take it personally if they match you with a salesperson.

Often, an agency has its own little rules. If you come in asking for a specific person because you either know them or you were recommended by a friend, most agencies will try to accommodate that request. Otherwise, many agencies have a "floor time" policy. Each employee, be they broker or salesperson, is assigned days and times when they are "on the floor." If a customer comes in during that time, that customer is theirs. You may walk into a busy real estate office, but out of twelve people sitting at desks working the phones, only two of them are "on the floor" when you arrive. If someone finishes their phone call and tries to snatch you up while the "on the floor" person has gone for a minute to use the bathroom, things could get quite ugly when they return to find you talking with some other salesperson who "stole" you. It's a funny business sometimes.

Don't be afraid to ask for an agent's qualifications. Do not be too quick to sign anything binding you to them personally until you know and respect their level of expertise and can get along with them. Remember—it's a buyer's market when you are looking for a real estate agent to represent your interests. Using California as an example, one out of seventy-four people there hold a real estate license. By the end of 2007, there will most likely be more licensed real estate agents there than actual property sales. Imagine! It's a pretty easy business to get in, but a hard business to *stay* in. As a consumer, you can be as choosey as you like. You are also not limited to just XYZ Real Estate. There are probably dozens of competitors in the same town, no matter how small the burg. Walk out of one and walk into another. Be comfortable. You may have to spend considerable time with this person and are likely entrusting them to one of largest financial transactions of your life.

Aside from salespeople versus brokers, there is still the issue of quality of service. Like anything else, there are some hardworking, ambitious hustlers with little experience who are going to be successful due to pure drive and high personal standards. There are others who may have been in the business for decades, but can't get out of their own way. One particular sales point is how well does this person know the neighborhood? They probably know *some* neighborhoods, but maybe not the one where you are looking to do business. See what they can tell you about the schools, the shopping, etc. If you are looking to sell, see if they know the street names and names of various developments. The perfect agent for you is someone who can, just off the top of their head, rattle off every house on every street and can tell you the last thirty homes sold there and what they went for. If you find that person, you've usually found a winner. They know the territory, which is half the battle.

Only one-third of all real estate agents make it in the business for more than five years. Some states do not even require that you have a high school diploma. Many people "try" real estate. Let's face it, thirty-five or fifty hours in a classroom is not onerous. Most halfway-intelligent people can study and pass a state exam. Lots of people looking for a part-time or a second job "try" real estate for this reason. Unfortunately, this is a major business transaction for you and you don't need someone who is not really qualified botching it up for you. Heck, you could have done that yourself! So beware of the real estate agent who also hands you the business card for the salon where she does nails or he sells men's clothing. This person is probably not strong enough in the real estate field to be your best resource.

Which finally brings us to Realtors®. **Generally speaking, a Realtor® can be either a salesperson or a broker. All that is required is that one joins their local, state, and national Realtor's® trade association and subscribes to their professional code of ethics.** I have read the Realtor's® code of ethics and I heartily agree with it. It does describe the proper way one should conduct oneself as a real estate agent and every person in that field should do so. As you will also note in the next subchapter, in most cases, **only a Realtor® may belong to the local MLS (Multiple Listing Service), which is still the main source for property listings.** Not all real estate agents or brokers are Realtors®, so in order to take advantage of this essential service, whether the person calls themselves a salesperson, a real estate agent, or a real estate broker, **make sure you are doing business with a Realtor® to get access to the best resources and the highest level of professionalism.**

Multiple Listing Service (MLS)

So why do I tend to recommend using a real estate agent and *how* do you use one?

If there was one singular benefit I would place above all others, it would be access to the *Multiple Listing Service,* or *MLS.* The MLS is usually run by a regional conglomerate of real estate agents, usually referred to as a local Realtor's® association or board of Realtors® who agree upon the rules of its usage. Furthermore, member users must also belong to the *National Association of Realtors® (NAR).*

The MLS is a master database of all homes for sale in a region, as well as an offer of cooperative compensation to the agent procuring the buyer. The depth of information in that listing is usually set in two tiers—that which is available to the eyes of the public (clients) and other information that is not (the cooperative splits, perhaps). The data can be sorted by the client's needs—searches can be done by price range, town, home type, or numerous other criteria. By and large, the MLS is free from federal or state legislation, but each regional MLS is governed by the broad rules of usage set forth by the NAR. Some of the generalities of those regulations are that Realtors® cannot exclude certain companies or individual real estate professionals for capricious reasons such as race, religion, or even simple professional jealousy or dislike.

After following the general rules and regulations of the NAR, many local MLSs draw up their own sets of rules for usage. Some of these may include what we call *"pocket listings."* **A *pocket listing* is when a real estate agent may withhold her listing from the MLS.** Now, why would your real estate agent want to do that? Simple: To try to get both ends of the deal and not have to split commissions with someone else or with someone at another agency. In some states or areas, pocket listings are prohibited. In others, there are strict rules for their usage, such as a short, finite period of time before any member of that local board of Realtors® must cease withholding the listing from the MLS. **A pocket listing hurts sellers. It only helps real estate agents.** If you live somewhere where pocket listings are acceptable, try to insist it be waived so that you can be up on the MLS immediately. Not being on MLS severely limits your exposure to potential buyers.

To have your home listed on MLS, you must be listing it through a licensed real estate agent who belongs to your local MLS; individual homeowners generally cannot submit properties directly to the MLS.

As a buyer, in some locales it can be challenging to get an opportunity to view the MLS except through a member real estate professional. In other places, gaining limited access to the MLS through the Internet is not a problem. In the end, though, you are, by and large, looking at properties listed with real estate agents and thus, if you want to buy one, you still have to do business with a real estate agent. As you know, as the buyer, you still do not have to pay a commission—that comes from the seller.

There have been some recent legal "wranglings" about the MLS. The NAR views it as both a data base as well as an offer for compensation to a buyer's agent (the buyer's agent's side of the split). Other people believe it is simply a data base. It will be interesting to see how the MLS might change in the future.

So, bottom line: **The MLS is the greatest thing in real estate since sliced bread.** It is one-stop shopping for almost all the properties you might want to buy, with the exception of those offered by an individual seller on their own. As a seller, it gives you exposure to more potential buyers than any other apparatus. And by and large, as I write this, you need to be working with a Realtor® in order to fully take advantage of it.

Experience, Knowledge, and Convenience

In addition to the MLS, here are some other amenities real estate agents provide:

For the seller:

Even if there is not always a perfect alignment of interest on setting and negotiating your selling price, good real estate agents know that there is more to a deal than just the price (although the price is paramount). They have been down this road many times before (you hope) and know what to do and how to negotiate around various issues that might crop up. If a buyer is picky, they will know the fair and common concessions needed to consummate the deal. On your own, you might give away too much or lose the deal by giving away too little.

Agents know how to sell a home. They may suggest some inexpensive amenities, such as making sure you clean up your lawn, staging furniture and decorating, what to leave out for all to see and what to hide, whether a fresh coat of paint might more than pay for itself, etc. First impressions mean a lot and good real estate agents know how to showcase your home.

Agents understand the local market. You might think you've got the greatest house in the world, but a professional will know its real value.

Agents know how to evaluate buyers. Again, you're a smart person; you can do this yourself. But a real estate professional knows all the specific questions to ask and how to ask them in order to determine whether you've got a poser or the real thing when someone claiming to be a buyer comes along.

Agents can play bad cop to your good cop when it comes to negotiations. If you get a low bid directly, you might get insulted. Hey, it's your home they're talking about! A real estate professional will just deal with the issues, not the emotions.

Agents frequently do "open houses," which entice and excite a whole lot of buyers. For you, throwing an **open house** might be a one-time thing and boy, you sure hope you do it right. An experienced agent has already done these many, many times and already knows how to do it right. They also often do "*Realtors'® open houses*" (sometimes known as "previews") early on in the course of your listing. This is when they will invite not buyers, but other *agents* to see your home. This is good because buyers' agents will bring their clients in later and the buyer's agent will know the house better in order to help sell it. An individual buyer who comes to a regular open house only represents themselves. If they don't like your house, the chain ends right there. Buyers' agents who come to a special "Realtor® open house" can bring by client after client.

A good agent will stick around with you throughout the entire process. They have a vested interest. They don't want the deal to go south once all parties are at the closing table—they've invested too much time by then. Again, with their experience, they should know all the tricks and know how to snuff out buyer shenanigans or suggest concessions on your behalf. They also know all the rules and regulations and will make sure that everything is consummated properly and legally.

In my opinion, second only to getting you listed in MLS, the most important thing a real estate agent can do is arrange the showings of your home. If you do everything yourself, selling your house can become your full-time occupation until the deal is done. An agent can make sure that buyers are only brought through when you are out at work—if that is your desire—or whatever else might be your preference. They consult with you, give you their recommendations, and in the end, arrange things to your convenience. Until you've gone through this, you cannot imagine the relief this can be.

Most of us end up selling one place and buying another. I mean, unless you like living in a tent in the woods somewhere. Sometimes the timing is less than perfect. A real estate agent can be a very good resource to work with if you need to move out of your house and chill out somewhere for a few weeks before you can move into your new home. They know and can help make arrangements for storage facilities, furnished short-term rentals, etc. Yes, you can do this all yourself—if you don't feel like working for a living for a while—but again, a good agent can be your one-stop contact for all your real estate needs and allow you to focus on living your life. It's a good thing.

For the buyer:

Again, they will act as your negotiator. And again, while they may not have a directly aligned interest (the more you pay, the more they get paid), they can still advise you as to what you should do if you find a crack in the ceiling, or if there's a sinkhole in the back-yard. They can suggest remedies and they can represent your wishes if you want to drive down the price. They will also know how long the property has been on the market—and not by simply asking. They will already have this data from MLS, while that information is often kept from clients acting on their own.

An agent can direct you to where to get answers about a neighborhood and its characteristics. Fair housing laws sometimes muzzle an agent from giving you their unvarnished opinion about an area, or even such factual information as crime statistics, etc. But...a good agent will know exactly where to direct you to get that data yourself, on everything from the state "report card" on the local school system, etc.

Agents can refer you to all the other professionals you may need in order to successfully and comfortably complete your real estate purchase. As previously stated, you may need to ask if there is a direct business interest, but agents are often a fountain of information when it comes to things both critical as well as banal such as movers, painters, masons, etc.

Limited Service Listings

A limited service agreement is a hybrid between selling your home yourself (FSBO) and using a real estate agent. Remember when I mentioned some exceptions to the rule whereby FSBOs were allowed to be listed on MLS? This is how it is usually done.

With a limited service agreement, an individual pays a one-time flat fee to a real estate agency simply for the privilege of appearing, via that Realtor®, on MLS.

Of course, not all limited service Realtors® only offer MLS listings. "Limited" is a relative term. Some offer an ala carte menu of services, stopping short of being what one might call a "full-service agency." If you want them to arrange an open house, you may pay them a little more; to arrange your showings for you, a little more again. It's all up to you. This is either done on a flat fee basis or a commission basis, but either way, it tends to be far less than the customary 4 to 7%.

How do they do this? While most full-service agencies have a regular brick and mortar office, companies that consider themselves "limited service" are often "virtual" companies. The person could be working out of their home and doing most of their work on the Internet.

Are they legit? Why, yes. They must be Realtors® in order to put you on MLS. They have received the same education and licensing and have agreed to abide by the same code of ethics.

Whether to go full-service or not is up to you. We've discussed the full palate of services one should expect from a full-service agency. If you found yourself saying, "That's all fine and good, but I don't really need all that," then perhaps a limited service listing is more up your alley.

One last thing…in order to make this all work well for you, you may still want to offer a "split" (for lack of a better word) to buyer's agents. Picture being in the MLS, but no full-service Realtor® shows your listing to their clients because if they show your house, they get paid nothing. It's like a tree falling in a forest—it makes no sound. Thus, you might save some money on the buyer's commission side with this sort of setup, but if it doesn't seem to be working, you might want to add in that you are offering a commission to Realtors® representing buyers. That should have them beating a path to your door, and you still end up saving some money.

Agency Agreements

This is the agreement a buyer or seller would have with their agent. Many states have standardized forms so that the wheel need not be reinvented time and time again. In other cases, it is the local, county, or state Realtor's® association. The time when I would be most wary would be if I were led to believe an agreement being presented to me was something this one individual or individual agency had drawn up. In such a case, check to see if your state or any of the relevant associations has a standard form and opt for that instead.

You may also find yourself using a real estate attorney at your real estate closing. If so, consider retaining his services early on in order to have him look over the agency agreement.

When you are selling your home and sign with an agent, it is important to note that in most states, you must pay that agent whether they actually got you the buyer or not. Example: You list with an agent. She brings some buyers by, she puts you on the MLS, but nothing happens. Then you're at a cocktail party and you meet someone who says their brother is relocating to your area from five hundred miles away and is looking for a house just like yours. Holy cow! You get the brother's number, invite him over to look at your place; he loves it and agrees to buy it from you. Your agent has not done a thing to bring in this buyer.

So what?

You are usually still responsible for paying your real estate agent, unless your listing agreement says otherwise.

These situations are too complicated with hearsay to rule it any other way. Once you sign that agency agreement, once your house is sold, that agent gets the commission noted in the agreement, period. The same holds true with a buyer's agent, except, of course, most buyers could care less because they aren't paying the commission out of their own pockets, anyway.

Double End, Dual Agency, and Transactional Agents

Only in real estate could such a thing happen—both sides of a major transaction represented by the same professional. Yet it happens rather frequently.

Example: You want to buy a house. You see a listing by XYZ Real Estate. You do not yet have a buyer's agent. You decide to check this home out. You call XYZ and they are MORE than happy to assist you. You tour the home and fall in love with it. But you checked your brain at the door. Why? BECAUSE THAT AGENT ALREADY REPRESENTS THE SELLER!!

So, what are the legalities here? The fact is, once you have sought out the services of that agent at XYZ, even though you have not actually signed anything, you have allowed them to "act" as your agent. Re-read that carefully and digest it. You have disclosed information to them about yourself ("I am looking for this, I want to spend that, etc.), you have asked them to assist you, and you have most likely asked them questions about the home. This means they have been acting, even if for just one hour, in the capacity of a buyer's agent. Now you are stuck.

If you try to wiggle out and hire some other agent to represent you now, the first agent will most likely pull her aside, explain what has happened, and the new agent you have tried to bring on board will bow out, citing a breach of professional ethics and courtesy.

So…now that you're in this pickle, can you make lemonade out of these lemons? Not really. The agent must, of course, make it clear to you (as if you didn't already know) that she represents the seller. Past that, she is bound by certain standards and practices to make a variety of other disclosures.

- She is not supposed to tell the buyer if the seller is willing to drop their price.
- She is not supposed to tell the seller that the buyer might be willing to bid higher.

- She cannot reveal personal information about one party to the other.
- She must disclose any known property defects to the buyer.

In plain English, while you are most likely legally protected against being robbed blind, you most certainly do not have a true advocate in your corner. There will be no hardball negotiations done on your behalf.

This is called "*dual end.*" The agency is acting as a "*dual agency.*" Agents love this, of course, because now they are getting two commissions instead of one. Oh yeah, baby! And the buyer, even more than the seller, runs the risk of being taken advantage of.

As to the seller, it is not the optimal scenario, either, but at least you know that no one is going to nickel and dime you. When we mentioned earlier about "pocket listings," this was precisely what we meant. By holding your sales listing out of the MLS for a period of time, your seller's agent is trying to get that elusive dual end deal. If she already has buyers under contract, she will call them up and tell them there's this "hot new house" on the market that she can get them in to see "exclusively." Also, a lot of buyers will simply drive around neighborhoods where they are looking for homes and may see the agent's sign on your lawn. "Hey, we didn't see this one yet on the MLS. Must be a new listing. Quick, let's try to get in to see it."

As a seller, there is not much you can do about this, outside of trying to protect yourself against pocket listings, as we discussed earlier. But buyers, you can definitely protect yourself.

If you ever get the urge to go see a house, even a model or an open house, do not do so before retaining a buyer's agent. One of the first things someone showing you a model, an open house, or one of their listings should ask is, "Do you have an agent?" If you say no, you could get yourself into this dual agency predicament. If you say yes, you are in the clear. Sure, you can visit listings and homes without your agent, though it is often best to bring them along. At the very least, you should have your agent call ahead for you so that there are no misunderstandings about your representation. But as long as you simply have one, you can tell that to the agent showing you the home and then the ground rules will be set. They, in turn, will not reveal too much information about the seller, and you will still get a chance to walk through the place and see if it's worth a second visit, perhaps with your agent along.

For those that are really impulsive and drop in on open houses the way some people cruise around for yard sales, I know of people who give a fictitious name or claim to have a buyer's agent even if they don't. I don't recommend lying, but what you're actually doing is protecting yourself from getting into a business relationship that you really don't want.

There is a new scenario in some states though, called the "*transactional agent.*" The differences between a transactional agent and dual agency are very, very fine. **While a dual agent represents *both* parties, a transactional agent represents *neither* party.** Confusing, I know. Their purpose is to simply act as a mediator and intermediary between both parties. The parties themselves do their own negotiating. The transactional agent simply conveys each party's wishes to the other. They may also suggest compromises to each side, but only for the sake of managing and facilitating the consummation of the deal, not to see that one party or the other receives greater or lesser benefit. The transactional agent does not have to protect anyone's personal interest in the deal or withhold personal information. He is a referee.

So, does this make a transactional agent a better deal for the consumer? Not necessarily. It's very similar to a dual agency in many ways. Usually, the transactional agent has been brought into the deal because he has a personal relationship with someone on one side of the table. That being said, no matter what representations are made as to neutrality, the agent could be leaning toward his friend's side.

Just like in dual agency, transactional agents must make disclosures to both sides as to their role. Some lawyers will tell you that, if you are an agent yourself, being a transactional agent may give you less of a chance of being sued by an angry client than being a dual agent, but again, it's a fine point. There are regulations as to the professional conduct of both dual agents and transactional agents and any intelligent or ethical professional will make sure to go by the letter of the law.

Transactional agents can be paid in a variety of ways, though many of them work on commissions exactly as a traditional agent does. Many Realtors® simply pitch the idea of acting as a transactional agent to their clients in order to collect a double end. However, for a successful agent that has lots of both buyers and sellers, it does give them more flexibility to sell their own listings, which is ultimately better for both sides.

At the end of the day, if you are a buyer, you are generally best served by having a buyer's agent to exclusively represent your interests.

Sales Contracts

Just as they have standard agency contracts, many states have standard buy and sell real estate contracts. It's a beautiful thing. I would not trust a lay person or even a real estate agent to draw up their own contract, even if the state allowed it. If contracts are to be drawn up by anyone, it should be a competent lawyer.

In some states, it is typical for both sides to be represented by attorneys at their real estate closing. Other states may more commonly use a representative from the title insurance company to act in a neutral capacity. If the contract deviates in any way from a state's standard contract, I would recommend retaining an attorney. Your real estate agent will often sit in at the closing as well to make sure everything is as had been discussed and agreed upon. By the time of closing, you should have some idea as to the level of expertise of your agent. If they are a sharp, intelligent professional, you should be all right. If your agent is a newbie who only got licensed a week ago, I would steer you toward bringing your own attorney to the table or requesting the agent to bring his supervising broker. Your agent alone would not be able to give you very good advice with that little experience.

One of the big things in real estate contracts that people need to be aware of is the *default provision*. You are often given a choice between *specific performance* or *liquidated damages.*

Default, of course, means that something has gone awry. The provision in the contract is to determine what to do about it. **"Specific performance" means that the non-defaulting party can legally compel the defaulting party to go through with the transaction.** This means that if you show up at the closing and say, "Braun, I'm sorry, but I can't come up with the money for your house," I can tell you, "Tough luck. You owe me X dollars as of this date. Give it to me now or I will sue and I will win." And I will.

"Liquidated damages" means that all I could do if you default is to keep whatever you have put up as an "earnest deposit." I could not go chasing you for the balance that you owe me.

It is clear which scenario benefits whom. Specific performance benefits the seller; a liquidated damage benefits the buyer.

Another common bugaboo at closings is the **square footage**. How was it arrived at? Did the agent measure it? Did it come from a home inspector? Was it from an appraiser? This should be disclosed at closing. Would it shock you to know that some transactions occur with the buyer truly believing he is moving into a 7,000 sq. ft. home when he is really moving into a 5,000 sq. ft. home? It happens. Sometimes it is fraud; other times it is simply incompetence. Either way, it is imperative for you to know the figures for certain. It will come back to haunt you in a dozen ways, whether it be when you try to put on an addition or do a tax appeal. **You have to know for sure the size of your property—both land and improvements (the structure).**

Another big disclosure is the **lead-based paint disclosure**. Without this form, the contract is void. Can you believe it? With the passage of time, this health issue has become less and less prevalent, but laws are laws and a closing "package" (the big pile of legal documents that must be signed at all closings in a given state) must be in compliance. Again, this is where an attorney sitting by your side can really help you.

Check out my website at www.BraunMincher.com for some examples of sample sales contracts.

Title Insurance

Title insurance **is an insurance policy to guarantee your ownership against claims, liens, or judgments that might arise after your purchase or loan has been completed.**

To go into more detail, when you purchase property, you want to be certain that the person selling it to you is the true owner. Scary thought, eh? There exists the possibility of complete and total fraud, whereby someone is trying to sell you their neighbor's house or something, but more commonly there are sometimes errors or little hidden "problems" with the true property ownership.

Examples of this might be that the selling party is incorrect in their presumption of where the property lines are drawn. There might also be another individual who is "on title," such as a parent who once co-signed a mortgage loan but whose name was never taken off. If so, that person must also approve the property sale. Another common issue is a lien placed on the property by someone who won a judgment against the present owner. It may be a workman who never got paid (this is called a "**mechanic's lien**"), taxes that are in arrears, IRS liens, or even deadbeat child support payments. People will often go to court for relief against a scofflaw and receive a lien against the defendant's property if the defendant loses and does not have cash in hand to fulfill the entire judgment.

All of these issues can cause you mountains of problems at closing. Simply put, you may have negotiated and consummated a deal with Joe Blow, the homeowner, but Joe's house is actually part-owned by the electrician who installed his hot tub five years ago. The title insurance company is retained to clear through these issues so that you have no such surprises at closing. Of course, if they find such problems, they will have to be cleared up before the closing, which may substantially delay the closing. If extremely problematic, these issues may cause you to want to cancel the deal entirely and you would usually be within your contractual rights to do so since, essentially, you had been led to believe that you were negotiating in good faith with the true and only owner of the property, which is now no longer the case.

There is, though, a way of plowing ahead most rapidly in a real estate transaction, if that is what is so desired by the parties. Title insurance policies often have "*exceptions*." Common exceptions are:

1. Easements, encroachments, overlaps, boundary line disputes, or other matters affecting title that a survey would disclose and which is *not* shown by the public record.

2. Rights or claims by parties in possession not shown by the public record.

3. Any lien or right to a lien, for services, labor, or material heretofore or hereafter furnished, imposed by law, and not shown by public records.

4. Covenants, conditions, restrictions, and easements which may exist on the land.

5. Easements or claims of easements not shown by the public records.

6. The property is subject to possible added or omitted assessments.

7. Defects, liens, encumbrances, adverse claims, or other matters, if any, created, first appearing in the public records or attaching subsequent to the effective date hereof, but prior to the date the proposed insured acquires the estate covered by the title insurance commitment.

Translation of the above from Legalese to English: The key words that appear in most of these are "public records." Most title companies will only be concerned with what is officially and legally listed with the county. If a claimant has not taken the proper legal steps to file their claim against the property or its owner and had that claim officially recorded by the county, their claim is very weak and really should not be of great concern to either party involved in the transferring of the property. Paying for an actual surveyor to do a survey is usually considered overkill. More often, both parties to a land sale simply rely upon how the property is described at the county courthouse. The last exception deals with matters that may occur between the date the title company completes its work and the actual closing.

So what about the insurance part? Ironically, *you* are paying for a policy that *indemnifies the title insurance company!* True, if the title insurance company does its duty and claims that the title is "clear" (no problems) and it later turns out that they were wrong, guess who pays to fix the problem? The title company. If you didn't have title insurance, it would be your problem. So, when you look at it that way, paying for a title insurance policy does give you peace of mind.

Unless you are buying some antique property (rare), the owner should already have their own title policy in place—which is not to assume these policies are transferable. Otherwise, you would definitely have to purchase a whole new policy to cover you. To clarify, the title insurance policy itself is not being transferred, but the existence of a previous policy on the property can affect the cost for the new policy that you purchase (more on this later). Also, know that the title company is not your perpetual big brother. They only evaluate the title situation at the time of a closing *looking backward in time*, be it a purchase or a refinance of a mortgage loan. Thereafter, the owner may get into all kinds of trouble with the property. That is not the title company's problem. They would only come back on the scene once there was another closing, or if a problem from before they did their last "title search" reared its ugly head.

Most mortgage lenders will not touch a borrower who does not have title insurance. I know, some people look for all kinds of ways to cut costs, but this is not one you should ever consider. Furthermore, even if you are paying cash for a property, you should still get a policy in order to verify issues with the present owner. Lastly, without your own policy in place, your property looks less desirable to a savvy buyer once you want to sell it because each policy delineates a benchmark. If you bought the property in 2002 and are selling it in 2008, the new buyer will primarily be concerned with the activity on the property between 2002 and the present. If you never got a policy, all bets are off and your buyer's title company will probably go back to the beginning of time out of the anxiety of wondering why you never got a title policy. If they convey this anxiety to your buyer, this may tarnish your deal.

Lastly, there is the cost of a title insurance policy. The price is based upon the price of the property and/or the size of the mortgage. If you don't say anything, you will most likely be charged a "new policy rate" on the total amount of your home purchase price. But you're smarter than that. Have your title company check to see how old any existing policies are. Maybe the seller just refinanced his mortgage a year or two ago. If so, policies revisited within a certain period of time—usually a few years—are considered to be "renewed" policies, even if the renewer is another party. The "new policy rate" is the highest rate. Any kind of re-issue, refinance, or renewal rate will be much cheaper. Mind you, your policy will be for the sales price of the property, thus, if you are paying $300,000 for the property and the previous owner had a recent policy put in place for $200,000, you would try to get $200,000 of your policy at the renewal or reissue rate, but you would have to pay the new policy rate for the $100,000 balance.

Title insurance is regulated state by state and their rate books are usually set by the state. By and large, you cannot really comparison shop based on price. But if you start asking about reissue or renewal rates and the company you have chosen starts hassling you, look around for alternatives.

Title insurance can be paid for by the buyer, the seller, or split. In every state, there seems to be a common practice, but there is no law. Thus, this becomes a negotiating point.

As previously mentioned, the cost of title insurance varies primarily upon the size of the policy (cost of the property and/or the amount being financed), and whether any part of the policy could qualify for the reduced re-finance or re-issue rate. Typically, though, policies themselves tend to range between $750 and $3,000. **Policy premiums are charged one time only and are not recurring.**

Transfer Deeds

A deed is a legal instrument used to grant an ownership. Deeds are best known as the method of transferring title to real estate from one person to another. They are sometimes also referred to as *transfer deeds* or *grant deeds*. The terminology varies from state to state.

In most states, in order to be valid, a transfer deed needs to contain six essential elements. Those six items are defined as:

- A written document.
- A clause that transfers title, called a *granting* or *transfer clause*.
- The names of the *grantor* and the *grantee* (the seller and the buyer, respectively). Remember the phrase "or's give and ee's receive."
- A description of the property being transferred.
- Execution, delivery, and acceptance. It must be signed by a competent grantor, meaning minors and those declared mentally incompetent cannot sign a deed.
- Grantor's signature.

A transfer deed is effective upon conveyance and acceptance—not necessarily the public filing date.

The most desirable type of deed is some form of **warranty deed**. With a warranty deed:

- The grantor states that the property has not been sold to anybody else.

- The grantor states that the property is not burdened by any encumbrances apart from those the seller has already told the buyer about.
- More importantly, the grantor will warrant and defend title against the claims of all persons. This means the grantor is guaranteeing the grantee that title is free of any defects that may affect the title.

A *general warranty deed* **offers the absolute most protection for buyers.** The seller is guaranteeing the sanctity of the title to that property since the beginning of time.

A *special warranty deed* **only guarantees the quality of the title since the owner has owned the property.**

Quit claim deeds **are used to convey any interest that the grantor *might* possess in the property.** The grantor might be a legal owner, or the grantor might never have formally been identified on a deed describing the property.

Quit claims are most often used during a divorce, to deed the property from one spouse to the other. If a married person holds title to a property as sole and separate owner, or perhaps if he or she acquired the property before marriage, the spouse not in title might be asked to sign a quit claim deed when the property is sold to a third party, just to make sure the spouse who was not on the deed does not later come back and lay claim to the property. Quit claims are just as often used to *add* a name to the deed, such as when a single person who owns a home gets married and wishes to add their spouse to the title.

Quit claim deeds get tossed around a lot and while they are fine for little issues such as adding or subtracting a relative's name on the deed, they can be dangerously overused. I can quit claim you the Brooklyn Bridge. By doing so, I am essentially saying, "Maybe I own it; maybe I don't; I am not representing that I do, but if I do, you can have it." Now you see how legally flimsy these instruments are. They are often used when there are serious questions as to the delineations of a property. Sometimes surveys disagree, or sometimes other factors come into play, such as coastal property being subject to soil erosion, or a dirt pathway being used by the owner for decades, yet technically not on his property. Quit claims, while not always able to clarify such matters, can at least allow the buyer to eliminate the future claims of someone who *might* be the owner of questionable pieces of land either adjacent to or on the periphery of a property.

Real Estate Closings

There are few things that vary greater from state to state than how real estate closings are handled and how much they typically cost. In some states, the title insurance company acts as a neutral paralegal or entity to talk both parties through the requisite paperwork, and their fees for doing so are split between both parties. Occasionally, such a party is referred to as a "*scrivener*." In other parts of the country, both parties retain real estate attorneys who sit in on the closing and each party pays, of course, for their own attorney.

In either case, it is important to shop around. Some states do regulate the fees title companies can charge, but more often, attorneys can charge whatever the market will bear. Even when a regulated title company does the closing, they may have the legal right to add on additional fees. The "regulation" in this case may only be a cap on how high any one of these fees may be, but often the inclusion of such a line item itself is ludicrous. Example: A state may allow a title company to charge for courier fees up to a certain dollar amount. Sometimes the fees are just being passed through at the request of the lender, so do not shoot the messenger. Before agreeing to pay for this, ask bluntly, "*Who* was couriered *what*? And *why*?" If they cannot offer proof and a satisfactory reason, ask them to take it off the closing statement. Do the same with any other unexplained fees that you see.

While there may be a whole pile of documents to sign, the master document listing all closing fees is the **HUD-1 Closing Statement**. It is a form that was created by and its use mandated by the federal government. It requires every fee to be spelled out and itemized. The numbers are usually filled in by the title company or some other entity administering the closing. Look it over closely and if you have questions, have them explained to your satisfaction. It would not be unreasonable to ask to review a copy of the HUD-1 at least a day before your closing.

Appraisals vs. Assessments

I rarely have a day go by when I don't have to correct someone misusing the terms "appraisal" and "assessment." The line will usually go, "The county has my property *appraised* for X dollars."

Counties generally don't appraise things. You will never see elected officials appearing on "Antiques Roadshow" on PBS setting a value on someone's old lamp. Counties usually "assess" things; and this assessment is for the purpose of taxation.

Your county sets an operating budget, just like any legislative body. Then it must raise money to pay for it. Counties use property taxes, or if by chance they do not, usually some governmental entity does, be it your local school district or someone else, and counties are charged with the responsibility of coming up with a relatively fair way of determining who pays how much. In order to do this, they must come up with very, very rough estimates regarding the value of everyone's property. These values are *relative*; for what it's worth, they could simply rank them, although that is not how they usually do it. The issue is to tabulate that there is, say, a small house, a large house, and a medium house in your neighborhood, and to make sure that the large house pays the most taxes, the small house the least, and the medium in between. They will also evaluate, in broad terms, the relative value of properties, so that a really, really nice new home pays more taxes than a really old decrepit one of the same size. They will also compare neighborhoods, assessing values to charge higher taxes on those whose homes are selling for more money and are thus more desirable, than neighborhoods where homes are selling for much less, regardless of any individual's personal opinion or preference of the properties in question.

Taken in total, counties use computer models to end up with assessments for every piece of land and every improvement (buildings that stand upon the land) under their jurisdiction. They do not actually see, measure, and evaluate each and every property individually.

This is in stark contrast to getting an *appraisal*. With an appraisal, you are paying a private professional to go into your house, take measurements, look at all the amenities (swimming pool, how many baths, type of flooring, etc.), evaluate the condition, and most importantly in the end, do a thorough analysis of all relevant recent home sales near your home in order to come up with an estimate of its value that is as accurate as is humanly possible, taking into account that anything in this world is only worth what someone is willing to pay for it.

In comparison, your county assessor may at best *drive by* your property. Heck of a difference, eh?

Bottom line: **The government roughly *assesses* you for taxes; you pay someone to do a thorough *appraisal* for the purpose of establishing a marketplace sales price or to substantiate its value for a lender.**

If you want to buy someone's property and they defend its value by stating, "Well, the county assessed (if they use the word right) it for X dollars," this should go in one ear and out the other. It is fairly meaningless, as it relates to the real market value of the property. So too, do not use this figure when setting the price for your own property. Most good real estate agents will recommend you pay for an appraisal or they may, of course, by virtue of knowing the neighborhood and the market, have a pretty good idea themselves of how to set the price so that you make a sale and get a fair deal. Real estate agents usually do this using what is called a "*Comparative Market Analysis*" or "*CMA*." Arguably, this may not be as good as an appraisal, but it takes into consideration what similar homes in similar neighborhoods during a similar time frame sold for.

Private appraisers charge varying rates depending upon where you live and whether you are appraising a small home or a large commercial property. A residential appraisal might go for between $350 and $550, while a commercial appraisal might run $2,500 or higher. Get recommendations, but remember that if you get that recommendation from, say, your real estate agent or your mortgage company, ask if there is a business relationship—they might be in business together. That said, I would get more than one name from more than one source and comparison shop, both for price as well as your impression of their expertise.

Property Taxes

Property taxes vary widely from state to state and even *within* some states. In Alaska, for example, only 25 of 161 municipalities actually *have* property taxes. This perfectly illustrates the total lack of uniformity on this subject.

Where property taxes do exist, they may be used for just as wide a variety of reasons. In New Jersey, the state with the highest property taxes in the nation, property taxes are used to fund literally everything: police, firemen, schools, libraries, parks, you name it. If it exists and it is provided by the local, county or state government, it is paid for by property taxes. Go to another state, and you will most likely encounter an entirely different set of circumstances. This is not to presume that these amenities come free in other states; it's just that each state and, again, even sectors within certain states, all come up with their own formulas on how to pay for things.

In the previous subchapter when we talked about assessments, we spoke of counties, for example, doing such property value evaluations. In a place such as Alaska, one must presume that it isthe municipality that is in charge of this. Again, variations are common.

The idea of a governmental entity doing an assessment is that, if there *are* property taxes, it is important to make sure everyone pays as close to their fair share as humanly possible. The problem arises when property changes hands. **If you buy a home, whatever you paid for that home is now factored into its new assessed value.**

Picture this: You buy a home for $450,000. The home next door, where your new neighbors have lived for the past twenty years, is virtually identical to your new residence. But *they* paid only $100,000 for the exact same house! This is perfectly natural. Markets change, economies change; bread and milk cost less twenty years ago, too. So what is the problem? The problem is that you may be paying four and one-half times the property taxes that your neighbor in the exact same house is paying!

What can be done? By rights, you and your neighbor should pay about the same in property taxes. But the whole thing has a domino effect. It doesn't stop with just your one neighbor; in the end, it affects every single home in the community. When this occurs enough times to create extraordinary discrepancies throughout the community, the county or municipality orders a **reassessment or re-evaluation** (both terms mean the same thing).

How often does this occur? If a market is relatively flat, it may not happen for quite a while, sometimes decades. If it is a frenetic market, it may occur far more often, sometimes as frequently as within two or three years. Once every four or five years is quite common.

Some communities have gotten quite computer savvy and have purchased software that allows them to make adjustments on the fly as new home sales occur. This can stave off a total re-evaluation even longer. Re-evaluations cost the community a significant amount of money, money that, ironically, drives up the community budget, thus forcing everyone to pay higher property taxes.

Some states or counties have adopted legislation that demands reassessments once their computer model shows disparities between recent sales prices and like-configured homes reaching a certain percentage difference, maybe 20 or 25%. Again, once things get really out of control, a reassessment is fairest to everyone.

There is a common misconception that a re-evaluation raises everyone's taxes. This is completely false. The only thing that can make taxes go up is for a town, county, or state's *budget* to go up. Yet what inevitably happens is that someone who bought their property many years ago will see a re-evaluation now listing their property as being worth more—*because it IS worth more now*. What they fail to realize is that ALL of the homes purchased in a long-ago market-place have been undervalued for taxation purposes. If anyone has been beaten up during this process, it is the guy who just bought a house yesterday and is paying an assessment based on what he just paid for his property, which will most likely be higher than anyone else in the neighborhood. Re-assessments simply level the playing field and make everything more fair to all.

Before we get any deeper into this subject, though, let's start with the basics:

- When you are buying a property, check to see if it is in an area where there are property taxes.
- Next, check to see approximately what the property taxes might be per year.
- Next, take into consideration this expense as you formulate your personal financial budget. Can you still afford this property once you add in what you will have to pay for property taxes? In New Jersey, maybe not. Many people in that state are paying double their mortgage payments per month in property tax assessments.
- Finally, PAY YOUR PROPERTY TAXES. You would be surprised to see how many people let this slip their mind and then suddenly a *tax lien* is placed against their property.

Property Tax Appeals

Okay, so your property taxes are too high. Aren't *everyone's* taxes too high? Is there anything you can do about it, short of moving? Yes, it's called a *"tax appeal."*

Property taxation allows you to do something you really can't quite do with any other form of tax that is placed upon you. Since your property tax is based upon how your property is valued, you can debate that evaluation of its worth. This is a formal process, not just calling up some complaint desk and whining.

The most important thing to note is that saying, "My taxes are too high; I can't afford to pay them," will not work. No one cares. Nor will saying, "It's not fair!" work, either. This is not because the powers that be are too callous and unfeeling—it is simply because these things are completely irrelevant. You also cannot negotiate a "settlement" or "work a deal" regarding property taxes. The property tax levy is the property tax levy, period. All that is subject to change is the fair market value of your property.

Your tax bill will always tell you the government's "assessed" (not appraised) value of your property. If the figure is about right, there's not much you can say. If it is far more than a rational person feels you could sell your property for today, then you've got grounds for appeal.

Some people hire a professional appraiser to help them prove their case. This is effective and efficient, but it is also costly. You may go to all the expense and lose, owing not only your same old tax assessment but the appraiser's bill as well.

But the government did not arrange matters so that only people wealthy enough to pay an appraiser every year could file a tax appeal. You can also represent yourself. What you need to do is find *comparable properties*. These are homes similar to yours that you feel have been assessed at a lower value than yours. The key word here is "similar." If you live in a three-bedroom ranch house with a two-car garage on a one-quarter acre of land, then that is what you should look for. Check recent home sale prices on such properties (this can usually be done very easily on a variety of internet websites). How do they compare to the assessment on yours? You may also check how your town has assessed your neighbor's similar property, even if it has not changed hands recently. How does the assessment compare? The bottom line is, **you only have a case if you can prove that similar, almost identical properties in the same area have been assessed at lesser value than yours.** In most cases, the "per foot" sales price is the commonly used measurement.

But let's get back a bit to the real nuts and bolts of how you go about doing all this. Step One: You get your property tax bill. Step

Two: You faint. Step Three: Your tax bill came from the tax assessor's office. Call him up. Tell him your plight. That starts the process. The tax assessor has an office. Make an appointment to go there, or follow the appeal instructions that came with your tax bill.

Once there, the first thing you want to do is make sure they have the basic raw data correct about your property. Would it surprise you to know that often times this information is critically wrong? Yes it is. You may be living in that three-bedroom ranch on one-quarter acre and the assessor's books say you live in a four-bedroom colonial on one-half an acre. These people try to keep track of massive amounts of data and errors are rampant. If you find an error you can substantiate, the tax assessor has the authority to make an alteration.

But it's not always that easy.

If the information they have on your property is basically correct, but you still feel you are improperly assessed, the assessor will inform you that your only recourse is to schedule a hearing before a board of review. There may be forms to fill out and this is the time when you really need to collect that data on comparable properties or "comps." Be thorough, or consider hiring a professional appraiser.

But what if you can't find true comps? An appraiser would know how to take similar yet unlike properties and make adjustments to compensate for their differences. Example: You have that three-bedroom ranch on a one-quarter acre, but the most similar property you can find is a four-bedroom ranch on the same amount of property. An appraiser can make modifications to standard formulas to draw a comparison between the two properties and then put it in a format that is self-explanatory and convincing to a review board. A professional and thorough presentation is important. It is not impossible to school yourself on such matters, but it takes time and effort. If you can save yourself, say, a thousand dollars a year on property taxes, though, it is time well spent.

Savvy property owners take advantage of the right to a tax appeal and do it often—sometimes each and every year

Unfortunately, it is sometimes the poor and the elderly—the people who need relief the most—who do not know of this process and do not take advantage of it. They most likely have the most glaring errors to fix, since they have not advocated for themselves. Don't let this happen to you.

Even if you are a renter, you can use this process. If there is a pass-through procedure whereby you, the tenant, pay property taxes or increases, look at how the building is valued. If you feel it is out of line, tell your landlord. A good and savvy landlord should take the ball and run with it. If property taxes are too high in his building, he may have trouble keeping it fully occupied. That's one heck of an incentive to do a tax appeal. Landlords can also use the income (or lack of income) of a property as a basis of appeal. If only half their building is occupied due to market conditions, they can sometimes get relief upon petitioning the board of review. Towns are often sensitive to a commercial landlord simply abandoning a property because it cannot sustain financial viability. This is how slums are created, and no town wants a slum.

Check your property tax bill each year. If you think the assessed value of your property is too high, appeal it.

Tax Liens

Okay, so you forgot to budget for your property taxes (assuming that your mortgage company does not automatically escrow them into an impound account on your behalf) and couldn't pay your bill on time. What happens now?

Although the process varies almost as greatly as property taxes themselves, there are a few commonalities. Usually, the county places a *lien* (a legal claim for payment, using your property as collateral) against your property. A tax lien actually supersedes all other liens, even your first position mortgage loan.

Once the lien has been in place a certain period of time (check with your state or county), a ***tax lien sale*** or ***tax deed sale*** (again, check where you live to see their particular methodology) is held.

Once more, various areas of the country conduct these sales following different protocols. What remains in common is that up until the moment a lien or deed sale is conducted, the county will happily take your money from you, with interest of course, if you decide to pay. In the end, that's all they want—your money. Furthermore, most communities want to move from lien to lien or deed sale as soon as possible because—they want money!

In a lien sale or deed sale, they are selling off your debt to someone else. Now, for those of you who always pay your bills on time, investing in tax liens is sometimes a nifty way to make money. Like all investments, it is not without risk, but some people make a nice little profit from it.

The sale is held and someone somehow (depending upon the protocols of your state) ends up holding the tax lien or deed on your property. They do this by (common sense) paying off your debt. Often times, there is a window of opportunity where you can pay whoever bought your tax lien exactly what is in arrears and that is that. Sometimes, interest on the debt begins accruing immediately. Eventually, though, if you continue to dally long enough, interest or further penalties will accrue. This is how the tax lien investor makes his money. I cannot emphasize enough, as a property owner, *do not get yourself into this type of situation.* **The interest and penalties will kill you.** Beg, borrow, or steal in order to get that lien taken off. Each day can cost you dollars you cannot afford.

A word of caution to potential tax lien investors: Remember that you have paid for and bought a lien for a specific amount of money covering a specific amount of time during which the property owner did not pay his or her taxes. But what happens if more tax bills come out? They will; they're like death and...uh, taxes. If the property owner gets back on track and pays his current property taxes, great. If he doesn't, YOU will have to continue to pay his property taxes. If you don't, there will be *another* tax lien sale and some other investor can buy out both the new taxes that are in arrears, as well as the lien or deed that YOU are holding. If you don't keep up with those taxes, you may have no further recourse in this matter. Of course, you'll still get out with what you put in, so you really won't go broke in this particular scenario. I thought it was worth mentioning, though, because some people have spread the rumor that tax lien investments are *really* easy money, and they're not.

There is a period of time during which the person behind on their property taxes is given to pay the new lien holder called the **redemption period.** Once the redemption period is over, the lien holder may initiate foreclosure proceedings. The proceedings (the costs of which must be paid by the lien holder, though a property owner may be required to pay them as part of buying back or *redeeming* his property) may result in either the lien holder acquiring title to the property (normally this will be a *"treasurer's deed"*—depending upon the state), or a tax deed sale of the property where the lien holder has the right of first bid (and may participate by making additional bids if he so chooses). During the period between the initiation of proceedings and actual foreclosure, the property owner still has the opportunity to repay the lien with interest, plus the costs incurred to foreclose.

Again, a warning to any would-be tax lien investors: Every tiny little arcane procedure as prescribed in the jurisdiction you are operating in must be followed to the "T" or your lien may be ruled invalid.

The rate of return on tax lien purchases can be enormous, depending upon the state you are operating in. Or, there may be circumstances where all you've done is loaned someone a lot of money interest free for a while.

Some experts tout tax lien sales as a means of acquiring property at highly discounted prices. In practice, the majority of liens are redeemed well before the property can be foreclosed, especially where a mortgage is involved, as the mortgage holder is secondary in line to a tax lien and is no way going to let you take away their collateral for pennies. Where tax deed sales are used to foreclose, numerous bidders participate, thus making the chances of actual acquisition remote, unless you are the high bidder. Finally, if the owner of the property declares bankruptcy, the bankruptcy court may lower the interest rate to be paid, or may discharge part or all of the lien, leaving the lien holder with nothing.

Property Tax Rates

The **property tax rate** is often given as a percentage. It may also be expressed as a *permille* (amount of tax per thousand dollars of property value), which is also known as a *millage rate* or *mill levy* (a *mill* is also one-thousandth of a dollar). To calculate the property tax the county or municipality will collect, multiply the assessed value of the property by the mill rate and then divide by 1,000. For example, a property with an assessed value of $100,000 located in a municipality with a mill rate of 20 mills would have a property tax bill of $2,000 per year.

There are three types of property:

- *Land.*
- *Improvements* **to land (immovable man-made things, a building being the most common).**
- *Personality* **(movable man-made things—say, an above-ground pool or a foundationless shed).**

Each type of property is assessed separately, yet taxed at the same mill rate. Your property tax bill will most commonly say, for example, "Land: $50,000, Improvements: $100,000." Thus, if you put an addition on your home—a new garage, perhaps—your land assessment will remain the same, but the value of your improvements will most likely increase.

If, while doing a re-evaluation, a tax assessor gains entrance into your home and notices physical upgrades, such as a formerly unfinished basement that has now been changed to a beautiful new recreation room, this may also increase the assessment on your improvements, or it may possibly be listed as personality.

There are also three types of land use:

- **Residential**
- **Commercial**
- **Agricultural**

Unlike property types, **each type of land use is taxed at a different mill rate.** While mill rate levy formulas vary from state to state, in most cases, residential land use is taxed at one rate and commercial at a much higher rate, the national average being around three times higher. Vacant land is also usually taxed at the rate reflecting its *"highest and best use"* (a commonly used land use law term). Thus, if it is possible, due to local zoning, to put a commercial building on the property, that piece of vacant land will be assessed as commercial, even if when it is eventually developed, a home is built on it. At that time, it would finally be re-classified as residential. In some states, though, *all* vacant land is assessed as commercial, which *really* stinks.

Bottom line: **It is possible for an acre of land with a large home on it to pay less property tax than an adjacent acre of vacant land.** Unbelievable!

The type of land with the lowest mill rate is agricultural. This fact, though, has been bastardized both through many states' legal and legislative systems as well as by citizens looking to pay as little tax as possible. On both sides of this dispute, the culprit is greed.

Here's how it works: In some states, the greed for higher property tax revenues has motivated legislators to only allow homeowners to have residential property of a certain size. Maybe they cap the amount of contiguous residential acreage one may have at, say, five acres. Anything more than that gets taxed as commercial. So if you own ten acres with a home on it in some rural area, you may pay for the residential improvement, five acres of residential land, and five acres of commercial land—even though you are conducting no commerce there. Unfair!

But sometimes there's a loophole.

The homeowner, in order to avoid taxes, researches the state's definition of agricultural land use. In some states, it is pathetically paltry. It may only be that the land provides its owner with as little as $250 worth of saleable produce, product, or income per year. So the owner plants a few tomato plants, gives a bag of tomatoes to his cousin Ernie each year, and Ernie, being the cooperative sort, gives him $250. The homeowner gives Ernie a receipt and makes a photocopy for his own records. At tax time, the homeowner shows the tax assessor the $250 receipt for produce and kazam! Our man is now a farmer. He has also probably saved himself thousands of dollars in property taxes.

Tax Increment Financing

Urban sprawl is happening all around our country. Everyone wants "new," and new is gained by taking green space, breaking ground, and building on it. Meanwhile, "old" just keeps getting older, and our older communities are going to seed. What can communities do to "redevelop" their aging buildings and properties, particularly in commercial areas and downtowns?

How about property tax incentives?

Tax increment financing (TIF) allows towns to create special districts and to make public improvements within those districts that will generate private-sector development. During the development period, the tax base is frozen at the pre-development level. Property taxes continue to be paid, but taxes derived from increases in assessed values (the tax increment) resulting from new development either go into a special fund created to retire bonds issued to originate the development, or leverage future growth in the district.

The tax freeze lasts for a defined period of time, as set forth in the redevelopment plan. At the end of that period, taxing jurisdictions finally enjoy the benefit of increased property values.

TIF districts may also use their dedicated funds to help finance improvements to buildings within the district that they have chosen to designate, yet not acquire by condemnation. This is often given in the form of matching funds. Example: A building owner is informed that if he or she makes façade improvements up to a certain dollar level, say

$100,000, the TIF will match the investment dollar for dollar (i.e. paying for up to $50,000 of the improvement to private property). This acts as an incentive for private investment by the building's owner at a discounted rate. The owner then possesses a building with an enhanced value. This value, though, will eventually be subject to a higher property tax assessment. In my experience, municipalities attempt to recover their grant over a three year period in the form of increased taxes. This makes TIFs ideal for developers who essentially see this as "free money," but not so good for the future owners or tenants who will actually end up paying the increased tax bill.

I have mixed feelings about TIF. It certainly creates opportunities for developers and redevelopers, but if you already own a viable property within the district, you may be encouraged to take on grant money for improvements that, while gratefully accepted, may end up pricing you out of a tenant once the TIF period ends and your property tax goes soaring skyward. My advice would be to be wary and try to get a handle on what the market for tenancy, both present and future, might be before getting involved in TIF. This also applies to remaining within such a district—this may be a perfect time to sell. Also, when a community decides to designate such a district, they often do so only after assessing public opinion, sometimes even putting it to a public referendum. Look at all the facts from the unblinking eye of a shrewd real estate investor before jumping on board. You may find yourself in a hot area that has "risen from the dead," or you may end up with a gorgeous, but empty building.

Selling Your Property

We've talked about real estate agents, real estate closings, etc. In each case, we've focused a lot on the buyer, but have also discussed the seller and his issues. Now let's talk a bit more about issues unique only to the seller.

In the process of selling your property, you may hear the phrases "*real property*" and "*personal property*." **Real property is fixed and** attached; *personal property* is usually mobile and unattached. Where this is likely to come up is in regard to items within your property. Most refrigerators that can roll out, be unplugged, and taken with you, are considered personal property. If a refrigerator is somehow permanently attached to the home (such as a built-in model), it is real property and stays. When selling a property, it is assumed that you are selling all real property. Ripping things like banisters, fireplaces, etc. off their moorings and taking them with you is not only boorish behavior, it would most likely be a violation of your sales contract. Even if it is possible to remove them, the buyer is assuming all real property to be his. Granted, anything is negotiable, but if I was a buyer and I allowed you to do such a thing at all (which I most likely wouldn't), I would demand significant financial consideration off the previously negotiated sales price, so much so that you would most likely say, "Forget it." As the buyer, I don't need you trashing the property as you leave.

Personal property is far more negotiable. Over the years, I've heard many buyers look at a fully-furnished room and say, "This stuff is great! Are you going to redecorate in your new place? If so, what will it take for me to persuade you to leave this stuff here and bundle it in with the property sale?" If you're lucky, your seller may throw in certain pieces of personal property you've identified simply to A) close the deal or B) save him the money of moving something he's not even that sure he wants to bring with him in the first place. On occasion, you can pick up some great stuff for cheap or even free. Items that frequently need to be clarified as to whether they are included or not are things such as hot tubs, washers and dryers and other appliances.

One of the most important things we should discuss regarding selling your home (rather than a commercial property or a residential property in which you do not reside) is the tax exemption on gain from the sale of your personal residence. This can be an incredible bit of financial knowledge, one which you should definitely remember and bring to your accountant's attention if you do sell your home, or if you do not use an accountant, one that you should definitely be aware of when you do your own taxes.

Under current tax law, if you sell your personal residence and you have lived there for two out of the last five years, the first $250,000 in gains (if you are single) or $500,000 in gains (if you are married) are not taxable.

A good example of a gain is when you "trade down." This is very common for empty-nesters or retirees. The kids are gone and they no longer need the big yard with the swing set and the home with five bedrooms. So Mom and Dad sell the family homestead—which has accrued in value very nicely over the years—to some new young family, and they pack up their things for Shady Acres Adult Community. They sell the homestead for, say, $500,000, but their condo at Shady Acres only costs $250,000. They have $250,000 in gains. Prior to the passage of fairly recent tax code legislation, Mom and Dad would have one heck of an income tax bill next April 15th. But now, all that money would be tax free, all the way up to $500,000 (for a couple). Nice.

For a person with good credit in an appreciating market, this tax exemption provides an incentive to move every two years or so. Example: You buy a home for $125,000 with 20% down ($25,000) and a $100,000 mortgage. You live there two years and, as we know about most mortgage products, you have paid an almost insignificant amount of mortgage principal. Your home has appreciated in value to $200,000. You sell. You now have $100,000 down payment for your next mortgage. If you can afford to pay the monthly PITI, you might now qualify for a $600,000 home with a $500,000 mortgage.

The best use of the tax exemption, though, is in selling down over and over again, every two years using the gains from the appreciated home sale to live off of or invest. There are some professional "fix-and-flippers" in this country that do just that. They are often professional or semi-professional craftspeople who buy a property at a low price, live in it while fixing it up nicely without spending too much money, then, in the right market, selling it for far more than they paid for and put into it. Then they take the gain portion, either live off it or invest it, and take the principal and use it to buy another slightly distressed property in order to fix it up as they live in it so that they can do the same thing all over again. Picture—you can make living in your house and puttering around in it your full-time occupation! And a comfortable one at that.

Finally, this tax exemption makes it profitable to build your own home. Think about it: Developers may make money because a new home can be sold for more than it cost to acquire the land and build upon it. Thus, by taking gains out of a home you have lived in that has appreciated in value, you are well-positioned to invest in building, and in the end, ending up with a home that is worth even more were you to sell it.

This tax exemption, coupled with record low mortgage interest rates, has been the engine that has driven our nationwide housing boom market.

There are also tax exemption benefits if you must relocate for employment. This kicks in if your employment changes by more than fifty miles. If you become disabled and must move into some sort of facility that provides health care, there are also tax exemptions to allow you to avoid capital gains when you sell your home. Bear these things in mind if they should ever happen to you. Consult with your tax professional for details so that you are sure to qualify.

Rental and Investment Properties

There are four major reasons why one should consider investing in rental real estate.

1. Appreciation – Given an infinite (and usually far less than infinite) amount of time, **real estate will appreciate in value**. When it appreciates while you hold it, you do not pay income tax on that appreciation until you sell it. You may even borrow against this appreciation, which, until the property is actually sold, is an invisible commodity.

2. Principal reduction – The presumption with any investment property is that someone other than you will occupy it. In order to occupy it, they must pay you rent. In theory, that **rent**

pays your mortgage. So, you borrowed money to buy this commodity (you got a mortgage loan), and *someone else is paying off that debt for you*. Where else can you get something for only 20% of its value (your standard down payment), get a third party to pay off the rest yet have no ownership interest (your tenant), most likely have that 20% initial investment also paid back to you by that same third party (most people charge enough rent to more than cover the monthly PITI, thus they eventually get made whole on the down payment as well), and…at the end of it all, the commodity is most likely worth more than its original value?!

3. Tax benefits – Although property usually appreciates in value, when you file your taxes, investment property is considered a *depreciating* asset, much like a car. This is reflected in your yearly income tax. According to the tax code, a residential property depreciates over 27 ½ years, a commercial property over 39 years. Only the improvement depreciates, not the land (buildings get old; land does not).

Example: You buy a residential property for $300,000. $50,000 is the value of the land; $250,000 is the improvement. $250,000 divided by 27 ½ years means that each year, you get to deduct $9,090.91 in *depreciation* from your income. This, despite the fact that the total value of the property has most likely *gone up*.

You also get all sorts of **business deductions** off the ownership of this property, such as advertising (for tenants), auto travel (to and from your house to the property), cleaning and maintenance, commissions to brokers or managers, legal and professional fees, mortgage interest, property taxes, repairs, supplies, and others.

4. Income – Landlords can make money. Obviously, if you had a rental property, you would try to charge enough to cover your PITI and any other expenses associated with property ownership (repairs, maintenance, utilities not passed through, etc.). But, if the market supports it, you would also be wise to charge more—enough to cover unexpected expenses that might arise as well as giving yourself some income. In a perfect world, the income from even one building or home would be substantial, but the truth is, it's usually not. Rents are market-driven and one cannot exceed the market and attract and keep tenants.

Of course, once your mortgage has been paid off, you really get some serious income, even off of a very small rental property. At that point, the majority of the rental income goes right into your pocket. Very nice. Of course, if you don't want to wait fifteen or thirty years to make the big income, the previous three reasons for real estate investment may have positioned you to sell at a significant profit due to favorable market conditions, making it wise for you to sell to an eager buyer before you have completely retired your mortgage loan.

1031 Exchanges

So you've invested wisely in real estate. Your mortgages may or may not be paid off. Life is good. Now you want to sell it all and make <u>mad</u> money. Ready to pay more taxes than you've ever seen before? I thought that would get your attention. Here come capital gains taxes, as well as your responsibility to recapture the depreciation you've been taking for all those years. Life can be cruel sometimes. But wait; there's a white knight riding in over the horizon.

Internal Revenue Code Section 1031 is one of the last remaining tax deferments (tax shelters). It is a powerful tool that allows investors to exchange any investment property for any other like-kind investment property. For your exchange to be valid, you must follow specific IRS regulations.

- The properties being exchanged must be of like kind (but not identical). For example, you may exchange land for an apartment building, a strip mall for an office building or an investment house for land.
- 90-Day Identification period – A taxpayer has ninety days within

which to identify one or more replacement properties. Identification must be made in writing. The taxpayer may identify up to three properties as long as their aggregate value does not exceed 200% of the property transferred by the taxpayer.

- 180-Day Receipt Rule – The taxpayer must close on the purchase of the replacement property within the *shorter* of one hundred eighty days after the first property was sold or the due date of the taxpayer's federal tax return (usually April 15th of the following year) for the year in which the relinquished property was transferred. Hence, the one hundred-eighty-day exchange period may be cut short for any exchange that begins after October 17th.

100% of the proceeds from the sale of your current property must be held by a third party *qualified intermediary (QI)* and applied toward your replacement property to get a full tax deferral. QI's are quite prevalent in the business now and many firms are sprouting up, specializing in guiding you through your 1031 (for a price—roughly around $500).

Your replacement property must be of equal or greater value to the property you have sold to get a full tax deferral. You must also have an equal or greater amount of debt and equity in the replacement property. Properties being exchanged must be held for investment purposes (personal residences are not exchangeable).

Granted, a 1031 does not completely cash you out of real estate investment, but they oftentimes allow you to move your assets into an investment situation that is more manageable for you once you have grown tired of the landlord game. Perhaps instead of a whole slew of college apartments dotted all over the map, full of party-throwing kids, you trade it all in for one nice, staid office building. Or maybe you really do want to start drawing down some of that cash by selling off properties. In that case, you may want to go the opposite direction—maybe you already own the one big office building. Trade it in for a bunch of smaller buildings, then sell those off gradually over time, spreading out your pain, if you will, tax-wise.

TIC Investments

"TIC" stands for "Tenants In Common." The term has been around almost as long as land use law itself. It is a form of property ownership for two or more owners. The individual interests do not have to be equal and the owners enjoy a proportionate right to the property. If a co-owner dies, title passes to the estate of the deceased owner (*not* the other partners) and the person named by the estate assumes their proportionate title to the property and becomes the new tenant in common with the surviving tenants in common—unlike *joint tenancy with rights of survivorship*, where ownership passes on to the other remaining partners. Each co-owner receives an individual deed at closing for his or her undivided percentage interest in the entire property. A TIC owner has the same proportional rights and benefits as a single owner of property.

TIC investments are similar to real estate limited partnerships, except that instead of becoming *partners* with someone else, you have your own deeded interest in the property. TIC investments are often done with large ticket properties, such as shopping malls or huge office parks—multi-million-dollar projects. A TIC "sponsor" does all of the legwork, then finds investors to buy "shares" of it and become TICs with them.

Because, unlike a partnership, you have just purchased real property, you are now eligible for a 1031 if you so choose. Spinning off of the last subchapter, many people with lots of smaller investment properties that they have had to manage by themselves for years and years are now using 1031 exchanges to shift them into TICs, whereby some large management company will take care of all the day-to-day property management and all the investor has to do is lay on the beach and collect monthly checks (in theory…).

Since TIC 1031s are fairly new, some issues are still being settled on the legal and governmental front. Real estate people view them as real property and want to keep selling them as such, collecting commissions as they go. Securities brokers are selling them as they would stocks, collecting commissions as well. At this point in time, about 30% of TIC investments are being sold by real estate agents and 70% are being sold by stock brokers. Perhaps the two entities will continue to be in this business, or some governmental edict will come down for one side or the other. Either way, though, they are a very interesting investment opportunity and are growing like mad.

Time Shares

I affectionately refer to these as "crime shares." Need you read on?

If you have been an adult for more than a few days, you have probably been approached to "invest" in one of these. The sales pitch is that you get something for free (amusement park tickets, a free night in a beachfront condo, ski lift tickets, etc.) and all you have to do is sit through a presentation—NOTHING TO BUY! NO COMMITMENTS!

There is no free lunch in this world. If you think you can outsmart these people by taking your free gift and running away without buying anything, you are nothing more than a Friday night beer and nickels card player going into a high stakes poker game with Amarillo Slim, Doyle Brunson, and Johnny Chan. You will walk out wearing nothing but your pride. Time share salespeople are the best. They can sell hamburgers to cows. Their commissions reflect this— they get paid top dollar and boy, do they earn it!

A time share is usually a vacation property in a resort setting, often times a condo. You are offered an opportunity to "buy a share" of a property, which they try to explain to you is "cheaper and smarter" than renting a hotel room. There is a lump sum cost up front, but one of the worst aspects of this "investment" is the annual maintenance assessment which, like most maintenance fees, is usually uncontrolled and is performed by a company that is in some way affiliated with the managing ownership company. **You do not own a deed, thus you do not really own a piece of property.** The alleged benefit is that you can use this place as your own for X number of weeks per year. BUT…everyone who has ever purchased one will tell you that only the least desirable weeks are the ones available when it's your turn to choose—Murphy's Law. And if you don't use those weeks, you *might* have the opportunity to trade them or sell them to someone else…but maybe not.

A time share is not an investment. Repeat this over and over until it makes as much sense to you as gravity. It is a vacation expense, period. You also may find it difficult to get out of a time share once you have gotten in. And while you are waiting to sell, you are still going to be assessed that maintenance fee which can be hundreds of dollars per year, for which you receive nothing of any value to you. Furthermore, that fee tends to rise yearly.

Time shares are not to be confused with *"fractional ownership clubs,"* **which I** *do* **endorse.** These are sort of the "rich man's time share." It is a partnership, you may even *own* part of it, and you take part in the appreciation. There are also very clear ways out. Because they involve actual ownership, though, you do have to put more money down initially.

Being a Landlord: Finding a Tenant

You can buy all the investment property you want, but if you have no one to occupy it, you've just invested in a money pit. Tenants can be a necessary evil, although I don't want you coming away from that statement thinking such relationships need always be adversarial. Some residential tenants are good, hard-working people who simply cannot afford a place of their own but have fine morals and ethics, pay their bills on time, and take good care of the property as if it were their own. Many commercial tenants simply eye the numbers prudently and realize that their business venture makes more sense to them were they to rent rather than buy. That said, they, again, may pay their rent on time and carry their weight without undo headache for the landlord.

How does one find a good tenant, or any tenant, for that matter? Newspaper ads are a staple of the game. Yard or window signs are excellent, as many people self-identify a neighborhood and then drive up and down streets looking for such things. Here in the new millennium, the Internet has created incredible opportunities to reach tons of people. As a landlord, you or your property management company (if you outsource such work) can have your own website that links from search engines via keywords. There are also websites run by third-parties, specializing in listing rentals. Go to my website at www.BraunMincher.com to see a current list. As many of these URLs come and go, Craig's List is a perennial favorite that seems here to stay.

Housing fairs are popular in some parts of the country. They are often targeted at a certain demographic, such as college towns having them for students, or areas of aging populace doing them for older folks looking to downsize out of their home, but who would rather invest their windfall and live in a rental. In any case, if you have multiple units available, taking out a booth at a fair may have its advantages in exposing you to a market.

Commercial rentals are a little different. While all of the aforementioned will also work for commercial investment property, a lot of people use a real estate agent instead. If you use a real estate agent to find you a commercial tenant, they will commonly charge as much as one month's rent as their commission, or 10% of the yearly rent. Many will try to get that per year, every year, for as long as the lease lasts. Some will even try to have a contract with you saying that they get it so long as that particular tenant is in your building, even if it is for fifteen or twenty years. You will have to really mull this one over if you are a landlord. In some markets, you are at a distinct disadvantage if you do not use a real estate agent because many businesses go directly to an agent in order to find available locations—sort of a commercial MLS. But as you can see, the cost can be prohibitive. This is why, while most real estate agents shy away from handling residential rentals, many specialize in commercial rentals because it can be so lucrative for them. I would obviously recommend that if you go this route, you cut the best deal for yourself—try to cap their commission on only one year's rental. Going beyond that, you've taken on a partner, not a service. On the other hand, if you have decided to go really strong into the commercial real estate investment field, you may be at a competitive disadvantage if you do not retain a long-term relationship with a commercial real estate agent who has a big local profile. They'll be placing tenants into everyone else's buildings while yours remain vacant. A vacant investment property is very bad news. See, there's no easy way to make money. You must think and weigh your options constantly.

Lastly, there are referrals. If you're a good, fair, generous (wisely generous, not stupidly generous) landlord, word of mouth will have tenants telling their friends about you. Some landlords even come up with certain incentives for their existing tenants if they can bring them good, new tenants. Nothing beats word of mouth in any aspect of business.

Once you have your rental property and a potential tenant in front of you, I cannot emphasize enough the importance of getting an application. It sounds so simple and so basic, but it baffles me how people will rent to people they don't know at all. When I watch the news, that always seems to be the case with serial killers: "Yeah, he seemed like the quiet type; kept to himself. No, I don't know where he came from. No, I didn't know he just got out of prison. He didn't seem the type."

There are standard rental application forms that are easily found on the Internet. Whether you use one of these or create your own, your goal is to get enough personal data so that you can run basic credit and background checks. There are companies that can do this for you and again, I list some agencies on my website at www.BraunMincher.com. Basically, you want to know this person's credit profile. If it's sterling, great; but expect that to be rare when it comes to residential rentals. Unless someone is either very young or very eccentric, renters tend to have less than average credit. Your job is to see *how* less than average it is, and whether you can afford to manage the risk.

As to a background check, no, you are not looking to have the police or FBI check out their entire life for you; that's not very good use of your time or money. You primarily want to know the last few places they lived. Hopefully, some of those were also rentals. Once you've gotten that info, you call the old landlord up and **ask the magic question: "Would you rent to them again?"** That's it. The answer is either yes or no. Your time is valuable. You don't have to waste it interviewing other landlords, asking about wild parties, was the tenant ever late with rent, or were they a chronic complainer. No one's perfect. The bottom line is whether they would rent to them again, period. If they would, then all the moaning and criticizing in the world doesn't mean a thing. Some people just like to gossip and complain.

Bear in mind that the decision not to rent to someone must not in any way be construed as being based upon race, religion, national origin, etc. If you turn down a tenant, keep a paper trail on file verifying your legitimate reasons for doing so; you may at some point be called upon to defend your actions. The same goes for evictions. It may even come up if you are the "old landlord" being asked by a "new landlord," "Would you rent to them again?" Tenants have been known to try to sue for defamation, etc. Keep everything factual, unemotional, and apolitical and you should be fine.

Property Management Companies

Property management companies can be a good idea if you have numerous rental units. These are companies whose sole job it is to be the day-in, day-out landlord, freeing you to do what it is you'd prefer to do with your time. Most offer an ala carte menu of services, from collecting rents to making repairs large or small, taking care of exterior maintenance (shoveling snow, cutting grass), finding you tenants, you name it. Depending upon how many of these responsibilities you give them, management fees to an outside company will usually range from 7 to 12% of the rent you are charging per tenant.

Management companies can have an effect on your tax situation as to whether you are receiving passive versus active income from your property. This may sound confusing, but **if you are *actively* involved in** managing your property, your property is considered *passive* income. Only in America. **Passive income is not subject to self-employment taxes (this is a good thing for you).** On the other hand, if you are not active in the management of your properties and simply turn that job completely over to a management company (a TIC investment would be a perfect example), you will most likely be re-classified by Uncle Sam as having active income and you will lose certain tax benefits. Talk to your accountant before retaining a property management company to see if this might affect you.

Investing in Rental Property—A Case Study

Return on Investment (ROI): A performance measure used to evaluate the efficiency of an investment or to compare the efficiency of a number of different investments. To calculate ROI, the benefit (return) of an investment is divided by the cost of the investment; the result is expressed as a percentage or a ratio. For example, if you invest $10,000 in something and sell it for $15,000, your ROI is 50% ($5,000). Obviously, you need to "annualize" this figure when you are evaluating different investments so that you get an apples-to-apples comparison.

Cash on Cash Return: A rate of return often used in real-estate transactions. The calculation determines the cash income (and later the profit) on the cash invested. For example, when you purchase a rental property, you might put down only 10 to 20% for a cash down payment and then use leverage to finance the balance. Cash-on-cash return measures the annual return you made on the property in relation to the down payment.

Gross Rent Multiplier (GRM): Another simple way to value and compare properties which uses the "gross" rental income rather than the "net" owner income (NOI) to value rental property. The GRM is calculated by dividing the value of the property by the monthly gross rental income; the lower the number the better. See the examples below. The GRM is not a very precise calculation, but can quickly tell you if a deal merits further investigation. As rule of thumb, I like properties with a GRM of 100 or lower, which means that the gross monthly rents are at least 1% of the property value. If you know of any investments with a true GRM of 100 or less, contact me via email through my website at www.BraunMincher.com! You can also use this same formula in reverse to determine the approximate value of a property based upon its rental income.

Example 1: If the sales price for a property is $200,000 and the monthly gross rental income for a property is $2,500, the GRM is equal to 80 (1.3% of the property value).

Example 2: If another similar property in the same area as used for Example number one generates gross monthly rents of $3,250, the approximate value of the property is $260,000 (the GRM is still 80).

Capitalization (CAP) Rate: A ratio used to estimate the value of income producing properties. The CAP rate is the net operating income (NOI) divided by the value of a property expressed as a percentage. For the buyer, the higher the CAP rate the better; for the seller, it is just the opposite. Net operating income is determined by subtracting vacancy amount and operating expenses from a property's gross income. Operating expenses include the following items: advertising, insurance, maintenance, property taxes, property management, repairs, supplies, utilities, etc. Operating expenses do not include improvements such as a new roof, personal property purchases, or mortgage payments (P&I).

Example 1: For a rental property that has a NOI of $85,000 and a sales price of $750,000, the CAP rate is 11.3%.

Since mortgage payments are not included in the NOI, it is important that the investment provides enough cash flow to cover these if it is to be financed. In past years, commercial investors would not even consider properties with a CAP rate of less than 10%, and a premium was placed on properties which offered a CAP rate of 16% or more (again, contact me via email through my website if you happen to know of any of these—they are hard to come by these days). However, with the appreciation balloon (bubble) of the past decade, it is not uncommon to see investors over paying for a 4 to 5% CAP rate, hoping that the property will appreciate in the future.

Sample Return on Investment (ROI) Analysis
Actual Residential Rental Property Owned, Managed & Sold by the Author

Year	Rent Income	Mortgage Interest	Other Expenses	Total Expenses
1997	$ 6,042	$ 956	$ 2,239	$ 3,195
1998	$17,540	$ 11,263	$1,629	$ 12,892
1999	$22,450	$ 10,848	$ 6,068	$ 16,916
2000	$22,103	$ 10,398	$ 1,849	$ 12,247
2001	$18,815	$ 9,907	$ 6,196	$ 16,103
2002	$24,844	$ 9,373	$12,822	$ 22,195
2003	$29,938	$ 8,791	$ 9,685	$ 18,476
2004	$ 8,640	$ 3,479	$ 1,135	$ 4,614
Totals	$150,372	$ 65,015	$41,623	$106,638

Purchase Date:	10/22/1997
Purchase Price:	$150,000
Sale Date:	5/3/2004
Sale Price:	$213,654
Months Owned:	80
Cash Down Pmt:	$15,000
Sale Profit:	$63,654

Annualized Cash-on-Cash Returns:

Operating Return	5%
Sale Return	64%
Overall Return	69%

Principal Payments	Cash Flow	27.5 Year Depreciation	Taxable Profit/Loss	Cash/Cash Return	CAP Rate
$ 373	$ 2,474	$ 1,138	$ 1,709	16%	2%
$4,689	$ (41)	$ 4,909	$ (261)	0%	7%
$5,103	$ 431	$ 4,909	$ 625	3%	8%
$5,555	$ 4,301	$ 4,909	$ 4,947	29%	9%
$6,046	$ (3,334)	$ 4,909	$ (2,197)	-22%	6%
$6,580	$ (3,931)	$ 4,909	$ (2,260)	-26%	6%
$7,162	$ 4,300	$ 4,909	$ 6,553	29%	9%
$3,168	$ 858	$ 1,151	$ 2,875	6%	4%
$38,676	$ 5,058	$31,743	$ 11,991	34%	8%

Overall Return on Investment:

Operating Return	$43,734
Sale Return	$63,654
Overall Return	$107,388
Total ROI	72%
Annualized ROI	11%

CAP Rate (Average): 8%

CHAPTER 5
CAR BUYING AND FINANCING

In previous chapters, we have talked about a variety of professions: mortgage brokers, credit repairers, real estate agents, etc. While by and far, people are honest and working to do the right thing for their customers, there are, unfortunately, some bad eggs in each and every bunch and folks will tell you horror tales about people in all of these professions. But no profession gets maligned as much as the stereotypical car salesman. Is it fair? Well, yes and no. By and large, airline food isn't very good, nor is high school cafeteria food. Does this mean that schools and airlines intentionally recruit really bad cooks? No. It's just the problems with a system where a mass quantity of people (travelers or students) must get fed a mass quantity of food—quickly and cheaply. So yes, while there are many fine and decent people who apply for sales jobs at car dealerships; in my experience, this has been the exception and not the rule. The car-buying game itself is an ugly one. The irony is that a truly good car salesman *and* dealership (i.e. one who uses a consulting approach and not just that of a hustler), will have a line of people wanting to buy cars and more referrals than he would be able to handle.

On a personal note, I absolutely hate the traditional and stereotypical car buying experience. You might think that a person like me who enjoys business would relish the opportunity to go mano-a-mano with a car salesman, seeing who can out-muscle the other over a dollar. No way. You can have it. It's demeaning and it's nauseating. I have better things to do with my time and there are better ways to do it, which I will explain.

I have had the pleasure of befriending a number of owners of car dealerships. Every one of them is a fine gentleman. It's the system that's broken. It is a very legitimate product sold by some of the most illegitimate means possible. A car is a high-end product. Its manufacturing requires highly skilled engineering and design; creativity, and technology at its finest. This is not something you can easily do for yourself—darn near impossible, in fact. So why the problem; the conundrum of a high-level product sold in such a snarky way? I wish I had the answer.

Unlike a real estate agent or a property appraiser, a car salesman requires little to no training, is only loosely (if at all) licensed or regulated, and is only minimally overseen by the government in his workplace duties. Even *manicurists* need licensing, training, and governmental oversight in most states. They're dealing with fingernails. The prices for their services are usually clearly posted on a sign on a wall the moment you walk into their salon. But selling something as expensive, complex, and dangerous as a car? It's the Wild, Wild West out there, and it has been forever. You're on your own, Jack.

In my experience, buying a car through the traditional means is an unpleasant and complicated experience. And who is at the greatest disadvantage when buying a car? The poor, the trusting, the naïve, and the honest—and the busy; folks too darn busy to go through such contrived contortions as they try to fend off trick after trick after trick, just trying to pay an honest price for a means of transportation. You.

But we must play with the cards we are dealt. Car buying may even take more time and effort insofar as tedious research than even purchasing real estate. If you fail to put in that effort, you might as well just hand the man (or woman) your wallet.

Research

Nuts and bolts time: Due to the power of the Internet, you can easily find out everything there is to know about every make and model of car that is or has ever been made. You can find out *exactly* what the car dealer paid for it. You can find out what rebates there are, you can, with a bit of time and effort, learn more about that car you've had your eye on than the guy trying to sell one to you. And when you go to buy a car, this is exactly what you have to do.

This should all be done in advance. Think about what kind of car you want and need. Don't wait until you go onto the lot to ponder whether you want a sedan or a minivan. Figure it out ahead of time. If you really have no clue as to what's out there, go visit car lots when they are closed. You've seen them. They can't put the cars away at night—they're too big. Stroll around on a Sunday or after hours. Assess your needs, and then see what's around.

Once you've found something you like, it is easy to find competitors. Almost every car is in a "class." If you find a particular Nissan model you like, Honda, Chrysler, Volkswagen, and half a dozen other manufacturers will have a comparable model. Check them all out online. See how they compare. Learn all the features and options. Find out how the experts, as well as the bloggers, have rated them. Study, study, study. Don't go to a car lot to ask questions. You can find the answers on your own. Knowledge is power. There's nothing they know on the lot that you can't find online.

It goes without saying that all this studying should include cost analysis. One manufacturer's car in the class you desire may be priced 25% higher than another manufacturer's. But is it 25% better? And if so or if not, by what standards? What are *your* priorities? Is it just price? Or is it horsepower? What about gas mileage? How have older models of the same make and model held their value? What about customer satisfaction after five years? It's all on the Internet.

One last item to research: Check out your local situation with auto sales taxes. Occasionally, the tax, if it exists where you are, fluctuates from city to city, county to county. Learn about this and find out if it affects where you buy the car or where you register it. If it is a registration issue, it may be cheaper to register it where you work or have an office versus where you live. I have seen sales tax rates in different areas within the same state vary by as much as 5%. This can mean a total price fluctuation of hundreds of dollars—real money.

Financing First

I'm giving this all to you in chronological order. Notice how we still have not stepped foot onto a car lot during regular business hours.

You're still not there.

Before shopping for a car, shop financing first. Know exactly how you are going to pay for the car before buying the car. The people who do it the other way around are generally not pleased with the end result.

In a perfect world, everyone would pay cash. Unfortunately, this is rarely possible.

- **There are 4 variables when buying a car:**
- **Price**
- **Down payment**
- **Monthly payments**
- **Trade-in**

As you can see, three of the four variables have something to do with financing. In fact, most car salesmen have what they call a "4-square worksheet." This is a rubric where they figure out how and where they can make their money off of you. If you whittle down the sales price, can they make it up on the trade-in? Or maybe on the down payment or the monthly payments? Dealers like to use the values in the Kelly Blue Book to sell you a car, but the NADA Guide for your trade-in. It's like a shell game.

The first way you beat the system is to reduce their four variables. The very best scenario is to drive them down to only one variable: price.

Then you can travel from dealership to dealership and be able to haggle on one common point and one point alone: How much for this car? Period. If they see that your hot button is getting a lot for your trade-in because you are emotionally attached to it or because you claim to have taken really good care of it, they may "over allow" the value on your trade, only to make it up on the price of the car. Reducing the negotiating variables is the key to success in this game.

So, if you can pay cash, you have immediately eliminated three out of four variables. But maybe you don't have that kind of money. If that's the case, let's look carefully at those other three variables. If you don't do this before walking onto the car lot during regular business hours, you may be a sitting duck.

First off, realize there are numerous other places to get car financing than at the car dealership. Having the car dealer finance you is putting two variables into play: down payment and monthly payments. The price of the car is a constant, so now you have three out of four. Bad news.

Car dealerships LOVE to finance your car, for the above reason. Many dealerships concentrate more of their advertising dollars on financing than on the cars themselves. You've seen the ads: "Bad credit? Been turned down for a loan? Then come to Sammy's Car Corral and we will have you driving away in a brand new car!" **The rich get richer and the poor get poorer because the world preys on the ignorance of the uneducated consumer.**

You should also beware of the "Buy Here, Pay Here" lots if you have less than perfect credit. Generally, these lots will finance you out of their own funds (usually at approximately 21% interest), but if you are even one day late with your payment you risk a repossession. Even if you do pay on time, it will likely not help your credit as many of these types of lots do not report to the credit bureaus. Finally, most of their cars will not be re-conditioned in any manner and will come without a warranty of any kind; you may have to learn the hard way the definition of "as is, where is."

Financing is often one of the first things a car salesman talks to a buyer about. This should tip you off. It can be a big profit center for them. Have your money matters in order *before* you get to the lot.

To understand better why this is so, realize that a car dealership usually has numerous sources of financing. You may believe it is only through the car manufacturer, but that is rarely the case. Furthermore, while they may advertise 0% financing or 1.99% financing, that is not guaranteed for all applicants, just like the come-ons from mortgage companies. The problem is, once you've gotten this deep into the process, it becomes increasingly difficult to extricate yourself from a deal when the dealership's financing guy comes back and says, "Well, we ran your credit information and we can definitely finance you, just not at 1.99%. The best we can do for you is 12%."

A dealership may have a dozen or more different financing sources, including multiple banks and credit unions. They run your credit numbers, get numerous quotes, and *then they often times add additional percentages to those quotes, or get a substantial commission back from the lender.*

Example: The dealership runs your numbers and Bank A agrees to loan you money for 6% interest. Bank B agrees to loan you money at 8% interest. The finance guy at the dealership tells you the best he can do is 8%. He then sets you up at Bank A. Bank A gets 6% interest, the dealership gets 2% interest (as an up-front commission payment), and you pay a total of 8% when you could have gotten 6%. *But you're never going to know this.* The dealership is under no obligation to share their internal numbers with you. You are using them as a loan broker on your behalf. All you have the power to do is say yes or no; take the deal or don't take the deal.

So if not from the car dealer, where *should* you get a car loan? If cash is the best and dealer financing may be the worst, here are the other four major players:

- **Bank financing**
- **Credit Union financing**
- **Online lenders**
- **Home equity loan or line of credit**

Banks: Most people already have a relationship with their bank. Maybe your bank is having a car loan promotion. Give them a call and see what they can do. Your bank will often ask you what make and model of car you are intending to buy, and whether it is new or used (I am not sure how the money knows the difference). Know this in advance. The bank will pull out the "blue book," the master bible of car values, and see what the "true" value of the car is. If you are buying a used car, they are more likely to have concerns about the make, model, and year of the car, since they don't want to loan you money that far exceeds the true and accepted value of the car. With a new car, this is not as much of an issue. Occasionally, though, the lender, be it a bank, a credit union, or an online lender, will only be concerned with the dollar amount you wish to borrow. Obviously, then, have an idea of what amount you want to borrow.

It has been my experience that **credit unions** actually outdo banks when it comes to car loans, particularly if you have good credit. The only downside to this is that many of them only offer their services to their members. However, many now have much more liberal requirements to join. Check this out.

Online lenders are the newest member of the club. I'm not talking about some crazy, no-name spam blaster offering to lend money. There are very large, well-known banks that advertise heavily on the Internet. They're trying to gain customers from outside of where they have brick and mortar branches, and car loans online has been a great way for them to do it. I have found many of these lenders to outdo even local credit unions when it comes to car loans. They can offer lower rates because they have lower overhead and specialize solely in car loans. The process is the same as if you walked into a local bank or credit union building. You fill out an application, you tell them what you are buying and at what approximate price, they run your credit numbers, and you get a price quote. This is a real pre-approval you can take into any car dealership, allowing you to act and be treated like a cash customer. Since these banks are heavily advertising car loans, they know the process and have lots of money to loan car buyers. They usually make the transaction very quick and very enticing to borrowers.

Lastly, we have **home equity loans or lines of credit (HELOC).** We've talked about them before. You borrow against your house and then your interest is likely tax deductible. Very nice.

In all of these cases, you are borrowing from some entity that has no relationship to your car dealer. Their only relationship is with you. That is what you want. In many cases, what you receive is, literally, a blank check, approved up to a certain dollar amount. All you have to do is fill in the name of the dealership once you've finalized the deal.

Almost all car financing is credit score driven. Thus, just like when getting a home mortgage, pull your credit score before looking for car financing so that you have an idea of where you stand before people start throwing deals at you. Don't take some other institution's word for what kind of credit you have. Know it in advance. This will also allow you to see if there are any mistakes on your credit report. If there are, it could take a month or two to clear them up and you don't want to have to take a bad deal because there is something bogus on your report. Different lenders use different credit bureaus and it is possible for your credit score to vary by as many as one hundred points between them; this could be the difference between 14% interest and 6.25% interest, so make sure that you check all three scores in advance!

Now, what if you do come in with your financing in place, but the dealer has that tantalizing "0% financing" sign waving overhead? What you could do is tell them you already have financing, negotiate the one variable of your deal (price), *then* show them your financing deal and ask them, "Can you beat this?" Once in a while, they can and will. Give it a try. Dealers *sometimes* can actually get you the best financing deal, just due to their sheer volume with certain lenders. Just be sure that you shop around first.

Another catch to low dealer interest rates is a short amortization period. You may have to pay it all back in only a year or two, whereas most car loans are for four or five years. This can cause some very high monthly payments.

One last thing to totally scare you away from dealer financing. In the upcoming section on "Psychological Warfare," I mention "**spot** delivery." Without giving too much away, the way it pertains to financing is that car dealers frequently shake hands with a buyer on a deal, then send you on your merry way, allowing you to drive the new car off the lot. Fine. But then he calls you a week later and tells you, "Sorry, but that 1.99% financing I thought I could get you got turned down. The best I can do is 12%." You're already driving the car! You've owned it a week. What do you do now? You scream and complain. The salesman informs you that the papers you signed said, "Subject to credit approval." Well, your credit wasn't quite approved.

You have two choices. Either you can roll over and agree to pay the 12% interest, or you can give the car back. If you choose the latter, you will most likely be charged some sort of "return charge" or rental charge, as well as some excessive fee for the mileage you put on the car. A cost of $50 per day plus $.50 per mile is typical. I have even heard of people getting sued by the car dealer.

If you are doing dealer financing, do not drive the car off the lot until the financing has been completely and totally approved, and you have signed the actual promissory note with the rate, payment, price and all other pre-determined numbers TYPED in on it. Obviously, you should also be sure that you receive a copy.

Although this takes us out of chronological order, there is also the phenomenon of auto "**refinancing**." This is geared at people who have already purchased a car and are paying a terribly high interest rate due to either a poor credit score or simple naïveté. Sometimes you'll see advertisements for companies like this; sometimes these companies buy a database that lists people who are paying high interest rates and *they* will call *you*. Companies like this are worth looking into, but be wary. On the plus side, they are often brokers who work with numerous banks and can get lots of quotes for you. On the negative side, these companies usually make their money by charging a processing fee. Add that processing fee onto whatever interest rate they can get you in order to calculate the APR, *then* see if they're able to get you a better deal. Again, you can also get an auto refinancing quote from your local bank or credit union for comparison purposes.

Trade-ins

Next variable elimination: Trade-ins. **Using your old car as a trade-in at the lot where you are buying your new car should usually be a last resort.** Even if you haggle a good price on the trade, I can almost guarantee you will get financially assaulted somewhere else on the deal. You've left the salesman and his manager too many opportunities to get you; it's just how the business works.

There is one financial planning aspect of this deal I must mention, though. If you live in a state where there is sales tax on cars, the value of your trade-in is usually exempted from sales tax. Example:

Car you wish to purchase:	$ 40,000
Value of your trade-in:	$ 15,000
Amount upon which you pay sales tax:	$ 25,000

Amount upon which you would pay sales tax had you not used the trade-in: $40,000

Calculate the sales tax in your city, county, or state and factor this in to your overall planning. This is literally like a 1031 exchange for cars. If you sell your old car privately, you are not entitled to this benefit. Because of this, you may want to consider a trade-in if the car you are replacing is of substantial value. For example, a $30,000 trade-in may save you upwards of $2,400 in sales tax, and that is probably the premium you would get for it if you sold it on your own, so it is about a wash. However, if you are considering a trade-in of a car for $2,000, you may be able to sell that privately for double and the lack of tax savings is negligible.

If this situation pertains to you, I would still not offer up information about your desire to trade-in early on in your negotiations. It is one of the first questions the salesperson will ask. Avoid it. Either say, "No, I have no trade-in," or "Well, I may have something to trade, but I'm not really sure about it at this time. Let's move on to something else." Then continue focusing on the sales price of the new car. Once you've established the sales price you want, *then* toss in that you have something to trade.

The most profit dealers make is on trade-ins. That's where they generally make their money.

If you do have a car you want to get rid of in order to have more cash for your new car purchase, consider selling your old car privately. Yes, there are downsides to this. You have to put out an ad either in the local paper, on the Internet, or both. You may have to meet strangers, some of whom may be stranger than others. If you don't want strangers coming over to your house to see your car, you may arrange to meet them in a neutral place. But then they may not show up and you've wasted your time. A lot of this is like selling your home without a real estate agent. The upside is you may get a good price without having to split it with anyone else. The downside is it eats up your valuable time.

For those not interested in putting a lot of time into private sales, there are private sales brokers who can assist. There is also the concept of simply selling to a place that buys a lot of used cars. With the private sales broker, you will be paying them a commission; with the lot that buys a large number of used cars, while you may have the advantage of it being a simple deal (you are only selling them your old car, period; no issues about new cars, financing, etc.) they are notorious for being the lowest possible bidder. I would only resort to this if you need to turn the transaction around immediately regardless of the sales price.

I've actually used eBay to buy and sell cars and I've had very good experiences.

Another potential drawback to private party sales is that, as the seller, you don't want to get into a financing situation—not unless it is a person you know, and frankly, even then you may run into big headaches. I would recommend pre-qualifying a potential buyer over the phone or Internet before wasting time with them. Either give them the selling price or the selling price range and ask them how they plan to pay for it if it meets their expectations. If they tell you something like, "Well, if I like it, I'll go down to the bank and <u>see</u>

(key word) if I can get a loan," tell them to arrange financing first before coming to see you. You don't necessarily need someone to come to your house with $10,000 cash, sight unseen, but you also don't want to reach an agreement with someone, then have to wait a month or two while they try to get financing. If you need that money for your new car purchase, it hangs you up tremendously.

Psychological Warfare

A car purchase should not be rushed nor should it be emotional. Mindset is key. You cannot fall in love with a car. There are others. There are also innumerable places to buy the same exact car.

In car buying, you must be prepared to walk away at any time during the process. This is a hard thing for most people to do. Dealers know that they have an 80% better chance of getting you to buy a car once you are actually there. But you must constantly repeat to yourself: "I can buy it somewhere else. I can buy it somewhere else." **Walking away is the ultimate weapon.** It is the nuke in your arsenal. It completely changes the playing field in your favor.

Your time is valuable. Car dealers know this. That is why they use it against you. A favorite tactic of the car salesman is to keep you waiting. Sure, they may be all over you when you first walk onto the lot. But after that, it's wait, wait, wait. There's a reason for this. The longer you wait, the more you look at your watch. The more you look at your watch, the more they feel you losing self-control. They know that other things will begin creeping into your mind. You have other places to go; other things to do. You begin to lose your focus. You're liable, once they come back to you, to rush through things just to get the heck out of there. And that's exactly what they want you to do. They want you to start melting down and saying, "Whatever, okay," to all kinds of ridiculous things they start tossing your way: extended warranties, rust-proofing, you name it.

This all begins once you have stepped off the lot and back into the showroom. They place you in (I swear this is what they call it) "the box"—a little cubicle. Sure, it looks innocent enough. There may be a bud vase on the desk and a picture of the salesman's loving family. It's all a ploy, though; no different than water torture. They are wearing you down, but politely. Even the family picture on the desk may be a ploy. How could a nice family man like this be a stone-cold game-player, sucking dollars out of your pocket like an industrial vacuum cleaner?

Again, remember that your best defense is the walk-out. This is not to say you should be in a rush to make your purchase and go, but remember that the game from the car salesman's point of view is to always have you stay a little longer than you really want to. That can mean stretching twenty minutes to thirty, or two hours to three. It's all relative. So when you get antsy, stand up and start back toward your car. I guarantee, the salesman will suddenly reappear and come running after you. Don't get mad; just tell the man (or woman) where you're coming from.

The closer you are to the end of the deal, the more likely it is you'll be tossed off to another staffer. You rarely consummate the deal with the salesperson you began with. A salesperson on the floor at a dealership has probably only been there for a few months at most. If they are good, they usually move up rather quickly, so finding a veteran floor salesperson is extremely rare. Expect each new person to contradict whatever the previous person agreed to. Then get up and walk out if you have to. They will usually give chase and the transaction will get back on track. If you really do have somewhere else to be at a certain time, just get up and go. If you have given them any personal information by this time, they will be calling you non-stop once you get back home or to your office. If you want to go back, that's your choice. I'm not above saying, "I will return tomorrow at eleven am to finish up. I know that what we have left to do should take only fifteen minutes. If I am not out of your office in fifteen minutes, you've lost the sale." Or don't go back. Buck the system. Personally, this is the part of the game I hate and refuse to play.

If you move for the door, whatever you do, do not allow them to "do you a favor" and take the car you had planned to buy home with you. This is a variation on the trick called "spot delivery."

The **"spot delivery"** is a technique that some unscrupulous car dealers use to get you to take delivery of a vehicle immediately after you agree on a car deal. Car dealers know that if you make a deal, then wait a day or two before picking up your vehicle—which is fairly common— there's a good chance (probably about 70%) you are going to have second thoughts and may possibly cancel the deal and start looking elsewhere. If you make a car deal and wait a few days before picking it up, you may mention the deal to someone who proceeds to tell you that you are not getting the best deal for one reason or another. You might also start thinking about all those car payments and decide you want to hold off. There are countless scenarios that may cause you to change your mind or get a case of "buyer's remorse." This is the car salesman's worst nightmare.

Car salesmen know they have to get you when you're hot or when you're all worked up emotionally. They don't want to give you time to think it over. They are going to do everything they can to get you down the road in your new vehicle right now. Everything is now, now, now! In the car business there's no tomorrow.

I've recently become a fan of the reality television show, "King of Cars." Basically, they profile Josh "Chopper" Tobin who runs the number one Dodge-only dealership in the nation in Las Vegas, NV. The guy is a car sales pro and a master marketeer; he has his own local TV show called the "Chopper Show," which features his staff dressed up in crazy costumes (i.e. the Blue Genie). The show focuses on the "sizzle" of a car sale. People get to hit the "gong" when a deal happens. All of his customers only seem to care about how much their monthly payment is, rather than the interest rate or the term, or even the price.... bad, bad, bad. His sales staff are all about getting the deal done, but nobody ever talks about finding the vehicle that is the right fit for the customer, or educating them about how the financing works.

Let me expound on this a minute, because it is so awfully, awfully important. I told you how important it is to arrange your financing first. Here's why; here's the psychological battle:

You walk into a car dealership. You see a new Lexus LS460L, all tricked out and loaded with every option. This is a $61,000+ vehicle.

This is not what you came on the lot for. You're heading over to the used car area to talk about that 2003 Nissan Altima. But the salesman sees the gleam in your eye, the look of desire and longing you can't control.

"How much can you afford in monthly payments?"

Let me stop you right there. **When at a car dealership, do not answer any extraneous questions.** Maybe you're a talkative guy and this would be totally unlike you. So what? Different landscape, different you. Outside of "How's the weather?" and "How ya doin'?" every question a car salesman asks you is *for a reason*. Once you understand that, you'll know that questions like, "So, what do you do for a living?" "Where do you live?" questions you hear every day, are loaded bombs in for his arsenal. Don't play. Get past them as deftly as you can without really answering. Talk about the weather.

The worst question, though, is a question like the one the salesman just asked you: "How much can you afford in monthly payments?" or some variation of the same. No matter what you answer, has he got a deal for you! See, he can get you into that new Lexus. Bet you didn't know that. If you can afford, say, $300 a month in payments, which is far less than any standard lease deal for such a car, he can find some way to put you in that car. How? Easy. Term, price, and interest. Instead of having a four or five year car loan, he can put you in a ten year. Anything's possible. Remember, he's got connections to multitudes of financing sources.

So you're thinking to yourself, "Hey, I was going to spend $300 a month in car payments anyway; why not roll around in that hot new Lexus?" Dumb, dumb, dumb. If you agree to his $300 a month deal (which you actually think is *your* idea), you allow him to set the retail price, set the interest rate, and set the term. You could be paying above sticker price, paying 17% interest (when you qualify for 7%), and, again, paying for that car for a decade or so.

If I were to run those numbers for you, you would faint at what you would end up paying for that darn car by the time you finally finished paying for it. You would be able to buy two of them at least. Furthermore, you satisfied your immature wants of today only. No fiscally intelligent person thinks that way. If you try to sell the car after a few years, what you will get in resale will in no way cover the balance left on your car loan. You will be paying for a car some other guy is driving, along with whatever new vehicle you purchase, unless you plan on giving up driving all together. Or…you'll drive the car until it drops, feeling lousy after a number of years because now you're driving the oldest car on the road. Once it finally dies, you may *still* be paying for it. All this, because you fell into the "what do you want to pay per month?" trap. Car salesmen know this. They live for it. Car you love + payment (not price, but payment) you love = fleeting happiness, followed by massive debt.

If you finance for five to seven years, you should plan on keeping that car for all but the last year, as cars generally depreciate faster than you pay them off. You will likely be "upside down" or have "negative equity" if you do 100% financing for five years and then try to get rid of it in three years. **Be sure you can live with the car for the *full* amount of time you are financing it.**

These are only a few of the issues a car buyer must deal with. You don't have to put up with this when you buy a sound system, a washing machine, or a tombstone. But when you buy a car, it's just game after game after game. We all should take public transportation!

The Blind Bid Process

Here's my favorite little trick for car buying. Don't want to waste your time in the typical car salesman's "box"? Don't want all the B.S.?

Get a fax machine. Program it to either go out "blind" (no return number or no ownership on it—your name usually appears at the top of the faxes you send), or to go out with the name of a fictional company. Do not have it go out bearing your name or the real name of your company or employer.

Set the machine to "broadcast," meaning to send out multiple faxes all at once. Then fax out a letter like this:

XYZ CORPORATION FAX

Any Town, USA

DATE: March 15, 20XX
TO: Fleet Sales Manager
FROM: XYZ Corporation

RE: Vehicle Quotation Request

XYZ Corporation is currently soliciting price quotations for the purchase of a new 2007 Honda Civic Hybrid Sedan. The desired vehicle shall have all standard factory options; navigation is *not* desired. Other options not desired, and not to be solicited in any manner during the sales or closing process, are as follows: extended warranty, brush guards, dealer added security system, paint sealer, fabric guard or undercoating. Any exterior color and interior color combination is acceptable.

If you are interested in providing a bid, please complete the section below and fax back to (888) 555-1212 within the time period specified below. It is our intention to complete this transaction within 14 days. Thank you for your consideration. NO CALLS PLEASE.

VEHICLE: 2007 Honda Civic Hybrid Sedan
OPTIONS: _____
COLOR(S): _____
Exterior: _____
Interior: _____
STOCK #(s):_____
PRICE:_____ $
Price Includes all costs, except tax and licensing
TERMS: _____ Certified Funds (Bank Draft)
CONTACT:_____
TITLE: _____
DEALER:_____
PHONE #:_____
Please fax to (888) 555-1212 no later than 5 pm on Wednesday, March 21ˢᵗ.

Let's examine what we are doing here. You get the names of every Honda (or whatever brand of car you want) dealer within a reasonable drive. You get their fax numbers (not hard to do. Try online or even call them. The receptionist will give you the data you want). The more the better. You are telling them EXACTLY what you want. You are telling them you are paying them in cash—they will be providing you with no financing. You have taken away three of their four variables—it's now all down to price only. And the best part—you are saving time and money in not having to drive around from dealership to dealership, playing games.

Does this work? My personal experience has been that 60% of the dealers will respond. That's good enough for me. You put the car dealers in a competitive bidding process. I just recently did this again for a friend. The price differences? The range from highest to lowest was $1,600 on the same $20,000 vehicle! That's an 8% savings—real money!. All of the prices were below the sticker price and I sincerely believe that every price was below what I would have gotten had I gone onto the lots to negotiate.

You can still use this method even if you *do* have to finance or trade-in. *Start* with getting the price out of the way via this method, then go onto the lot only to negotiate that other variable or variables, knowing that the big one is already out of the way.

Finally, another alternative to the traditional car dealer that I feel is worth mentioning is the use of reputable car brokers who do all of the shopping for you and take most of the brain damage out of the equation. These people know the industry, are not brand-biased, know the games (and how to play them) and can usually save you money because they have "wholesale" relationships with the dealerships. Please visit the "Links" section of my website at www.BraunMincher.com for some additional information.

How Car Dealers Make Money

I try to cover this in every section of this book. **When doing business with anyone, try to figure out exactly how they get paid to determine your alignment of interest.** As you've already seen, this is a less simplistic thing than you might imagine at first glance, and seeing the whole picture is important to you understanding where your financial interests are aligned.

So how do car dealers make money? By selling cars, of course (they also make money in lots of other areas such as financing, parts and service, too). But let's break it down. There's a profit on the selling price of the car. This is basic retail. The dealer buys the car for X dollars; he then sells it for X dollars plus $1,000, or something on that order. But unlike most pure retail transactions, there is more to this than meets the eye when it comes to cars.

Would you be surprised to know that car salesmen are often paid a sliding commission percentage based upon the dollar-amount profit?

Example: The salesman negotiates a selling price with the buyer that creates a retail profit of $750 for the dealership. The salesman gets, perhaps, a 20% commission ($150). If the salesman creates a retail profit of $1,000, he may get a commission of 25%. If he creates a profit of over $1,250, he may get a commission of 30%. It's almost like a progressive income tax, only it's an asset, rather than a liability. Thus, it is very, very easy to see how the salesman's interests do not align with yours. Not only is he highly motivated to make a sale, he is *very* highly motivated to get the absolute highest retail profit off the sale of that car. He is being paid a very good incentive to do so.

Once you've finished with the salesman, you may think it's all over. No, not by a long shot. Next you are led into another room, another box, where you get to spend time with the "F&I Guy," which stands for "Financing and Insurance." His job is usually to sell you lots of extra stuff that you may not need. He makes money on financing; he makes money on all the add-ons, better known as "after-market accessories." Rust-proofing, VIN etching—a new one where they will etch your Vehicle Identification Number (VIN) into your windows—a process that probably costs about $30 to do, but for which they charge $500-$600, fabric-guard, undercoating, extended warranties, etc. If someone has invented it, they've got it on their little inventory sheet and the F&I guy will probably try to sell it to you. In each case, the add-ons, of course, cost you more, but the F&I guy also gets a separate commission on every add-on he gets you to buy, so he's a highly motivated seller.

I recently helped a friend by setting her up with a blind-bid fax. From the responses, we picked out a dealership and felt we should have been in and out in a matter of minutes. No way. They still led us into the F&I box. I immediately said, "We don't need this meeting. We already stated very clearly what we wanted and what we did not want." The F&I guy replied, "By law, we have to describe to you and offer you each of these additional features."

There are no laws stating that you have to be offered undercoating or extended warranties. This is another psychological ploy. The best way to sell something to someone is to tell them that you are doing them a favor, or that some "big brother" figure has insisted that you be "sold" this product for your "consumer protection." It sounds good, but it's a scam. Shut it down firmly.

Bottom line: **You generally do not need any of these after-market accessories, and you can usually purchase them elsewhere for a fraction of the cost.** Extended warranties are arguable. I know some people who say that it saves them from un-budgeted repairs, but on the whole, they are simply profitable for the dealer to sell.

As good as the salesman out on the floor or on the lot is, it's the F&I guy in the back room who is the pro of pros. As a businessman, I respect his abilities, which is why he should be feared. The sales manager can also fall into this category as well.

One final sales tactic is the classic "bait and switch." Dealers will specifically buy a stripped down "Ad Car" so they can advertise it as being unbelievably cheap. However, once you get there and find out that it does not have A/C, power windows, a CD player, a sunroof or any other options, you get steered to the more expensive model. Make sure you read the fine print in any ads, and if it seems too good to be true, it probably is.

New Cars vs. Used Cars

There's an old adage saying that the moment you drive a new car off the lot, it massively depreciates in value. The adage is true. That is why I prefer "newer" <u>used</u> cars.

One of the best incentives for me, personally, in buying a used vehicle is the opportunity to deal privately and not have to go through the whole rigmarole of dealing with a commercial car dealership. Me and another regular guy, one-on-one, just doing business. That's the way I like it.

Whether you buy privately or through a dealer, a car that is one or two years old is usually a very good deal. If you are worried about getting a car that has been wrecked, then cosmetically fixed up, **there are on-line sources where you can run the VIN and see the car's accident record. With any used car, this should be a mandatory exercise for you, the buyer.** Beware though, if the car was wrecked and the guy had his "buddy" fix it; that may not show up on the report. The same goes for somebody who may have paid cash to the body shop for a repair, rather than filing an insurance claim. If a car has ever been painted, that decreases its value substantially.

There is a misconception that only poor folks buy used cars. Nothing could be further from the truth. Some of the savviest guys I know only buy used. With car leasing as popular as it is today, car lots are full of low-mileage cars only one or two years old—as many companies rotate their leased fleets that frequently. These cars are usually a good deal. Some of the people most likely to consider only new cars are those who are insecure about their income and feel they need a new car to justify their self-worth. This is buying on emotion, which is *always* a dumb idea.

Personally, my newest vehicle is three years old. Please understand that I practice what I preach as it relates to not having to buy every new car that comes out.

Buying vs. Leasing

The big tease about leasing is it allows you to drive a more expensive car than you can really afford. Car leasing is the "designer mortgage" of the auto world. It appeals, again, to the person who feels the need to be behind the wheel of that new BMW, year after year. I mean, what spells "success" more than a new car every year or two? But again, that's emotions talking, not financial acumen.

Leasing is also good if you are in a situation where you can write the entire transaction off to your business. As I said before, many "company cars" are leased. When this occurs, every aspect of the transaction—from down payment to insurance, to gas, to monthly lease payments—is written off as a legitimate business expense.

The downside to leasing is that you never have any equity. If you own a car or cars and need money quick, you can sell one. You cannot easily re-sell your leased car—you don't own it. Leases also usually have a rather low mileage formula. If you are a traveling salesman who drives all over kingdom come in a year, leasing will kill you. Most leases only allow around 10,000 to 15,000 miles per year. Anything over that sends the pricing sky high when you go to return the car at the end of the lease, unless you have pre-negotiated additional mileage. This is something you agree to when you sign the lease.

If you do put on a ton of business miles per year, go with owning versus leasing. You still get to deduct all documented car expenditures. The key word there is "documented." The IRS requires you keep a written mileage log and jot down every business mile you used and what it was for. This is also true if you lease a car for business. The IRS has a right to investigate whether you really used it exclusively for business purposes.

Whether you buy or lease, or whether the car is owned by a company you own or if it's just under your own name, you can deduct car expenses for business travel. Log everything accurately. The current federal tax code presently provides an allowance of 48.5¢ per mile. Now, gas may be high, but not *that* high. That rate was arrived at in order to compensate for gas, insurance, car payments, wear and tear, etc. Your accountant can assist you in evaluating whether to use the allowance formula or to take your actual car costs per year (gas, car payments, car insurance, repairs and maintenance, depreciation, etc.), then calculate the total miles you drove that year and what percentage was for business, and then list that as a tax deduction. Too many people fail to take advantage of this opportunity each year.

Manufacturer's warranties are usually still in place for slightly used cars. Having less of a warranty is a gamble, but the odds of a warranty coming into play pales in comparison to the depreciation of the car once it leaves the lot. I still say that used is the better deal.

Holdbacks, Rebates, and Incentives

Here are more variables thrown into the car-buying stew.

Years ago, savvy car buyers would go into battle with car salesmen, volunteering to pay a certain dollar amount "over invoice." This was a game of chicken whereby the buyer dared the seller to show him what he actually paid for the car. This information also eventually found its way onto the Internet.

***Dealer holdback* is a percentage of either the manufacturer's suggested retail price (MSRP or "sticker price") or invoice price of a new vehicle that is repaid to the dealer by the manufacturer.** Contrary to what some consumers think, **the holdback itself can't really be used as a bargaining chip.** However, knowing about it might help you get a better deal on a new car.

Dealerships must have an inventory on hand so that consumers can browse and ultimately select a vehicle. Dealerships must pay for this inventory (or the interest under a "floor plan" financing program) when it is obtained from the manufacturer, and the amount it pays is the price reflected on the invoice from the manufacturer to the dealer, the so-called "invoice price."

With the introduction of holdbacks some years ago, most manufacturers *inflated* the invoice prices for every vehicle by a predetermined amount (2 to 3% of MSRP is typical). The dealer pays that inflated amount when he buys the car from the manufacturer. But later, at predetermined times (usually quarterly), the manufacturer reimburses the dealer for that excess amount. This is the "holdback," so named because funds are "held back" by the manufacturer and released only some time after the vehicle is invoiced to the dealership.

Holdbacks enable dealerships to advertise "invoice price" sales and sell their vehicles at or near invoice and still make hundreds of dollars on the transaction. Dealer holdback allows dealers to advertise attractive sales. Often, ads promise that your new car will cost you just "$1 over/under invoice!"

Bottom line: It is good to know the dealer's invoice price on a car. But that information is a little less valuable today than it used to be. Find it out anyway, and also see if you can research what, if any, holdback there is for the dealer.

Rebates are programs offered by manufacturers to customers to stimulate sales. Go online and search them out to find out if the car you are interested in has a rebate promotion going on at a given time. Beware that there may also be strings attached, such as that the rebate is only for college graduates, active military members, etc.

Incentives may include special lease rates, financing rates, or even some form of advertising underwriting for the dealer. Again, these can sometimes be researched online. If you know that your local dealer is getting a lot of money this month to advertise a certain model of car, you can try to use this to your advantage if you come in to buy that particular model.

I like rebates a lot. I especially like it when they come with few or no strings attached. The F&I guy may try to get me into his financing program, even tease me with incredibly low car loan rates—lower than I got online or at my local credit union. But take the time to research all the numbers. Here's an example of a situation I checked out.

	2.9% Dealer Financing	Take the Rebate & Finance Elsewhere
Vehicle Price	$20,000	$20,000
Trade-in Value	$2,000	$2,000
Rebate	$0	$3,000
Amount Financed	$18,000	$15,000
Term (months)	60	60
Interest Rate (APR)	2.9%	5.9%
Monthly Payment	$322	$289
Total Cost of Loan (P&I)	$19,358	$17,358

In many cases you're better off taking the rebate and financing elsewhere at a higher rate.

CHAPTER 6
INSURANCE

Insurance. The word alone causes one of two reactions—sleepy-eyed boredom or hysterical fear. Most people are either over-insured or under-insured. Worse yet, most have no idea which of the two they are. In some cases, they are both: Over-insured in one part of their lives, yet under-insured in another.

Real life scene: You go to a dinner party at a friend's house. Over salad, someone mentions they just had terrible flooding in their basement. "So," they say to you, "Do you have flood insurance?"

A look of panic sweeps your face. *No, I don't think I do. Should I? I mean, I don't live near any body of water. Still...ommagod!* If you are like most people, you swing into action. You immediately go home and...crawl under your bed and start to pray.

Instead of flood insurance, I could just as easily substitute Disability Insurance, Life Insurance, an Umbrella Liability Policy, etc. Most people not only do not fully understand these things, they get bored when someone tries to explain such things to them, until one day when they have a panic attack concerning one or more of these.

Fact: A lot of the aspects to our financial literacy are less than scintillating. Face it, Hollywood will never release a blockbuster movie called, "Catastrophic Care Insurance." But insurance is important and you should never fear the knowledge, nor panic because you do not already possess the knowledge. This stuff is easier than you think, and there are lots of good resources to make it easier to understand, including this book. Come on now, crawl out from underneath your bed and let's talk about it.

Health Insurance

Fact number one concerning this or any other kind of insurance: **The fundamental concept of insurance is that it balances costs across a large, random sample of individuals.**

The science of insurance is that one can track the frequency with which almost anything occurs. Fact: One hundred percent of people eventually die. Do one hundred percent of all people get cancer? No. Is cancer costly to treat? Yes. Thus, a company that sells health insurance can look at the numbers and hypothesize what percentage of people they sell health insurance to will probably get cancer. This gets even more scientific once it breaks down to what age group is more likely to get cancer, where do geographic cancer clusters exist, what kinds of people get what types of cancer, etc.

Frankly, though, we know that the larger the sample—the more people who are in a group—the less likely it is that statistical abnormalities will occur. Example: Perhaps (I don't know the real numbers, so I'm making this up) the total percentage of non-smoking people between the ages of forty and sixty in Colorado who get lung cancer is 2.25%. But if I only select fifty random people from Colorado in that age group, I could end up with zero who develop lung cancer, or I could have twelve people. But if my sampling goes up to five hundred people, chances are that my numbers have a greater chance of reflecting the calculated average. And if I get five thousand people or fifty thousand, the chances of hitting that 2.25% mark increases even more. *The more people, the more statistically accurate the data.*

This is how insurance rates are calculated. This is also how some people bargain for discounted rates for their insurance—by being part of a group, such as when an entire factory gets group health insurance. The larger the group (or employer), the greater the chance that the group as a whole will be closer to the calculated average incidence of adverse medical occurrences. Thus, people who work for a big company such as Nike may get a better deal on health insurance than people who work for Joe's Butcher Shop on Main Street, Anyville, Ohio. The insurance company wagers that out of a large enough group of people, only X percent will need a certain type of treatment, and thus the payment for that treatment will be spread around throughout the entire group. In other words, the healthy people end up paying for the unhealthy (or unlucky).

The one great benefit to working for a company or being a part of some kind of group is that **if you qualify to be in the group, you cannot be refused health insurance.** Let me be clear on this. **If you, as an individual, try to get health insurance, you *can* be turned down by an insurance company.** The most common reasons for being turned down would be a pre-existing condition (you are already sick), an unhealthy lifestyle (smoking, skydiving, etc.), or even age (the elderly get sick or injured more often than the young). But…if you work for the Whiz-bang Widget Company, and all Whiz-bang employees get health insurance after ninety days, then you, regardless of the above conditions, will get yourself some health insurance. You qualified to be part of their group once you worked there ninety days.

Some organizations and professional guilds also offer group health insurance. Check this out if you are self-employed, unemployed, or work freelance but belong to an organization that may offer such an optional benefit to its members. If for some reason you do have a health problem or some other issue that might have otherwise excluded you from being insured or insured affordably, see if there are any exclusions allowed for members of that organization. These sorts of groups may not have all the protections of a group of employees.

Now, allow me to hit you with some **important facts and figures:**

- Over the next decade, health care spending in the United States will double, to more than $4 trillion a year.

- 90% of what we spend on healthcare is spent in our last year of life.
- Today, most comprehensive private health insurance programs cover the cost of routine, preventive, and emergency health care procedures, and also most prescription drugs.
- Monthly premiums can cost from $150 for a healthy, single employee to over $1,500 for a family whose members live a less-than-healthy lifestyle. Smokers pay substantially more. Women and those with families pay more.
- There is a widely reported Fidelity statistic that claims the average retiree will need $250,000 for Medicare premiums, deductibles, co-payments and uncovered drug costs.
- According to the recent United States Census Bureau figures, approximately 85% of Americans have health insurance. Approximately 60% obtain health insurance through their place of employment or as individuals, and various government agencies provide health insurance to over 29% of Americans. In 2005, there were 41.2 million people in the U.S. (14.2% of the population) who were without healthcare insurance for at least part of that year.
- Of the people who show up in hospital emergency rooms, only one out of seven have health insurance.
- Medicare – This is a government funded program to help insure the elderly (age sixty-five and older).
- Medicaid – Instituted for the very poor in 1972, this is a state administered health insurance program for certain low income individuals and families. The number of providers accepting Medicaid has decreased in recent years due to relatively high administration costs and low reimbursements.

Allow me to cover a few simple terms. With health insurance, **a co-payment or "co-pay" is when there is a minimum dollar amount that the patient must pay for every doctor's office visit or prescription.** This can range from zero (no co-pay at all) or something minimal like $5 or $25, to as high as $50 to $100. In the case of a $50 to $100 co-pay, the patient may literally be paying for a basic procedure or medication, such as an in-office well-visit or a generic drug, completely out of their own pocket. Hospitalization or any form of overnight care may have a separate type of co-pay, such as $100 or $200 per night for residing in a facility. The co-pay only covers the doctor's time for a visit in the office (such as when you go in because of a cold or for a physical); the cost for any tests, X-rays, procedures or the like are paid for separately and are subject to the annual deductible, which is explained below.

A *deductible* **is the maximum amount of money per year that a patient pays in full out of their own pocket before their health insurance begins to pick up the balance.** This is done cumulatively and usually on a calendar year basis. For example, if you have a $1,000 per year deductible, it may take you a number of doctor's visits, lab tests, procedures and prescriptions before health insurance begins to pay for anything.

Usually there is a maximum out-of-pocket payment for any single year ($1,000 to $5,000), and there can be a lifetime maximum (such as $1 million, $5 million, etc.). In some cases, you will also have "co-insurance" which means that you split part of your deductible with the insurance carrier after reaching a certain threshold. For example, between $3,000 and $5,000 per year, you each pay 50%, and then the insurer pays 100% of anything over $5,000.

There is no excuse for anyone not to have some form of health insurance, even if it is an inexpensive plan with a high deductible only to cover catastrophic happenings. That being said, it somehow became expected for employers to provide health care for employees as a fringe benefit. While **employers are not required by law to provide health insurance,** they may have a difficult time finding good employees if they do not. Unfortunately, the rising cost of health care premiums is having a very adverse effect on all business and their ability to afford to properly staff their businesses. Premiums tend to rise at a rate of almost 20% per year, every year. Incomes and revenues don't, but insurance costs do. Ask any employer what their main business concerns are these days, and I guarantee that health insurance costs will be high on the list.

Unfortunately, the cause of most of this is the unthinking individual, or what I call "Generation E;" E for Entitlement. Example: You are offered two jobs, both at the same salary. Both jobs offer health plans, but one offers a plan with no co-pay and a $200 per year deductible. The other employer's plan has a $50 co-pay and a $750 per year deductible. Which one are you going to choose? Of course, you're going to pick the employer with the more generous health plan.

That part's all well and good. The bad part is what most people then do with that health plan. They stub their toe; they run to the emergency room at the local hospital. Why? No appointment necessary and it's one-stop shopping. If they need an X-ray, it's there. If they need an orthopedist, there's one there, too. The problem is, emergency room care is priced far, far above regular doctor's office care. But why should they care? It's not costing them a dime! They have no co-pay. And everyone gets at least $200 worth of medical care in a year's time, so there's literally no deductible. Like a hog at an all-you-can-eat buffet, they just smile while they get that toe looked at. There was no motivation whatsoever for them to simply pack it in ice at home, check it again after a few hours, and then, if they really thought something was broken, go to their primary care physician. Nope, they've got this medical Gold Card that someone else pays the tab for. Life is good.

As a society, we are our own worst enemies. When our toe-stubber gets downsized, it will never occur to him that his cavalier attitude about health care may have been the reason his employer could no longer afford the same sized staff he once had.

Believe it or not, it's not the guy who gets cancer that messes up the health insurance system; it's the toe-stubber. Patients with *real* health problems need care anyway. They are a static statistic. There's no gray area of "does he need care or is he taking advantage of the system?"

In my humble opinion, there needs to be a move toward health insurance being for catastrophic illness and injury only, rather than toe-stubbing and diarrhea. As a self-employed person, I have set up my own health insurance to reflect that philosophy. Check-ups are good; well-visits are fine. But if they are free, people abuse them. By making my own co-pay very high and my own deductible high, I have lowered my monthly insurance premiums considerably. If you are self-employed, consider doing the same. If I ever get into a car accident or get some exotic disease, I am fully covered. But I pay for my sore throats out of my own pocket. Some people refer to this as a "**catastrophic policy.**" Instead of paying a lot in monthly premiums, I do gamble, but ever so slightly. Being young and healthy and with no dependents, I have a $5,000 yearly deductible. My monthly premiums are less than $100. So long as I have $5,000 (in either cash or credit) at my disposal to cover sore throats and stubbed toes, I'm good. Anything bigger than that, and I'm covered by insurance.

People will tend to overuse medical care when the out-of-pocket costs are small. If the healthcare recipient is not directly involved in payment of healthcare services and products, they are less likely to scrutinize or negotiate the cost of healthcare received.

Still, there may always remain a basic unfairness to healthcare and health insurance. Refer to the statistics above regarding the uninsured. Technically, if an uninsured person shows up on the doorstep of a hospital emergency room, someone has to take care of them. Hippocratic Oath and all. This is, of course, not free, in the purest sense. You and I pay for it—indirectly, but still, we pay for it.

A bit more about being uninsured. What you've read so far may lead you to believe that being uninsured is pretty cool. I mean hey, you show up at the emergency room bleeding, they're going to patch you up no matter what. But do you really think it ends there? No way.

The hospital will bill you. And bill you. And bill you. If you do not pay, they will send you to collection. All this demolishes your credit and indirectly causes other patients to pay your bills. Remember what you've learned about how credit works. Many of your other financial commitments, such as your car insurance and your credit card interest rates, will skyrocket, costing you tons of money. Continue not to pay, and the collection agency will take you to court. If you have assets or a job, the court will move to seize your assets and *garnish your wages* (this is where the court will legally force your employer to give a portion of your paycheck to the people you owe before it gets to you). The only way you can stave off this onslaught is to declare bankruptcy. **Unpaid medical bills are the single most common reason for personal bankruptcy in this country.** Bankruptcy is not only harder to declare these days due to recent federal legislation; it is the ultimate credit rating killer. **When you play around with being uninsured, you are playing with fire.** Chances are that you will eventually lose, no matter how young and healthy you are today.

Back to employers…**while employers do not have to provide health insurance for employees, if they do provide it, it must be for all employees who qualify by definition of employment.** English translation: There are now laws and regulations on the books that state that an employer cannot only pick out the employees he likes and offer them health insurance. It's all or nothing. An employer cannot discriminate against those who earn less than others—giving a plan to executives but not entry-level employees. And above all else, an employer absolutely cannot give the plan only to the unwell or the well, for this is the basic tenet of insurance itself—that risk must be spread among all. The only thing at the discretion of the employer is that he may require that an employee be employed for a certain length of time before they are offered this benefit, or that the employee be full-time versus part-time.

Some employers attempt a compromise regarding health insurance. If they cannot afford it as a salary perk, they may still form a group and negotiate group rates with an insurer, with the employees paying their own premiums. Unless a better deal comes along somewhere else, employees should still appreciate this because it does offer them better rates than if they were to go it alone. Also, as we said before, you cannot be turned down if you belong to a group. Some go even further and offer a shared payment—perhaps the employer pays half the monthly premium (or a set amount per employee) and the employee pays the balance. As long as all employees have the same deal, it's all fair and legal. The same situation would be true if you got into a group plan through an organization or guild. Since they're not your employer, they wouldn't be paying your premiums, but you would benefit from a negotiated group rate.

A relatively new wrinkle on all this is portability of health insurance. If you have a plan through an employer and you leave their employment under most circumstances, they must offer you the opportunity to continue to receive health coverage. No matter what the financial arrangement was while you were an employee, though, once you have been terminated or have left voluntarily, the only way you can stay on the plan will be to keep up the payments—100%— out of your own pocket. As long as they offer that plan and you offer to pay, you can continue on this way for up to eighteen months. You may have heard of this referred to as "**COBRA**." Impress your friends by informing them that COBRA stands for Consolidated Omnibus Budget Reconciliation Act of 1985.

One of the things about health insurance that is confusing is that there is no single, simple type of policy. There is no "30-year fixed rate mortgage" when it comes to health insurance. Every plan is a "designer mortgage." They're all different. They all have different combinations of co-pays, deductibles, riders, and services included or excluded. Some cover chiropractic care, some do not. The same goes for mental health care, dentist visits, optical, homeopathic care, health club membership, etc. Prescription drugs may or may not be included. If something is not included, it is sometimes available in a separate plan for additional cost—on and on.

This is one of the main reasons that working for a company that has a good health plan and gives it away to you, the employee, for free or for a reduced rate, is great. Big employers usually have a Human Resources person right on staff who handles all this craziness. They negotiate with the various insurance companies who solicit their business. Believe me, it can be a full-time job, especially when that person is also expected to have to explain the plan to employees and be their ombudsman when things go awry (which they sometimes do). Yes, if you're self-employed, unemployed, or free-lance, you have to do it all yourself, but you absolutely have to do it. Life is too risky.

How Do Healthcare Providers Get Paid?

This is where I usually talk about alignment of interests. But in healthcare, it's a little bit different, because we have the insurance companies and their salespeople, and then we have the healthcare providers. Let's talk here about the healthcare professionals.

Just like anyone else, a healthcare provider can *bill* whatever the market will bear. If I can get you to pay $150 to turn your head and cough, no one says I can't. BUT...then there's insurance. While I may "bill" $150 for this service, they may only decide to *pay* me $40.

So what happens? I get this question almost daily, usually from some frightened young person who has just gotten a statement from their insurance company that said that a doctor billed them $500, but their insurance company only *allowed* the doctor to be paid $200. Do they have to pay the doctor the remaining $300 out of their own pocket?

The issue is whether the doctor (in this case) is "**in-network**" or "**out of network**," sometimes also known as "**participating**" or "**non-participating**."

Being a "participant" or "in-network" is like free advertising—except it's not really free. Let me explain. Let's say you need a pain management specialist. You don't know any. You have health insurance. Your insurance provider gives you a catalogue each year or a web address that lists a whole bunch of pain management specialists in your area who are "in their network." If you go to one of them, these are people who have negotiated in advance to take whatever payment the insurance company has deemed reasonable and customary (whether it's fair or not remains to be seen).

On the other hand, maybe your best friend recommended another pain management specialist, but he's not in that little catalogue. He's "out of network." Sure, you can still go to him, but two things will likely happen. One, he will likely make you pay whatever he charges right up front. Have that credit card ready. Then he will give you a paid-in-full receipt that you can submit to your insurance company so you can get reimbursed. The second thing that will happen is your insurance company will reimburse you *part* of what you paid, which is what the *insurance company* feels is the "fair price" for that procedure. Trust me, that price is always lower than what the healthcare professional regularly charges. Or, if you're lucky, the healthcare provider will be a little bit nicer and agree to send in the bill to your insurer anyway, and they will pay him less than he usually charges and once he gets that, he will bill you for the rest. The bottom line, though, remains the same—you will be paying a significant amount of money out of your own pocket. Why? Because **every healthcare provider bills more than the insurance companies have contracted to pay!**

This was supposed to be the wonderful idea behind Health Maintenance Organizations (HMOs). They were supposed to "negotiate lower fees" for healthcare services. Well, they sorta did, but they sorta didn't. See, the "in-network" guys figured they'd make it up on volume. That little catalogue would send a ton of patients their way. So what if they were only getting 40% of what they felt was a fair price—it was better than sitting around twiddling their thumbs, losing money. That catalogue was advertising.

But everyone's business model is different, and every business goes through cycles and changes due to market conditions. And yes, the healthcare field is a business, just like selling cars or building tree houses. What is the incentive for an already successful healthcare provider to accept lower payments? Answer: none whatsoever. So if my appointment book is packed, I'm not going to take any insurance, especially low paying insurance. I'll charge what the market will bear. Some guys start off accepting insurance, then opt out. Others go the opposite way, only taking insurance once their practice starts to go downhill for one reason or another.

So to answer the opening question, if you get a statement from your insurance company (known as an "Explanation of Benefits" or "EOB"), saying you (they) have been billed $500 for a procedure but the insurance will only pay $200 for that, if the provider was in-network, you're off the hook; keep your wallet in your pocket. If the provider was out-of-network, start writing a check. And don't worry that you will have a tough time figuring out the lingo on their statement. When they want money, insurance companies and healthcare providers make things very, very clear and easy to understand.

But there's a trick I'd like to teach you. See, what if a healthcare provider charges $500 but will accept $200 for the same thing from an insurance company—but you're either uninsured or you carry a policy that he does *not* accept?

Try negotiating.

Yes, I know. It will make you feel cheap; it will make you feel like you're buying a used car again. But think about it: This guy gets two vastly different prices for the same service. Shouldn't *he* be the one who feels embarrassed, not you?

I've done this with mixed success, which is to say I feel it's always worth a try. When you go into a provider's office, look to see if there are any signs that he takes *any* type of insurance. They often have decals or signs somewhere. If not, don't be afraid to ask when you make the appointment or once you get there. Mind you, some medical providers do not take any insurance, period, and there's not much you can do there (insurance generally does not cover elective procedures, such as plastic surgery). But there are a lot out there who participate with a few companies, just not all of them.

Ask what the cost for the procedure is. Then ask what the insurance price is. Trust me, you won't get immediate cooperation, but try. Say, "Look, I know you take Oxford Insurance, but I either have no insurance or insurance that you do not accept. If I had Oxford, what would be the charge?" Expect more hemming and hawing. Then hit them with this: "Listen, I see you take MasterCard. If you put this through to insurance, you and I both know you'll have to wait weeks and months to get your money (some providers have been known to wait as long as a year to get paid). I am willing to pay you with this very credit card (from which I get Frequent Flier Miles) today, payment in full, if you can give me the Oxford

Insurance price." I have also had good success with calling the billing office after the bill for my portion has arrived and explaining to them how that is such a substantial amount. They generally offer the option to spread the payments out over three to six months (interest free), and then I ask them if I could get any discount if I gave them a credit card number right there and then. More than half the time, they take off an additional 10 to 25%. I did this recently for a $10,000 medical procedure. I ended up paying less than $5,000.

Now does it sound like a dumb or embarrassing idea?

This is called "***patient negotiation***." You may not have ever heard of it before, but try it. It could be the wave of the future in healthcare for consumers. You have nothing to lose by asking for a discount.

In a recent instance where I attempted this and was thwarted, someone in the health provider's office said, "We can't do that. It's illegal." Bull. I asked them to tell me which law said so, and they could not provide it. With some limitations, patient negotiation is perfectly legal. If a doctor gives his own family free care, is that illegal? No. If he discounts his fee to his best friend, is that illegal? No. Their fees can be negotiated no differently than if they were selling jewelry or steel-belted radials. The key is to be persistent, and as time goes on, health care providers will continue to see the benefit in lowering their prices to patients who pay promptly.

The other issue to understand with healthcare providers (the broader term I use to describe doctors, hospitals, pharmacies, etc.) is that they make their real money on items not covered by insurance. See all those ads for corrective eye surgery? Many ophthalmologists in America are spending tons of money advertising this procedure. But that can't be the only thing they do, right? Right. They do eye exams, remove foreign objects from your eye, treat glaucoma, remove cataracts, the works. But all those other things are covered by health insurance. Health insurance does not cover corrective eye surgery! An ophthalmologist can charge whatever the market will bear for corrective eye surgery, but just like in any business, competition has brought down prices.

Now watch for all the advertising you see or hear about any medical procedure. I can almost guarantee you that anything that is advertised is not covered by most insurance plans. That's why it's being advertised. It's their profit center. In most cases, these are called "*elective procedures*." Elective procedures are the things that put the new Jaguars in the garages of doctors, and there is nothing wrong with this. Understand that the doctors of today have a much tougher time staying in business than their predecessors. Medical school costs more (it is not uncommon to come out with loans of $200,000 or more). Malpractice insurance is expensive. And, dealing with payment issues from insurance companies takes a lot of overhead. No wonder doctors are focusing on elective procedures just to stay in business.

Lastly, there are the horror stories of patients being billed for tons of tests and procedures that they really didn't need, or maybe were not even performed. It's a horrible thing and yes, unfortunately, it goes on every day. Although not the norm, sometimes you'll see where an egregiously greedy provider will get snagged by the authorities, but many get away with it. This is not to say that healthcare professionals are bad people, but every field needs oversight and vigilance. You must be an educated consumer to represent your interests!

This happens a lot with insurance companies because they are not physically in the room with the patient or the practitioner. There have even been fraud cases where the patient has been complicit. Imagine this: A doctor is taking care of you and he says, "Your insurance company allows me to bill them for a such-and-such test. You don't really need one, but they pay me $250 for administering it. If it's okay with you, I'm going to put down that I did one, then I'll split the money with you. How's that sound?"

Pick yourself up off the floor. Things like this are lower than low, but they happen. In the case above, obviously the right thing to do is not only not to participate in this fraud, but to contact your insurance company as well as the state medical board. But most times it is less obvious than this. When you get your billing statement, check to see what you were billed for. Does it all make sense to you, or do you have questions? You have a right to ask; you have a right to know. Unfortunately, when insurance is involved, most patients only care whether the insurance company paid the bill or not. If it was a million-dollar bill, they could care less as long as someone else picked up the tab. This is unfortunate but true, and our society's attitude toward it needs to change.

When the bill is going to you, though, it's a different story. You *must* ask questions every step of the way. This does not mean you need to be rude, but you have a right. Understand what is being done to you and why and how much it costs. If it was any other kind of purchase, this is what you would do. But when it comes to healthcare, we often shy away. I optimistically wait for the day when providers post a standard price list for one and all.

Even if your insurance is paying for things, I would still recommend you act as if you were paying for everything yourself. It may appear on the surface that you're not paying for it, but in truth, you are. You pay for it in the form of premiums that go up every year. If we all did this, healthcare costs would become far more contained. Billing errors are rampant in the healthcare industry, and there are even companies that specialize in auditing such charges.

High Deductible Health Plans (HDHP) & Health Savings Accounts (HSA)

Wow, look at all those random capital letters in the subchapter title. Frightening, huh? Well, they're not as bad as they look, and they can save you a bundle on healthcare.

I mentioned that for myself I have a **high-deductible health plan (HDHP) combined with a health savings account (HSA).** This is becoming the wave of the future and for that reason, there are starting to emerge more formalized ways of putting such a program together for one's self, coupled with other healthcare planning apparatuses.

The truth is, most healthy, non-geriatric people only spend or need to spend about $1,000 per year on health care. This is what the actuarial tables tell us (actuarial science is the science of insurance and probability. It is the methodology of figuring out the rate of incidence of almost anything—car accidents, getting struck by lightening, or catching a cold). So...run the numbers. If you have a super-deluxe health plan with all the bells and whistles, and a low or no co-pay as well as a low deductible—say $250—it may cost you, as a single individual, as much as $500 per month in premiums. That's $6,250 per year (including the deductible). If you fit the typical profile and only need $1,000 worth of care per year, you just flushed $5,250 down the toilet.

I, on the other hand, only pay around $82 per month for my high deductible health plan. I pay for all my own healthcare needs up to the first $3,000 per year. I pay 50% for my costs between $3,000 and $5,000 (this is called "co-insurance"). If I ever exceed $5,000 per year, my "high deducible" health plan kicks into high gear and picks it up 100% of everything above that amount. Thus, my maximum amount of out-of-pocket expenses per year is $4,000, while my yearly premiums only total $984.

A Health Savings Account (HSA) is a medical savings account available to people who are enrolled in a qualifying High Deductible Health Plan (HDHP). The funds contributed to the account are not subject to income tax, but can only be used to pay for qualified medical expenses. HSAs were established as part of the Medicare Prescription Drug, Improvement, and Modernization Act of 2003, so they are relatively new.

Prior to this, there were similar programs called "Cafeteria Plans." **A Cafeteria Plan is a payroll deduction, like income taxes. The money is tax free so long as you use it for health-related expenditures *in the same year you set it aside.*** The problem to this is obvious—what if you don't get sick? Cafeteria Plans encourage people to spend money on healthcare services whether they need them or not. Not a very good concept. Cafeteria Plans are still around, but new legislation has given us better options.

Although both use pre-tax funds, HSA's are an improvement over Cafeteria Plans, as the excess funds are allowed to roll over from previous fiscal years and remain your property. In fact, the excess funds can be used similar to an IRA (Individual Retirement Account). Deposits to an HSA may be made by any policyholder of a Qualified High Deductible Health Plan (HDHP) or by an employer on behalf of a policyholder. If an employer makes deposits to an HDHP on behalf of its employees, non-discrimination rules apply just like any other health insurance program—that is, all employees must be treated equally.

Under current tax law, the annual contribution limits to a HSA are $2,850 for an individual and $5,650 for a family. Again, these contributions are tax deductible, which means that they reduce the amount of income you pay tax on, thus saving you money. If the policyholder ends participation in the HDHP, he or she loses eligibility to deposit further funds, but funds already in the HSA remain available for use.

A High Deductible Health Plan (HDHP) coupled with a Health Savings Account (HSA) provides traditional medical coverage and a tax free way to help you build savings for future medical expenses. When put to work together, a HDHP/HSA gives you greater flexibility and discretion over how you use your health care benefits.

For a plan to qualify as a HDHP there must be annual deductibles of at least $1,100 for an individual or $2,200 for a family. Depending on the HDHP you choose, you may have the choice of using in-network and out-of-network providers, just like any other plan.

When you enroll in an HDHP, the insurer determines if you are eligible for a Health Savings Account (HSA). Those who are enrolled in Medicare are not eligible for a HSA. You can pay your deductible with funds from your HSA, but you cannot pay your HDHP premiums. If you have a HSA, you can also choose to pay your deductible out-of-pocket, allowing your savings account to grow tax free.

On the topic of the tax implications of your yearly spending on healthcare, ordinarily, medical expenses, including insurance premiums, are not tax deductible until they exceed 7.5% percent of your income. However, if you are self-employed or your employer offers a Cafeteria

Plan, you can get a tax break without meeting the threshold—and of course, HSAs are not taxed.

Going back to my own personal healthcare program: Since I use a HSA as well as a HDHP, if I do, in fact, have to ante up that first $4,000 in healthcare costs in a given year, I can take that money out of my HSA, which is pre-tax dollars, rather than using money on which I've already paid income tax. Meanwhile, I put $2,850 per year—the maximum allowable—in my HSA. Again, I do not pay income tax on this money, and I can roll it over and keep adding to it if I do not use it in a given year. This allows me to build up a nice little healthcare nest egg grown with money I never had to pay taxes on. For example, if I gross $50,000 at my job per year, but put in the maximum $2,850 to my HSA, I will only pay income tax on $47,150 in earnings, and this would save me approximately $855 in taxes. This is a great savings plan over time; frankly, you can say it's like having another IRA (we'll get more into IRAs and other retirement savings vehicles in upcoming chapters). **You do not have to contribute to it every year** if for some reason you cannot afford to, but again, if you can, it is a great way to save and avoid taxes. **You may also invest the money in your HSA, allowing it to earn interest and grow even more.** Also, it is important to note that electing to have a HDHP does not mean you *must* have a HSA; it simply means you are *allowed* to have one.

Another advantage to HSAs: While the money must be used for healthcare-related expenses, the definitions of such expenses are greatly widened. For example, your regular health plan may not cover over-the-counter medications, acupuncture, corrective eye surgery, contact lenses, or eyeglasses. The money in a HSA *can* be used for those things and many more. When setting one up, check to see if there are other opportunities, as well as limitations.

At the age of sixty-five, you can elect to begin withdrawing money from your HSA if it has grown significantly enough and you want the funds for something other than medical expenses. At that time, you would simply declare the money to be income and pay normal income tax on it.

The bottom line is that this "wave of the future" is to encourage individuals to be more responsible for their own basic healthcare needs, while utilizing health insurance only for catastrophic care. I endorse this heartily.

Medical Tourism

Medical tourism is a specific term, but before I delve deeply into it, let's discuss those two words separately.

Tourism: You go on a vacation (outside the country). Medical: You get sick there. Does your health insurance cover you outside the country? Maybe yes, maybe no. If not, don't panic. *Travel insurance* is relatively inexpensive, but making sure your healthcare issues are in order before a trip is just as important as packing your toothbrush or your shoes. On recent business trips that I have made out of the country, travel insurance has cost me about $1.75 per day for half a million dollars worth of coverage. When shopping for this kind of insurance, make sure it covers "*repatriation*," which is payment to fly you back home quickly if it is decided by you, a doctor in another country, and a doctor back in the States, that you would be better served getting treatment back home.

"**Medical Tourism**" **is going abroad to receive healthcare in other countries.** This year alone, upwards of five hundred thousand Americans are expected to travel overseas to get their bodies fixed, at prices 30 to 80% less than at home. With places like Costa Rica, the Dominican Republic, India, the Philippines, and Thailand pitching their low-cost care, Americans are expected to help turn global medical tourism into a $40 billion-a-year industry by 2010. This has also created a brand-new business opportunity: medical tourism agencies. Not only do these companies act as middlemen between patients and foreign physicians, but they also find hospitals, schedule surgeries, buy airline tickets, reserve hotel rooms, and, yes, even plan sightseeing tours for recovering patients. Most importantly, they aim to reassure customers that cheap does not equal poor quality.

Many of the practitioners at these overseas hospitals studied at the best American and European medical schools. Also, the top medical schools in countries such as India are every bit as good as those in our country; I have been there and can personally vouch for this.

A patient can go to India for a hip replacement that costs about $13,000, including airfare and a twenty-day hotel stay. The estimated cost in the United States for the surgery alone? $40,000!

The biggest market for medical tourism is uninsured retirees ages fifty to sixty-five for whom Medicare hasn't yet kicked in, the self-insured, and those seeking elective procedures such as cosmetic surgery.

To be sure, the medical tourism business is risky. Most insurance companies don't yet offer medical tourism policies, but that is changing rapidly. Some of the reasons the cost is so cheap is that there is no billing (you pay cash on the barrel), few carry medical malpractice insurance like in the U.S., and there is minimal insurance industry overhead. These things lower cost, but up the risk to the patient.

Some of the ways to reduce the risk are to use a well-respected medical tourism agency, and make sure the hospital you will be using is accredited. Outside of that, though, fans of this concept brag about healthcare like one would never find in the USA: two or three nurses all to yourself, recovery in a five-star hotel room instead of a hospital room, and five-star restaurant food. Worried about a language barrier? A good medical tourism agency will make sure you deal only with English-speaking doctors and nurses. All of this for 20 to 30% of the cost for the same service here in America.

Just like a regular travel agent, a medical tourism company makes its money by getting commissions from your destination. In this case, the foreign hospital, doctors, hotels, and airlines kick back about 10 to 20% of what you spend to the travel agent. Nothing at all wrong with that; again, this is the same thing that happens when you book a trip to the Bahamas for fun and sun.

Life Insurance

As with most insurance polices, life insurance is a contract between the insurer and the policy owner (policyholder) whereby a benefit is paid to the designated *beneficiary* (or beneficiaries) if an insured event occurs which is covered by the policy (i.e., death). Exceptions may include claims relating to suicide (within one to two years), fraud, war, riot, etc.

As part of the application, the insurer receives permission to obtain information from the proposed insured's physicians. This is not a good time to lie about issues such as drug use, prescriptions for depression (even sleeping pills), mental health issues, etc.

Many companies use four general health categories for those evaluated for a life insurance policy. These categories are Preferred Best, Preferred, Standard, and Tobacco. Preferred Best is reserved only for the healthiest individuals in the general population. This means, for instance, that the proposed insured has no adverse medical history, is not under medication for any condition, and his family (immediate and extended) has no history of early cancer, diabetes, or other conditions. Preferred means that the proposed insured is currently taking medication for a medical condition and has a family history of particular illnesses. Most people are in the Standard category, one step below. Profession, travel, and lifestyle factor into whether the proposed insured will be granted a policy and into which category the insured falls. For example, a person who would otherwise be classified as Preferred Best may be denied a policy if he or she frequently travels to a high risk country. Underwriting practices can vary from insurer to insurer, which provides for more competitive offers in certain circumstances.

It was once popular for people to offer to "buy" your life insurance policy from you, meaning, they would give you cash in order for you to designate them as the beneficiary. Think for a moment and you can see the potential for danger in this sort of business relationship. You have a million dollar life insurance policy, you need money, I give you $100,000, and when you die, I get $1 million bucks. Now if *I* run into some money problems and you're still hanging on…Not a pretty picture. Insurance companies know this and are trying to clamp down on it, lumping it into a big basket called "insurance fraud." It may not belong there in the classic sense, especially if everyone is above board about reporting it, but it still causes discomfort for insurers. For one thing, insurers bank on a certain percentage of policies lapsing. Consider this: You have no heirs. You have that $1 million dollar life policy. You're old, so it's costing you thousands of dollars per year in premiums. And for what? It only pays out if you die! Pays out to whom? Not you; you're dead! So you stop paying the premiums. Insurance companies *want this to happen*. It is one of the few cases where a company *wants* to lose your business. Thus, as this loophole closes up, your beneficiary should have an easily explainable relationship, such as blood, marriage, etc., and not simply commerce.

One exception that may remain in this strange category is naming a charitable organization as your beneficiary. If you keep paying the premiums, or if you designate the beneficiary organization to keep them up, and the beneficiary is the church down the lane or the American Cancer Society, insurance companies may have some bad publicity if they try to prevent that sort of thing.

Also, you definitely cannot take out a life insurance policy on someone else without that person's permission (i.e., you could not take out a policy on me because you drew my name in a morbid "death pool" of some sort). You need to have what is called an "insurable interest."

Term Life Insurance

"*Term*" life insurance provides for life insurance coverage for a specified term of years for a specified premium. The policy does not accumulate cash value. In this way, it works exactly like car insurance. If you don't have an accident, there is no pay-out. If you do not die before the term is up, your beneficiaries receive nothing. Term is generally considered "pure" insurance, where the premium buys protection in the event of death and nothing else. Term insurance premiums are typically low because both the insurer and the policy owner agree that the death of the insured is unlikely during the term of coverage. The premium can remain level or increase. *Guaranteed renewability* is an important policy feature for any prospective owner or insured to consider because it allows the insured to acquire life insurance even if they become uninsurable.

A version of term insurance which is commonly purchased is *annual renewable term* (ART). In this form, the premium is paid for one year of coverage, but the policy is guaranteed to be able to be continued each year for a given period of years. This period varies from 10 to 30 years, or occasionally until age 100. As the insured ages, the premiums increase with each renewal period, eventually becoming financially unviable as the rates for a policy would eventually become absurd. In this form, the premium is slightly higher than for a single year's coverage, but the chances of the benefit being paid are much higher.

More common than annual renewable term insurance is *guaranteed level premium term life insurance*, or "level" term; where the premium is guaranteed to be the same for a given period of years. The most common terms are 10, 15, 20, and 30 years. In this form, the premium paid each year is the same. The longer the term the premium is level for, the higher the premium, because the older, more expensive to insure years are averaged into the premium.

Level term insurance is what I personally suggest for most people.

For myself, I do not even bother to carry life insurance. Why? I'm young with no dependents; nobody relies on my income to live. I have enough assets to plant me and mark the spot. There is no other reason for my life to be insured.

Were I to have a spouse who did not work outside of the home, or if I had children, life insurance would be more imperative. The entire point is to have your passing not be financially devastating to your heirs, dependents or other loved ones.

There is another position, though, on this circle of life. Picture being seventy years old, your spouse has passed and your children are grown, earning money of their own, and furthermore, you still have assets to pass on. Do you know what life insurance premiums would be by this age? Around $1,200 per month. Per month! What the heck do you need that expense for? Let the darn thing lapse and use that $1,200 per month for something you'll benefit from—'cause you certainly get nothing out of your own life insurance.

Here's another demographic. I remember back when I was just a kid. A friend of mine—eighteen years old—told me he had life insurance. Sure, it was cheap—about $18 per month. But even then I realized that this was a dumb idea. "Who is relying on your income? You hardly even *have* an income! You could do something with that $18 per month. Not much, but something." He was throwing that money away. If he died, his parents could afford to bury him. Other than that, his income sustained no one, not even himself. Sometimes I actually wonder if people think life insurance guarantees you'll stay alive!

Which brings up the last category of people who may or may not need life insurance: young children. A good argument can be made that it assures "permanent" life coverage, regardless of changes in their health condition or dangerous future occupations or hobbies. There are also several "life events" (i.e., marriage, birth of a child, etc.) that allow the coverage to be increased at later dates, as well as a savings component of the policy. Again, unless you cannot otherwise pay for their funeral, this may not make sense; each person just needs to evaluate their situation. Keep in mind though, a child produces no income; thus, their monetary contribution to your household will not be missed. **This is the main reason to buy life insurance: To pay for your funeral and to replace your income to your beneficiaries if the other assets in your estate do not otherwise do so sufficiently.**

Whole Life and Universal Life

"Whole life" **(permanent) insurance provides for a level premium and a cash value table included in the policy guaranteed by the company.** The primary advantages of whole life are guaranteed death benefits, guaranteed cash values, fixed and known annual premiums, and mortality and expense charges that will not reduce the cash value shown in the policy. The primary disadvantages of whole life are premium inflexibility, and the internal rate of return in the policy may not be competitive with other savings alternatives. Premiums are much higher than term insurance in the short-run, but cumulative premiums are roughly equal if policies are kept in force until average life expectancy.

"Universal life insurance" (UL) is a relatively new insurance product intended to provide permanent insurance coverage with greater flexibility in premium payment and the potential for a higher internal rate of return. A universal life policy includes a cash account. Premiums increase the cash account. Interest is paid within the policy (credited) on the account at a rate specified by the company. This rate has a guaranteed minimum, but usually is higher than that minimum.

Stay away from "accidental death or dismemberment" (AD&D)— they rarely pay because so few things are included.

What makes Whole Life and Universal Life attractive is that they are sold to people as savings vehicles. "It's not just life insurance; it's a savings account!" Well, as savings accounts, they're not so good. Better than sticking money in a mattress, perhaps, but not by much. Also, while you do have the opportunity to borrow against them or draw money out of them, the premiums are far higher than with a term policy. Other income tax saving vehicles (i.e., IRA, 401K or Roth IRA) appear to be better alternatives for value accumulation, at least for more sophisticated investors who can keep track of multiple financial apparatuses.

Now, as to Braun's infamous "alignment of interests/how do people get paid?" section on life insurance. **Life Insurance is sold, not bought.** Agents sell the vast majority of life policies written in the U.S. because the life insurance industry has a vested interest in pushing high-commission (and high-profit) whole-life policies. Up-front commissions to the agent are typically 100% of your first year premium. Fortunately, most states have a right of rescission period (thirty days is typical), in case you change your mind. Unlike health insurance or auto insurance, life insurance does not get renegotiated and renewed, in the traditional sense, each year. So, when a life insurance agent makes his sale, he keeps getting commissions for decades. Decades! And since the terms are laid out right upon sale, there is very little "buyer's remorse" or switching companies. As each year of your life goes by, simply purchasing life insurance will get harder and harder—you're getting older! Thus, all the push is put into the initial sale. Imagine if a diner only had to cook you up one good meal and then you'd sign a contract binding you to them for eternity. The waitress could be rude, the food could be undercooked; it wouldn't matter. You'd be locked in. That's sometimes how life insurance works. Your only interface from then on may be that bill that comes monthly, quarterly, or yearly. After that, it will just be your beneficiaries chasing them for the pay-out (which they tend to be pretty good at, at least if you deal with a solvent, established, major company).

The costs of life insurance range widely. First off, bear in mind how many factors enter in to rate quotes: your age, your health, your occupation, hereditary diseases, etc. But outside of that, shop around. A $250,000 term policy can easily range anywhere from $20 per month to $80 per month—a 400% difference. A universal life policy for the same amount (which is *not* a large amount) could begin at around $120 per month and skyrocket to over $250 per month.

Furthermore, one must consider the amount of insurance needed. How many children do you have? Does your spouse work? Will you need to pay for child care were you to die tomorrow? How much do you have in your estate *without* life insurance? In some cases, *you* are your family's only asset. Without you, they have nothing. In such a case, more life insurance would be prudent—at least until you put more assets and equity into your portfolio. This, of course, is a situation you should avoid or try to extricate yourself from as quickly as possible. **Life insurance alone is not proper financial planning.**

Premiums paid by the policy owner are normally not deductible for federal and state income tax purposes. Proceeds paid by the insurer upon death of the insured are not included in taxable income for federal and state income tax purposes; however, if the proceeds are included in the "estate" of the deceased, it is likely they will be subject to federal and state estate and inheritance tax. The tax ramifications of life insurance are complex. The policy owner would be well advised to carefully consider them. As always, Congress or state legislatures can change the tax laws at any time.

If you are smart with the money you have today and you get rid of your mortgages, car loans and credit card debt and put money into retirement plans, you don't need insurance thirty years from now to protect your family when you die. There are better ways to both spend and invest what you would have paid for monthly life insurance premiums.

Disability Insurance

Disability insurance. So many people assume they have it, yet most people do not. For starters, **disability insurance insures your income.** Your health insurance takes care of your medical bills. As to other issues, sure, you can afford to get sick and miss a day of work now and then, even if you are self-employed and a sick day is a day without income. But if you are laid up for a long time—maybe even forever—what are you going to do for money? How are you going to pay your bills? That's what disability insurance is for.

Let's start off with some important bullet points:

- **There are two major types of disability insurance: "*long term*" and "*short term*."**
- **Short term is usually for a few months; long term is usually until you turn 65 and become eligible for Social Security and/or Medicare, or for the rest of your life, if you become permanently disabled.**

- Disability benefits are generally not taxable income *unless* your employer pays the premiums.
- Disability insurance replaces 45 to 60% of your gross income should a sickness or illness prevent you from earning an income in your occupation.
- You should not shop for disability policies on price alone—it's complicated and you get what you pay for.
- Renewability is a very important aspect to a policy.
- The renewability of a plan is broken down into three different categories:
  - *"Non-Cancelable"* – The premium rates are fixed for the life of policy. This is the best and most expensive coverage.
  - *"Guaranteed Renewable"* — The premium rates increase annually. This is more affordable than Non-Cancelable, but you may be priced out once you reach a certain age.
  - *"Conditionally Renewable"* – The worst. Each and every year, your insurer can raise your premiums to the sky or simply drop you completely.

Regarding renewability, most long-term policies use a *"90 day Elimination Period,"* meaning, you do not get any benefits for the first ninety days you are out of work. This explains the reason for the existence of both long-term and short-term policies. Most people are apt to only purchase a long-term policy, which is more of a "catastrophic" policy, covering you if you should be permanently disabled or out of work for an extremely long time. A badly broken leg, for example, would not cause a permanent disability; you would likely be back at work in a matter of weeks—a month or two at worst. You can regard this as similar to a deductible on your health insurance. You are personally responsible for the initial term of your care.

Most people get a long-term policy covering them until they turn age sixty-five, then go on to Social Security and/or Medicare, a government healthcare program. Others choose to buy a more expensive policy that covers them for life.

So, since we all earn different amounts of money, do we all pay different premiums for long-term disability insurance?

Yes.

The thing to bear in mind when purchasing disability insurance is, "How much will I actually need?" This is a reflection on your personal financial planning. Do you have a lot in the bank? Maybe you don't need so much disability insurance then, even though you are a high earner. On the other hand, maybe you don't want to tap into all your savings were something to happen to you. Also, there's the issue of what sort of lifestyle do you wish to continue if physical tragedy befell you. Further, there is the case of whether or not you have income-producing assets. Some people are able to live off of income derived from investments; thus, they do not actually *have* to work in order to retain a financial status quo in their lives. This is something we should all aspire to, but few of us attain. Finally, you should determine the definition of "disability"—does it mean that you cannot do *any* type of work whatsoever to qualify, or does it mean that you are still considered "disabled" if you are able to work a different type of job (i.e., fast food) than what you do currently (i.e., construction)?

So, for example, I have a friend who is a dentist. His profession earns him a nice living and he wants to continue that lifestyle no matter what may happen to him. He pays $800 per month for disability insurance. Yes, that's a lot of money, but again, he earns a lot and he wants to keep on earning it if he gets into a car accident or has a stroke or something of that nature. His policy also covers him until the day he dies.

By the way, bear in mind the obvious: Once you put in a claim for your disability policy, your premium payments are suspended. How can you pay them; you (sort of) don't have an income!

Bottom line: Some type of disability insurance is a good thing to have, unless you are, as previously stated, living largely on investment assets. The more you are living paycheck to paycheck, though, with you as your only income-producing asset, the more you need disability insurance and the more important it is that you have both a short-term policy that picks up quickly after an incident, as well as a more catastrophic long-term policy.

Despite this, only thirty to forty percent of all workers have long-term disability insurance. Disability insurance is perhaps the most undersold insurance in America today. There is a misconception that health insurance and disability insurance are one and the same, although nothing could be further from the truth. I believe this confusion stems from many health policies mentioning long-term care, as in long-term *health* care, such as extended injury rehabilitation, long hospital stays, or extreme and lengthy treatments such as chemotherapy or radiation. Again, health insurance pays for your health care; disability insurance replaces your income—two completely different things.

Putting aside that the greatest variable to disability insurance is the amount of income the insured wishes to be guaranteed, the average monthly benefit for non-cancelable (fixed rate/cannot be canceled by insurer) individual disability insurance is $4,250, which carries an average annual premium of approximately $1,700. The average monthly benefit for guaranteed renewable (variable rate/cannot be canceled by insurer) is $1,500, for an annual premium of $525. Premiums seem to be rising at a rate of about 7% per year, although, with non-cancelable, that rate of change is most likely to rise greater as the insured ages.

You know that famous television commercial duck who quacks "AFLAC?" He's shilling for the biggest name in short-term disability insurance. Short-term disability insurance, as previously stated, tends to only be for three to six months. The way most savvy people who are reliant on work-income do it, they get a short-term disability policy that has a very short elimination period, perhaps as little as two to four weeks. They then arrange to have a long-term policy that kicks in the moment the short-term policy ends. There is no reason to have overlapping coverage, just consecutive coverage. In this way, they save some money by having an elimination period of as long as seven or eight months on their long-term policy.

There is a rumor around that disability insurance is unnecessary because of Social Security. The problem with this urban legend is that with Social Security, one must prove utter and complete disability, which is the inability to do *anything*. In other words, if you lose your legs, even though you used to make a living as a truck driver, the government could say you could still work as a telemarketer. See what I mean?

Others will say, "But aren't these sorts of catastrophes what Worker's Compensation is for?" Worker's Compensation Insurance is compulsory for almost every employer in the nation to provide for almost every employee in every state in the union. Unfortunately, it only covers you, the employee, for *job-related sickness or injury*. Furthermore, those benefits are limited to the express purpose of patching you up and getting you back to work ASAP. Worker's Comp is also a battleground. Employees who fall down the stairs at work fight to be declared permanently disabled, while their employers hire private investigators to try to catch the employee jet skiing while on vacation.

But consider the myriad of things that could happen to you that could happen *not* due to your employment: Cancer. Heart attack. A major car accident over the weekend. But for as much as I want you to strongly consider disability insurance, the possibility of disability is also one of the prime reasons you should also have an emergency savings fund of a few months salary set aside, and/or a HELOC in place. Think of those Elimination Periods. Also consider what happens if you are living so tightly paycheck-to-paycheck that even two weeks lost income could decimate you and your credit. You must strive to eliminate this kind of stress on your life. You must have lifelines and life preservers.

Property and Liability Insurance

Property and Liability Insurance is also known as "Hazard Insurance." Mortgage lenders require this. Your property is the collateral on their loan, meaning, they own a piece, if not all of it. They have to be sure that asset, that collateral, is insured against fire or other damage.

If you recall back when we discussed mortgages, we talked about PITI. Insurance is the second "I." When your mortgage payments are in a PITI format, you get a yearly statement from your insurer, but it is your mortgage lender that actually pays the insurance premium out of monies you have sent to them. Your lender will usually break up the payments into twelve installments, although most insurers only bill annually. If you are not in a PITI escrow setup, you will get the bill yourself and have one large payment to make all at once, unless the insurer has a payment plan available. Sometimes when payment plans are available, insurers charge a small premium—interest—in addition to the actual billed cost.

Either way, mortgage lenders will be strictly monitoring that a policy is in place. And while you will usually have free reign to contract with whichever insurer you wish to do business with, your lender will oversee to make sure that their interests are adequately covered—they won't let you get off on the cheap and only cover a small portion of the property's value.

Property Insurance coverage can include losses occurring to your home, its contents, and your loss of the property's use (additional living expenses—what happens if it burns down? Where and how will you live?).

Your policy will usually also, or *should* also, include liability insurance for accidents that may happen at the home or on the property. Trips and falls are the most common—someone slips while descending your outside stairs and breaks a hip. They sue; you're covered. This, too, is important to your mortgage lender. If you are sued and lose, again, they do not want the property taken as compensation for the injured.

Typically, exclusions on property insurance are claims due to "*Force Majeure*": earthquake, flood, "acts of god," or war. In each of these cases, though, separate policies *can* be purchased. These can be expensive and it is worth thinking long and hard about them before expending the money. For example, in case of war, you may not have a lender left standing to have to worry about. Earthquake insurance is typically predicated upon your property's location: If you are on the San Andreas Fault Line, this would be prudent. If you are in Eastern Ohio, earthquakes are probably non-existent or incredibly mild.

Flood insurance is a far different matter. Similar to earthquake areas, yet far more common, *"flood zones,"* **also known as** *"flood-plains" or "lowlands"*, are mapped by the county or state in which you live. If you live in such a zone, your mortgage lender will insist that you get flood insurance as a condition for lending. Most commercial insurance companies will not even sell flood insurance, particularly to properties in flood zones. To take the place of private enterprise, the federal government sells its own flood insurance. One major problem for all involved is that the government's payoff cap is currently only $250,000. This means that if you have a big million-dollar-plus mansion overlooking the ocean (or even a modest house in areas like San Francisco), if the local river were to rise rapidly due to heavy rain and flood your home, you would only get a small portion of its value back. Mortgage lenders take this into consideration and borrowers often find that they cannot finance such properties as fully as they would like, having to instead put down all but $250,000 out of their own pocket, while designating the mortgage lender as the beneficiary of the policy.

Another complaint about the government flood insurance program is that some people keep filing claim after claim. Since the government is prohibited from running programs like this at a profit, the National Flood Insurance Program is run at a loss. This loss is made up by taxpayers like you and me, most of whom do not live in flood zones. Taxpayer groups have lobbied that certain properties should simply not be continuously rebuilt and rebuilt, only to be destroyed again and again because they are so precariously located.

National Flood Insurance premiums are expensive, running around $150 per month. Additionally, just getting standard hazard coverage when you have property in a floodplain can be astronomical, when the insurer takes into consideration the location. Yes, those properties with ocean, lake or river views are great, but their cost goes far beyond their simple property value. I met a fellow recently who owned a $400,000 home on the ocean in Florida (not an exorbitant price). Luckily, he did not have a mortgage on it, which would have *forced* him to insure it. He told me that when he went to price out homeowner's policies for his own peace of mind; combined with a flood policy, his premiums would have been $18,000 per year. That's insane! And so, he chose to go without insurance at all. We call this being "*self-insured*." If anything goes wrong, he pays for it himself, and in his case, he had the resources to support this. Some people will actually set up a separate bank account for such a purpose, will pay into it with regularity just like a standard insurance premium, and then arrange with their accountant to attempt to tax shelter as much of these dedicated funds as possible under prevailing tax code.

If you do not live in a floodplain, but have heard tales of people in your neighborhood having basement flooding problems or worse, you may have an easier time finding a private insurer. On the other hand, something to consider is to compare the price of this kind of insurance, multiplied by the number of years you believe you'll live in that home, and then compare that to how much it would cost to better waterproof your basement and other potential problem areas of your property. It may be cheaper to better protect the property than to insure it against flooding. Also, insurance will usually only pay to patch up the problem, not completely remedy it from happening again. Constant water damage will eventually erode the value of your property, making it more difficult to sell at a fair price.

In general, Property Insurance premiums are based upon:

- The insured value of the property
- Your selected deductible
- Your claims history
- Your credit rating (I told you to be careful about this)
- The property's proximity to a fire station
- Whether or not you have an alarm system or fire sprinklers
- What are the building's materials? Wood burns while masonry does not.
- Any multi-policy discounts.

Let's look more closely at the above list. As to deductibles, bear in mind Braun's law of understanding how people get paid and whether there is an alignment of interests. Sellers of property insurance work on commission. The higher the premiums, the higher their commission. **The lower the deductible, the higher the premium, the higher their commission.** See how the logic flows?

A super-low deductible on property insurance might be something on the order of $250 per year. Do you really need that low a deductible? If you raise your deductible to $500, $1,000, $2,500, you usually lower your premiums by 5 or 10% with each of those jumps.

Personally, all my properties have a $2,500 deductible. As both a homeowner as well as a real estate investor, I have negotiated discounts with my insurer by bringing her all of my business, as volume will always get you better prices. Thus, you would be correct in saying that I am "self-insuring" all those $2,500 deductibles. As noted before, I also have high deductible health insurance and I will soon tell you about how I have set up my automobile insurance (hint: It's much the same way).

Someone else might tell you that this is reckless, but I would disagree. My insurance moves are part of an overall plan of fiscal conservatism. I do not overspend on luxuries. I'm a saver. I have chosen to position myself so that I have enough assets and savings so that I won't go broke on insurance premiums. Yes, folks, insurance can kill you. I know, insurance people will tell you that to be heavily insured is what a prudent, conservative person would do. In some cases, I beg to differ.

Consider this: Your insurance premiums do not earn you interest. They do not grow for you. They grow for the *insurer*. I take the money I would have spent on higher premiums and put it in the bank or invest it in growth assets. I put that money to work *for me*. Am I still insured? Hell yeah! But I am insured for catastrophes, not daily annoyances. If I get a broken window, I buy a new one. It's not a thing that happens everyday, but if and when it does, I can afford to purchase a new one—I've saved for it. If a toilet breaks while I'm on vacation and water goes through the ceiling, creating a hole and water-damaging the room below it, that's a big job that will cost thousands of dollars—new floor, new ceiling, new toilet. For *that*, I have insurance.

The only caveat to this is that some mortgage or auto lenders will insist that you carry a particular minimum insurance deductible. If that is the case, the situation is out of your hands, although I still go up to the maximum they allow. You can also negotiate—in life, it never hurts to ask.

Claims history involves something called a CLUE Report. **CLUE stands for Comprehensive Loss Underwriting Exchange. CLUE is like a credit score for the insurance industry.** You can shift from insurer to insurer, but this report follows you everywhere. What are insurers on the lookout for? People who file a ton of claims, that's what. Sure, the need to file claims could be pure bad luck, but more often it reveals a person who either is trying to "jake" the system by taking advantage of insurers, or it is an irresponsible person who does not take intelligent precautions and care for their property.

Just like credit reports, **you are entitled to one free CLUE report per year.** Information on a report generally stays for five years. Check out my website at www.BraunMincher.com for links to where to get yourself a copy of your free report.

People who are claims-free or close to it will pay less for insurance than people with a lot of claims. Now, this brings up another topic for consideration. Sometimes, it is wiser not to put through an insurance claim if by doing so it may raise your premium or cost you your coverage.

Example: One of my rental properties had a sewer backup that caused damage. The total bill was $4,000. With my $2,500 deductible, I would have paid the first $2,500, then submitted the bill to my insurer so they could pay the remaining $1,500. However, if I had one more misfortune within two years, my premiums would have shot up significantly or I may have been dropped by my insurer altogether. What if a year later one of my rental properties burned to the ground? Was it worth $1,500 to avoid that roll of the dice? If I didn't have $1,500, then no. But since I did, I wasn't going to take the chance. I paid the whole bill out of my own pocket and never filed the claim. I figured I'd save it for something more substantial, if it were to happen.

This is a particular quandary for real estate investors. Due to CLUE reports, the insurance industry indirectly forces owners of multiple properties to pay for small-ish things themselves while only using hazard insurance for devastating losses, such as total or near-total losses. Even though you will have separate policies on all of your properties, having claims show up allows insurers to raise *all* of your premiums, or drop *all* of your policies, just like with credit cards.

Is this fair? I believe it is all a balancing act. The perspective from the insured's point of view is simple: Why should I be punished when bad things happen to me? Isn't that the entire reason I buy insurance in the first place? On the other hand, from the insurance industry's point of view, the system, without checks and balances, can easily get out of hand. Want a new bathroom? Stick a T-shirt down your toilet and then flush it. Water damage—the most common non-total-loss claim—will probably ruin your entire bathroom. Your insurance settlement will usually be for replacement value, not actual value. No, that still won't get you solid-gold shower fixtures, but it *will* get you new ones. But don't do this.

I've already bemoaned the over-importance of one's credit score to things completely unrelated to it, such as it affecting your insurance premiums, but I mention it again to report the truth, whether it is a truth we like or not.

Want to build that dream house in the middle of nowhere; be like Thoreau and commune with nature away from noisy neighbors? Be prepared to pay extra for it. Insurers don't like when, say, a small fire will likely cause a total loss because you are so far away from a professional firefighting unit.

Insurers love fire alarms, burglar alarms, and fire sprinkler/fire suppression systems. If you are buying or building, take these into consideration, price them out, and see if their costs are a better investment than higher insurance premiums. Again, since premiums do not grow for you and improvements to your property do, and since what you save on premiums can be invested elsewhere, these can be very prudent expenditures.

Real numbers: I built a pretty nice house a few years ago and installed a sprinkler system. The system cost $11,000—a lot of money, but a one-time expenditure—and it saves me 15% in premiums per year. Something to think about.

Building materials? Don't be afraid to call an insurance agent and get data on what to look for and what to avoid when purchasing property. This could be the tipping point when choosing between Property A and Property B, even if they are priced the same. If building from scratch, get your insurance company as well as your architect involved from the start and share with them your concerns. The right materials could save you tens of thousands of dollars in premiums in upcoming years. Insurers are rarely loathe to pay you and your property a visit. It benefits them as well as you.

Live in a condo? You still need property insurance. Yes, part of your HOA (Home Owner's Association) fees likely goes to property insurance for the general property, but you, the tenant/owner, are still usually responsible for "the unfinished drywall in," meaning, everything within the interior four walls. The insurance you pay via HOA fees will be for a liability policy for the exterior of the property as well as hazard insurance for the exterior of the structure ONLY. Read the fine print. You still need your own coverage.

Renter's Insurance? I say don't leave home without it. It's cheap—most policies are less than $15 per month—and landlords do not provide coverage to tenants. A landlord may, at most, provide coverage to the exterior property as well as a limited liability policy, but if you throw a party and someone leaves drunk and gets killed in a car accident, you, my friend, are liable. You should be insured for that via your own liability policy. In a less severe example, remember that rental units are more often found in less-affluent/higher crime areas. If someone breaks in and takes your stereo, TV, computer, and jewelry, you're out of luck unless you have renter's insurance.

Own some recreational vehicles like jet skis, ATVs, etc.? Get insurance. We do dangerous things on these as it is. Imagine if you let someone use one of your "toys" and they get badly hurt. You get sued. If you have a liability policy, you're covered.

Umbrella Insurance

I won't make bad jokes about umbrella policies being for a rainy day or anything corny like that, but they are a worthwhile investment.

Umbrella insurance refers to insuring more than one property or thing as opposed to insuring only one. For example, as previously stated, you might get a discount for insuring both your house and car rather then insuring them with separate policies. Typically, **an umbrella policy is pure liability coverage over and above the coverage afforded by the regular policy, and is sold in increments of one million dollars.** The term "umbrella" is used because it covers liability claims from all policies underneath it, such as autos and homeowners policies. For example, if you have an auto insurance policy with liability limits of $500,000 and a homeowner's policy with a limit of $300,000, then with a million dollar umbrella, your limits become, in effect, $1,500,000 on the auto policy and $1,300,000 on a homeowner's liability claim. Umbrella insurance provides broad insurance beyond traditional home and auto. It:

Provides additional liability coverage above the limits of your homeowner's, auto, and boat insurance policies.

Provides coverage for claims that may be excluded by other liability policies including:

- False Arrest
- Libel
- Slander
- Liability coverage for rental units you own

I strongly advise getting an umbrella policy. The main thing you are insuring against is a lawsuit, and America is the most litigious country in the world. People sue over everything and if a suit gets before a jury, juries love to dole out enormously large settlements. People who slip and fall in front of your property no longer sue for just their medical bills and loss of income—perhaps, $10,000. They sue for millions—and often get it. An umbrella policy, depending on the insurance company, can give you an additional $1 to $5 million dollars in liability protection for a cost of around $300-$900 per year.

Automobile Insurance

Some of the best advice I can give you regarding auto insurance would be to simply repeat much of what has been said about all other insurances. **Lowering your deductible raises your premium.** Unfortunately, just like there may be limitations placed upon you with homeowner's insurance if you have a mortgage, an entity helping finance your car may also mandate that you have a certain minimum deductible on your auto policy. If you are paying cash, though, the choices are all yours.

Regarding choosing whether to put through a claim or not for fear it might raise your premiums or cost you your policy entirely, there is a lot of misinformation out there. For one thing, if you and another driver are in an accident together, you MUST file a report, beginning with calling the police and having them assess the situation as a neutral party. If one driver in a two-car accident files and the other driver doesn't, the non-filing driver can get in big trouble. If the filing driver states to his insurer that you asked that he not report the incident or you tried to offer money to settle outside of insurance (offered him a bribe?) you can also get in big trouble.

On the other hand, a one-car accident—say, you ran off the road and smacked into a tree—gives you more options. Unfortunately, those options must be decided on *immediately*. For your insurer to file a proper report and decide a claim, they must usually have a police report in hand. If you drive away from that tree, go to a body shop, and THEN decide to report a claim, your insurer may not cover you. You failed to follow proper procedure.

Automobile insurance is mandatory in every state. But does that mean that every person and every vehicle is insured equally? No.

What each state requires by law is a "*liability policy*." Minimums are set by each state, but the distinction of exactly what this covers is *damage to the other guy*. Liability means that *you are liable*. It is *your fault*. If you don't brake quickly enough and rear-end the car in front of you, it's your fault. Claims are filed and your insurance—not his—pays for damages to his car. The same goes for doing property damage to someone else's property (for example, hitting their tree), or hitting a pedestrian or causing injury to a passenger—whether they were in your car or the other driver's car—if you were considered liable for the accident.

The determination of who is liable in a multi-car accident is usually decided by each driver's insurance company, using the police report as a neutral retelling of the tale. Insurers, though, are prone to battle these things out with one another. Being too easygoing when paying out claims can bankrupt an insurer. Extremely negligent liability can also be grounds for criminal action as well as civil (for example, if the police determine that you were drunk when you ran over a pedestrian).

Even when an incident occurs that is, in the purest sense, no one's fault (you swerve to avoid a downed tree during a severe storm and skid into another vehicle), fault is still assessed to the person or vehicle that caused it. Using the above example, if the other car was standing still and you lost control and ran into it, you are liable, even if Dale Earnhardt, Jr. himself could not have prevented the accident.

Some states have what is called "***No Fault Insurance***." This is an interesting concept whereby, again using the above example, you would pay for the damage to the car and driver you hit, while the other driver's insurance would pay for damage done to you and your car. No fault would be assessed, thus the name. These states (there are currently twelve of them) feel this concept helps unclog the court system when agreements cannot be made as to who was truly at fault in an accident.

Notice that all we have spoken about thus far is auto liability insurance. So what happens if all you have is a liability policy and you have a one-car accident, hurting no one or no one else's property but your own?

Open your wallet and pay for it.

This is an option chosen by many drivers, particularly those with older vehicles that have little to no "blue book" value (the "Kelley Blue Book" is the master automobile "bible" that determines the value of a car based on its make, model, age, condition, and mileage). Imagine this: You wreck your 1997 Geo Metro that has 200,000 miles and tons of body rot on it. It would take $4,000 to fix it. The car is worth $0. *Why insure it?*

The insurance you carry on your own vehicle is called "Collision/Comprehensive" or sometimes just "Collision." In the above example, money spent on buying a collision policy for that Geo Metro would be money flushed down the toilet month after month. When you wreck it, kiss it good-bye and use that $4,000 toward a new car; you needed one anyway.

In case you were worried I forgot about something; if you are asking, "Yeah, but forget about the Geo; what about me? That accident broke six of my ribs and punctured my lung," I've got you covered. Actually, your insurance has you covered. Your liability policy would cover your injuries. Provisions on your health insurance might also pick up some of the slack. Add to that your short and long-term disability policies. See how important all these insurances are? While I have encouraged you not to overspend on them, you cannot underspend, either.

Now forget you own an old, dingy car. If you have a newer car that is still being financed, your lender will give you no choice but to get full collision insurance. Even if you bought such a car with cash, if it still has a significant value to you, I would recommend carrying collision. Think about it: You have a new $45,000 Volvo in great condition. To carry full collision (total replacement), it costs you, say, an extra $200 per month. That's $2,400 per year. If it is totaled after nine months, what do you plan to do, reach into your pocket for another $45,000 for a new one? *This* is what insurance is for. Yes, those premiums add up over time, but as the value of the car decreases, so can the cost of the collision component if you keep on top of the situation. And yes, eventually you may decide it is more prudent to do away with it completely. This is the intelligent way to handle car insurance.

The "comprehensive" aspect of "Collision/Comprehensive" Insurance is insurance against car theft, but usually also covers vandalism, broken windshields, a fallen tree and the like. The two are usually bundled together since common sense dictates the following: Why would you insure a valuable car against one thing and not the other? The decision to eventually abandon collision/comprehensive would involve the decision to de-value damage or total loss to the vehicle, whether it was via an accident or theft or vandalism.

Look at state minimums on your auto liability insurance. The minimum is usually set far too low to be realistic in this "sue everybody" society. Again, remember to bring your umbrella…policy. It's good on a rainy day. Research state liability minimums yourself, then decide the best way to cover yourself. This is not an area to be too frugal. Even if you do not cause catastrophic injury to another driver or passenger, if you hit a $90,000 Mercedes and you only have your state's liability minimum of $50,000, you'll be digging $40,000 more out of your own pocket unless you're insured for it.

Planning on **renting a car?** Before you do, check your own policy and see if it covers this. Most policies do. The car rental companies will rarely tell you this and will try to sell you that additional $12 to $15 per day rental insurance. Why buy it if you don't need it? The same holds true for borrowing the car of a friend. Know your auto insurance policy to understand what you are covered for and what you are not. People borrow each other's cars from time to time. Don't do it if you're not insured—the same goes for if you are the lender of the car. Check, check, check your policy first.

Also, check out your credit card coverages. They often cover rental car insurance. Find out before doling out.

Just like everything else we've covered, your past history will dictate the rates you will pay. Auto insurers will take into account your credit score (which may be totally unfair), your CLUE report (still a bit unfair), and your driving record (right on point). DUI's (Driving Under the Influence of drugs or alcohol) will shoot your premiums sky high—usually as much as 300% higher. Another good reason to not drink and drive.

Car insurance policies are usually annual or semi-annual. If you own multiple vehicles, try to set them all to have common expiration dates. This way, it is easy for you to remember when it's time to comparison shop for new rates. And yes, this is something worth doing each and every year. Bring your old policy with you, as well as any records you might have about your past year's driving record or any incident reports. Set up appointments with a few different insurance agencies in your area and see what they can do. You could save a few hundred or even a thousand dollars a year. I actually take this a step further and have *all* my insurances come up for renewal at the same time. Again, the idea is that if there is a different policy expiring every other month, you will be less motivated to comparison shop. If you know July 31st of every year is your Insurance Day, you can spend time throughout July shopping around. This is easy to do. If you buy a new car March 1st, only get a policy that is pro rated until July 31st. That will get you on board with your other policies when you celebrate your personal Insurance Day. And remember, when you can wave the possibility of multiple policies in front of an insurance agent, they are more highly motivated to get you the best deal possible.

Insurers usually give you the option of paying your premiums in installments or all at once. If there is no penalty or interest for doing it on installments, by all means go for it, but this is rare. So, **if there are fees involved with installments, just pay it all at once to save some money.**

Expensive cars are more expensive to insure than cheaper cars. Yeah, I know; common sense. But consider it when you are vacillating on whether to buy that prestige car or the cheaper, practical car. The cost difference will not simply be the dollar difference you pay the car dealer—the cost difference keeps on coming for as long as you own it.

If you ever have anything inside your car that gets stolen, that is usually not covered by your auto policy, but by your homeowner's policy. So, too, if you go with a high deductible and you get $100 worth of CDs stolen, pretty much kiss those babies good-bye.

With collision/comprehensive policies, your insurer will only be insuring the value of the car at the time you insure it. This means that if your four-year-old car gets totaled, you will not get enough money to buy a brand new version of that same car. You will get the replacement value of that four-year-old car. Also, if you heavily financed your car and it is worth less when it is wrecked than what you owe to the bank…tough on you. Of course, insurers have thought of this. They sell a product called "*Gap Insurance*," which pays the negative difference between what you owe and what the car is worth for insurance purposes. If, and only if, you find yourself in this sort of financing quandary, this can be a good idea to explore.

CHAPTER 7
TAXES

America has one of the most complicated tax systems in the world. Politicians will say that this is true in order to achieve parity and fairness, but unfortunately, cynics are often right when they say it has been designed to reward certain behaviors and punish certain others (think cigarette taxes). It also rewards and punishes certain people, often unfairly. It is too often used to create social policy, leading to conflicting "loopholes." Its raw complexity alone favors the fiscally educated and those who are wealthy enough to afford the best financial advice money can buy.

Taxes have been a cornerstone in the history of our country and, in fact, it was the cry of "taxation without representation" that set us adrift from Mother England back in 1776. The Boston Tea Party was over a special tax dispensation given to the East India Tea Company—a "sweetheart deal" that allowed one favored company to avoid the same taxes that other companies and merchants had to pay.

One major problem we all face is that it is hard enough just *making* money. That alone can fill our heads and consciousness completely as we struggle through our days. It barely leaves enough room in our brains for considering the tax implications of what we earn, how we earn it, and where we put it.

In this chapter, let's go over the types of taxes we pay, how they are calculated, and what, if anything, we can do in order not to pay more than our fair share of them.

Income Taxes

"There is nothing sinister in so arranging one's affairs as to keep taxes as low as possible."—Judge Learned Hand, 1934

I shall not attempt to teach you to become an accountant in this chapter, but I will give you enough information to be an informed layperson.

The first national income tax imposed in the United States was in 1862. The Internal Revenue Service (IRS), our nation's tax collector, arguably has more raw power than almost any other government agency. They have the ability to seize property and income in order to enforce the tax laws. When things go badly for you, bankruptcy may stave off most of your creditors, but nothing staves off the IRS.

There are a lot of people I would consider messing with in this world, but one I would not is the IRS. While I agree with the quote from Judge Learned Hand that begins this subchapter, bear in mind the following: You can gather together a dozen tax attorneys and a dozen accountants to debate how to shelter your assets and declare deductions on your behalf. From this you will most likely get two dozen different tax-planning strategies, none of which would likely be considered technically "illegal." At worst, the IRS might read over your tax return, disagree with your professionals' interpretation of the tax code, and mandate that you remit to them more taxes along with some penalties and interest. This is bad, but not necessarily debilitating. On the other hand, all twenty-four of your experts would be in total agreement on one solitary thing: **If you do not properly declare all of your earnings, you stand to get in big, big trouble.** Jail-time trouble. Yes, I know, some people are in what is commonly referred to as a "cash business," and yes, some of them feel no guilt at stuffing some of that cash in their pockets without reporting it as income. But that's them, not me. Me, if I get some random $50 rebate check for some piece of equipment I bought (and took a business deduction for), I declare that as income. I don't mess with the IRS. I have too much to lose. So do you.

With the increased complexity of tax laws, most people probably should use a tax professional such as an accountant, enrolled agent or CPA at tax time. Only those in extremely uncomplicated taxation scenarios should consider going it alone, even with the assistance of well-supported commercial tax-filing software programs such as Turbo Tax, Secure Tax, or H&R Block's TaxCut On-line. A professional tax preparer I interviewed indicated that a client last year, using one of these programs to prepare his own return, unknowingly under reported his income by $40,000. Outside of those options, though, only those just starting out in life with no dependents, no mortgage, and no itemized deductions (i.e., young minimum wage earners who flip burgers) should sit down and try to do their own taxes assistance-free. Those sorts of people luckily can still fill out the "short form"—the aptly named IRS Form 1040EZ.

April 15th of each and every year is known, unofficially, as National Tax Day. This is the date when income taxes must be filed and paid. Many post offices actually stay open until midnight that day to accommodate late filers. I do not necessarily condone waiting until April 14th to begin starting to organize your taxes. No decent accountant will likely have the time to touch you then and if you quickly rush in to try to learn a new software program or do it all yourself, you will probably miss a lot of things and either mess yourself up or make mistakes that will get you penalized.

On the other hand, you Johnny-come-latelies can always file for an extension. The "second" National Tax Day, the one for late filers, is October 15th. But there's a catch: **The IRS allows you to request and be given an extension to October 15th for the filing of your paperwork, but payment of your *taxes* are still due April 15th or else you will be subject to penalties and interest.** This is a classic Catch-22. The reason most people file for an extension is that they either let things go or else they have complex taxation situations where they cannot get all their paperwork together by April 15th. That being said, how can you send in money if you don't know how much? Some wise folks deal with this by estimating their tax payments and sending that in on time. If they are short, the penalties and interest will only be on the amount in arrears. If they overpay, they will get a refund. By the way, a little known fact: If you are getting a tax refund, you do not need to file for an extension and you face no penalties or interest since, obviously, Uncle Sam owes you, not the other way around. But be careful with this one; you could be wrong and if you do owe money, even a slight amount, you could end up owing much more due to penalties and interest.

A lot of people have no idea about some basic tax terminology and what, exactly, we are taxed on. Perhaps this chart will help:

GROSS INCOME (Money received from all sources)
– LESS: ADJUSTMENTS (Alimony paid, IRA deductions,
    HSA deductions, Early Withdrawal Penalties,
    Tax paid on Self Employment, Moving Expenses paid,
    Education Loan Interest paid)

ADJUSTED GROSS INCOME (AGI)
– LESS: STANDARD DEDUCTIONS or
    ITEMIZED DEDUCTIONS (Whichever is greater)
– LESS: PERSONAL EXEMPTIONS

TAXABLE INCOME
x TAX RATE (See Tax Brackets Below)

GROSS TAX LIABILITY
– LESS: TAX CREDITS

NET TAX

Okay, let's go over the terms:

Gross income: This is the raw amount of money that you made or acquired. This would be all of your salaries, fees, royalties, dividends, interest income, miscellaneous income, life insurance proceeds, alimony or child support received, *net* money (profit or distributions) received from businesses, investments, etc. If it was money and it landed in your pocket and/or bank account, it probably begins as Gross Income.

Adjustments: There is a lot of confusion as to the difference between Adjustments and Deductions. Their effect on your taxation situation is similar: They both reduce your taxable income. I have listed on the above chart some of the most common adjustment items. An accountant, tax professional, or tax software program will assist you further in determining what an adjustment is and what a deduction is and what, unfortunately, is neither.

Adjusted Gross Income is a "stopping point," although you are far from finished yet. Despite this, many applications for credit, college financial aid and such, will ask for this figure even though it is not the final figure upon which you pay income tax. Thus, it does serve a purpose.

Standard Deductions or Itemized Deductions: A *"deduction"* **is something that the IRS deems exempt from taxation for one reason or another.** In their infinite wisdom, the IRS decided to make their job slightly easier by assuming that most Americans have *something* in their fiscal profile that would be considered a legitimate deduction. Thus, they created the *"Standard Deduction."* **Standard Deductions range from $5,150 for single taxpayers to $10,300 for married filing jointly (as of 2006 federal tax law).** To simplify this, if you were married and the two of you earned $10,300 or less, you would be considered to have earned zero for the year and would certainly owe no taxes. If any federal taxes were withheld from your paycheck, you would get all of that back when you filed your tax return.

Most people compile their actual deductions, then add them up to see if they are less than or greater than the Standard Deduction. If what they have is less than the Standard, they are allowed to simply take the Standard. If it is more, it would be wiser for them to *"itemize."*

Major types of qualified deductions that you can itemize include:

- Major medical expenses (*above* 7.5% of your Adjusted Gross Income)
- Home mortgage interest expense (up to $1 million on your mortgage, and $100,000 in home *equity* indebtedness)
- Property taxes
- Charitable gifts (usually limited to 50% of your AGI)

- State and local income taxes
- Reasonable and necessary business expenses

A few other common deductions that may require a bit more explanation:
Home Office Deductions: Although not technically an "itemized" deduction, both the self employed *and* employees who use a portion of their home for business purposes can get a deduction for the use of a home office. However, this one scares some people because they erroneously believe it draws unwanted attention from the IRS, but in truth, it is quite legitimate if reported properly. Some of the keys are that a substantial portion, if not all of your business, should be done from your home, and it is mandatory that this business is done in a *dedicated* room used *exclusively* for business, not a shared room. If you sit at your dining room table and write out bills, this will not fly, but if you have an actual office in your house where you do actual office work, you're on the right track. You will need to measure that office, then consider the percentage of the house that office space takes up (10%? 15%?). If you have a dedicated phone line, you can easily separate off that particular utility. In most other cases, though, you will be using that space percentage as a multiplier. Example: If your office is 10%of the total square footage of your house, then it uses 10% of your heat, electricity, water, homeowner's insurance, repairs, Internet, all other utilities, etc.

Gambling losses – Who'd have known? Yes, you embittered gamblers, you can report that terrible run you had in Vegas to the IRS and deduct it from your yearly earnings. The only caveat here is that you must report *all* your casino action, not just that one bad loss. If you won, you are supposed to report that, too. Also, if you lost $3,000 on Friday, but won $5,000 on Saturday, you cannot just list the $3,000 loss. Technically, you are still up $2,000. If you gamble a lot and want to take this legal deduction, you should keep a running tally of your yearly action, with dates and locations. *Gambling losses are only deductible against declared gambling winnings; they do not offset any other income.*

Next we subtract **Personal Exemptions**. Exemptions also reduce your taxable income. Generally, you can deduct $3,400 for each exemption you claim (federal tax code as of 2007). You generally can take one exemption for yourself and, if you are married, one for your spouse. You generally can take an exemption for each of your dependents. A dependent is your qualifying child or qualifying relative. If you are entitled to claim an exemption for a dependent, that dependent cannot claim a personal exemption on his or her own tax return. You get less of a deduction when your adjusted gross income goes above a certain amount. For 2007, this phase-out begins at $112,875 for married persons filing separately; $150,500 for single individuals; $188,150 for heads of household; and $225,750 for married persons filing jointly or qualifying widow(er)s. However, you can lose no more than two thirds of the amount of your exemptions. In other words, each exemption cannot be reduced to less than $1,100.

Now, according to the chart, we are left with our **Taxable Income**. THIS is what we actually pay income tax on (almost). How much tax you ask?

2007 Federal Tax Brackets (Single)
Note: There are slightly different tax brackets for those who are married

If your taxable income is between:			Your tax bracket is:
$0	and	$7,825	10%
$7,826	and	$31,850	15%
$31,851	and	$77,100	25%
$77,101	and	$160,850	28%
$160,851	and	$349,700	33%
$349,701	and	above	35%

For this next step, take your taxable income and multiply it by the proper tax rate and you're almost finished. This multiplication will give you your **Gross Tax Liability**. But you're not quite done yet. Lastly, we subtract out your Tax Credits. **A Tax Credit is an amount**

by which tax owed is reduced directly, dollar for dollar. There are numerous examples of tax credits, but let me list a few:

- **New Baby** – This is not a deduction, but a dollar for dollar subtraction off of your taxes. If you have a baby during a particular tax year, you may subtract $1,000 off your tax bill. You would be surprised at how many late December C-sections are performed in hospitals in order to qualify for this tax credit before the year is up.
- **Earned Income Tax Credit** – The Earned Income Tax Credit (EITC) is a federal income tax credit for low-income workers (under $38,348) who are eligible for and claim the credit. The credit reduces the amount of tax an individual owes, and may be returned in the form of a refund.
- The credit for the **elderly or disabled** is a tax credit that many elderly or disabled individuals may receive. According to the IRS, an individual must be over the age of sixty-five or must be under the age of sixty-five and be permanently disabled to receive the credit. Certain restrictions and requirements may apply.
- Taxpayers with or without children may also be eligible to receive an **education credit**. Education credits are designed for individuals who have paid for themselves, their children, or their married partners to receive an education. The amount of credit will depend on a number of factors including tuition costs, admission fees, books, and school supplies.

NOW you are finally left with your **Net Tax**. If you have been paying estimated taxes throughout the year, or if your employer has been withholding and thus paying your income taxes for you throughout the year, that amount is subtracted from your net tax to give you your bottom line for the year. The reason most taxpayers like to have their income taxes withdrawn during the year in some way or another is so that they are not hit with a huge tax bill on April 15th that they have not saved up for. On the other hand, overpaying throughout the year is no virtue either. Why loan Uncle Sam money *interest free* that you could be doing something practical with? Whenever someone brags to you about what a large tax refund they are getting, remember this: It is a fool that treats the IRS as a savings account. Even the worst savings account in the world pays at least a *little* bit of interest. The government will happily hold your money all year long, but will not ever give you a cent of interest back. Take this into consideration when having deductions made throughout the year by your employer or if sending in estimated tax payments. A perfect scenario is to end the year owing nothing and getting nothing back—zero-sum tax planning.

Some of you may have heard of the **Alternative Minimum Tax (AMT)**. It was passed in 1969 to ensure that upper-income taxpayers paid at least some income taxes. Up to that point, taxpayers skilled at finding enough in itemized deductions, income exclusions and tax credits would sometimes manage to avoid paying any income taxes at all. The lack of indexing for inflation combined with the growth in incomes over the past thirty years, has resulted in many more taxpayers paying the AMT. By 2010, thirty-five million individual taxpayers are projected to be subjected to the AMT. The tax rate for the AMT is 26% of the first $175,000 of ordinary income that exceeds a certain amount of exempted income ($33,750 for single taxpayers to $45,000 for married taxpayers filing jointly).

My concern about the state of the Alternative Minimum Tax is that, because of lack of indexing, almost *everyone* will soon be considered wealthy. Are they? No, certainly not if other tracking numbers indicate that the disparity between the rich and the poor in America is growing. You can't have it both ways; it's either one or the other. The AMT needs to be addressed and modified.

State Income Taxes: In addition to federal income taxes, all but a handful of states (nine) also impose state income taxes that range from 1% to 9%. Luckily, state income tax paid is subtracted when figuring your federal income tax. Most states also have a far less complex taxation formula with less loopholes and "gotchas."

Gift Taxes: You can give (or receive) up to the annual exclusion of $12,000 tax free, meaning, you can give away $12,000 per year to someone, or someone can give you up to $12,000 per year ($24,000 to a married couple) and it will not count as income. This is a strategy used by some parents who wish to help out their children by giving them some money from time to time. **Gift taxes, if any, are paid by the giver, not the recipient**, thus the need to be aware of the $12,000 ceiling. Some people hear that they can give an annual amount to their child "tax-free" and wonder if this means they can claim a deduction for such gifts. The bad news is that there is no *deduction* for gifts—except gifts to qualifying charities. Also note that although there is no tax on these gifts, they do count towards your lifetime estate tax exclusion, which is currently $2 million.

Another interesting thing to note is that **the IRS will actually *do your taxes for you*, if you so desire.** Weird, huh? But yes, you can send in all of your raw data and ask Uncle Sam himself to "be your accountant" and figure out what you owe or what he owes you. Elvis Presley was famous for doing this each and every year of his adult life. If it sounds like letting a wolf mind the henhouse, though, you're right. It was said that Elvis was America's number one taxpayer. I guess one should be loath to trust the IRS to find the maximum deductions in order for you to pay the least amount of income tax.

So exactly where do our taxes go? According to the Federal Office of Management & Budget:

National Defense	21%
Social Security	21%
Medicare	12%
Income Security	13%
Health	10%
Net Interest	9%
Other	14%

Capital Gains

When you invest in stocks, bonds, real estate and other capital assets, you may also owe "***capital gains taxes***" on the profits from the sale of those investments. Capital gains rates are designed to encourage long-term investing. Most people can get a significant advantage from holding stocks, real estate or other investments for more than one year. The tax rates that apply to net capital gains are generally lower than the tax rates that apply to other income and are called the "***maximum capital gains rates.***"

Generally, **if you sell an investment asset at a higher price than what you paid, you earn a capital gain. If you sell at a lower price than what you paid, you earn a capital loss.** Losses can offset gains, so if you lost $50,000 on one investment, but made $50,000 on another, you pay no capital gains—you ended up even. Investment income is tallied and totaled and you pay on that total. Capital gains taxes are not added on top of ordinary income taxes; that would be double taxation. With limited exceptions, so too, a capital loss cannot *lower* your ordinary income tax. Income is one issue, capital activity is another.

The length of time that you hold your investment determines whether your capital gain is treated as a long or short-term gain. The IRS sets the cutoff period at one year. That means that **if you hold a capital asset for more than one year (i.e., one year and one day), the capital gain you realize on its sale is considered a "*long-term capital gain.*" "*Short-term capital gains*" are those that you earn on sales of one year or less.**

Short-term capital gains are taxed as ordinary income, no different than salaries or any other income. Long-term capital gains, however, are taxed at a preferential rate. For all but the people in the 10 and 15% tax brackets (the lowest), the long-term capital gains tax rate (as of 2007) is typically 15% on the sale of stocks, mutual funds, rental real estate and similar investments. Investors in the 10 and 15% tax brackets (there aren't many) currently pay a long-term rate of only 5%. These rates are considered to be historically low (during the 1970s, the top rate on capital gains was 40%; in 1918 it was 77%), and many experts anticipate that the rates will be raised sharply within the next few years. Thus, for investors with appreciated assets, this might be the time to think about disposing of those while the tax consequences are relatively low.

Interesting Note: Lower-income investors get an even better investment sale deal in 2008. That year, filers in the 10% or 15% tax brackets (those who make less than $31,850 per year) will pay *no tax* on sales of long-term holdings. Hence, if you fit into this category and have some appreciated stocks or a business to sell that year, you will do so tax free!

Let me introduce two important terms here: "***Progressive taxation***" and "***regressive taxation.***"

Income tax is a progressive tax. The more money you make, the higher your tax rate. Your income progresses, your rate of taxation progresses.

A tax is considered regressive when it has a worse impact on lower wage earners than higher wage earners. Example: You and I both buy a burger and fries. The state where we bought it has a 6% sales tax on fast food. The bill is $10. We are each charged $10.60 ($10 plus $0.60 tax). I earn $100,000 a year. You earn $20,000 a year. That tax just hurt you more than it hurt me. I am more able to pay it than you. That sixty cents is a higher percentage of your yearly income than my yearly income. Sales taxes are a regressive tax because they are a *fixed rate* and apply to everyone equally, regardless of income. This comes up a lot when people begin suggesting raising gasoline taxes to encourage less use of foreign oil or to stem pollution. Such a tax would be devastating to the poor, who can ill afford it. On the other hand, the guy with the twelve Hummers will just laugh and keep driving. Again, government attempts to control behavior via taxation, but sometimes it backfires.

I'll give you another example. One state tried to raise revenues by adding on a new tax on boats. Actually, the term they used was "yachts." Now, who isn't in favor of taxing some arrogant rich guy who owns a "yacht?" What happened? Guys who could afford yachts decided not to buy them that year. Who did this hurt? The boat makers. What did the boat makers do? They laid off their help. What sort of people were laid off? Guys making working wages. So in order to tax the rich, the state ended up unemploying the poor.

Capital gains taxes are, presently, a regressive tax because they are less than income tax. And while people in the lower brackets get a better deal than those in the upper, this is somewhat disingenuous because very few people who earn less than $31,850 per year can afford to invest in real estate, stocks, or bonds. They are usually just struggling to eat, have shelter, and be clothed.

On the other hand (lots of hands in this discussion…) having capital gains rates lower than income tax rates does encourage investment. Furthermore, remember one important thing: **You are not charged capital gains tax until you *sell* an asset.** If you bought stock at $1 a share in 1965 and it has split twenty times and is now selling at $100 a share, so long as you continue to sit on it, you have nothing to worry about. Your worries (we should all have such worries) will come when you decide to cash in. The same goes for your $10,000 rental house that you could now sell for $450,000. No capital gains until you sell.

Unlike salary and other income, capital gains can be "sheltered" somewhat. I already went over 1031 exchanges for trading investment real estate properties. So long as you keep trading around and keeping your money in play, you do not pay capital gains until you finally turn it into cash and stick it in your pocket. Capital gains can also sometimes be deferred, the payment spread out over time. Some people also arrange to be paid in installments on a large capital transaction so that the tax, again, is spread over time. Finally, some people give some of their equity away to a charitable organization, which in turn is not only a tax deduction, but if partial ownership is given, the capital gains situation is again altered in the individual's favor.

Depreciation

When a business spends money for a service or anything else that is short-lived, this expenditure is usually immediately tax deductible as an expense. However, when a company buys an asset that will last longer than one year, like a computer, car, or building, the company cannot immediately deduct that large cost and enjoy an immediate large tax benefit. Instead, the company must *depreciate* the cost over the depreciable life of the asset, taking a tax deduction for a part of the cost each year. Eventually the company does get to deduct the full cost of the asset, but this happens over several years. A computer may depreciate completely over five years; a nonresidential building, usually 39 years. Depreciation values and practices are governed by federal tax laws which must be monitored continuously for any changes that are made. Accounting bodies, too, have developed standard practices and procedures for conducting depreciation.

A little pontification here: I tell people all the time that one of the goals of life should be to be financially independent. In order to do this, "employee mentality" must be erased. So many of us go through life and through school being taught that our goal should be to "get a good job." But our economy keeps rolling because we are a nation where people "create" good jobs, instead of just working at a job someone else created. Sure, working one's way up an organization can feel very "comfortable." Someone else takes all the risk, right? Wrong. We are accepting risk every day we wake up, whether we realize it or not. Maybe today will be the day that company you work for goes under. Now *that's* a heck of a risk, a risk made ever riskier because we, as only a small cog in a big machine that we do not control or own, have very little to do with the overall success or failure of it. Furthermore, our nation remains great because yes, indeed, it does actually encourage and reward people for "taking risks," risks such as entrepreneurialism. Remember what I said about taxes in general, that our tax code rewards certain behaviors and punishes certain others? Depreciation is a great example of this. **Businesses can depreciate hard assets. Individuals generally cannot.** When the XYZ Corporation buys pencils, paper, computers, refrigerators, trucks, what have you, they can write it off either immediately or over time. You, my friend, my individual friend employed by someone else, cannot. What for a company is a deduction of some sort, for you as an individual, is merely an expense. Companies *invest* money in these items. Individuals just *blow* money on these very same things. How ironic that, depending upon the role we have chosen to play in life, doing the exact same thing can in one case be prudent and wise, and in the other case be needless and wasteful.

Is there something you can do about it? Certainly. You could chuck it all and start your own business. Just about anything you can do, you can do just as easily for yourself as for someone else. Think about it. School teacher? Start a private tutoring service. Truck driver? Buy or lease your own rig; get your own routes or become a sub-contractor. I could go on and on. If the thought still scares you, bear in mind that many people begin by "keeping their day job" and starting their own business on a small scale—moonlighting. If you do this, you can realize enormous tax benefits almost immediately. For a small amount of money, you can set up a simple corporation—an S Corp or an LLC (more on this toward the end of this chapter). Then, when you buy equipment, it is a business expense. See, Uncle Sam is encouraging entrepreneurialism. You may eventually not only employ yourself, but employ others as well, creating jobs. You will have more control over your future because *you* will be making the important business decisions, not someone who doesn't care at all about your personal health and welfare. Your employer may send your job overseas. You wouldn't do that to yourself, now would you?

You can never depreciate your personal residence.
You can never depreciate land.

There are a number of different methods for depreciating goods. The depreciation method that you use for any particular asset is fixed at the time that you first place that asset into service. Again, most of this should be done with the advice of a tax professional, but it is important that you understand some of the terminology.

"Modified Accelerated Cost Recovery System" (MACRS) categorizes all business assets into classes and specifies the time period over which you can

write off assets in each class. For example, vehicles or computers may be depreciated over 5 years, while office furniture and fixtures are depreciated over 10 years. If you do not claim the equipment expensing deduction (Section 179 deduction), the IRS generally wants you to use the MACRS deduction.

"Straight Line Depreciation" or *"straight line amortization"* is the simplest deprecation method. Basically, it **just spreads out the cost of an asset equally over its lifetime.**

For the *"Declining-Balance Method"* **of depreciation, the fixed asset is depreciated by a progressively falling rate.** A constant percentage rate is calculated from the expected useful life and a given multiplication factor. This is multiplied with the falling net book value of the fixed asset.

The Declining-Balance Method:

- Results in relatively large amounts of depreciation in the early years of an asset's life and smaller amounts in later years.
- Is an accelerated method.
- Assumes that assets are most efficient when new.

Type of Property	Method of Depreciation	Depreciable Life in Years
Land	Not depreciated	N/A
Residential rental real estate (buildings or structures and structural components)	Straight line	27.5
Nonresidential rental real estate (commercial)	Straight line	39
Shrubbery, fences, etc.	150% declining balance	15
Furniture or appliances	Double (200%) declining balance	5-7

Section 179 Deductions

"*Section 179 deductions*" are my favorite tax deductions of all. **They allow many businesses to *immediately* deduct the cost of certain types of goods and property on their income taxes as an expense (rather than requiring the item or property to be capitalized and depreciated over time).** For 2006, the maximum deduction for the year was $108,000. Up to $25,000 of the cost of vehicles over 6,000 lbs (passenger SUV's, etc.) can be deducted using a Section 179 deduction. Work trucks weighing at least 6,000 lbs (with at least a 6 foot bed) or vehicles (i.e. buses, tow trucks, etc.) over 14,000 lbs are deductible up to the total $108,000. This deduction was enacted decades ago to assist small businesses with purchasing a vehicle for work use. Again, this is our country encouraging certain behaviors via taxation. Businesses purchasing things keeps the economy rolling. Recessions get exacerbated when businesses, because times are bad, stop making purchases. This, in turn, hurts the business that makes or sells another product and so on down the line.

A note here: As more and more large SUVs (Hummers, etc.) come on the market as passenger vehicles, the Section 179 deduction for vehicles has been modified in an attempt to exclude vehicles that would appear to be for standard passenger use only, as the government's intent was to encourage the purchase of work vehicles (trucks, ambulances, etc.) not just big SUV gas guzzlers. Before you try to use this tax strategy for a vehicle, check with your tax professional to make sure the vehicle you wish to purchase qualifies.

This tax strategy has been great for small businesses in particular. As a year comes to a close, a business can look around, assess its needs, and, perhaps, buy as much as $108,000 worth of new equipment—equipment that can have a long useful life, or be used up rather quickly—and write the entire amount off in that same year. No, it's not free money, technically, but it means that: A) a business that has over $100,000 in liquid assets can spend it rather than be taxed on it; or, B) the business can finance over $100,000 worth of capital expenditures and immediately write off that amount on its corporate taxes.

The only potential problem with Section 179 accelerated deductions is that you are more likely to run into the need to *"recapture depreciation"* if the asset is sold. If you happen to sell off that asset during its "useful life" (this is its useful life as determined by the IRS, not its real useful life. If you can keep a vehicle running twenty years, more power to you.), you will need to "recapture" its depreciation. The same holds true for property.

When assets are sold, the difference between the selling price and depreciated costs (known as the "basis") is gain subject to tax. Any past depreciation is first recaptured (usually at a 25% rate), followed by either short or long term capital gains tax (the long term capital gains rate is currently at a historically low 15% for most taxpayers).

For assets other than buildings, the gain attributable to the prior year's depreciation is "recaptured" as ordinary income. The balance of the depreciation is capital gain. For example, if someone owns a $20,000 business machine that has been depreciated $12,000, his "adjusted basis" is $8,000—the machine is technically worth $8,000. It matters not what someone is willing to pay for it. If he sells the equipment for $10,000, he has ordinary income of $2,000, upon which he must pay tax. Alternatively, if he sells the equipment for $25,000, his ordinary income (Depreciation Recapture) is $12,000 and his capital gain is $5,000.

If a taxpayer sells investment real estate that was partially or fully depreciated, the depreciation will need to be recaptured, which is typically done at a 25% tax rate.

Thinking about going into the oil, gas, or mineral mining business? A natural resource can, potentially, be exhausted. The amount of the original deposit is hidden from view and thus necessarily unknown. In taxation, *"depletion allowance"* is a deduction allowable to an owner of oil, gas, mineral, or timber property (depletable property). It allows an owner to recover the capital cost of the natural resource property as he exhausts the natural resources. This is in contrast to depreciation deduction provisions that deal with the wear and tear and deterioration of tangible physical property that result in the shortening of its useful life.

Sales Taxes

Sales tax is normally a tax on consumption and is usually charged as a percentage. You buy a thing, the thing is subject to sales tax; the thing costs $100, if the sales tax in that state/county/community is 6%, you pay $106.

There is no national sales tax. All sales taxes are either state, county, local, or sometimes even just a geographic section of a town or city. Most states have sales taxes, although five do not (Alaska, Delaware, Montana, New Hampshire and Oregon). Each state has its own sales tax rate and list of items subject to taxation. For example, most states exempt food from sales tax, although some do not. Some states also tax different goods or services at different rates. The whole system is very confusing, especially for travelers, although I believe it is important that a person at least know about the sales tax implications where they live and work.

It is usually up to the merchant to oversee the charging of sales tax and the remittance of said monies to the taxing entity (government). This is also where the terms "*wholesale*" and "*retail*" come into play. If you are in business and you buy things in order to sell them (envision a shoe store that must buy shoes first from a manufacturer before selling them to the general public), you do not pay sales tax on those items since they are intended for resale. In such a situation, you may be required to fill out certain tax exemption forms to verify that you are, indeed, a reseller (retailer), but this is nothing more than a small annoyance and is usually only done one time per vendor. Of course, if a shoe store owner buys paper towels to keep his place clean, he must pay sales tax on such items. A retailer can only be exempt from paying sales tax on things he is *reselling*, not things he is *using*.

The manufacturer does not charge sales tax to the (confirmed) retailer. On the other hand, some companies are manufacturers in name only. Picture the "shoe manufacturer" that really only buys shoes made in some Third World country, then sells them from their

American warehouse to retailers across the country. This, too, is considered "wholesaling," and is, as we said, exempt from sales tax. It is always the end user—the consumer—who pays sales tax to the person or entity that directly provided him with the good or service.

Sales tax is generally only charged on tangible items. You generally do not charge sales tax on labor, ideas or concepts. Certain services, though, usually charge sales tax. One of the most common is hotel and motel occupancy taxes—a type of sales tax. A night's stay in a hotel room is not something you can hold in your hand, but it is still usually taxed. Occupancy taxes are frequently higher than the state sales tax, as most cities and towns add a local portion onto the state portion.

The idea of a county or town adding on their own sales tax is quite conventional. For example, one may live in a state with a 4% sales tax, a county with a 2% sales tax, and a town or city with a 1% sales tax. When they go to Main Street to buy a box of pencils, they are charged not 4%, but 7% sales tax, with that money going back to three different government entities.

This alone should be cause for some serious purchase planning on your part. If your town or city charges sales tax and the next town over doesn't…as long as you don't lose what you'd save in gasoline (which can be quite a concern these days)…get in your car and save some money. On most cash and carry transactions, you simply pay what the sales tax is where you make the purchase.

With cars, though, it is often a little trickier. For example, you generally pay sales tax where you *register* the vehicle. If you've bought it out-of-state, the dealer will have to issue you a temporary permit and have you sign something stating that you intend to register it in another state, so they don't have to collect the sales tax.

If you buy from a private party, you'll be paying the sales tax when you register the vehicle anyway, so it doesn't really matter where you've bought it, excepting that you are *supposed* to get a temporary permit from the DMV (Department of Motor Vehicles) of that state to drive it home—if, again, the purchase was made in a different state. Private sellers usually do not have to report or collect sales taxes, whether it is for vehicles or for when they have a yard sale.

Lastly, on the topic of car purchases and registrations, check out whether there is a difference in the sales tax where you live versus where you work or own other property. If there is a difference, when you go to register your car, use the address with the lowest sales tax as the registration address. Yes, you can do that. It can, in actuality, save you hundreds of dollars, considering the size of a motor vehicle purchase. In fact, some savvy people factor in the local and/or county sales tax when deciding upon where to live or establish a business. One could say that this is a way in which the taxpayer can send a subtle message to the local government.

Speaking of interstate commerce, many people do not realize that their home state may have tax obligations for goods purchased or otherwise acquired without payment of sales tax to their home state. For instance, even though you pay no sales tax when you shop in Montana, your purchases may be subject to "**use tax**" when you bring them home to one of the forty-five states that *do* have state sales tax. Use Tax and Sales Tax are usually the same rate and on the same list of goods and services subject to taxation.

The citizens of some states also have Use Tax obligations in their home state when they purchase items in other states that have a sales tax rate simply *lower* than their home state's.

Now, this all being said, except for very large items such as vehicles, most people do not self-report and pay out this additional money to their home state if that state has such Use Tax policies. But…lack of Use Tax awareness costs state and local governments millions of dollars in tax revenues each year. When people fail to pay their fair share, everyone else's tax bill goes up and the state has to get the revenue from somewhere, somehow.

Many Use Tax states even go so far as to expect you to report and pay sales tax on privately purchased goods, such as that yard sale I mentioned a few paragraphs back. So, too, goods purchased out-of-state by subscription, from a mail order catalog company, or over the Internet. Some of these "virtual" retailers will actually collect the sales or use tax of the state you are having the product delivered to. The next time you make an on-line or mail-order purchase, check the fine print and see if it says, "Residents of X states, add 6% sales tax; residents of Y states, add 7.5% sales tax, etc." But if the retailer does not do this, yes, certain states expect you to declare it and pay it on your own.

All of which brings us to more discussion about mail order purchases, be they via the Internet or even if they involve a face-to-face transaction that is being shipped to another state or locale. In most cases, if you are making a purchase in Location Y, which has an 8% sales tax, but are having it shipped to Location Z, which has a different sales tax, the retailer will either A) charge the sales tax of Location Z. This will usually only happen if Location Z is in the same state and the varying tax rates are known to the retailer, or...B) the retailer will charge no sales tax. Again, the place where the goods are being shipped may have laws stating that you should pay the local sales/use tax rate, but you're basically on your own. I know many people who have a friend or relative that lives in another state. They go into the local shopping mall, buy a ton of clothes, then have them shipped to their Aunt Mary in the next state and avoid paying sales tax. I'm not endorsing this, but it does happen.

One last wrinkle to this is that you are most likely not to be charged any sales tax if the retailer in question does *not* have a location in your home state. If they do have a location there, they will usually charge you your home state's sales tax rate.

Most states do not charge sales tax on labor, but this gets a little fuzzy depending upon where you live. For example, some states require repairmen to charge a sales tax on their endeavors, not just on parts. In most other states, this is not the case. In the end, the true onus is on the service giver. If someone charges you sales tax and they do not report and remit that money to the state or other government entity, they can get in heinous trouble. If someone charges you sales tax on a good or service that is not taxable in that locale, they can also get in incredibly big trouble. If you are ever in doubt, check it out—that's what the Internet is for. If you feel you've been scammed, report it to the proper authorities.

Finally, Special Taxing Districts are examples of certain areas within a town that may have a different sales tax rate. Often times it is a *higher* rate, with the excess meant to be set aside for private security, capital improvements, or to pay off bond debt for improvements that have already been made. While this looks to be fine and good for the area in question, it is not conducive to the consumer, and if enough consumers feel that way, they may vote with their feet, go elsewhere to shop, and the redevelopment experiment will have been a bust.

In other cases, the sales tax may actually be *lower*. Some states do this in order to encourage shopping in a depressed area. See again what I mean by taxes being used to encourage or discourage certain activities? They're not just about raising money; they're about crafting behavior.

Payroll Taxes

You get a paycheck. Unless you are considered a freelancer or an independent contractor (more on this shortly), the *employer* who gave you the check will have taken out deductions. You will then be disappointed at the difference between your **gross** (what you got paid) and the **net** (what you *really* got paid, after taxes and various other things were taken out). Some of you might even be angry at your boss, thinking he ripped you off. I mean, you negotiated to work for $10 an hour, you worked forty hours, but instead of getting $400, you got something on the order of $340.

Hold back your indignation. Your employer got an even worse deal on this than you did. The reality is, employers pay out—to *somebody*—about 15% more than what they negotiated to pay *you*. That means, in the above case, your employer is actually parting with about *$460* per week, not $400. This cost to the employer is known as *burden*. It's lonely at the top.

This may come as a surprise to you. It may even sound erroneous to you. Take out your past pay stub. If you look for that additional 15%, you won't find it there. Is Braun lying? Nope. Sit back and learn.

Like the bandleader says, let's take it from the top. You start a new job. Your employer will have you fill out a **W-4 form**. This is a federal government form that assists your employer in properly figuring out how much tax to withhold and remit on your behalf. A question you will be asked on this form is, "How many deductions do you wish to declare?" **Whenever possible, claim the maximum number of exemptions applicable to you.** The greater the number of (legal) exemptions, the better. The idea is to not "loan" Uncle Sam money during the year. As I've said before, the IRS does not pay you back interest on money you've lent them. You should be saving money throughout the year as it is. That way, if you do, indeed, end up having to owe a bit of money to the IRS at the end of the year, you will have it available.

At the end of the year, your employer will give or mail you a **W-2 form**, another government form that provides you with a grand total of that year's income and deduction activity on your behalf. You will need this when doing your tax returns. If you worked for multiple employers, you will get one from each of them.

If you are a freelancer or "independent contractor," you will usually just provide the employer with your social security number and they will, in turn, give or mail you a different form, a **1099 form**, at the end of the year. Again, if you worked for multiple employers, you will get more than one 1099, or a combination of W-2s and 1099s. 1099s will not show any taxes taken out; they will only list the gross amount you have been paid and by whom. Independent contractors are responsible for remitting their own payroll taxes (both the "employee" side, and the "employers" side, known as "self employment tax").

You should receive from your employer(s) your W-2s and 1099s no later than the end of January. That being said, this is frequently not the case. On the other hand, if an employer takes egregiously longer than January 31st to deliver your forms to you (March?), you have every right to confront him and, if the delay continues, you would not be outside your rights in contacting the local IRS office. This will probably not keep you in the employer's good graces, but it might also indicate that something is quite amiss and should be looked into.

Your own personal records of earnings should match up with the W-2s and 1099s. Most tax professionals would advise you to go with the "most accurate" figure, if you cannot resolve the situation with your employer. The late reception of your forms or significant deviations between your records of earnings and your employer's records could be an innocent clerical error, or it could be some form of fraud. **In the end, though, it is you who is responsible to make the most accurate disclosure of your personal financial affairs to the IRS.** Remember what I said before: A lot of tax-related issues are open to interpretation, but gross earnings are not.

A lot of people debate the definition of what is and what is not an "independent contractor." In each case, there is a fiduciary issue as well as a legal one. Some employers will wish not to have to offer you certain employee benefits (health insurance, etc.), and will thus try to claim you are not really an "employee." This is generally not in your best interest. On the other hand, if you are, indeed, something other than a full-time, year-round employee, you may prefer to be an independent contractor to avoid certain deductions from being made out of your paycheck. These may include union dues, pension plans, etc. The legal issues are that in some cases, being an employee bundles you up with the employer if the employer gets sued for some form of malfeasance. In other scenarios, being an independent contractor actually leaves you open to *more* liability. For example, certain "Good Samaritan" type laws actually place more responsibility upon a total stranger than upon a co-worker or employer. In Minnesota, a court ruled that an employee was acting in an acceptable manner when he waited an hour to call an ambulance when another employee collapsed to the ground, while noting that according to state law had a passerby stopped, investigated the scene, and showed the same lack of care and concern, there would have been far greater liability. This country is full of strange laws.

If you are ever given a choice between being an employee or an independent contractor, take a moment to consider all the facts and get some outside opinions from professionals you respect. It could be a very important decision.

The following are the most common deductions made from your paycheck as an *employee*:

1. Social Security
2. Medicare
3. Federal income tax
4. State income tax

Additionally, the following are the most common payroll expenses of an *employer*:

1. Social Security
2. Medicare
3. Unemployment (Federal and State)
4. Workers' Compensation

Social Security refers to social welfare services concerned with social protection, or protection against socially recognized conditions, including poverty, old age, disability, unemployment, families with children and others.

Medicare is the federal health insurance program for people who have reached retirement age.

Social Security and Medicare are bundled together on your pay stub and called "*FICA Tax*" (Federal Insurance Contributions Act).

Federal Unemployment Tax (FUTA) is a tax used for state and federal administrative expenses of the unemployment program.

State Unemployment Tax is a state tax used to pay benefits to unemployed workers.

Workers' Compensation is an insurance program that pays medical and disability benefits for work-related injuries and diseases.

Federal Income Tax (already covered)

State Income Tax (already covered)

Social Security, Medicare, Federal and State Unemployment, and Workers' Comp are all set up as a flat percentage of your earnings. There is nothing you can do to lower your contribution rates, nor are the rates indexed for income—the rich, the poor, and everyone in between all pay the same percentage rate, although there are some earnings caps in some cases.

As previously stated, your employer (if you have one) makes contributions above and beyond your personal contributions *on your behalf.* This is to say, because you are on his payroll (i.e., he has ten employees) he pays more than if you were not on his payroll (i.e., he has nine employees).

Here is a table showing sample contributions for a typical employee (I have used a single person with no exemptions, living in Colorado, earning $75,000 per year):

PAYROLL TAXES			
	Employee	Employer	Total
Social Security	6.2%	6.2%	12.4%
Medicare	1.45%	1.45%	2.9%
State Unemployment (varies by state)	0	2.2%	2.2%
Federal Unemployment	0	0.8%	0.8%
Workers' Compensation (varies by vocation risk)	0	4%	4%
Subtotals	7.65%	14.65%	22.3%
State Withholding (approx)	4.5%	0	4.5%
Federal Withholding (approx)	19.5%	0	19.5%
Total	31.65%	14.65%	46.3%

Limits and explanations for the above chart

- In 2007, Social Security is only paid on the first $97,500 of earnings.
- Medicare has no annual limit.
- State Unemployment – varies from state to state. I have used my home state of Colorado as an example. In 2007 in Colorado, it is paid only on the first $10,000 of earnings.

- Federal Unemployment in 2007 is paid on the first $7,000 of earnings (maximum of $56 per year).
- Workers' Compensation premiums vary based on risk and vary anywhere from a total of 0.3% to 10%. Higher risk occupations require a higher premium than those with little risk.

One of the most important things you should take away from all this is what a large percentage of your income is taken up by payroll taxes, and also that your employer pays measurably more than simply what you see as being your gross salary on your paycheck. Em-ployees cost a lot of money, which is why automation and shipping jobs overseas keeps certain employers viable. This is another reason why everyone should consider not having to simply rely upon an employee's salary in order to live. That's not living; it's risky surviving.

Other things that add to an employer's burden are:

Training – Once you are hired, it will take you a while until you are of any real value to your employer. Despite this, you begin drawing a salary from day one. In fact, as you are learning your new employer's systems, you are probably taking up excess time of your employer or some other employee assigned to you, thus robbing them of *their* efficiency. This is additional money lost by the employer.

Vacations – Aren't they great? But while you're lying on the beach in St. Bart's, who is doing your job? Either someone else is trying to do the work of two people, or it's simply not getting done at all. This also costs your employer money.

Sick Days – See above. Whether they're real or you're just too tired to get up some Monday morning, when your boss is down a worker, it costs. I mean, these are *paid* vacation days and paid sick days I'm referring to.

Health Insurance, Pension, IRA, or 401K Savings Plans – They call them perks, they're used by employers to compete for talent with other employers, and sometimes, these extra benefits can only be bestowed upon the *employer* as an employment benefit if he also offers them to the *employee*. They often carry a direct monetary cost if the employer chooses to contribute to them either fully or by some sort of cost-share or match, but they always carry an administrative cost.

So yes, all you employees; I'm here to come to the emotional rescue of your much-maligned bosses. You think it's all fun and games for the big boys? Well, it's not, particularly when it comes to taxes.

Self-Employment Taxes

I've spoken about and encouraged you to consider being the boss, not simply the underling. In most cases, this will not mean that you will be able to find investors to stake you enough so that you can open a one hundred-employee operation on Day One. And as businesses go, a one hundred-employee business is actually considered small. No, most people who begin their own businesses start out with only one employee—themselves.

So what are the tax implications?

To begin with, corporations—typical "C" corporations—are subject to "**double taxation**." This means that a corporation pays tax once when it shows a profit. Then when it distributes the dividends, the shareholders have to report and pay tax on that income again when they receive it. Double taxation; once at the corporate level, and then again at the shareholder level. All companies with over one hundred shareholders have to be a "C" corporation (smaller companies can get away with being other types of legal entities. These companies can, luckily, avoid double taxation.).

I felt it was important to mention this, but again, a business with one hundred shareholders or more is something to aspire to, and if you're nearing that point already in your life, your financial education is probably far more advanced than what we are covering in this book.

Back to you, the independent practitioner, the one-man band. You may choose to set yourself up as a "**sole proprietorship**," a "limited liability company" (LLC), or as an "**S Corporation**."

A sole proprietorship basically means that a person does business in their own name (although they may do business under a fictitious trade name) **and there is only one owner.** A sole proprietorship is not a corporation; it does not pay corporate taxes. Instead, the person who organized the business pays personal income taxes on the profits made, making accounting much simpler. A sole proprietorship need not worry about double taxation like a corporate entity would have to, but you are subjected to personal liability.

What is usually more recommended for this person is to form a *"Limited Liability Company"* or *"LLC."* This strategy offers the sole proprietor certain liability protections if sued. It also makes it easier for him to borrow money for his business. Finally, it also opens up the possibility to selling shares of his business to others. It certainly makes a clear distinction between what is personal and what is business.

A person running a business as a sole proprietorship or a limited liability company is generally considered self-employed for tax purposes. The self-employed are usually required to pay estimated income taxes quarterly. They pay both the "employee" and "employer" portions of the FICA tax (Social Security and Medicare) on any salary, since they are considered both the employer and the employee. An employed person pays 7.65% (6.2% for Social Security and 1.45% for Medicare) through a paycheck deduction, and the employer pays the other 7.65%. The self-employed person pays both sides of this tax, or 15.3% total. However, since half of this *"self-employment tax"* is allowed as a deduction against self-employment income, only 92.35% of the self-employment income is taxable at 15.3%, an effective tax rate of about 14.13%.

Unlike a regular C corporation, a *"Subchapter-S Corporation"* generally pays no corporate income taxes on its profits. Instead, the shareholders in the S corporation pay income taxes on their proportionate shares (at their individual tax rate), called **distributive shares**, of the S corporation's profits. Shareholders must report the income—and pay a related tax, if any—regardless of whether the shareholders receive distributions from the S corporation.

The sole shareholder of an S Corporation is not considered self-employed. Such a person is considered an employee of the corporation and does not pay self-employment tax, but instead pays FICA tax on any salary or wages (matched by the corporation) at half the tax rate at which the self-employment tax is imposed—7.65% each by employer and corporation, instead of the 15.3% self-employment tax.

Many self-employed people choose to incorporate to reduce this tax. Before incorporation, a self-employed person making $100,000 in business profit would pay 15.3% of that profit in self-employment tax, or $15,300. But with an incorporated business, the business can pay the owner $50,000 in salary and $50,000 in dividends (called "distributions"). The owner pays 7.65% of the $50,000 in salary and his corporation pays the other 7.65%, for $7,650 total. **Distributions are not subject to self-employment tax**, so there is no FICA/Medicare tax on the $50,000 in distributions. Thus, the business owner may save $7,650 in taxes. However, tax laws can be tricky, and do change, so it is always advisable to seek the advice of a competent accountant in making the decision to incorporate for the purpose of saving tax. Also, these particular types of entities have some complicated tax rules about the allocation of "salary" and "dividends," and you would be well advised to consult a tax professional who is familiar with this.

Self-employed persons are sometimes eligible for more deductions than an ordinary employee. Travel, uniforms, computer equipment, cell phones, etc., can be deducted as legitimate business expenses. However, again, the advice of an expert may be worth the money it costs.

"Passive Income" such as real estate rentals, dividends, interest and capital gains, are generally NOT subject to Self Employment Tax. This means that if you owned a business and you also owned the building you did that business in, any "rent" (assuming it is not above the market rate) is NOT subject to Self Employment Tax, and thus, saves you significantly.

CHAPTER 8
INVESTING FOR THE FUTURE

Do you know who thinks about retirement? People getting close to retiring. This is sad. To begin getting your financial affairs in order when you're in your fifties is a *lot* of dollars too little and a *lot* of days too late.

Perhaps it is the concept of retirement itself. When we're in our twenties, nothing could be farther off. Even death is more on our minds, often each time we get on a busy highway with crazy drivers streaking past us. But retirement is...well, that's for old people, right?

So allow me to propose to you a different mindset. Don't think of it as retirement. Think simply about **investing your money**. "Invested money" is "growing money." You can earn tons and tons of money, but if all you do is spend it, you are not truly rich. Wealth is defined by how much money you have on hand at any one time. If you make $10,000 a week and blow it each week, you are not wealthy. If something happens and you no longer earn that kind of bread, you're in a pickle. Lots of guys working on Wall Street during the Go-Go Eighties learned this the hard way.

Furthermore, let's actually take on the "R-word"—retirement. What if you do keep making and spending that $10,000 a week every week until you can no longer work? What do you do then? That's what I'm talking about. You could sell off all your expensive toys and live decently for a few more years. But actuarial tables tell us that Americans are living longer and longer and longer. Once you're down to your last Ferrari and all your vacation homes are gone, where do you go next? Let's see if I can help you plan better for the future.

Investing is Saving, and Saving is Investing

Investment, it has been said many times and in many places, is about *paying yourself, and specifically paying yourself first.* When you buy that new car, you are really not paying yourself. You are paying the *car dealer.* Sure, you're getting a nice gift in return. But *you* paid for it, so it's not much of a gift. And yes, you do need something to get you from here to there, but let's face it, some of us go a bit overboard; am I right?

The greatest balance to all this is no different than with dieting. Think about it. Why do most diets fail? Because dieting suggests denial. If we starve ourselves and when we do eat, we eat none of the things we like, we are punishing ourselves. Most humans can only do this so long before they just say, "To hell with it," and find themselves at the take-out window of a Taco Bell at one a.m..

Saving and investing is the same thing. If you think it means dressing in rags, walking ten miles to work, and living in a crack house while you put 90% of your paycheck into some form of savings for that "rainy day," you're going to snap one day and blow it all on a personal jet you can ill-afford to store and fuel.

So it is all about balance. Can this be easily achieved? Well, let's explore further why investing is worth your while in the first place.

Investing, especially when started early, can create serious wealth that allows for career choices, flexibility and the opportunity to pursue your dreams. Investing consistently *now* will give you the resources for future things such as buying a home, opening a business or starting a family.

Time is the #1 key to creating long-term wealth. With this one edge, anybody can do it, regardless of occupation or income. Investing requires time, consistency and discipline. Using one of the many savings calculators available online, here is an example:

Monthly Savings:	$ 300
Starting Age:	30
Retirement Age:	65
Number of Years:	35
Annual Yield:	8%
Ending Balance:	$ 688,165

Note: No allowances were made for inflation or income taxes.

Looks good, wouldn't you say? Now, run the numbers again, this time starting your savings at age twenty-five instead of age thirty (five years earlier). You end up with $1,047,302! That's 52% more!

If you were to retire at age sixty-five, kept that $1,047,302 principal intact, created a conservative investment portfolio that paid out, on average, 8% per year (and that happens to be a rather conservative growth rate), you could receive $83,784 per year in payments to live on (not adjusted for inflation), each year for the rest of your life. That's not half bad! By that time, you'll most likely only be taking care of yourself and, maybe, your spouse. And if your spouse received this book as a high school graduation present and started saving at age twenty-five also, together you'd be able to draw down $167,568 per year! Not bad money for not working. And remember, I didn't even *mention* touching the principal.

By starting early and investing consistently, you too can become a millionaire with even a modest savings of $10 per day. Break down the $300 per month by either earning more or cutting back on things like "designer coffee," partying/alcohol, eating out, expensive designer clothes and other unnecessary luxuries that you have nothing to show for. Think about this the next time you hand over $10 for one of the above.

Investing and creating wealth requires that you live within your means and save (i.e., not spend) a material portion of your earnings. This is where many people today have a problem in the never-ending quest to keep up with the "Joneses"—large houses, nice cars, luxury vacations, and other indulgencies that they cannot afford. There is nothing wrong with having these things if you can really afford them. But we have become a society accustomed to instant, rather than delayed, gratification. The two things that help people get ahead the most are education and delayed gratification. This brings back that word "balance." Starting with something as relatively inconsequential as $10 per day will feel as painless as that super-sized double mocha half-caf latte, coupled with a fresh scone and a bottle of water—you know; that snack routine that's become a part of your daily ritual. And you know about rituals—once they become habitual enough, we don't even notice them anymore. *That's* how you should think about saving. Make *that* the ritual. Besides, it's a lot less fattening.

Ever hear of John D. Rockefeller? At one time he was the richest man in the world. In fact, I recently read that, adjusting for inflation and factoring in percentage of the world's total wealth, he was at one time the richest man who *ever* lived—far richer than Bill Gates or any other more recent contenders to the throne.

Let me share with you two legendary Rockefeller tales about creating wealth. As a very young man, Rockefeller kept a diary. He logged in every single cent he ever acquired or spent. And when I say "cent" I mean "cent." If he bought a penny candy, he wrote it down. Once he started doing this, he was amazed at how much money he completely wasted. From that realization on, John D. Rockefeller continued to live his life with that sort of obsessive attention to the value of each and every penny. Now, we can look at this and say, "Wow, that's a little over the top." Okay, so maybe it is. And no, I don't have a book like Rockefeller's where I list every penny I find lying on the street. But look at the bigger lesson to be learned. We all waste money. If we took a closer look at that, we would not find ourselves saying, "I can't save. I don't earn enough." Sure you earn enough. That's not to say you shouldn't want to earn more, but if you never *pay yourself*, then no matter what you earn, *you don't earn enough.*

Another Rockefeller tale. Rockefeller is the reason we have all the anti-monopoly and anti-trust laws that we have today. Rockefeller, like every businessman, depended upon other businessmen, other vendors, in order to run his own companies. Eventually, he realized that if he bought out the vendor, he had more control over his own financial destiny. But buying other businesses meant going into areas in which he was not yet an expert. But sometimes expertise is all about common sense.

Rockefeller was in the oil business. Oil was stored and transported in barrels—old wooden barrels at the time. Rockefeller eventually bought out a barrel-maker and began making his own barrels.

Well, the old man himself came down to the barrel-making plant and watched the men making the barrels. He couldn't help but notice that each craftsman slapped a different amount of solder on the metal bands that held together the wooden slats. Remembering his log book where he tracked every penny he earned or spent, Rockefeller began taking into account that metal solder indeed had a monetary value and he was having millions and millions of barrels made on his behalf.

Rockefeller went down onto the factory floor and asked a foreman how many drops of solder it took to make a barrel that held. "I have no idea," the man answered. Rockefeller suggested that the man make a new barrel from scratch right then and there and to count exactly how many drops of solder it took. The foreman complied. They then filled the barrel with oil to make sure it held. It did.

Rockefeller then ordered the man to make another barrel, this time with one less drop of solder. Again, the foreman complied. Again, the barrel held. Rockefeller then ordered the foreman to keep doing the experiment until he finally made a barrel that would not hold, each time methodically counting each little spot of metal solder. Finally, they reached the point where they knew exactly the minimum number of spots of solder a barrel required in order to do its job. "Now," said Rockefeller, "I want every single barrel made exactly that way. I do not want a single drop less nor a single drop more used to make one of my barrels."

Maybe you're reading this and saying, "Wow, that's way too obsessive compulsive." Well, what if I were to tell you that the savings Rockefeller gained from this experiment, multiplied by the hundreds of millions of barrels his plant made, earned the man tens of millions of dollars. Tens of millions of dollars simply by counting and controlling the number of spots of solder on a barrel!

Taking control of the solder being used on his barrels caused Rockefeller no pain. He wasn't giving up something he couldn't live without. It was not a "starvation diet." It was simply another example of how he took notice of wasteful spending and corrected it. I, too, have used this type of practice many of times in my own businesses with great success. You can do this as well. And when you do, the savings you discover should be put aside for investment.

Somewhere along the line, "saving" became a bad word in this country. Right now, Americans' savings are in negative numbers. Rephrased, this means that Americans spend more than they earn and more than they save. This is a formula for disaster. Creating wealth is not about conspicuous consumption, it is about savings— money in the bank. With that comes security, flexibility and options—a life free from unnecessary stress.

Do you keep a change jar? A lot of people do. When it gets fairly full, put it into some form of savings. It adds up. We all have the opportunity to "do a Rockefeller" and save money painlessly. There's an old adage: Take care of the pennies, and the dollars will take care of themselves.

I'm sure you're wondering, "Okay, so if I make a commitment to saving, *where* do I save that money? How do I invest it?

Let me make clear that this book is not at all intended to be an investment guide. The library and your local bookstore are already bursting at the seams with those kinds of books, and companies like Fidelity and Charles Schwab offer lots of free online resources. I have nothing new or unique I can add to that discussion. Should you read some of those books and take advantage of those resources? Definitely! What I will say is that you should stay away from crazy, risky stuff. If it sounds too good to be true, then it usually is. When you are starting out in the savings game, take it slowly and conservatively. Once you've built up some savings, then you can get a little more creative;

a little more risky with a small portion of your portfolio. But right off the bat...how about making sure you've got a nice cushion in your checking account? That's as basic a start as there is. Don't let that thing go down to zero each and every month. Carry a positive cash balance and, as we covered in previous chapters, see if you can find a checking account that, perhaps, pays a bit of interest if you keep a certain level of balance within it. But don't think that a checking account full of money is the best way to save. Even if you can find interest-bearing accounts, the interest rate will be minimal at best. Also, the best and worst aspects to keeping a lot of money in checking are that it is the easiest money to access. This is called "liquidity." While one should always have *some* liquidity, there is always the temptation to take very liquid assets and spend them, defeating the entire program.

Traditional savings accounts will often have a slightly higher interest rate than an interest-producing checking account; but in both cases, we are still talking relatively small potatoes. As I write this, rates average slightly less than 5%. Nonetheless, when you are first starting out and need liquidity as well as lack of risk, this is another reasonable avenue for your savings. Once you've accumulated some money in a regular savings account, you may wish to explore other higher growth savings options such as money market accounts and certificates of deposit.

I know you've heard this word long before you probably even knew the meaning of it. The word is "diversify." The concept is that one should not put all of their savings in one place (including under your mattress). No, savings accounts in FDIC (Federal Deposit Insurance Corporation) protected banks will not disappear (you are insured for up to $100,000) but other investments *can* go south. Just look at people who had their entire life's savings invested in Enron or WorldCom and you'll know what I'm talking about. Spread those savings around. One thing may earn you 5% interest, while another earns 25%, and yet another *loses* money. That's why we diversify. For this exact reason, I suggest that people not have more than 20% of their portfolio in any single investment.

As we move along through this chapter, we will go over some basic types of investments, as well as discuss other savings vehicles that are available—some of them potentially through your place of business. We will also talk about government programs aimed at helping make sure that Americans do not retire in total poverty. But let's hope that's not you.

But if I can emphasize one single thing, it's that automatic weekly or monthly investing for long-term savings is the only way to properly prepare for your financial future. It's easy to say, "Oh, when I get my big tax refund, I'll put that money into savings," or "If I get that bonus at work, I'll invest that." That sort of thing is sporadic and it never really works. For one thing, it means that we plan to take a "present"—some not totally expected fiscal windfall—and put it aside for a rainy day. What we're more likely to do is spend a large part of it celebrating our good fortune. But besides that, these are things we can't bank on. Ten dollars a day, saved by giving up "Happy Hour" after work or that latte on the way in to the office—that we can count on. **Save regularly…and watch it grow.**

Many employers can arrange to deduct money from your paycheck automatically and place it electronically into a savings vehicle for you. If you are self-employed, you can still arrange for money to be deducted automatically each month. This is a great plan to force regular savings. This is you paying yourself first. Do it! **Having money deducted electronically for the purpose of saving is far better than relying on yourself to do it manually.** With a manual deduction, there's too much of a temptation to fiddle with things and skip a month here and there. **The formula for success is automation and consistency.**

Social (In)Security

Why bother saving? There's always Social Security, right?

Social Security is a social insurance program funded through dedicated payroll taxes (via FICA—the Federal Insurance Contributions Act). Tax deposits are formally entrusted to the Federal Old-Age and Survivors Insurance Trust Fund. The program was initially signed into law by President Franklin D. Roosevelt in 1935 as a measure to implement "social insurance" during the Great Depression of the 1930s, when poverty rates among senior citizens exceeded 50%. Payments to current *retirees* were (and continue to be) financed by a payroll tax on *current* workers' wages, half directly as a payroll tax and half paid by the employer.

Payroll taxes were first collected in 1937, also the year in which the first benefits were paid. The original 1935 statute paid retirement benefits only to the primary worker. Many types of people were excluded—mainly farm workers, the self-employed, and anyone employed by an employer of fewer than ten people. These limitations, intended to exclude those from whom it would be difficult to monitor compliance, covered approximately half of the civilian labor force in the United States. Critics have even called Social Security a compulsory wealth transfer mechanism.

In 1939, the Act was amended in three important ways:

- The widowed, nonworking spouse of someone entitled to an old-age benefit also became entitled to an old-age benefit.
- Survivors (widows and orphans) became eligible for a benefit.
- Retirees who had never paid any FICA taxes became eligible for old-age benefits. This feature was very popular among the millions of elderly Americans hardest hit by the Great Depression.

The earliest age at which (reduced) benefits are payable is sixty-two. Full retirement benefits depend upon a retiree's year of birth. Those born before 1938 have a normal retirement age of sixty-five. Normal retirement age increases by two months for each ensuing year of birth until the 1943 year of birth, when it stays at age sixty-six years until the year of birth 1955. Thereafter the normal retirement age increases again by two months for each year ending in the 1960 year of birth, when normal retirement age stops at age sixty-seven for all born thereafter.

The normal retirement age for spousal retirement benefits shifts the year-of-birth schedule upward by two years, so that those spouses born before 1940 have age sixty-five as their normal retirement age.

A worker under age seventy and eligible for retirement can delay receiving benefits past full retirement age, and thereby increase the worker's eventual retirement benefit and the surviving spouse's benefit (delayed retirement credit).

Although Social Security is sometimes compared to private pensions, this is not a correct comparison, since Social Security is social insurance and not a retirement plan. Throughout a worker's career, the Social Security Administration keeps track of his or her earnings. **The amount of the monthly benefit to which the worker is entitled depends upon that earnings record and upon the age at which the retiree chooses to begin receiving benefits.** For the entire history of Social Security, benefits have been paid almost entirely by using revenue from payroll taxes. This is why Social Security is referred to as a pay-as-you-go system.

In 2004, the U.S. Social Security system paid out almost $500 billion in benefits. In approximately a decade (2019), payroll tax revenue is projected to be insufficient to cover Social Security benefits. **Don't count on Social Security when you retire…the system may be bankrupt by then.** In fact, according to the Social Security Administration website, unless changes to the system are made, benefits will be reduced by 26% in 2040 and could continue to be reduced every year thereafter. Check your calendar and check your birth date. Are you planning to retire after that time?

The worker-to-beneficiary ratio has fallen from 16.5-to-1 in 1950 to 3.3-to-1 today. Within forty years it will be 2-to-1. With this ratio, there will not be enough workers to pay scheduled benefits at current tax rates. In short, the system is currently broken, and it soon may be bankrupt. **I am not telling you this to send you into a panic; I am telling you because you must put this benefit out of your mind.** Forget about it. If it's there when you retire, use it for groceries and be glad for it. **But it is not a retirement strategy.**

Why am I down on Social Security? I'm actually not. It came from a very nice and warmhearted gesture. The problem is, the numbers no longer hold up today. People are living longer, and the Baby Boomers are now retiring and they didn't produce enough offspring to join the workforce and help support their retirement. For that, dear readers, is the crux of the system. Today's workers pay for today's retirees. I once read where someone suggested that people receiving Social Security benefits should be shown on each check they receive exactly how much of "their own" money they are getting back from the system, and how much is from the rest of us who are still working. For after a certain number of years, people do, indeed, begin drawing out far more—even calculating interest—than they themselves paid in.

Longevity (thank you, modern medicine and science) has caused a big shift in the actuarial table, and is probably the biggest single reason the system is in disarray. Retirement age may now be shifting to sixty-seven, but in truth, were we to use the calculations FDR put in place in 1935, we would be raising it to around seventy-eight. Should our government drastically raise the age at which one may receive benefits in order to save the system? I can't really answer that question. The problem is, it is hard and, frankly, unfair to change a system midstream. If citizens are paying into this program with the expectation of retiring at age sixty-five or sixty-seven, is it right that they should find out at age fifty-nine that the game has been changed and now they must plan to work until seventy-five or seventy-eight? I don't think so.

I don't mean to use this book for my personal political pontification, but my suggestion is simple and was stated succinctly a few paragraphs ago: **Don't depend on the Social Security system. You simply must be in charge of your own retirement.** Anything you get from the government should be considered gravy, not the entire meal.

As stated before, the amount you may draw out per month is dependent upon your wages during your working years. But that said, the truth is that the amounts being paid out today are barely enough to keep elderly people from living out in the streets. It is a social safety net, but nothing more. Imagine that spend-a-holic non-saver who earned $10,000 a week and spent it all suddenly retiring and being forced to make due with around $1,500 per *month*. That's one heck of a shock to the system.

As a small anecdote, if you're a Libertarian/anti-Big Brother-type, you might be enlightened to know that Social Security numbers were never intended to be used for identification. Their primary purpose was to track individuals for taxation purposes. In recent years, though, your Social Security number has become a de facto national identification number. Apply to go to school, even a public school (I'm not even talking college here), and you have to present that number. Apply for loan? Show the man your number. Buy a car? Get it insured? Gotta have that number. An American simply cannot be an American today without that little nine-digit number.

Company Pension Plans

Okay, so while I'm in the midst of debunking the retirement myths of the last few generations, allow me to now eviscerate "the company pension plan." Yes, between Social Security and the company pension, we would be set for good. That's what Americans were told and many believed it. Frankly, for a short window of history, it was true. But unfortunately, those days are now over.

A pension is a steady income given to a person by virtue of their previous employment, usually after retirement. These are generally funded through labor unions, the government, or through the former employer themselves—sometimes as a pure benefit or sometimes via an employee contribution matched by the employer. The concept of the company pension went along with the classic "gold watch" for fifty loyal years of service. That was what America was once built upon—the lifelong employee. For a time, most American parents taught their children that this was why they should "get a good job," and this was what *defined* a good job. A "good job" involved working for a big "stable" company that not only provided wages, but also a retirement plan. All you had to do was get hired, then show up for work each and every day for the rest of your productive life and everything would be set for you. No cares, no worries.

This is no longer the case today. True pension plans have been almost entirely replaced by 401K plans and IRAs (definitions and entire dedicated subchapters to follow). Most younger workers are NOT covered by an old-fashioned company pension that pays benefits upon retirement. Some of the biggest traditional pension plans still in existence are through major unions such as those for teachers or government employees. Also, non-unionized government employees still do rather well with these programs in most cases.

Furthermore, we are very much in the age of "Future Shock," that is, too much change in too short a period of time. Few companies are truly stable. It has been said that fifteen years from now most Americans will be working in industries that *do not even exist today*. Starbucks only began in 1971 and didn't expand to multiple cities until 1987, but look at them today. Microsoft was only founded in 1975. Google just began in 1998. Fifteen years from now, even these big names may seem quaint and antiquated.

The point I am trying to make is that "The Big Boss Man"—your employer as some surrogate parent figure—is a thing of the past. You work for him (or her) and the employer gets from you what they need and you get from them what you need. In each case, the needs are immediate and immediately gratified. But there isn't much of a tomorrow. Tomorrow is no longer guaranteed. **Only *you* can guarantee your own tomorrow.**

Pension funds usually invest in large real estate projects, like shopping malls and high rise buildings and use the return from that investment to fund payments. But if you read the newspapers, you will recall that some pension funds have been horribly mismanaged over the years, and workers' contributions or contributions made on their behalf have been squandered in highly speculative ventures—or stolen outright.

The point here is that, if you do happen to work in an industry that provides a pension plan, you have no control over the management of that money. Repeat: You are not in control. Your opinion does not count. In upcoming subchapters, we will talk a little about things like mutual funds, where you are investing in some expert's opinion of which stocks and investments should provide the best possible return. But even then, you can pull your money out and "ride another horse" if you don't like the results of that expert's investment picks. You can't do that with a company pension. You're along for the ride, good or bad. Personally, I like a bit more control over my own future than that.

In addition, pension benefits, combined with health benefits and other perks, have crippled some of America's greatest companies. Large and powerful unions forced large employers, such as those in the automobile industry, to provide incredibly lucrative compensation packages for their rank and file employees. These benefits far exceed what might be considered free market-driven wages and benefits for unskilled or semi-skilled workers. This may have been good for the workers (while the party lasted), but it eventually ruined the companies themselves. Consider companies such as General Motors. Instead of being a manufacturer of cars, GM is more like a healthcare/pension company that just *happens* to also make cars. Tons of retirees drawing large pensions has contributed greatly to large layoffs of current employees, outsourcing of manufacturing, and the inability of domestic manufacturers to compete with savvy foreign companies. It is said that approximately $1,000 of the cost to build each GM car goes directly into retiree benefits.

The bottom line: Do not depend on Social Security OR a company pension plan (if you are one of the few who still qualify for one) for your retirement. Take responsibility for your own retirement by saving ...starting NOW!

401(k)s

When someone starts to drone on about what you *shouldn't* do, it can be difficult to stay awake sometimes. Human beings were meant to be proactive. Don't just tell me what *not* to do; tell me what *to* do.

Here's one of the first things *to* do: Get yourself a 401(k).

Here's what it is: First established in 1981 with final regulations in 1991, **a 401(k) is an employer sponsored retirement plan** named after a section of the US Internal Revenue Code (Section 401, Paragraph "k"—duh). Would you believe that Japan also has 401(k) programs modeled after the U.S. system and they, too, call it a "401(k)"—even though that number and letter correspond to absolutely nothing in that country? Some trivia with which to impress your friends.

A 401(k) is usually set up by a private corporation—not a government entity. For certain selected occupations, there are similar plans that work much the same way, but are given different names. For example, **403(b) Plans** cover workers in educational institutions, churches, public hospitals, and non-profit organizations, and **457 Plans** cover employees of state and local governments and certain tax-exempt entities. The self-employed are also eligible to setup their own 401(k) programs. Individuals or employees themselves are not eligible to sponsor their own 401(k) plan.

A 401(k) allows a worker to save for retirement while generally deferring income taxes on the saved money, growth and earnings until withdrawal, with the theory being that most people's post-retirement income tax bracket will be less than it is today. This makes sense for the individual when one considers that it is logical to earn more money when working than when retired, right? So the idea here is that **no income tax is withheld on the money contributed *in the year that money is put into the 401(k).*** Furthermore, some people retire to states that do not have income taxes, since income is taxed on both a state as well as a federal level (with the exception of the no-income-tax states that were explained in a previous Chapter).

However, there is a new "**Roth-401(k)**" (named after a U.S. Senator by the name of...Roth). With this program, taxes are paid *now*, but *not* on the growth or withdrawal in the future. Wrap your mind around this twist: You put $1,000 in today. It produces earnings and grows in value. Eventually, due to appreciation, you get to withdraw, say, $10,000 from that original $1,000 investment. Forget tax brackets—the tax on $10,000 is larger than the tax on $1,000, right? That's how the Roth program works. Using the aforementioned example, with a Roth IRA, when you draw out that $10,000, you pay *no taxes*, because you *already* paid taxes on the $1,000 you started with way back when you put that $1,000 in.

Because of this new wrinkle, Roth 401(k)s are becoming immensely popular. What you might be wondering is how does one designate which of the two programs one participates in. The way that works is this: Your employer (not you, unless you are self-employed) sets up the 401(k) or Roth 401(k) program. Setting up either such program requires the filing of certain forms with the IRS—an employer can't simply say, "If you want, you can give me some of your money, I'll add some of mine to it, and we'll invest it together and call it a 401(k)." It doesn't work that way.

It is possible that your employer will give you a choice between a traditional 401(k) and a Roth. You can see the advantages of both, though, and even if you favor one more than the other, they're both good retirement vehicles.

If you are self-employed, or if you are the employer, then you must mull over the differences and decide which way to go. A good professional financial advisor and/or accountant can then help you set it up and make sure all the proper forms have been filled out and filed.

Usually, the employee can select from a number of investment options, such as a variety of mutual funds that emphasize stocks, bonds, and money market investments. Some plans also offer the option to purchase company stock. **The key here is, the employee—you—gets some choice as to how the money is invested, and if you leave, you can take it with you.** This, again, is in contrast to a company pension plan where you have no control over how the money is invested.

This is also where that word "diversify" comes up again. **Again, it is best not to have more than 20% of your money in any one stock, fund, or investment apparatus.** Think about the people who tied up all their benefits in Enron or WorldCom stock.

Assets held by the plans are generally protected from creditors of the account holder (i.e., if you get sued or go bankrupt). In other words, **if you declare bankruptcy, your 401(k) cannot be touched. In the case of EMPLOYER bankruptcy, assets in a 401(k) are protected, while**

pension plans usually are NOT (another advantage of 401(k)s over traditional employer pension plans).

Here is the biggest benefit to a 401(k): **Many companies "match" an employee's contributions, up to 1, 2, 3% or more of their salaries. This is like "free money" for the employees, and you are *crazy* if you do not max out these contributions! The "match" is also tax deductible to the company.** Like health plans, this is an important employee perk, and many employers are offering it in order to get quality employees.

Despite this, unlike health care benefits, some employees don't bother getting involved in their employer's 401(k) program. This is insanity. I am urging you to be a saver anyway; why not invest in a program where some of your savings may, in fact, be matched by someone else? Picture putting $50 a week into a savings account, and then handing *your employer* some deposit slips so that *he or she* could *also* put $50 per week, every week, into YOUR savings account. Mind-blowing, isn't it?

Other employees still leave money on the table by only "dipping their toe in the water" with 401(k) investment. At a minimum, I strongly urge you to put in as much money as your employer will match. Using the previous example, what if I told you that if you put in up to *$100* per week, I would *also* put $100 per week into *your* account. If you only put in $50, then that is all I would put in as well. Why, then, would you stop at $50? Put in whatever *I* am willing to put in. Take my money, please. It's like the reverse of the street person standing on the corner asking for spare change. A 401(k) is like a rich guy standing on the corner handing *out* spare change. Take it!

Furthermore, money placed into your interest-bearing checking or your regular savings account is not tax-deductible or tax-deferred. A 401(k) is. Earn $50,000 a year and put $5,000 a year into a savings account, you still pay income tax on $50,000. Earn $50,000 and put $5,000 into a traditional 401(k), you pay income tax on only $45,000. Which is better?

You can contribute up to $15,500 to a 401(k) in 2007. This will be indexed for inflation in future years, increasing in $500 increments. For

2007, the maximum total contribution (what both you and your employer can contribute) is the lesser of your total annual earnings or $45,000. Employees are generally able to contribute up to 15% of their earnings to a 401(k).

With a traditional 401(k), you <u>must</u> start to draw out assets after reaching the age of 70½, but can do so as early as 59½ in most cases. **Only a Roth IRA is not subject to minimum distribution rules.** There is a specific calculation that the government has devised that dictates how much money must be withdrawn from your 401(k) upon reaching this age of (assumed) retirement. The penalty for not doing this—50% of the amount that should have been withdrawn—is one of the most severe that the IRS levies. So, remember that this program does have certain rules and regulations that must be followed. Following them is not onerous, so don't be scared off. But bear in mind that they are there.

If you really need to get at your 401(k) money early, there is a 10% penalty for early withdrawal, in addition to ordinary income taxes on that money, which is considered regular income upon withdrawal. There do exist, though, some exceptions for borrowing for home purchases, secondary education expenses, medical care and the like. Check with your accountant or your employer's human resources (HR) person before contemplating early withdrawal.

If you change jobs, you can take your 401k with you. This is important, as some people are under the misconception that they must either stay at a job they dislike so that they do not lose that money, or that they MUST cash out that money and pay a 10% penalty if they leave that employment. Not to worry, the government has already addressed that issue and you are covered. If your new employer has a 401(k) Plan, you can convert yours into theirs in what is called a "Direct Rollover." Even if your new employer does not offer a 401(k) program, you can still do this via something called an individual IRA Rollover (more on this later). You even have the third (and least desirable option) of keeping your 401(k) with your old employer. For obvious reasons, this is not a great idea since you would most likely lose daily controls over that money's management.

Too many people ignore all of these options and simply cash out and pay the 10% penalty. Dumb, dumb, dumb, dumb. Worse yet, some then take that money and say, "Wow, what a windfall! I think I'll go out and buy a boat." You've now just thrown away a whole lot of savings, defeating the whole concept.

This is a major hurdle in savings and investment mentality in general. When we are children, parents often tell us, "If you want that expensive toy, you're going to have to save for it and buy it your-self." On the surface, this is good parenting in its attempt to mold young people's minds about hard work, saving, and reward. The problem is, the reward is *too* easily obtained and has negligible value. So the kid saves for that hot new toy. He buys it. Six weeks later, he's bored with the toy and it's thrown into the back of the closet. The kid hasn't learned to save for anything of important lasting value, such as LIVING. And this is hard because the younger we are, the less we think about tomorrow. Oh, we might think about tomorrow, as in *actual* tomorrow. On Monday, we think about Tuesday. What we don't grow up thinking enough about is Tuesday, sixty years from now; when we're old and can no longer work.

Another catch to the whole "leaving my old job and taking with me the 401(k) I had there" is simple housekeeping. **Make sure the check for your cash-out (it is still a type of cash-out, unless you decide to leave it at your old employer) is written out to the new plan and not to you personally. If it is made out to you, you will have to pay the 10% penalty and the income tax. Or, better yet, go the "Direct Rollover" route and never even touch the check.**

401(k)s are great and you should avail yourself of them. The tax advantages, whether you are using a traditional or a Roth type, are substantial. Again, this is an example of the government creating incentives and disincentives to direct the populace to do certain things and not do certain other things. As Social Security continues to have its problems, the federal government is hoping to have as many people saving on their own—and they consider a 401(k) something that you do on your own, even though it usually involves an employer. In this way, if Social Security benefits need to be cut more in the future, less people are likely to be adversely affected. In fact, as you may know, Social Security benefits are now taxed if one's total income from all sources exceeds a certain level. It's a give away/take away. Social Security is fine for people who are truly indigent—it keeps them alive. I hope it stays in existence for their benefit. But for the rest of us, all signs are pointed toward us forgetting about it and taking care of *ourselves*—with the occasional governmental incentive.

Individual Retirement Accounts (IRAs)

Do I like 401(k)s? Yes, I do. They're a great long-term savings vehicle. Yes, I know that long-term savings can be a bore. Besides, Mom and Dad and rich Uncle Harry are going to die someday and leave you with cars, houses, and tons of money that *they* saved. Life will be a dream.

Think again.

Our parents and grandparents had "saving" drilled into them. After the Great Depression, Americans learned to hold on to every penny.

Not today.

We are Generation E—the Entitlement Generation. We assume that our ancestors will have put so much money away (those tightfisted little Depression babies) that they'll die with tons left over for us.

Guess again.

Thank medical science. Thank a lot of things. But Americans are living longer today and healthcare costs are skyrocketing. The cost of living during the last decade of life is extraordinary. Do you really think Mom and Dad are going to forego buying themselves medicine so that they can die quicker to satisfy *your* laziness and inability to prepare for *your own* future? Fat chance. Death is more likely to be long, drawn out, and costly, rather than quick and cheap.

I mentioned in the last subchapter that we learn as kids to save for *things*. But 401(k)s and Individual Retirement Accounts (IRAs) are all about saving in order to live out our lives comfortably after we've stopped working. Retirement, that nasty, far-away word, is lasting longer and longer because of medical breakthroughs. Gone are the days when "Old Bob" retired from the accounting firm and was dead within six months. Now Old Bob will probably be tooling around for another thirty years. How is he going to pay for it? How are *you*? Better think about it now, because, as I showed you at the beginning of this chapter, the sooner you start, the easier it is. It's called interest. Finally, not interest you owe, such as on a mortgage loan or a credit card, but interest you *earn*—money in your pocket—eventually—if you start saving now.

An Individual Retirement Account—better known as an IRA, can be set up by an individual with or without company participation. In fact, employer participation, either in setting up the fund or in providing matching contributions, is rare. This is the first major way in which 410(k)s and IRAs tend to differ. An employer *can* set up and match funds in an IRA, but they rarely do, as 401(k)s are the more typical vehicle for employer participation.

Like a 401(k), an IRA is a retirement plan account that provides some tax advantages for retirement savings. Yes, you can save money anywhere and in any way you choose. But the reason I am telling you about 401(k)s and IRAs is because, unlike simply investing in stocks, bonds, money markets, real estate, etc., these are mechanisms that have been created by the federal government to encourage long-term (i.e., retirement) saving. The IRS typically does not encourage you to invest or save your money in general, but these are specific programs where they do exactly that. These, then, should be your financial foundation. Begin with using what Uncle Sam hands you. Just as I said about not leaving money on the table when we spoke about employer contributions to 401(k)s, not taking advantage of the tax breaks that the government offers you is saying no to free money.

Subject to certain income limitations, you can usually have both an IRA *and* a 401(k) and in fact, I encourage you to do so. *Uncle Sam* encourages you to do so. That is why they both came into being. These two programs do not conflict with one another any more than buying lunch at McDonald's today and Wendy's tomorrow conflicts. You can do more than one thing and it's all good. It's *diversification*.

Your best possible position would be to max out both of these programs each and every year. You may not be able to do so, but think of this as a goal. Remember, you're going to live to one hundred five, right? I hope you do, but you still will need enough money to get you there.

For 2007, the IRA contribution limit is 100% of your earned income or $4,000, whichever is less—*unless* you are 50 or over, when the limit rises to 100% of your earned income or $5,000, whichever is less. Unfortunately, the deductibility of contributions also phases out as you hit higher income brackets.

As you can see, IRAs are not always the place to dump tens of thousands of dollars. The government wants you to save for your retirement, but they don't want to give you *too* much of a tax break—or *you'd* break *them*. Still and all, to be able to "tax shelter" some of your money for retirement is a good thing and you should take advantage of it.

There are a number of different types of IRAs which may be either employer-provided or self-provided plans. The types include:

- **Individual Traditional IRA** – contributions are often tax-deductible (often simplified as "money is deposited before tax" or "contributions are made with pre-tax dollars"); all transactions and earnings within the IRA have no tax impact, and withdrawals after retirement age are taxed as income.
- **Individual Roth IRA** – contributions are made with after-tax dollars; all transactions within the IRA have no tax impact, and withdrawals are usually tax-free.
- **SEP IRA** – a "Self Employed Pension" provision that allows an employer (typically a small business or self-employed individual) to make retirement plan contributions into a Traditional IRA established in the employee's name, instead of to a pension fund account in the company's name.
- **SIMPLE IRA** - a simplified employee savings plan that allows both employer and employee contributions, similar to a 401(k) plan, but with lower contribution limits and simpler (and thus less costly) administration. Although it is referred to as an IRA,

it is treated separately. SIMPLE stands for "Savings Incentive Match for Employees" and it is generally used at companies with less than one hundred employees.

- **Self-Directed IRA** - a self-directed IRA is one that permits the account holder to make investments on behalf of the retirement plan. The beauty to this plan is that you can invest in things such as real estate and other more exotic investments rather than simply stocks, bonds, or mutual funds.

Let's concentrate on the first and most popular two types, the Traditional IRA and the Roth IRA. Here, in as simple of terms as possible, are the differences:

The biggest difference between the Traditional and Roth IRA is the way the U.S. government treats the taxes. If you earn $50,000 a year and put $2,000 in a Traditional IRA, you will be able to deduct the contribution from your income taxes (this means you will only have to pay tax on $48,000 in income to the IRS). At age 59½, you may begin withdrawing funds but will be forced to pay taxes on all of the capital gains, interest, dividends, etc., that were earned over the past years.

On the other hand, if you put the same $2,000 in a Roth IRA, you would *not* receive the income tax deduction that year. If you needed the money in the IRA account, you could withdraw the principal at any time (although you will pay penalties if you withdraw any of the earnings (growth) your money has made). When you reached retirement age, you would be able to withdraw *all* of the money (principal *and* growth) *100% tax free*.

The Roth IRA makes more sense in most situations. Unfortunately, not everyone qualifies for a Roth. A person filing their taxes as "single" can not make over $95,000 per year. Married couples are better off, with a maximum income of $150,000 yearly. There are no income restrictions with a Traditional IRA, but there can be deductibility limitations for high income earners.

Lastly, a Traditional IRA requires that you *must* begin withdrawing money by age 70½. With a Roth, you can begin withdrawing money *anytime* after age 59.

I know this may sound odd, but some people have more than one IRA for one reason or another. Perhaps it is a married couple where there is a program at each person's place of employment. The deal here is that no matter how many different IRAs you have, you still can't contribute more than $4,000 (or $5,000 if you are older) per year *total*.

IRA's of either type can be opened through a bank or brokerage house. If you are interested in holding stocks or bonds in your IRA, it may be wiser to open an account with a broker. It should require no more than a few minutes' visit to the local branch office, or a trip to their website. Minimum opening deposit requirements differ by institution, but are dramatically less than other types of investment accounts.

There is no reason for anyone to not have an IRA. Whether you are doing a Traditional IRA or a Roth IRA, there are tax advantages and incentives to use these vehicles to save for retirement. The contribution limit per year is small—this is not a program in which "only the rich" can get involved. The maximum contribution for most people is less than $77 per week or $11 per day. That's one fancy snack per day. Take that money and put it toward the future. Besides, if you give up that designer coffee, two after-work beers, or bag of doughnuts, you'll also lose weight and live longer!

Differences: More on 401(k)s vs. IRA's, Roths vs. Traditionals

In school, they call this "compare and contrast." My personal recommendation is that since a person can contribute to BOTH a 401(k) and an IRA, they should. But here is a side-by-side comparison.

- 401(k)s are generally sponsored by an employer, while an individual can setup their own IRA.
- 401(k)s have higher contribution limits than IRA's. The maximum individual contribution toward a 401(k) is $15,500 per year, while the maximum potential contribution to an IRA per year is only $4,000 or $5,000.

- Anyone, regardless of income, can participate in a 401(k). Once your salary exceeds $150,000, you can no longer contribute to an IRA. The money still in your IRA is, of course, still yours, and if your yearly income drops back under $150,000 again at some point, you can begin putting money in again.
- 401(k)s require a custodian, usually a brokerage or investment house such as a Charles Schwab, Fidelity, Merrill Lynch, etc. There is an administrative fee that can be quite substantial—a few thousand dollars per year is common, and there is a lot of paperwork. For this reason, 401(k)s are most common for larger employers—at least twenty to twenty-five employees. Smaller businesses will more often opt for a Simple IRA instead, which has minimal administrative fees and much less paperwork.
- There are both "Traditional" and "Roth" type 401(k)s and IRAs. Participants can usually direct their contributions to be put into either one of these types of accounts, or split between both.
- Traditional 401(k)'s and IRA's: Pay tax later on BOTH principal and growth appreciation.
- Roth 401(k)'s and IRA's: Pay tax now on contributions only (principal).
- With a Traditional 401(k) or IRA, the contributor gets a tax deduction in the year that the contribution is made. For example, if you earn a $50,000 salary and contribute $2,000 to a Traditional 401(k) or IRA, you only pay income tax on $48,000 income. However, when you start to draw out of your account upon retirement, you then pay ordinary income tax on BOTH your original contributions (which you previously received a deduction for), as well as the growth (gain) on the account over the years. The theory behind this is that your income tax bracket may be much less when you are retired, and thus, you will pay a lesser tax *rate*. However, the flaw with this theory is that you are now paying income tax on all of the growth as well—if you have your account for many years and the investments have performed well, you will have a *large* tax liability.
- With a Roth 401(k) or IRA, the contributor does NOT get a tax deduction in the year that the contribution of principal is made. For

example, if you earn a $50,000 salary and contribute $2,000 to a "Roth" type of 401(k) or IRA, you pay income tax on the *full* $50,000 of income. However, when you start to draw out of your account upon retirement, you then pay NO income tax on EITHER your original contributions *or* the growth (gain) on the account over the years. For people who will likely build up a significant account over a long period of time, or others who will still have substantial income during retirement (i.e., rental real estate income, royalties, interest income, etc.), this is usually the preferred type of plan.

- The resulting compound growth, <u>without taxation</u>, can be a major benefit of the Roth plans over long periods of time.
- A Roth plan allows you to withdraw your contributions (principal) at anytime, penalty free.
- With a Roth IRA plan, you do NOT have to take mandatory distributions at age 70½. If you do have a Roth 401(k), which does have mandatory distribution requirements at age 70½, you can then convert it to a Roth IRA.

Simplified Comparison Example of "Traditional" vs. "Roth" IRA:

Annual Contribution:	$ 4,000
Annual Growth Rate:	10%
Years Until Retirement:	30
Federal Income Tax Rate:	31%

Traditional IRA/401(k):	$ 499,404
net money to be withdrawn at retirement (after taxes)	
Roth Type IRA/401(k):	$ 723,774
net money to be withdrawn at retirement (after taxes)	
Difference:	$ 224,370 (45%)

Here is the point of this comparison, which obviously favors a Roth plan. Say you have a Traditional plan. You put in $4,000 a year for twenty-five years. Each year, your taxable income is reduced by $4,000. That's great. You pay a little less tax during those years that you are working.

Now you're retired and you contributed a principal of $100,000 (twenty-five times $4,000). Well-managed, that account may now be worth $1,000,000. You are now MANDATED to start taking that money out at a certain age, and you must PAY TAXES on ALL OF IT—the $100,000 principal as well as the $900,000 gain/growth/interest. The tax on $4,000 in any one given year is far less than the tax on $1,000,000, even granting for the fact that you will probably not be drawing it out all at once. This is why, **by and large, Roth plans—if you are eligible to use them—are superior to Traditional plans.**

The only people I would recommend using a Traditional plan versus a Roth is someone who is older, has just started making some significant income, and needs the tax advantages now, rather than later, since their contributions will not have all that long to grow and by the time they begin drawing out of the fund, they will, indeed, be in a lower tax bracket.

529 College Savings Plans

This is the third in our list of most important long-range savings plans. And yes, like the first two, it does not provide you with immediate gratification. No new Porsche in your garage, no new garage to even put one in. But these savings vehicles are the difference between *wealth* and *earnings.*

I keep preaching this, but **making lots of money means nothing if you don't get to keep any.** In none of these chapters do we discuss how to earn a living or how to get a job. That's for someone else in some other book. I am assuming you work for a living. Maybe you work for someone else or maybe you work for yourself. Throughout your life, you may do a little or a lot of both. You may earn hundreds of thousands of dollars per year, or you may never crack six figures. But none of this has much to do with *wealth.* **Wealth is whether or not you have what you need *when you need it.*** When you *lose* that six-figure job is when you are going to need *real* wealth. If you ever get a catastrophic costly illness and cannot work for two years, that is when you are going to need *real* wealth.

The difference between earnings and wealth is the difference between wants and needs. I *want* a vacation to Hawaii. I *need* a heart transplant. *Needs* are best met through savings and investment. *Wants* are met through spending.

For this subchapter, allow me to assume you have gotten married (or have made some sort of relationship commitment) and have decided to have children. Private colleges in America today cost approximately $45,000 per year. Figure on a 4% yearly rate of inflation and you can start to guess how much it will cost by the time your child is ready to attend college. And if you have more than one child…The mind reels.

Does your child *need* college? Although there will always be exceptions, that seems to be the majority opinion in our ever-changing world, full of emerging technologies and global finances that get more complicated by the day. In fact, there are so many people with undergraduate degrees wandering around today that now the badge of honor when applying for a skilled job position is to have a Masters or a PhD. Generally speaking, more schooling equals more money.

The trick to using a 529 College Savings Plan, one of a variety of college savings vehicles, is not to start it once your child is a junior in high school and already has a good idea of what he or she wants to do with his or her life. It's to begin saving as quickly as possible, such as when the child is born. Setting one up and making contributions to it is a better use of the money from that baby shower you just came home from than buying a few dozen more stuffed toys.

A 529 Plan is a tax-advantaged investment vehicle designed to encourage saving for the future higher education expenses of a designated beneficiary. It is named after Section 529 of the Internal Revenue Code (have you noticed a pattern of incredible lack of creativity in the world of taxes and finance?). Each state generally has its own types of plans.

Generally, the features of these plans are:

- You pay no taxes on the account's earnings. Generally, the

money grows federal and state income-tax free.
- The child doesn't have control of or access to the account—only the parent/sponsor/guardian does.
- If the child doesn't want to go to college, you can roll the account over to another family member.
- Anyone can contribute to the account.
- There are no income limitations that might make you ineligible for an account.
- Most states have no age limit for when the money has to be used.
- If the child gets a scholarship, any unused money (up to the amount of the scholarship) can be withdrawn without paying any penalty. All that must be paid at that juncture is regular income tax on the proceeds.

Summary: With higher education costs continuing to soar, **a 529 Plan should be opened for each child at birth.** Family and friends wanting to give gifts throughout the life of the child should be encouraged to contribute to the plan. If started at birth, annual contributions of at least $3,000 ($250 per month) should be made to insure adequate funds available for when the child goes off to college. Quite simply, there is no downside to opening up a 529 Plan for each of your children as soon as they are born or adopted.

So, how do you go about opening a 529 Plan?

Each of the fifty states has its own version, most with many options to choose from. Some plans are offered only to state residents, while others are open to anyone. Some states tax withdrawals from out-of-state programs, while others don't. All but a handful of states also offer an income tax deduction.

Is there any way to cut through all the clutter to find the best plans? Yes. Like finding out about the best of anything, go onto the Internet or watch for current cover articles on major and reputable financial magazines such as *Fortune* or *Kiplinger's*. What was good two years ago may not be so good this year. Some savvy investors end up opening accounts in other states that allow participation to nonresidents.

To properly evaluate the quality of a state's 529 Plan, one must focus on the quality of the mutual funds offered in that state's plan and the annual fees charged. Some of the best plans use low-fee funds from major, historically well-performing mutual funds. However, there is usually only a limited selection of funds, and in most cases, you can only change the allocation once per year. The worst states charge big fees on top of the funds' fees, while other states charge next to nothing. **Avoiding high fees is the first rule of 529 selection.**

The second rule is to **steer clear of funds sold through brokers.** These generally entail paying upfront sales commissions known as "loads," and the continuing annual fees are often larger than those of plans sold directly to investors by the providers. Fees can chew into your earnings. If your plan were to return, say, 8% a year, a single $1,000 contribution would grow to nearly $4,000 after eighteen years. Add a 2% fee, cutting the return to 6%—and you'd end up with just $2,850.

Damage from fees is especially bad when returns are relatively low, and most experts think a typical mix of stock and bond funds will return less over the next decade or so than in the past.

Of course, a high-fee plan can be a winner if its returns, after fees are deducted, still beat the competitors. But many of today's 529 plans have not been around long enough to establish any clear track record.

In the long run, then, it's probably best to pick a plan using low-fee index-style funds that simply try to match the performance of specific segments of the stock and bond markets.

Stocks, Bonds, and Mutual Funds

I probably should first apologize for using a number of terms in some of the preceding subchapters with which you may not be familiar. These are the kind of financial terms that, perhaps, make your eyes glaze over while your head nods knowingly, despite the fact that you have no idea at all what the words really mean. These words can also cause anxiety, panic, and a general feeling of inferiority because of our ignorance of them, thus the reason why we nod as if we know all about them anyway.

Well, I'm here now to give you a VERY brief summary of what some of these terms mean, bearing in mind my promise that this is NOT a book on how to make a killing as an investor. Sure, some people like Warren Buffett have done just that—one of the world's richest men despite listing his occupation simply as "investor." His brilliance in this area is unparalleled. I wish I could say the same for myself.

Yet Warren Buffett is a man to be admired because of a number of reasons, not the least of which is his solid, feet-on-solid-ground approach to life. Mr. Buffett, despite his billions (not millions, but *billions*) has lived in the same modest home in Nebraska (yes, I said Nebraska—I have been there and it looks just like a regular house— no gates, no staff quarters, no pretentious statutes). He drives himself to his office each day in a very un-flashy car, and believes in making prudent and often downright conservative financial investments. One of his favorite quotes is, "Only buy something that you'd be perfectly happy to hold if the market shut down for ten years." What Warren Buffett is talking about is <u>saving</u>—long-term investing—not making quick hit-and-run financial killings.

Here we go:

Stock – A stock is a small ownership of a portion of an individual company. Companies may choose to be either publicly traded (i.e., anybody can buy or sell them on a stock exchange) or privately owned. Stock prices may go up or down, depending upon the *perceived value* of partial ownership of the company in question.

Bond – A bond is a fixed interest financial asset issued by governments, large companies, banks, public utilities and other large entities. Bonds pay the bearer (essentially you are a "lender") a fixed interest percentage amount at a specified end date—for example, you can purchase an 8% 3-Year Bond. Bonds have different ratings and do carry varying degrees of risk. Municipal bonds, issued by towns to finance capital projects, are generally tax free, but have lower rates of return. The tax-free aspect, though, is enticing to someone in a high tax bracket who needs some financial planning and tax-planning assistance. Someone only earning enough to be in the 15% tax bracket should probably not be tying up their money on the relatively nominal returns of tax-free municipal ("muni") bonds.

Mutual Fund – Mutual funds are portfolios of multiple company's stocks, picked and managed by a professional fund manager. Each company's stock within the portfolio has a different value that will fluctuate. The mutual fund's share price is determined by its net asset value, which also fluctuates with the circumstances of the various companies within the fund. Mutual funds offer a lot of diversity.

Put simply, instead of picking individual stocks yourself, some people choose to "place their bets" with a professional stock-picking firm, so to speak. The performance of the fund itself can also be tracked, not only day-by-day/hour-by-hour as individual stocks are, but more importantly, on a quarterly or yearly basis. A good mutual fund will perform well year in and year out; providing, usually, a more stabile investment for the individual than having that individual picking their own stock or stocks.

Index Fund – An index fund essentially matches the market. It has no manager in the traditional sense and is simply made up of representative amounts of each stock in the index. The most well known are the Dow Jones Industrial Average (DJIA) and the Standard and Poors (S&P) 500 index. The "500" are the 500 largest publicly traded American companies. **With an index fund, you are essentially wagering on the stock market as a whole.** An index fund buys equal shares of each of these stocks, which really spreads your risk around.

"No-Load" Mutual Funds – A no-load mutual fund is one which does not impose a sales or redemption charge, selling and redeeming its shares at net asset value.
English translation: A "load" can be a sales fee. Think of it like a tax. You make a $1,000 investment into a mutual fund that has a

"Front End Load," and you might only be investing $950, while the "load"—the remaining $50 fee—is the commission paid to the broker who sells it to you. There can also be "Back End Loads" where you are paying the same such fee in addition to or instead of the front end load when you go to sell or redeem your investment.

Look for "no load" mutual funds. Watch out for any fees or commissions that will reduce your earnings!

Company Stock "Options" – An employee stock option gives you the right to buy ("exercise") a certain number of shares of your employer's stock at a stated price (the "exercise" price) over a certain period of time (the "exercise" period). For example, if your company gives you 100 "options" at $1 each, and your company's stock (after your hard work) becomes worth $5 per share, you can make $400 by exercising your options. You get to buy $5 stocks for $1 each. Lots of newer companies do this for their employees in lieu of cash bonuses or higher salaries. When the company grows and grows, this can be great. Imagine having stock options when Microsoft, Apple, or Yahoo was just getting off the ground. On the other hand, weighing two job offers—one from a start-up offering a horrible salary, but stock options, and another with a high starting salary, it can be a tough choice. Not every new company becomes a Microsoft.

The most prudent, basic investment is an indexed fund. Historically, since 1926, index funds—the stock market as a whole—have had an average annual growth of about 11%. Now you see how something as relatively safe and conservative as this far outperforms a regular savings account or interest-bearing checking account, which languish at around 4 or 5%. Granted, there were some times in the late 1990s where index funds were over 30%, while there were a few times some years ago where they were negative 20%. But year in/year out 11% growth—over an extremely long period of time—is a good deal.

Now, as previously stated, I realize that all these possibilities can be frightening. That's okay. What's not okay is if your fear of them causes you to not participate in your employer's 401(k), or for you to not invest in an IRA. These savings vehicles will, most likely, be invested in stocks or bonds or mutual funds or index funds. That's Ok. My recommendation to you would be to try to direct your personal funds toward an index fund as your first choice, and a good, reputable mutual fund as a second choice.

By the way—**beware of "privately created" mutual funds**. Really. It is possible for Joe Stockguy—the market know-it-all who bores everyone at cocktail parties—to set up his *own* mutual fund and try to get other people, such as you, to invest in it. Joe Stockguy may be a legend in his own mind; maybe he's even made some incredibly lucky stock picks over the years. But that does not make him a Vanguard, Smith-Barney, Salomon Brothers, Oppenheimer, or Janus—some of the biggest names in the business. When those companies name a new fund manager, it is like the naming of a new Pope. White smoke billows from the top floor of their fifty-story office towers. Trust me, if our friend Joe Stockguy was wise enough to get that gig, he wouldn't have time to be talking to either of us.

Speaking again of 401(k)s and IRAs, **resist the temptation to invest all of your money in your own company's stock plan** (think: Enron, WorldCom, etc.). Sure, you want to be a "team player" and of course, you feel that being an employee there, you have some inkling of what's going on behind closed doors and that you yourself are making some contribution to the success of the company. Dream on. Remember the 20% rule and diversification. Unless you are the company president or the Chief Financial Officer (CFO), you may actually have less of a perspective and less impact on the bottom line than someone outside of the company.

Generally speaking, **picking individual stocks is NOT the best choice for the average investor.** Sure, it looks like fun, and some people get really excited watching a stock ticker each day. But it has also been proven that certain primates without opposable thumbs can be just as lucky or unlucky at picking stocks as the average investor. My advice would be that once you've maxed out your yearly contributions to your 401(k) and IRA and if you have some other money lying around to play with, then fine, knock yourself out and pick some stocks in which to invest. It's more likely to make money for you than simply spending it on things you don't really need. If you do so, it is not recommended that you have more than 20% of your portfolio with one single stock. Again, the word "diversify."

But please, remember this: **Get an IRA, get a 401(k), make sure they are invested prudently in index funds or well-established mutual funds, and then max them out every single year. Start doing this early in your life and keep doing it for your entire life.** If you do not make enough money to max out these investments each year, do not invest in any other gambles (individual stock picks, etc...). Exercise self-restraint. Do not be bullied into doing dumb things with your money to show-off. **Manage your risk by taking as little risk as possible.** 401(k)s and IRAs, invested in index funds and well-managed mutuals, are as small a risk as one can reasonably find.

Stock Brokers and Financial Planners

Now for one of "Braun's Favorites:" How do people get paid, and is there an alignment of interests?

Financial planners and stock brokers usually work on commission. Just like in insurance, some of these commissions are very lucrative and do not necessarily indicate an alignment of interest. **Most financial planners and stock brokers make money on you when you make a transaction, not just when those transactions are profitable for you.** In this situation, where is the incentive to give you the very best possible financial advice? If I am a stock broker, I can tell you to buy a great stock that I believe is going to go up in value, or I can sell you a "dog stock" that no one wants—and I still get paid the same. Nice work if you can get it. However, there are becoming more and more "fee only" investment advisors that charge a flat rate for their services, and I generally like this option the best if you are seeking investment advice.

I'll tell you a personal tale of woe. I bought a stock once that

I thought was going to be a winner. It was in an industry in which I was involved, so I wasn't just throwing darts at a board. I went to a stock broker and bought $1,500 worth of shares. I also paid him a sales commission on top of the $1,500.

Well, the stock tanked. The value of my holdings had gone down to $180 and it didn't look like it was ever going to come back. I called my stockbroker and asked him to sell it for me so that I could use it for a tax write-off. I anticipated receiving a check for $180—the current value of my holdings. I got a check for $-0-. His fee for selling those shares was...$180.

Now, in that story, *I* had been the one to pick the "dog" stock. But one must be wary, also, of stock brokers or financial planners who have a corporate or personal interest in a particular stock. This relationship may not be readily apparent and might not be fully disclosed in the kind of detail you might wish for it to be. The broker may, in fact, be getting paid a company "bonus" for selling one particular stock over another. There are millions of tear-filled stories of "boiler rooms" (there's even a movie of the same name) where stock brokers cold-call people, hyping a stock—a stock whose price may be artificially inflated by virtue of those very same calls. In other words, "value" is based purely upon perception, not reality. If I can be convincing enough to get enough people to buy stock in a company that is going down the drain, I can be holding enough of that stock myself so that not only can I get commissions from you when A) you buy it and B) you sell it, but when the stock "artificially" rises enough, I can sell you *my* shares and put even *more* money in my own pocket. It's dirty, but it happens.

So what are your options? Generally, the large discount brokers (i.e., Charles Schwab, Fidelity, ScottTrade, AmeriTrade, E-Trade, etc.) are a good fit for the average investor. They have great research online, online trading and expert help if you need it—kind of an ala-carte offering. As the word "discount" infers, their costs and prices are very competitive compared to a "full-service" broker.

If you have a complex enough financial situation, you should think about a "fee only" financial planner like I mentioned previously, rather than one who makes a commission whenever you buy or sell. This should be your next step up after discount brokerages and should only be considered once you are dealing with moving around hundreds of thousands of dollars. The idea here is that you should not want to pay a commission on each transaction, but rather, you pay them an hourly fee, a monthly fee, or a yearly percentage of the total assets. Because of this neutral fee structure, they are more likely to represent the best interest of the client, rather than seeing a commission each time a transaction takes place.

When you start getting substantial assets (i.e., $1 million or more invested), you will generally pay a trust company to administer your investments and they will get paid yearly a flat percentage (i.e., 2-6%) of your total assets. This means that the return they need to achieve for you needs to be more than this to cover their fee.

In the end, when it comes to choosing stocks, bonds, or mutual funds, you have to do a lot of due diligence yourself—and the Internet has made that incredibly easy to do. These "experts" do not necessarily have financial interests that align with yours. If you buy a stock from them that loses money, *they* do not lose money. If that were the case, it would be a whole different ballgame.

So in Conclusion...

If your employer offers a 401(k) or a SIMPLE-IRA, invest the maximum company match, or you are leaving money on the table. Matching money is free money.

- There are HUGE tax incentives that allow your retirement savings to grow—if you take advantage of them.
- Talk with your company HR person to make sure that you are taking full advantage of the plans and benefits they have available.
- Use your tax refund to fund an IRA—NOT to take a vacation or buy yourself an unnecessary material possession. The same thing is true with promotions or raises. Just because you start to *make* more money does not mean that you should *spend* more money.

- If you have children, start a 529 Plan for college as soon as possible.
- Just as compounding interest works AGAINST you when you BORROW money, it works FOR you when you INVEST money.
- Time is the key! The fact that you are young gives you a huge edge if you want to be rich in retirement…IF you do something about it.
- Retirement planning has become more consumer-driven. Unlike the previous generation who had company sponsored pensions, YOU must take responsibility for your own savings—nobody else is going to do it for you.
- Invest automatically (have the money automatically deducted from your paycheck so that you never even see it or miss it). If you start early (such as when you are 25), it is relatively easy to have a million (or two!) by the time you retire.

CHAPTER 9
WILLS, PROBATE, & PRENUPTIALS

Leave it to a single guy like me to finish with death and marriage, in that order. In my own defense, there's a method to the chronology of this entire book. First, you must grow up, wake up, and begin to understand money. Then you must properly work your way through some of life's basics: credit cards, cars, homes, insurance, taxes and saving. Maybe it's just me, but I think you should have your head properly wrapped around all those important issues first before you start dragging some other poor soul into your life.

Now, as to the dying part…well, that can happen at any time; in fact, it could happen before *or* after you decide to enter into the ultimate "joint venture." So let's talk about death…and marriage.

Estate Planning

Ever go to an estate planning seminar? Zzzzzzz. It's a hard topic to make scintillating. Nevertheless, it's a sign of immaturity to avoid all topics that do not get our juices flowing. Our boredom is another person's opportunity to fleece us. Furthermore, this is a topic most people do not want to think about. I mean, this is about what happens *after* we die! Shouldn't that be someone else's problem—especially when we are young?

But EVERYONE should address it early on, especially the healthcare portions. **If you have a spouse, kids, or substantial assets, you need to have a will in place. No matter your net worth, it is important to have an estate plan in place.**

The first thing you should do is **keep an updated inventory of your assets.** This means your car, your valuables, collectibles (those old comic books and baseball cards you knew would be worth a lot if you held onto them long enough), and so on. The documentation of your ownership of these (things such as the title to your car) should be put in a safe, yet easy-to-find place—easy for the people you *want* to have find them to find them.

Sure, I know, some of us are sloppy. "Functional sloppiness" is when we manage to pay our bills on time and can lay our hands on certain things like warranties and licenses if need be—usually in one of many piles laid in a corner somewhere. And yes, you've probably taken some heat about that at one point or another in your life. But hey, you're functioning, right? You've got good credit, you get all your work done, and you meet your deadlines.

But what if you keeled over tonight? Think about it (but not right before you go to bed—you may have trouble sleeping). How the heck is anyone else going to be able to figure out your "system" (and I use that word loosely)?

Should you care? I guess that all depends. Do you have a Mickey Mantle rookie card (worth tens of thousands of dollars) shoved at the bottom of some drawer somewhere? Even though it's worthless to *you* once you're dead, didn't you want your kid brother to get it? Well, that might be hard if the cleaning person throws it out with all the rest of your junk.

Even if we're talking about things of purely sentimental value, sentiment *has* value. Photographs, trophies, keepsakes. Maybe once a year, think in terms of inventorying these things and putting that list in a safe place so that someone you care about can find it easily. And certainly, do the same by recording the location of documents for things of undisputed value—your house, your car, etc.

There is also the issue of your bills. I know, death is the greatest way for you, personally, to get out of debt. But those debts may still continue to accrue, and somebody might be left on the hook for them—usually your spouse, if you have one. Picture some of the most disastrous situations people have left their families in when they died suddenly (or even not so suddenly). Maybe you had a post office box where you had all your bills sent. Maybe your spouse never had a key to said box or didn't even know about the box. Then you die, the bills keep coming in, and by the time your spouse or some other responsible party hears about the backlog of debt, your accounts have already been sent to collection, and *their* credit has been destroyed. Not a pretty picture. Not nice at all.

Even if there is no other "responsible party" (someone who is co-signed to a debt), leaving these things in limbo will substantially eat into your estate. Why would you want faceless creditors to get more than they deserve from what you've left behind? Wouldn't you rather it go to someone you cared about? And what about time? An estate cannot be settled until everything is, well, settled. If some bank somewhere is still bellyaching about money owed to them on some loan no one can find any documentation on, it could take years for your loved ones to ever get a cent or an item that you left behind. Yes, even your sentimental things could be withheld if a creditor puts a lien against your estate. They might figure the thing has value and this is just one of the ways that they can collect what is owed them. If you think about it; you can't blame them.

Passwords! Here's something no one had to think about fifteen or twenty years ago. If you do online banking or online anything, what is going to happen if your passwords die with you? Even e-mail! That may even be more frustrating than the secret post office box. Your responsible party (if there is one) will know there's e-mail piling up somewhere, but will have no way at all of getting to it. The cost of hiring computer security folks who can hack into things isn't cheap, and your heirs may have to jump through a lot of hoops to get someone to break into everything in a legal manner—lots of official forms and so on. And even then, the hackers may not know what they're looking for! I heard of a recent situation where Hotmail would only *close* the account of a deceased person, rather than give his family access so that they could notify his friends. Imagine the emotional toll of your friends not even knowing you died, because no one knew who they were and/or how to contact them.

I keep a list of my passwords, my accounts, and the "hiding places," of my important things—along with what those important things are—updated and printed out once a year, and then I put that list in a safe deposit box. I have multiple responsible parties (most people use a spouse and/or family members) who have keys to that box or who know where a key can be found.

Safe deposit boxes are great, and are very easy to obtain. Go to your local bank, walk in and ask for one. Their cost is negligible. They are usually priced by size. Start with a small one, then get another one or a larger one as needed or if needed. If you are paranoid, most banks may even have certain security measures as part of their protocol, where you indicate who has keys to your box. That person may have to show ID in order to even *get* to your box, even if they *have* the key. Simply put, most banks have a person on staff who is more than happy to discuss the options they have available. Safe deposit boxes are a money-maker for them. They will be happy to help you.

The bottom line here is to be considerate of your family, friends, and loved ones. If you leave behind anyone that you love or care about, why do things to unnecessarily burden or upset them? It's bad enough that they will be grieving for you. Why add to it with a whole lot of other headaches? It's just not right.

Wills

"A will is a dead giveaway." (Famous bad pun)

Estate planning *now* will make the entire process easier for your heirs and may prevent disputes or confusion as to your intentions. The ultimate estate-planning tool is a *"will,"* also known as a *"last will and testament."*

A will tells everyone exactly how you want your assets to be distributed upon your passing. Without a will, your estate will likely have to go through a much more complex version of "***probate court***," which is a time consuming process wherein the court decides what happens to your money and your stuff.

Dying without a will is known as being "*intestate*;" not "interstate;" that would be if you died on a state border; but "intestate." Either way, it's a bad thing.

Why? Well, let's look at some of the most common categories of situations that may be present upon your demise:

1. You are married and you die.

When this happens and you did not leave a will, most states will try the simplest route and pass all your assets to your spouse. This is probably fine in most cases, but consider all of the possibilities. What if you wanted to give that baseball card collection to your kid brother, but your wife and he are not speaking to one another. Cross that off the list; it isn't going to happen. Your brother can sue and a bunch of lawyers will get more money than the cards probably are worth; but basically, your lack of planning just blew it for your brother.

What if you were in the midst of a divorce? What if you were separated? What if you had kids? What if they are estranged from your spouse? What if you had kids from a previous relationship? What if your parents were destitute and you wanted to provide for them as well, but again, your spouse and your parents had "issues?"—What if; what if; what if?

Your lack of a will sends everything to a neutral party—a judge—who simply wants to follow standardized patterns in order to get your case the heck out of his courtroom. And these patterns *are not necessarily what you had wanted*!

2. You are unmarried and you die.

Generally speaking, without a will your estate will go to your children, if you had any, or your parents if they are alive. If you have children who are minors and your parents are still alive, your estate will most likely be given to your parents and your parents will be given custody of your children, with the proviso that they (as grandparents) are expected to use some of your estate to care for them. But who is going to oversee this? See, it all gets tricky, sticky, and rotten—and all because you didn't write up this simple document expressing your wishes.

But what if you had no children and your parents predecease you, which most parents do? The probate court will start looking around for a more distant relative. If you had siblings, they'd be the logical choice. But what if the closest they can find is your idiot cousin Melvin, the guy you once loaned $10,000 which he never paid you back? Yep, he'd probably get it all; everything you ever worked for.

What if you're gay? There's a *whole* other set of issues. Imagine your life-partner and Cousin Melvin fighting it out in court over your assets. Not a pretty sight.

3. You're married and both you AND your spouse die at the same time.

The two of you are in a car wreck and both die (sorry to be so morbid this entire chapter). If you had minor children, what happens to them? Depending upon what state you live in, a court—maybe the probate court, maybe a similar court—would have to take up that issue as well. If your parents are alive, they would be a natural choice. But what if both *your* parents and your *spouse's* parents are alive? Who gets the kids and the money? Another sticky wicket. And what of godparents? Maybe you didn't want *either* set of grandparents to raise your children; perhaps they're too elderly. And remember, godparents are chosen when your children are first born. Maybe that was many years ago and you don't even *speak* to those people anymore. And if you have multiple children, you probably have multiple godparents for them. Do you want your children split up? This stuff just gets worse and worse.

Bottom line: There is absolutely no intelligent reason not to have a will. Complex probate stinks! You do not want your estate going there under any circumstances. It will tie things up for a long, long time and there is no possible upside.

Yet still, you challenge me. "But Braun, I don't have much."

So what? **A will is probably the cheapest thing you can ever purchase from a lawyer.** And the less you have—the less complicated your estate— the less he or she will charge to help you write one up.

What you should keep in mind, though, is that **a will should be revisited every few years.** By getting one as early as possible, the basic template has been set up. Now all you have to do is modify it as you undergo major life changes.

So today, you say, you don't have much money or many assets. But you keep working and hey, you start to gather some. Let's imagine you're single and you set up that first will and it said your primary beneficiary was your parents, and if they pre-decease you, you want your assets to go first to your kid sister, then lastly to the American Cancer Society. That being said, there's really nothing to change—any and all parties will simply get more as you earn and gather more. By the way, **charities are usually a very good "final choice" for your inheritance.** There are also some significant tax benefits for doing this when an estate is in excess of $2 million. If you only designate certain people and none of them are alive when you die (they may even all be with you— what if you're all on the same airplane and it crashes…isn't this a fun chapter?), do you know who gets your money? Uncle Sam! Can you believe it? Now, I love my country, but I'd rather designate a charity I believe in before I'd simply let the government take my estate and use it to buy $1,200 toilet seats. But merely having more money and stuff doesn't absolutely necessitate changing your will.

Examples of major life changes are:

- A person you've designated as an heir dies.
- You get married.
- You have children.
- You get divorced.

Someone you've designated as an heir has a major change in *their* life. Picture this: Say you designate your kid sister as your sole beneficiary. If she marries and she predeceases you or dies with you, *her husband* may become *your* sole beneficiary if he is *her* sole beneficiary. If this is not what you want, you should have your lawyer use language to curtail such an event.

You have a falling out with someone you've left all or part of your estate to and no longer wish for them to receive anything.

What is also of utmost importance is…what good is a will if no one knows where it is and what is in it? You must make sure that someone handles this! This, too, should be a staged process, subject to modification in case of major life changes.

Many people simply designate their primary beneficiary as the *executor* or *executrix* of their estate. This makes them your **Personal Representative**—somebody you name to handle your affairs after your passing. They will usually deal with the courts, your attorney, trustees if any exist, etc. Depending upon the size of the estate they are settling, they may get paid a small stipend, although this is usually only if the designee is not a family member or if the size of the estate is quite large.

Although your beneficiary may also be your personal representative, unlike a simple beneficiary, you have to let them know they have been so designated. Think of the tree falling in the forest—if your kid sister does not know where your will is, what good was it to name her your executrix?

Furthermore, you can't expect a charity to be your personal representative. Your "last choice" here should instead be someone like your attorney, or even your local banker. Both parties are very experienced at such duties, and you may even want to push them ahead of some of your beneficiaries in the pecking order you set up. I mean, if at the time of your passing your only heirs are your ninety-year-old parents, they may not have the faculties to administer your estate. The same goes for a child. Just think about those clichéd movie scenes where the rich old guy dies and everyone—even the widow—sits anxiously in the attorney's office waiting for the reading of the will. That scene is cliché because that's how most people with sizeable estates do it. It's the way to go.

That, logically, brings up another major "life change": What if you designate your attorney and THEY die? It happens. Again, keep abreast of these things and make modifications as you go on through life. It's not that hard, it's not that expensive, and you'll be glad you did. There is no excuse for not having a will—do it today if you do not already have one in place.

Dividing Up Your Stuff

So now you know to have a will in place, no matter how young you are; no matter how "poor" you are. AND you know to make sure someone knows you HAVE a will as well as where it is located. Lastly, you have a personal representative to "quarterback" the execution of your will.

So, is there anything else you should know about what to put in that will?

Of course.

Some people keep it all really simple. They do nothing more than say, "I leave everything to my husband Marty," and that is that. As previously mentioned, you may want to put in contingencies if Marty predeceases you before you have a chance to modify your will, or if you die together.

Some people divide up the net proceeds of their estate in percentages. Maybe you have no spouse, no children, no living parents, but three siblings. You may simply want to say, "I leave 33.33% of my net assets to each of my three siblings," and you're finished. The only problem with this is that it may require the liquidation of all of your assets. This may or may not please everyone involved. In other words, you can't give someone 1/3 of a car—the car would have to be sold.

Where this becomes a problem is if one of your heirs wants something and does not want its cash value. Using the above example, what if your older brother really *wants* that car? He'd have to do some horse-trading with your other siblings in order to figure out a way for him to drive off in it. This can often times cause problems.

The same is true for things of sentimental, rather than monetary value. Even if you don't have a lot of money, you may know that your youngest sister could really use your old apartment furniture, your older brother would really appreciate your music collection, and your middle sister would cherish your scrapbooks and other memorabilia. You can make life easy on everyone if you simply state these things in your will. Again, if things ever change, you can make modifications as time goes on. But **there is nothing worse than families fighting over an estate.** Do them all a favor and take the issue out of their hands.

Now, there is no need to go overboard. If you start creating a seven-tiered back-up plan for your music collection ("If David dies before me, it goes to Carol. If Carol is dead, it goes to Ned, etc.") and every other thing you own, your attorney will start charging you more money for all the hours he has to put into this encyclopedia-sized will of yours. It's simply not worth it. If a certain person has their eye on something and you want them to have it, designate it and move on. Most attorneys will even give you a simple form that is attached to the will to detail this, so you can modify it yourself without having to visit their office each time you make a minor change.

Again, bear in mind that your debts must be paid before anyone can revel in your booty. If you owe MasterCard $6,000, that gets paid before your brother gets paid. So, too, any outstanding mortgages, car loans, etc.

Funny, but some businesses *love* dead clients. It's easier to collect from an estate than a living, breathing person. **Law dictates that all debts must be paid by the estate before it can be distributed to its designees.** All a creditor has to do is present their bill, then sit back and wait. With a human being, they might have to chase them, haggle with them, etc. But not with an estate, excepting if the debts outweigh the size of the estate itself. That happens, too. So if you live life with lots of debt, you might think you're leaving your family or friends a lot when you pass, but they may never see a dime of it. That's something to think about.

By the way, an "*estate*" is a generic term for all that you leave behind. Don't think cinematically of some big mansion like "the Wayne Estate" in Batman comic books. Your "estate" might be nothing more than the $1,000 in your checking account and some beat up furniture.

As to personal responsibilities for debts, think about debts where you left behind a specific co-signer/co-debtor, as well as if you ever co-signed any notes yourself and what happens if that person dies. Sometimes it's hard to turn down a friend or relative who asks you to co-sign a loan for them, but think about what would happen if they died suddenly. You would be left 100% on the hook for that debt, unless you are somehow able to extract that money from their estate. This is not good.

If you still want to help out and be a co-signer for someone, ask that contingencies be set up in *their will* to cover the possibility of their dying before the debt is paid in full.

It's YOUR Funeral

Funerals cost money—too much money, if you ask me. The problem is, the funeral industry can sometimes prey upon the bereaved. They show caskets to people in deep mourning and if they try to pick out a simple one, they sometimes get a response on the order of, "What, didn't you LOVE them?" as if love is measured on how much you spend on some box that will just go in the ground in a matter of hours.

Funerals are a personal issue, to say the least. Some people could care less, and rightly so. I mean, it isn't like you're going to see your own funeral. Many people simply designate that their personal representative takes care of all funeral arrangements and leave it at that. If the representative wants to blow through money they themselves could otherwise be inheriting in order to give you a big "Hollywood send-off," then so be it. If you are leaving them money, they can blow it any way they choose. As they say, you can't take it with you.

Other executors would rather just throw you in a pine box and toss you behind the nearest dumpster. Again, you may not care and you certainly aren't going to be an active participant. Funerals are for the living.

On the other hand, you may have certain particular wishes, and those wishes should be included in your will. Here are some to consider:

- Organ donation. How do you feel about that?
- Death notices. Some people actually write their own obituaries. Others are more concerned that certain people are contacted so that they may have the opportunity to properly mourn.
- Wakes, memorial services, and open or closed caskets. There is an ala carte menu to choose from. Do you have a preference?
- Cremation? It's one of the less expensive funeral options.
- Where do you want to go (and I don't mean heaven or hell)? If burial, do you have a preferred cemetery? A plot? You might even want to think about this in advance and, perhaps, buy one, if you are particular. If cremation, where do you want your ashes to go? Lots of choices there.
- Do you have a strong opinion on the budget for your funeral? For example, even though you know that your spouse would like a big gala send-off for you, you might feel that is not in her long-term best interest and wish to override her via your will.

Would you believe that, due to the high cost of funerals, some people actually have a separate "funeral fund"—kind of like a "Christmas Club" at a bank? You can do that, especially if you want something big and extravagant. I also hear that "pre-paid funerals" are becoming popular. Outside of that, though, usually just making the aforementioned decisions and codifying them in your will should do the trick. Again, the cost of all this comes out of your estate first, before the division of the remaining assets, so take that into consideration if there is a loved one you want to help out financially. A $50,000 funeral means you'll be leaving someone $50,000 poorer.

But what if you don't *have* any assets to pay for your funeral? It happens. If you have a will and designate a representative, even though you state that you want a solid gold casket, if the money isn't there to pay for it, it would simply be up to your representative to make their own personal decisions and carry them out. Some people actually *cost* their loved ones when they die. They leave behind nothing but debt, and the closest relatives have to chip in just to toss them a decent funeral. This is very sad, but very true.

If you are worried about, again, having NO money to pay for a funeral and no rich or generous relatives to pay for it for you, a number of things may happen. If you have life insurance, some of the proceeds may pay for it. Governmental benefits, such as social security or veterans benefits may also help pay for minimal funeral costs (a whopping $255). A good source of information in this instance is, in fact, your local funeral director. Along with pushing those solid gold caskets, they also have to advise the less wealthy, and they usually know where certain subsidies can be found.

What about the Kids?

If you are a parent of minor children, drop everything and make your children your first priority. Nothing compares to this when deciding what you'd like to see happen once you've passed on.

As I've mentioned before, if you and/or your spouse die intestate and you have minor children, it can be a total nightmare—far worse than figuring out where your money goes. **The moment you have a child, you MUST draw up a will and you MUST designate who shall care for them and raise them.**

Like everything else, you must be very careful to have back-up plans in case you do not get a chance to update your will if your designee predeceases you, or if you and that designee or designees die together. I advise numerous back-up plans—first choice, second choice, third choice, and so on. And far more importantly than with deciding who will get your money, you MUST let these people know that it may be your wish that they become parents to your child or children. Unlike money, which everyone will take, some people who you love and respect may, for one reason or another, not want or may not feel they are able to parent another child. Know this in advance; don't let them start putting your kids into foster care when you die because you didn't know they felt this way.

This is also an issue that may be subject to greater alteration and variation as time goes by than deciding who gets your stuff. If you have living parents, they may be one of your first choices. But by a certain point, you might be of the strong opinion that Grandma and Grandpa are no longer capable physically or mentally. In the reverse, a sibling who was "only a kid" when your children were born might have grown into a very mature, responsible person by the time your oldest child reaches the age of ten or twelve. At that point, they might make a fantastic parent for your son or daughter or brood of many.

I've mentioned godparents before. Keep an eye on this situation, too. If good old Joe, who was your best pal in college, suddenly develops a drinking problem, you might not want him to have your kids. The same goes for their spouses. Your sister might make a great mom, but what if she just made the unwise decision of marrying some recently paroled sex offender. Keep that will updated!

If you have children, this will also impact greatly where the money from your estate goes. First off, if they are minors and you have to designate someone to raise them, the party you are saddling with that responsibility is going to need more money in order to do it; more mouths to feed, more clothes to buy. Make sure your will reflects that.

The other issue is one of passing along your money to your children. You certainly want them to be able to live well and healthily and to get the education they deserve. But you don't want them becoming spoiled rich kids without values. Giving kids a substantial sum of wealth can actually be a burden. It's a tightrope, even if you are alive, let alone dead.

The best solution is usually in the form of a *trust*, or multiple trusts. A *Living Trust* can also allow your estate to bypass the probate process altogether. This is where a good estate attorney can be invaluable. The best ones are often a good personal representative to administer such a trust.

A trust is a fund that is set up and managed by a designated trustee. That trustee is like a money manager, but you don't want them doing stupid things with your money like blowing it down at the track. Your will might reflect that you want your children's portion of your estate to be put in some very stable, conservative monetary investment, where it will grow.

Then there would be the issue of disbursement. You want to make sure their new guardians have enough to raise your children until they're eighteen. You'll want some more available for education (college, trade school, etc.) after that. Finally, if there is any left—and especially if there is a LOT left, you might want to dole out the rest piecemeal so that your children do not become overnight millionaires. Overnight millionaires tend to end up with a lot of problems. Just look at past lottery winners for some unflattering examples.

I advise maybe apportioning out some money at age eighteen—particularly if they do not decide to go to college, then perhaps another portion when they turn twenty-one, and another at age twenty-five. Some people even stretch this out to age thirty. But you get the idea.

And whatever you do, make sure you leave them a copy of this book so that they know how to handle that money!!!

Finally, like in the last subchapter, you might be wondering, "But what if I die and don't have enough money to care for my kids until they can pay their own way through life? We're young and we're just living hand-to-mouth right now."

Here's the answer. You might want to take this into account when designating their guardians. I hate to put it this way, but Howie and Lisa might be great people, so great that they wouldn't have the heart to tell you that taking care of your son or daughter in addition to their own might just put them in the poorhouse, unless you have the money to stake them. On the other hand, Paul and Lana might be very wealthy, yet still have the values you know you want your children to develop. Maybe they would be a better choice, and frankly, Howie and Lisa might even be relieved.

But if this does not reflect the choices put before you, bear in mind that Uncle Sam knows that children in poverty are bad for his image. Social Security and other governmental programs are available for children whose biological parents are deceased. Whoever you designate to raise your children, if they are not easily able to do so monetarily, should know to look into what assistance is out there at the time of your demise. Good sources of information about this are again, believe it or not, funeral directors. Also, your estate attorney might be able to help them. Lastly, this is the kind of question your local U.S. Congressman's office gets all of the time. That sort of thing defines "constituent services," and constituent service is why 95% of them get re-elected every two years.

Of course, I hate to say, "I told you so," but the moment you have children, you need life insurance. Remember that from a few chapters ago? So make that one of the bedrocks of your estate planning. Do it for the children.

Death and Taxes: Keeping the Buzzards at Bay

By planning in advance, you can take advantage of the "*federal estate tax exemption*," which has been rising gradually and will hit $3.5 million in 2009. Unless congress passes new laws between now and then, there will actually be NO estate tax in the year 2010. In fact, there is a running joke with CPAs and attorneys right now about that being the year to die (or "kill") if there is a large estate. They openly wonder (in jest) how many wrongful death suits there will be after that year.

What this means in plain English is that in 2009, the first $3.5 million you leave to your heirs is tax-free. If you die and leave your two daughters $3,500,000, they don't have to pay any taxes on that income. It doesn't matter how it is split. The splits have nothing to do with it. The issue is one of the *estate* being taxed, not the individual receiving the estate.

This is similar to when you hit a big jackpot at a casino. If you win a bit here and there, the casino pays no mind. If you can win some and you decide not to declare it as income, well, that's between you, the Lord, and the IRS. But if you win big, the casino takes you in a little back room…and rubs you out. Only kidding! No, instead of having you walk around with tens or hundreds of thousands of dollars or more in cash, they "do you a favor" and cut you a check—AFTER taking out taxes and having you fill out forms for the IRS. Estate tax is the same way. You can "win small," but you can't "win big"—tax-free—at least not until 2010.

So the joke about killing or being killed in 2010 can just as easily be reversed as to say that everyone will be kept on life support until then so that when estate tax ceases to exist, everyone can finally die in peace. I must tell you, though, this whole thing is a political hot potato, and I wouldn't bank on the estate tax going away and staying away forever.

That being said, there are numerous ways that people with large estates can attempt to keep them in tact for their heirs. For example, you can state that the maximum allowed by law without estate tax be distributed, and then have the rest set up in a trust. This trust can, for example, hold the balance of your assets until such time that they can be distributed without the recipient having to pay estate taxes. Really good estate attorneys know a lot of other tricks, both legal and semi-legal (stay away from the latter). If you have this kind of money (over $3.5 million in assets), you can afford to get an opinion or two. But before you go running off half-cocked, remember that the first $3.5 million is still safe. If you have that or less, don't worry yourself.

On the plus side, inheritors of certain assets receive a "hidden" bonus, called a *Stepped Up Basis on Inherited (Appreciated) Assets.* Here's how it works: Grandpa bought a building for $100,000. It is now worth $1 million dollars. He already may have taken advantage of all the depreciation he could possibly get from it. Whether he did or didn't, though, matters not.

Grandpa dies. You inherit the building. This $1 million asset (today's figures) is part of that $3.5 million ceiling of what can be passed on without estate tax. BUT…you get to start *depreciating* that asset for your own income tax purposes once you get it, starting from that $1 million figure. This is a good thing for you.

I've mentioned *trusts* and *trustees.* A trustee may be given broad powers to benefit the beneficiaries of the trust. They can make monthly payments to the beneficiaries or lump-sum distributions at certain times, such as giving your money to your children as they reach certain ages.

You can broaden and sharpen your trustee's powers even more so. You may do things such as direct them to evaluate the stability or maturity of an heir, allowing the trustee discretion if they feel that giving an heir certain amounts of money at certain points in their life would not be in their best interests—consider an heir who develops a gambling or drug problem. You might direct a trustee to simply evaluate not the heir as much as the amount and reason for the request for distribution of assets—think about an heir who wants to give a million dollars to some televangelist. In this sense, you can ask the trustee to act as *loco parentis*—a parent in place of yourself. Simply put, there is a lot of flexibility in trust situations, and they further point to the need to keep your final wishes up to date, both in terms of prevailing law at the time, as well as the life situations of your heirs.

Trusts are not just for the "rich"—if you have a net worth of at least $100,000, you might want to consider one.

One caveat of a trust is that you must transfer your assets into the trust. This even includes your house. You should discuss all this with a good estate attorney before jumping into things—your accountant as well. Make sure you have the kind of flexibility while you are alive that you want to maintain depending upon how you are moving your money around.

Bear in mind that you do not have to place *everything* you own into a trust, although whatever is not in the trust will not have the protection of the trust. The thought of placing one's home into a trust while they are still living and still living *in it* turns some people off, and rightly so. I might add, though, that many trusts can be revokeable, meaning that if you want to tap into the equity of something within your trust, or sell something within your trust, you can take it out in order to do that.

Do not try to set up a trust by yourself. The cost to have an attorney set up a trust usually ranges from about $1,500 to $3,000 or more, depending upon its complexity.

Trusts can be very creatively designed. If you have multiple children and each has a different story—one is totally self-sufficient, another has mental health issues, another is basically fine, but lazy—a trust and a trusted trustee can manage your estate using the same sort of discretion that you exercised throughout your life.

In previous subchapters, we mentioned **gifts** and **gift taxes**. Most gifts are not subject to the gift tax. The federal gift tax exists for one reason: to prevent citizens from avoiding the federal *estate* tax by giving away their money before they die.

Currently, you can give gifts of up to $12,000 each year to any number of individuals. You and your spouse *together* can give up to $24,000 a year. If you have five hundred friends on whom you wish to bestow $12,000 each, you can give away $6 million a year without even having to fill out a federal gift-tax form. That $6 million will be out of your estate for good. But if you made the $6 million in bequests via your *will*, the money would be part of your taxable estate and would trigger an enormous tax bill.

Your estate is the total value of all of your assets, less any debts, at the time you die. Under the laws in effect for the tax year 2009, if you die with an estate greater than $3,500,000, the amount of your estate that is over $3,500,000 will be subject to a graduated estate tax that climbs as high as 45%. That $3,500,000 is an *exclusion*; meaning that the first $3,500,000 of your estate does not get taxed.

So why not give all of your assets to your heirs before you die and avoid that estate tax? Clever idea, right? But the government's ahead of you. As noted above, you can move a lot of money out of your estate using the annual gift tax exclusion. But **you may only gift any one person $1,000,000 per lifetime before you must begin paying a tax on lifetime gifts. That rate is the same as estate tax rates.**

Bottom line: **You can avoid some estate taxes by giving your wealth away over time, but there are still some limitations.**

There is one last quirk I want to touch on regarding the buzzards that swoop overhead when our demise has either occurred or is imminent. One of the fastest growing industries in America today is that of retirement homes and communities. Some of them are utterly fantastic. Gone are the days of hell holes and dog food for Grandma. Now Grandma can live out her days as if she's on a luxury cruise every day until the end of her life.

But there's a catch. There are some very straightforward payment programs for these retirement villas, as well as some very creative ones. The creative ones can benefit you as easily as they can literally own you. In some cases, you must make the retirement facility the *sole beneficiary* of your estate—regardless of the size of that estate. For the poorer person who lives a long time after entering the facility, this is a grand deal. For the wealthier person who lives a rather short time, it can mean an incredible windfall for the facility, while leaving the deceased's loved ones with empty hands and mouths.

If you have a lot of money in the bank or wherever, and you want to finish out your days in one of these retirement facilities, check out their policies long before you start packing your bags to move in. What you discover might be worth discussing thoroughly with a good estate planning attorney who may have some good ideas for you to get what you want for yourself (a nice place to make your final home) as well as for the heirs that you love, by protecting some of your assets via trusts and so on.

Power of Attorney

Power of Attorney is an issue that comes up not only at one's demise, but probably even more often while one is alive and vibrant. **A Power of Attorney (POA) is you giving someone else the right to act on your behalf in a legal situation as if they were you.**

There are many different types of Power of Attorney and it is important to know the difference, especially in case of your demise.

First off, a **Power of Attorney is a document.** *General Power of Attorney* **is something that gives another person absolute and total power over all of your affairs. It is not limited in any way.** THEY are YOU. That person can sign any contract, can borrow money, can do anything you can do, using your signature.

The way they would accomplish this would be to sign their name, then state they are the "*Attorney in Fact*" for you. Example: I might sign as "Braun Mincher, Attorney in fact for Abbott Costello." I then simply would have to have that formal, signed, notarized document from Abbott Costello granting me his Power of Attorney.

A General Power of Attorney is so all-encompassing as to be dangerous as hell. The need for one is extraordinarily rare. What is far more common is a *Limited Power of Attorney*, **which is sometimes also referred to as a** *Special Power of Attorney.* **A Limited Power of Attorney is a legal document that states that the holder can be allowed to sign for another person only in one specific instance or category of situation**—there are really no "rules" for this sort of thing, it is simply whatever you want.

One of the most common instances of use of a Limited POA is for a specific real estate transaction. Spouses do it for one another all the time. Say you are buying a piece of property and the closing keeps getting delayed and delayed. You have other business that will be taking you out of town. You've been waiting so long for this real estate closing that you don't want to be the one to have it cancelled and rescheduled again, so if it hits on a day when you'll be away, you draw up a limited POA designating that your spouse can sign for you *in this instance only*, and you're on your merry way.

Limited (*very* limited) POAs are commonly given to entities such as title insurance companies at real estate closings for the purpose of fixing typos and such. What if after you've signed everything, the title company discovers that on one page out of five hundred your address is listed as 231 Main Street instead of 123? Without granting them a limited POA, you'd have to trudge on in and initial the correction. Not a good use of your valuable time, and errors like that happen frequently.

Would you believe that a General POA usually stays in place until you physically wrench it back from the hands of the person who has it? Yes indeed. Further reason that this is something not to be messed with. A General POA is like a nuke in your personal legal and financial arsenal. You don't give your nukes to just anybody.

That being said, I actually have a General POA in my safe deposit box. Why? Only the people I trust most in the world have access to and knowledge of that box. Having a General POA in there can assist in tying up the loose ends of my estate if I become ill or incapacitated before dying (a POA expires upon the death of the grantor). Furthermore, while I am still lucid, if some great business opportunity finally comes together while I am, say, out of the country, I can call my representative and tell him to go to my box, grab that POA, and sign as me so that I don't miss out on some important deal. By having it be a General, rather than a Limited, it becomes a "jack of all trades" document that I don't have to redraft every time I decide to take a vacation or business trip.

And if I don't get it back from my representative upon my return, I start breaking kneecaps. For this reason, I also recommend placing an expiration date on all POAs.

A few last things on General and Limited POAs. I don't recommend letting your real estate agent have your POA. It's a conflict of interest. I have my real estate broker's license and I've even turned down people who asked me to act on their behalf in this manner. I'm not even crazy about assigning a POA to my attorney in a real estate deal. Assign it to a trusted friend or relative—spouses, of course, are the best. Outside of a spouse, it pays for the person with your POA not to have a personal financial interest in the transaction in question.

Durable Power of Attorney and Living Wills

Ah, now for some really sticky stuff; stuff that's been in the news a lot these past few years. What happens when you're almost dead, but still technically alive?

A *Durable Power of Attorney* is similar to a General POA, but is instead limited to your agent being able to make *healthcare* decisions about you if you are unable. For example, if you are in a coma and unable to communicate, your designated agent can choose whether or not to pull the plug. The word "durable" means that it will remain in effect or *take* effect if you become mentally incompetent.

I cannot minimize the importance of a Durable POA, as well as a Living Will (more on that in a minute). Most older people realize this and have them in place. But younger people still incorrectly feel they're invincible. Do you know the number one cause of death for young adults? Auto accidents. Have you ever known anyone who was in a catastrophic automobile accident? Sometimes the luckiest people are the ones who die instantly. Accident victims can be in comas, vegetative states, or simply be so physically and mentally wracked and twisted that they are no longer the same persons they were before—at least for a while, but maybe even for life. Many older folks understand that Alzheimer's disease and other types of senility can rob them of their mental faculties. But catastrophic injuries can render younger people the same.

As I write this, I realize that this is a very touchy subject. Many people have very strong religious beliefs that impact upon this topic, and I respect that. In fact, it is from that respect that I am even more insistent that you consider having both a Durable POA and a Living Will. The following is attributed to none other than Mother Theresa herself, a devout Catholic nun:

"5 Wishes" Document (Mother Theresa)
1. **The person I want to make care decisions for me when I can't**
2. **The kind of medical treatment I want or don't want**
3. **How comfortable I want to be**
4. **How I want people to treat me**
5. **What I want my loved ones to know**

The concept of a Durable POA or a Living Will is not to be confused with taking a stand in favor of euthanasia, which was not within Mother Theresa's personal belief structure. That is a common misconception, and for that confusion to stand in the way of you having these two documents in place is tragic. It is, in fact, your opportunity to say exactly how it is that YOU feel about this issue and tangential subjects as they pertain to you. If you NEVER want ANYONE to pull the plug on you, how will anyone know?

A *Living Will* is also known as a *"Declaration as to Medical or Surgical Treatment"* or an *"Advance Medical Directive."* **This document**

lets everyone, especially your doctors, know your wishes if you are terminally ill and unable to make decisions yourself. It includes such things as your wishes for nutrition, pain medication, etc. It can also include a *DNR—a Do Not Resuscitate* order. But again, note this fact— a Living Will does not LIMIT itself to directing medical personnel ONLY not to resuscitate.

Lack of a living will, even at a young age, is not recommended. Does everyone remember the Terry Schiavo "media spectacle" in 2005 over the controversial removal of her feeding tube? In 1990 at the age of twenty-seven, she collapsed outside her apartment from no apparent trauma, suffered brain damage, and was in a permanent vegetative state for many years. Her husband wanted her feeding tube removed; her parents and family did not. After *fifteen years* of costly court battles, and despite intervention from both the Governor of Florida and the President of the United States (who happened to be brothers), the feeding tube was finally removed and she died shortly thereafter. Most of this strain on her husband, family, and the court system would have been avoided had she had a simple Living Will expressing her desires—whatever they might be—should something unthinkable like this happen.

Almost any lawyer is capable of drawing up both a Durable POA and a Living Will, although these forms have become so standardized that templates are available for free online download from almost every state as well as most every hospital.

In going back to Mother Theresa's 5 Wishes list, consider them one by one. Item one speaks to the issue of having a Durable POA in place. Like your will or any General or Limited POA, **a Durable POA is only of value if someone knows of its existence.** When you decide who that someone or those ones might be, contact them and have a frank and open discussion with them. Be sure that they not only know you have this document in your safe deposit box, but are also informed as to what it says. What you *don't* want is to designate someone who is diametrically opposed to your wishes and will not enforce or make any pertinent parties aware of your true wishes. If you want the plug pulled and this person says, "I could never do that to you," then find someone else. This is serious stuff.

There is also a lot of nuance to all of this. The person given your Durable POA should be competent to quarterback your entire situation the way that you would have wanted. This is no time for not wanting to hurt someone's feelings. This person could be making major business decisions as well as health decisions on your behalf. That lovable boob you have beers with after work might not be the best fit for this job.

As to item two, it might surprise you to know that Pope John Paul II, while not indicating a desire to be euthanized (pulling the plug), which would have been against the stance of the Catholic Church, did indicate that he simply wanted to be "made comfortable." In other words, there was no plug to pull because no machines were ever hooked up. It's a subtle difference that sat well with his personal faith and, in fact, might well be shared with many other individuals also.

On the other hand, this is where we do run into the decision of whether one wants to be hooked up to machines and kept that way indefinitely or not. More and more people are leaning toward inserting DNR language into their Living Wills and instructing the persons in possession of their Durable POAs. Without a DNR, medical personnel will continue "*heroic means*" (a legal and medical term) unless instructed otherwise.

Again, regarding subtlety, some people indicate things such as getting more than one medical opinion, or there being a certain period of time during which they are comatose or living on some form of life support before wishing for a plug to be pulled. You can be as specific as you desire, or you can simply talk it out with the person you give your Durable POA to and allow them to use their best judgment, based upon the discussion you two had together.

Hospitals are becoming so sensitive to this issue nowadays that it has become pro forma for them to ask whether you have these two documents in place even if you are going in for the most basic procedure. Obviously, this can be rather frightening when you are simply getting your tonsils out or a broken bone set. In their eyes, though, not having a Durable POA and a Living Will in place is like not having health insurance. Responsible people simply don't live that way.

Prenuptial Agreements

Okay, so now you're wondering why this topic is in the same chapter as discussions about death. I could try to muster up a good joke, but I will spare you for the moment.

This chapter is all about your *estate*. Your estate is most certainly an issue once your die, but it is also a *living* issue, one that is always around. Whatever you own or owe today, while you are alive and reading this, is your "estate." Your death is cause for the *transference* of your estate. So is your marriage. And that's why we're here.

If you are getting married, a prenuptial agreement can protect your assets. It is a contract between two people about to wed that spells out how the assets will be distributed in the unfortunate event of divorce or death.

Should you have one? I can't really tell you the answer to that any more than I can tell you whether you should have a DNR in your Living Will. These are personal decisions that sometimes even have religious overtones, and I do not go there. That being said, some situations are more logical for such a legal agreement than others.

If the two people about to wed come into the marriage with disproportionate amounts of wealth, it begs the question. Think of the recent Paul McCartney divorce. It boggles one's mind to think that one of the wealthiest entertainers in the world could marry someone with literally no assets at all and not have a prenup. On the other hand, few people who marry young, who both come into the relationship with little to no money, bother forging such an agreement. Despite this, even those people may find significant financial issues down the line that they wished they had negotiated in advance.

Example: Sometimes one spouse pays for the other to go to school to get an education that enables them to earn tons of money. What, then, is the value of this monetary contribution that came when it was so sorely needed? What about the spouse that earns lots of money, but volunteers to take an earning hiatus for the sake of raising children? How much more could that person have earned had they kept working?

I could go on and on and I certainly do not wish to weigh in on who is right, who is wrong, and who deserves what in these or any other hypothetical situations. But many people go the route of the prenuptial agreement.

If you do see the value in this, **an attorney should draft the document and each party should then have their own individual attorney review it.** Nothing gets a pre-nup tossed out of court faster than if it was drawn up by *one attorney*, representing *both sides* at the same time. And even then, prenups can still be held unenforceable by the court, so nothing is guaranteed. This is another reason why, unlike a will or a Living Will, I am not emphatically pushing you to have one. Some states and some judges literally laugh prenuptial agreements out of their courtrooms—and that can be their judicial prerogative.

All this being said, nothing can kill romance faster than discussion of a prenuptial. If you really want to go this route, bring it up early on and see where things go. If it doesn't fly, weigh your options carefully. It could mean you are marrying a gold-digger, or it could mean that your money means more to you than your relationship. Neither situation is a good one.

Some of the most prudently drawn prenuptials utilize a sliding scale based on the length of the marriage. If the marriage lasts one year, the assets are distributed one way; two years, another way, and so on. The longer the marriage lasts, the more commingled the estate becomes and the harder it might be to differentiate what truly belongs more to one than the other. But from the outset, **both parties should make it clear within the document what it is, monetarily, that they are bringing to the relationship.** Even if a judge throws out the agreement, he may still take into consideration this accounting of assets at the beginning of the marriage if he is asked to adjudicate the divorce settlement.

Would you believe that some people wait until their wedding day to spring a prenuptial upon their betrothed and soon-to-be-married? Yup. Is this a good idea? Nope. Want to stand in a church announcing that the wedding is off? Probably not. Furthermore, nothing could bring into question the legitimacy of such an agreement more than evidence that it was presented under such a scenario of obvious duress.

If you are worried about your assets and your estate when you are about to enter into marriage, consider drafting a prenuptial agreement and discussing it with your intended well in advance. They might go for it, they might not. Only you know for sure, and even you might not know unless you broach the subject.

CHAPTER 10
YOUR KEYS TO FINANCIAL SUCCESS

This book has been laid out in such a way that if there is a particular topic that interests you, you can jump right to it—sort of like a reference book. On the other hand, if I had my way, I'd wish for you to start at the beginning and go straight on through, for so much of it builds upon itself. Your financial life is like that—if you want to buy a house, you probably need a car as well. If you buy one, the other, or both, you will need insurance. You will also be dealing with credit. And how could you possibly be talking about cars or houses if you don't also have savings? On and on and on. Have you ever heard the phrase, "a house of cards?" That's what life is, in so many ways. Every individual component relies upon a multitude of other things, or else the entire structure falls down.

So if you've gotten this far, I hope you've read all of the chapters and please, use it as a reference book as well. Refer back to the sections you need, when you need them. Trying to memorize this entire tome would be almost impossible, I know.

In each chapter, I've tried to keep the concepts as factual as possible. Sure, you've gotten some "Braun-isms" along the way. It's almost impossible to not let your own personal feelings and opinions come into play when discussing topics about which one feels passionately—and there is nothing I feel more passionately about than the American public's need to gain a strong personal financial education.

But now it is my turn. No more facts and figures. What I'm about to give you here are the concepts I would share with you if we were sitting across from one another in a local diner, sipping our coffees and spouting off about life and living. What you won't get from me are opinions about sports, pop culture, the weather, or even politics. But now it's philosophy time. Let's talk money, growth, success, and the responsible pursuit of happiness!

Spend Wisely

I do not consider myself to be "cheap," but rather just shrewd. **I generally buy the best quality I can afford when I make purchases, and I ALWAYS get the best deal.** This does not always mean the CHEAPEST, because there is sometimes hidden value. You have to become good at distinguishing the difference.

For example, I travel a lot on business. I'm sure you've heard of "no frills" airlines. Hey, God bless them. This is a need that should be addressed and when one company in this market niche folds, another comes along to take its place. There will always be people who need to get somewhere fast, even if it is on a "flying bus."

But it's not for me.

When I'm doing business, I need to arrive on time, be safe, be calm, and not appear frustrated. I need to look and feel good. *This is a priority for me.* For no matter what business you are in, we are all in the business of sales, in one way or another. Personally, I can't sell my best if I'm an hour late, sweating like a hog, wearing a wrinkled suit, and feeling like I might punch the next guy I meet right in the nose. This can be the difference between a successful business trip ($$$$$) or an unsuccessful one ($).

Now, do I *over-spend* when I fly? No, I don't do that, either. I've learned all the tricks for getting the best airfares on carriers I've grown to trust. A few mouse clicks here and there and I can find out the reputation of an airline I may not have flown before. I can compare prices, I can figure out the optimal lead time to book flights and the best times of day or days of the week for the best fares, etc. That's the shrewd part. See, **any fool can be cheap.** "Cheap" and "shrewd" are as different as chicken and ice cream. Sure, they're both food; but personally, I don't care for a banana split as my main dinner course.

Now, do not misinterpret this subchapter to be about the narrow topic of air travel. Look around at your life and see where the importance lies. I know; it's so easy to justify *any* purchase. "No, really, a big fondue kit will force me to invite more people over to my house, and that will help me break out of my shell socially, and I can then make lots of great business contacts, and my life will improve because I will be making lots more money and *it will all be because I bought the world's biggest, best, and most expensive fondue kit!*" Don't laugh; I've heard worse.

Ever go to high-end gadget shops? I'm a guy, and guys LOVE gadgets. But, you have to ask yourself, do you *really* need a multi-speed electric nose hair clipper? I mean *really?* So what we have are the questions of:

- *What is it you <u>really</u> need?* along with
- *What level of quality do you <u>need</u> in such a purchase?* and finally
- *How do I get the quality I need at the most affordable price?*

Once you've set your priorities and answered these questions, do your due diligence. Don't let savvy shopping be only hit-or-miss luck. Even a broken clock is right twice a day. You can do better than that. If you've come to realize that a well-made business suit is important to your success in life, then study, research, and analyze how, where, and when to make such a purchase. The time spent doing that will be time well spent. **Get the *quality* you need for the *right* purchase at the *best possible price!***

Accept Responsibility

As I said in the beginning of this book, we of the current generation are known as "Generation E," with the "E" standing for "Entitlement."

Responsibility is something many have forgotten long ago. Nothing is anybody's fault. When something goes wrong, fingers are pointed everywhere except where they belong, which is often right at our own chest. Finding a scapegoat to blame is more important than fixing what is wrong. It just sickens me.

When I do business, there is a reciprocal arrangement I enter into that is often unspoken, but simply demonstrated by how I conduct myself. If you tell me that you are coming to work on my chimney at 10 am Tuesday, then I expect you there anywhere between 9:45 and 10 o'clock, period. Nothing else is acceptable. I will hold your feet to the flame (in the chimney example, this may, in fact, be literal). Conversely, I will do the same for you. If I say I will be at your office to install a phone system on a certain day and time, I will be there, come hell or high water. And how hard is that, really? Think about it. If you know a trip usually takes thirty minutes, give yourself an hour to get there. Traffic is unpredictable. **Calling to say you're stuck in traffic is no excuse when you are doing business with me.** And please, administer the same pressure on me. I can accept it. *I accept that responsibility.*

If you arrive early, your client may be pleased. If not, I'm sure there are some business calls you can make on your cell phone while you wait. Maybe you were worried you wouldn't have time for a quick snack; well, now you've been handed the time. You won't get low blood sugar so you'll do an even better job. *See how well things work out when you work them out well?*

If you DO make a mistake, admit it and try to work it out. Don't make up excuses—what's the point? If I back my car over your new flower garden, does it really matter that the sun was in my eyes, or that I had just gotten an upsetting call on my cell phone? No matter how you look at it, my car just ran over your flower bed. As a person who accepts responsibility, I should simply offer to replace your flowers. That's that. Furthermore, think of all the litigators you'll put out of business. If everyone conducted themselves this way, half the lawyers in America would be working at other jobs.

Failure to accept responsibility actually costs you more money in the long run. I'm a landlord. My tenants are given certain responsibilities along with the basic responsibility of paying their rent on time. Some have to water the lawn, cut the grass, or most importantly here in Colorado, shovel the snow. These things are written into my leases, but not because I'm looking for cheap labor. The snow shoveling, for example, is required by municipal ordinance. Snow must be cleared within a certain amount of time after a storm or else A) there will be a management fee and B) the city will shovel it for you—for a much higher price than the open market will bear.

If my tenants don't want to shovel the snow in front of their property, right off the bat they have the opportunity to rent from someone else who does not require it. I don't hide these things on my leases. They're plain as day and I make sure my tenants are well aware of them. But having accepted the responsibility, it is far cheaper to simply go out for thirty minutes and shovel than get a very large fine and shoveling bill from the city. And no, when you're my tenant and you make the wrong decision, I really don't sympathize with you. When it snows here in the Rockies, it doesn't just fall in front of one building. We ALL have to shovel.

Companies no longer accept responsibility. What ever happened to "the customer is always right?" Sure, there are some customers who border on the downright criminal in their demands, but more often than not, customers simply want a fair deal. This also applies when mishaps occur. If I order a chocolate milkshake and you bring me a strawberry shake, all you have to do to make me happy is accept responsibility, take back the strawberry, and bring me back a chocolate one as quickly as possible. If you do, I'll be a happy customer who will return again and again, and I will likely even send you referrals. To err is human, to forgive divine. To make me feel like it was my fault, or to argue with me, or to give me dirty looks, or to spit in my shake when I'm not looking is not right. Furthermore, my demands are reasonable. Like the snow shoveling example, the cost to make me happy is another shake, nothing more. What's the wholesale cost on that, eight or ten cents? Conversely, multiply the profit the business can garner from me if I remain a regular customer who comes in every week or two for the next decade. It's no contest. **Accepting responsibility is usually the least expensive and most effective option in the long run.**

Our disposable society needs to hang on to some of the permanence that made it great. Sure, companies come and go, but they need not. Take a consumer electronics store. Certainly, technology will constantly change (anybody want to buy a Beta VCR?), but the concept of consumer electronics should be around for as far into the future as I can imagine. Thus, businesses should not consider themselves to be disposable entities that do not have to nurture customers. **"Customers for Life" always used to be the goal of business, and that goal should remain intact.**

Accept responsibility for your life. You are owed nothing. If you live in America, you are blessed with a free public school system and minimal social safety nets for your health, nourishment, shelter, and retirement. But no one owes you *wealth*. You are given opportunity to *achieve* wealth, which is a rarity in much of the world. Be grateful for it.

***Work* for what you want.** To get to the top, you must start at the bottom. Do the best job you can. Find ways to make things better. Work hard and do not waste your life away. Sitting around and playing video games all day is not a good use of your time! It is okay to relax once in a while, but do something productive and fulfilling with your time.

A good, hard-working handyman I use did some work at an apartment I rent to college students. When he presented his itemized bill to me, it looked like this:

Vanity:	$318.00
Vanity Top:	$ 99.00
Faucet Set:	$ 59.00
7 Hours Labor at $35 per hour:	$245.00
Watching Your Two Tenants Play Video Games for 7 Hours:	**Priceless**

Okay, so he stole the last line from a TV commercial, but the best laughter comes from truth. The truth was, while this blue-collar guy was working his tail off, these two college guys did nothing but play video games like a couple of brainless couch potatoes. Should they have pitched in and helped the handyman? Not necessarily, although if they had shown initiative and expressed to me a willingness to do their own repairs, or to do some repairs on my other rental units, I would have paid them handsomely. Heck, if they had done it enough, they could have lived rent free! Now *that's* taking responsibility.

So maybe these weren't the world's handiest guys. They were attending college. Shouldn't they have been doing some homework? Studying? Reading? Trying to cure cancer? Somehow I doubt that future Nobel Prize winners waste seven straight prime-time hours making little cartoon men jump up and down. I have a funny suspicion that once those particular guys managed to get out of college, they were hard-pressed to earn the $35 per hour my far less-educated handyman does. And yet they probably look down their noses at him. Entitlement. What a concept.

Make a difference. Leave a positive mark on society. Take initiative; be a self-starter. Be persistent. Be passionate. Work long, hard hours until you have met your goals. These are the tenets of success and wealth-building. When you do these things, you are accepting personal responsibility for your own future.

Be honest and ethical. People will always try to teach you short-cuts in life. It takes a solid base of morality, ethics, and the willingness to investigate all claims, in order to know the difference between a savvy tip and something that could land you behind bars. Scams are everywhere, and what is most dangerous about them is that they are so seductive. Something for nothing. Con artists have been around for-ever because of one thing: greed. Yes, if you ever watch a scam being run on some TV news program, even though they set out to vilify the con artist, cons always work because the "mark" wants something for nothing. That's the inducement that blinds good people to bad ideas. So what, then, does that say about the "mark," the dupe? It means that on some level, he or she is almost as unethical as the con.

Know the difference, then, between a logical suggestion such as, "You might want to consider leasing equipment rather than buying," and "Hey, do you wanna know how to fleece the IRS?" Granted, this is an obvious example. If something looks less cut and dried, take the *responsibility* of doing research. If you make bad decisions in life because you didn't do your homework, it is no one's fault but your own.

Learn the trade before you learn the tricks of the trade. Fight for what you believe in. Set precedence. **Each day of your life, you are making a reputation for yourself.** Sure, some things can be out of your control. You might call out a crook who attempted to rip you off, and suddenly you turn around and *he's* trying to ruin *your* good name by telling everyone who will listen that *you're* the crook. What could be more infuriating? But time is the great equalizer. Time acts as judge, jury, and executioner. If you take responsibilities for your actions, if you do the right thing, eventually, the truth will win out. A lie can hurt your reputation for a short time, but in the long run your reputation is your own making. Make it a good one and it will be a good one. But reputations, like money and wealth, are earned. Just as you are not entitled to a pot of gold, no one is entitled to a good reputation. Those things are earned. If you do everything I've outlined in this book, but don't accept responsibility, your character flaws will always drag you down and keep you from living the life of which you dream.

Every business I ever worked in, I made paying my bills on time the most important thing on my professional "to do" list. You would be surprised at how much that contributed to my personal success. If I dealt with a vendor and he had one widget left on his shelf, and he had to ship it to me or to some other guy, and that other guy was always making his payments thirty days late, sixty days late, who do you think always got the last widget? Me. Little things like that can be the difference between success and failure in business.

Now picture that other guy who wanted that widget. Now he's waiting and waiting for it and I can only imagine he's blaming the vendor, he's blaming me, he's blaming the weatherman, he's blaming God; he's blaming everyone but himself. He's not taking *responsibility*.

Protect Yourself

- Be a savvy consumer.
- Do your research.
- Make educated decisions.
- Ask questions.
- Beware of scams.
- And when things don't go your way, don't be afraid to walk away.

This goes a step beyond simply accepting responsibility. It can be a nasty world out there. While the majority of people you will do business with are completely honest and perform with integrity, some are not and do not. It doesn't hurt to be wary. Trust is earned. Remember what I said about reputations. **Don't just buy into an "honest face." Make sure there's an honest person wearing it.**

I sometimes drive people crazy by proceeding slowly. If I'm buying a house and there's a stack of papers half a mile high in front of me, what's my rush? It's *my* time; it's *my* money. If I want to read it all, I'll read it all. That's my prerogative. And if someone wants to rush me, that'll usually make me go even slower. Is this passive/aggressive behavior? Not at all. I simply figure that anyone who doesn't want me to read through contracts must be hiding something from me.

If I have a question, I ask it. **The only dumb questions are the ones you *don't* ask.** Everyone is so worried that people will think they're stupid. Frankly, I don't care what you think of my I.Q. If I'm buying your property or your business, or I'm purchasing insurance or a service from you, I really could care less if you think I'm stupid or dense because I'm not buying into your logic.

Don't be insecure. I know; it's hard. We grow up wanting everyone to like us. But be liked for the right reasons. I honor the commitments that I make. That's a likeable quality as far as I'm concerned. I expect the same of others. That sometimes makes me unpopular. I accept that. You have to as well, if you want to be successful. Otherwise, you are placing a big "Kick Me" sign on your back.

Don't be afraid of your gut (unless it is unhealthily large and bloated). Sometimes I sit across from someone and I just have a gut instinct that this is not a trustworthy person. If that's your first instinct, it's more frequently correct than incorrect. If your sixth sense tells you to be on alert, then be on alert. And if things begin to go south, abort, abort, abort! We have instincts for a reason. Nothing will make you kick yourself more and longer than ignoring your internal warning signals and winding up in a horrible business deal.

Get second opinions. Surround yourself with people you can trust. Rely on personal recommendations. Remember what I've been saying all along about alignment of interests? If I need a good estate attorney and I have a friend who is a podiatrist and I trust and admire him, I might ask him who he uses and is he happy with him. Unless the podiatrist tries to send me to an estate attorney who is also his brother-in-law, I feel protected and secure that I have asked a neutral source who has no personal agenda. There *is* an alignment of interest—he has no immediate monetary stake in the transaction. If we are friends who respect one another, he may ask me next week if I can recommend a good roofer. If we both continue to give each other good business leads, we will also continue to be friends as well as continue to do business with one another.

Still, don't be lazy. Protect yourself. Maybe ask *two* friends for recommendations for professional services or whatever it is you need, particularly if it is a major purchase. Then, do some independent research as well. No one watches your own back as well as you do.

Am I paranoid? No, I don't think so. But wary, be very wary. Careful—that's an even better word. Be careful. Bad decisions can be costly. No, I'm not talking about going to one gas station, filling up, then driving another few blocks and seeing gas for two cents per gallon less. Big deal; so what? I'm talking about major business and life decisions. Get a lousy building contractor and it can over-cost you tens of thousands of dollars and keep you in litigation for a year or two. These are not the kinds of decisions to enter into lightly. Protect yourself!

Know what you want and what you need and demand that you get it. Some people might call you a jerk for doing this, but I believe it is all in how you present yourself. I don't walk into a store and immediately slam my fist on the counter. Heck, I don't slam my fist on the counter even if some catastrophe has occurred. That doesn't get you your way; it just makes you look like a raging lunatic.

If I go into a men's clothing store and I say that I want tan chinos without pleats in the front, then that's what I want. If you, the salesperson, want to try to educate me that pleats are in this season, that's fine, but only up to a point. I'm never averse to learning something new. But, perhaps I really don't care about what the current issue of *GQ* is saying about pleated pants. I don't want pleats. At this point, either sell me what I want or I'll go elsewhere. And like the old saying goes, I don't go away mad; I just go away.

I had a horrifically scary business transaction recently where I am incredibly glad I stood my ground. Looking back on it, I wonder out loud how many other people would have simply allowed themselves to be bullied.

I bought a used motorcycle from a dealer. He said he wanted to "mail" me the title in a couple of weeks, and I told him that he would need to give me the clear title that very day, to which he reluctantly agreed. I tried to register the vehicle the next day, but could not do so because the title still had a lien on it! This is called "title kiting," and it is one of the new automotive scams sweeping the nation. I won't get too deeply into it, but basically, people have started selling cars to which they do not possess clear title. Maybe there is a lien on the title, or perhaps the car is being held as collateral—sort of like in a pawn shop. Most commonly, it might involve you buying a car and your money being used to pay off some other debts—maybe to the car dealer's loan shark. Then you have to wait for the next guy to pay for *another* car before the car dealer can use *his* money to purchase or clear the title on *your* car. Any way you slice it, it's a mess and it's completely illegal.

The dealer I bought the motorcycle from didn't want to give me my title right then and there, like I asked. He said, "By law, we have thirty days to mail you the title." And he may have been legally correct. *But that was not what I wanted.* I'm Braun and this is what *I* wanted and how *I* wanted it done. If push came to shove, I was prepared to turn on my heels and leave. There are a lot of motorcycles in the world. I could buy another one elsewhere.

You must always remember: *you* are empowered to act this way, too. You don't have to be a millionaire to want what you want and get what you want. The poorest person in the world can still make a stand that he or she is not going to be pushed around or bullied. **In a transaction or conflict, no one is going to empower you but you!**

Frankly, the motorcycle dealer has his rights, too. If I had said, "Not only do I want clear title, but I want the keys to your house," he would have been right to tell me to jump off a cliff. And I would respect him for feeling that way.

Back to the story…I wanted to pay for the motorcycle by credit card. Remember, my credit card company gives me added consumer protections against fraud. "No," the dealer said, "we don't take credit cards." I considered my options and offered him a check, which he accepted, but I still was not going to leave with that motorcycle unless he gave me a title. Again, I could have buckled, but I didn't. I was prepared to stand my ground until it became obvious I would not get a deal that I could live with. Was that to occur, I was ready to walk.

Well, you already know the climax of the story: the title was not clear. Because I paid by check (my second best option next to a credit card), I immediately stopped payment on it before it cleared. This is not very hard to do, although it does cost a few dollars. But when you're making a purchase for several thousand dollars, what's a small bank service fee?

I called the dealer up and told him what had happened and that I had stopped payment on the check. Needless to say, he was not a happy camper. Again, the bullying began. He became very threatening and said that he was turning the case over to the District Attorney and he would sue me as well. Note to readers: No one threatens lawsuits more often than crooks. Prepare to deal with it. When it happens, find your "happy place" and calm down. If you're in the right, you will almost always win out in the end.

Since I'm not a lawyer, I called one that I trust and told him what happened. In order to put myself in the best possible legal position, my lawyer had me write out a new check to his law firm's trust account for the amount of money in question. We both feared that if I simply returned the motorcycle at this point, this crooked guy would probably deface it intentionally when my back was turned, then try to sue me for damages. My lawyer then sent the dealer a registered letter explaining that the money was being held in escrow and that once he provided me with clear title, the law firm would release the funds to him.

In the end, it all worked out. Was I happy? Not really. The whole thing wasted a lot of my valuable time. Was the dealer happy? No, because I caught him in the midst of a scam and if I wanted to waste more of my time, I probably could have made a ton of legal trouble for him. But I'm not about vengeance. **Revenge isn't cost-effective**.

Bottom line: I protected myself. If I had not been a prudent consumer, I would have been out thousands of dollars. The art of the deal (stealing a line from Donald Trump) is not simply getting what you want, but getting it the *way* that you want. I could have allowed myself to be bullied by this dealer and in the end, I eventually might have ended up with the motorcycle and a clear title—*maybe*. But that's not how I roll. Fair is fair and if I buy something, I'm buying it without undisclosed liens. Those are my terms.

Beware of bullies. The world is full of them. The thing always to remember is that this is a civilized society. Usually, no one is going to punch you in the nose if you stand your ground in a negotiation. If they do, they go to jail for assault.

Speaking of Donald Trump, I'm reminded of the late Merv Griffin (Huh? Bear with me; this will all make sense in a minute). Merv was a D-list actor and big band singer when he first got started. A chubby guy with no overpowering talent, he wasn't going to ever become a big Hollywood star. Eventually, he morphed into a

TV talk show host, where his friendly and non-threatening manner made him a hit with housewives across the nation.

Then Merv found his true niche. He loved games and he eventually developed the TV game show "Jeopardy," followed shortly thereafter by "Wheel of Fortune." Suddenly, Merv was a billionaire entertainment mogul. He invested his money wisely and his fortune grew and grew.

One day, Merv decided to enter the casino business. He made a move to take over Resorts International, a major player in the casino game. Unfortunately, at that very same moment, Donald Trump was trying to do the very same thing (See, I told you I would tie them together.).

Now, Trump is a tough-talking New Yorker and Merv was, well, a little guy, much older, and more than a little on the effeminate side. In a street fight, I'd have bet on Donald Trump, no question about it. But like I've been saying, life is not a street fight.

As Merv tells it, "The Donald" called him up screaming and yelling, threatening and bullying every way he could—the kind of treatment that had cowered so many other businessmen Trump had conquered over the years. Merv simply chuckled. He responded, "Donald, you've got a fleet of sharp-toothed lawyers and so do I; so let's stop the bellowing and talk business." In the end, Merv got Resorts International and the everlasting respect of Donald Trump. Now, if a guy like Merv can stand up to a guy like Trump, you can stand up for what you believe is right, too.

In the end, think things through. Consider where you are vulnerable. Cover your flanks. No one watches out for you better than you—but only if you're paying attention to the details and looking at all the angles. And if you're not sure about something, get some advice, then get some more advice, then research, research, research. **Anyone can become an expert at anything if they're willing to invest the time.**

Live Within Your Means

"Living within your means" is a mantra I've infused into a lot of previous chapters, but admittedly rather obliquely. If, for example, you own a house that costs you three quarters of your monthly income (mortgage, insurance, taxes, upkeep), then you don't own the house; the house owns you. This is not a way to live.

What really gets to me is that **some of the poorest people I know make the most money.** The house example is the best. Living here in Colorado, Boulder is one of the most affluent communities around. The average home there is around 4,300 square feet. That's a nice-sized house. I recently read that most new residential home construction in Boulder is averaging around *8,000* square feet. That's a *heck* of a nice-sized house. But here's the rub: Neither the average nor the median income in Boulder has risen significantly, if at all. Does this mean that you can now get an 8,000 square foot house for the price of a 4,300 square foot one? No way! Those houses cost a lot more, and thus, people are putting a higher percentage of their income into the roof over their heads.

This is dumb.

But it's not just the big ticket items such as homes and cars, although they're the worst offenders. People waste money all the time.

Credit cards are the root of all evil. I'm convinced of this. Go to the mall, pull out that card, buy something here and there, then here and there again, and pretty soon what seemed like a little impulsive trip just cost you a lot of money. Make only the minimum payment per month on that credit card and keep spending like that and what do you get? Right—*more credit cards.*

To truly achieve wealth, drop the credit card mentality. Only buy what you can easily pay off the moment you get that credit card statement. And **make a budget!** This is so basic. Sit down and look at the entire picture every few months—this exercise doesn't take long to do. How much is your housing? Your car and transportation costs? Your TV and Internet? Food? Clothing? Utilities? Rattle off every single category of "where your money went" and take a cold, hard look at it. Are you happy with what you see? If so, you probably didn't need this book in the first place. But most people are less than happy with their financial picture. A budget is a good place to begin.

If your house is killing you, owning you, then downsize. If it's your car or cars, do the same. Trade in the Beemer for a Honda, if that's what you can better afford. But so many times it's the little things. Food—do you eat out a lot? If yes, why? Eating in is far cheaper than eating out. It is not unusual in this day and age for a family of four to spend $2,500 or more on food each month. If that family could find a way to cut that food bill in half, they'd be $1,250 per month richer. That's real money!

How do you do it? Simple. First off, really think about those meals out. Are they for business lunches? Those may be fine. If you're picking up the tab for a client, that's a partial tax write-off. But if you're going out to a restaurant for lunch—even a fast food place—by yourself or with your co-workers, you are wasting money. Brown bag it to work. It's even cheaper than a Happy Meal.

What about the groceries themselves? Eggs are eggs. Milk is milk. Are you going to the cheapest place in your neighborhood to buy those things, or do you not even *know* which place has the best prices for food staples?

Clip coupons.

I'm not telling you to be miserly. I'm telling you what to do if you look at your monthly expenditures and you don't like your personal profit and loss statement. So many people look at these facts staring them right in the face and say, "But there's nothing I can cut." I'll guarantee, if you called me up and asked me to come over and look over the same things you were looking at, I could show you a ton of things you could cut if you were highly motivated and ready to make changes in your life.

There's even a show on TV where a guy literally does that. A fellow named Larry Winget has a show called "Big Spender" on the A&E Network. He shows up at people's houses and puts them on a "tough love" spending diet. And what he finds would amaze you. There is fat in all of our living budgets—mine included. But luckily, I've reached a point where I'm not staring up at the ceiling when I should be sleeping, shaking from the cold sweats because I have no idea how to make my next mortgage payment. So if I want to fly first class, I can afford it. But nothing is more mind- boggling than the guy with the cold sweats and the looming mortgage payment sitting next to me in first class, telling me his problems. It makes me want to toss him out of the plane!

"We have met the enemy, and he is us." — Pogo

"The only person that can drive you into debt is you." — Braun

Do you really need "name brand everything?" Take the classic polo shirt. I'll grant you, they're all cut a little differently and we all have different bodies, so maybe one brand fits you a bit better than another. But seriously…I find more people hung up on whether the little logo on the left nipple is a polo player, an alligator, a yacht, a moose, a name (BOSS, DKNY, etc.) than anything else. Now, if it's because the alligator is on sale this week and is cheaper than the yacht, great; you've proven yourself to be a good shopper. But if it's because you think one is more "prestigious" than another, I hope you can truly afford it. If you can't, just remember—it's just a shirt. The only people who get close enough to you to see the little logo probably already like you.

I'm not embarrassed to shop at Wal-Mart. I don't know where this fad started, but I don't understand it. Some people have political issues with Wal-Mart and so be it. But whatever they're griping about—if it's true at all—is probably also true about Target, K-Mart, or a dozen other retailers in the same category. We're talking discount stores for basics. *You don't need designer socks!* Need some tube socks? Go to Wal-Mart or K-Mart. You can probably get a 12-pack for two or three dollars. And you won't have to buy tube socks again for another three or four years. This is smart consumerism.

Sin may be fun in moderation, but it is also costly. Cigarettes, liquor, gambling, lap dances. All expensive.

Peer pressure? All the guys at the office are going out after work and you don't want to be the "un-cool guy?" So go with them, but order a club soda. It's the cheapest thing you can get at a bar and still be allowed to take up a stool. Your co-workers may think you're a recovering alcoholic. Believe it or not, people actually have grown to respect that. It means you've lived a little, but now you've grown up and taken responsibility for your life. That could make you management material! And who is more popular nowadays than the "designated driver?"

And if you're single, do you know the best thing about Happy Hour? Finding the one with the big free food buffet! I've known young single guys who have been able to scarf down an entire free meal for the (Happy Hour reduced) cost of a $1.25 club soda!

On the other hand, when you're actually eating out in a restaurant, forget that club soda entirely and simply drink water. No, not that designer bottled water! They *charge* you for that. And you know where most of it comes from, don't you? The same spigot that your free water came from!

I travel a lot. Do you have any idea how much luggage can cost? Every product that exists, there are low-priced models, medium, and high. So ask yourself; do I really need a $1,500 bag when a $200 one would do? Frankly, I'm a guy who, even though I can afford the $1,500 bag, simply can't abide the apparent (to me) waste of money. Luggage doesn't last forever. I know, longevity is a major selling point for high-end goods. But once the $1,500 bag gets banged and smashed around enough by the baggage handlers, it eventually starts to look like crap, too. So what if it lasts a year or two longer? For the math to work out in its favor, it would have to last over seven times as long as the $200 bag for it to make financial sense. That's asking a lot.

I could make an entire book out of this topic alone. Suffice it to say, there are ways to save on EVERYTHING. The question is, where are you at with your personal budgeting? Do you have money left over after all the bills are paid each month? Are you carrying balances on your credit cards? Are you religiously contributing the maximum to your IRAs and 401ks? If not, then look at all the ways you can cut, cut, cut. This is how "living within your means" is defined.

If you are in a personal financial crisis, you have to cut your expenditures quickly and viciously. But if your only complaint is that your savings is not as great as you'd like it to be, then analyze that budget of yours and see where you can make some painless surgical cuts. It's easily doable.

Make More Money

All right. Tens of thousands of words into this book and you've learned a million ways to save money—to spend less and to "live within your means." Now let's try an earth-shattering concept; a creative alternative that is rarely discussed: Why not make MORE money?

I doubt most people are maximizing their income. If you work for someone else, one of the easiest ways to do this is **ask your boss for a raise.** I am shocked at how few people ever do this. Perhaps it's a holdover from the days when unions ruled the land and collective bargaining dictated how, when, and how much everyone would make, no matter how well or badly they performed. But let's take you, a person who is doing a good job and working hard. You're probably not a member of a union (their numbers are presently dwindling in America), so no one's got your back except the man in the mirror. I'll bet you've been trained to pull out the local Want Ads or go online and look for a new job in order to make more money, rather than ask your boss for a raise. This is crazy!

Your boss will rarely just offer you more money unless you ask for it. Why should he? By not asking for more, you're telling him that even *you* don't believe you deserve it!

I know, asking the boss for a raise is like asking the most attractive person in school out on a date. A lot of people get all choked up and befuddled. Not to worry. It's not that hard.

First, be honest with yourself and ask yourself what, if anything, you have done to *deserve* higher wages. Maybe you really *don't* deserve more. If so, look at your own shortcomings and figure out how to *add value to your workplace*. Is there an additional skill you could learn? Are you working as hard as you possibly can? Could you put in more hours? Maybe you're having trouble getting the hang of something. If so, ruminate upon how you could get better at it. Depending upon your occupation, maybe it would pay for you to take some of your work home and practice until you gain greater mastery over a certain skill. Or perhaps there's a guidebook you could buy and read. Maybe there's a more experienced mentor you could seek out and ask for assistance.

Here is another funny story that actually happened to me several years back, and it is one that my close friends still talk about. I had a housekeeper who cleaned my house every couple of weeks. She barely did an acceptable job, only putting forth the most minimal of efforts, and if I'd had the time, I would have found a replacement, but I was busy building a business and this was not a priority. One day, after a hard day at the office, we crossed paths when I came home and she made a comment to the effect of, "I see you have gotten some nice things around the house recently, so you must be doing pretty well. How about giving me a raise?" Obviously, I was put off that this person made judgments about me and simply thought she deserved a raise since she thought I could afford it. Unfortunately for her, this strategy backfired and I finally made the time to find her replacement. The moral of this story is that if you are only giving a marginal work performance, you may not *deserve* a raise and you also may not like the outcome if you demand such a thing.

There's nothing worse, nothing more lame, than to go up to the boss and say, "I need a raise because I've got lots of bills." That's a "pity raise." Do you really want the boss to think you're pathetic? Is that a good long-range plan? I don't think so.

Worse yet is, "I deserve a raise because I've been here a year." SO WHAT?! Simple longevity is no reason for reward; not in my book. Use either of these two methods and you'll be lucky to keep the salary you have, let alone increase it.

If you want a raise, build your case as to why you have earned it. Then ask for an appointment with the boss in order to present that case. That case presentation should be the same as a sales presentation, and IT IS. You are selling YOU. It doesn't matter that the boss knows you already. The argument is that he doesn't know enough about you to understand how fabulous you are and *what value you bring to his business.*

Notice how both times above I mentioned the word "value," I

italicized the phrase. I know that *you* value *you*, but the opinion you have of yourself that you're a great guy or gal is meaningless in this situation. *Are you valuable to your <u>employer</u>?* Now, before you answer that in the affirmative, understand what I *really* mean by this question. If you're a receptionist and you simply walked off the job without telling anyone, now being without a receptionist would prove that your *position* had value. But the question really is, "*did <u>you</u> bring <u>value</u> to the <u>position</u>?*" Did you do whatever you were asked to do with such aplomb that you were able to add "extra value" to the job? Did clients see the boss and say, "Wow, what a great receptionist you have! She was so nice and friendly. She offered me coffee or tea. She recommended a good place for lunch. She let me know exactly how long I'd be waiting. She made coming to do business with you a joy and a pleasure." *That's* bringing value to your job.

But still, even the best sales pitch for a raise is not always successful. Maybe the boss has a counter-argument of where you let him down. If so, listen intently. This is the area where you are being told to improve. Do it, then re-approach the raise issue again later.

Other times, the boss will give you a more nebulous answer, or simply an excuse. "Times are tight. The company isn't doing well right now. Can't afford it." If that's the case, pose the question: "What can I do to help? What more can I do in order to be of greater value to the company?" In short, ask what you have to do in order to *get* a raise.

An even less confrontational way of earning more money within a firm is to **keep on the lookout for job openings in higher positions.** Be aware of what's going on around you. If your immediate supervisor is rumored to be looking for a new job elsewhere, picture yourself doing his or her job. Do you have the skills? Again, don't look at this like, "Well, I *deserve* his job if he leaves." You don't "deserve" anything. You earn it!

Maybe there's an issue of education. Maybe you've hit an invisible ceiling to your success because you don't have certain schooling or training. If so, figure out what you can do about it. **Some big companies even assist ambitious employees by contributing to**

their advanced schooling or training. Ignoring such a benefit is no different than passing up an employer-contributed 401k. You're leaving money on the table!

If, on the other hand, you own your own business, or if you work on commission…**increase your sales volume!** There must be a thousand good books on salesmanship out there. If you haven't availed yourself to a few, perhaps you should look into it. Some people are naturals at sales, yet could always use a few good tips to improve their game. Others find sales to be an unnatural act, and reading up or seeking out a strong mentor can be just what is needed.

Maybe you don't actually work on commission, but you are still in the business of sales, or in a position to bring in more clientele for your employer. As to sales volume, this is a great quantifier when you want to approach you boss about a raise. While platitudes about, "I'm a team player," or "Customers really like me," can be debated, numbers don't lie.

As to bringing in new business or simply being innovative, I think most employers would be open to "sharing the wealth" if you could find a way to show them a significant increase in productivity, profitability, or client volume. Obviously, if you are self-employed, you should *always* be on the lookout for improving the bottom line. Too many people don't understand the difference between "working hard" and "working smart."

It's hard to disparage "working hard," but doing it in an ostrich-like fashion (head buried in the sand) rarely leads to wealth and success. **"Working smart" means that your head is always up, eyes wide open, looking to maximize every possible way of improving your bottom line.** Are there more cost-efficient ways of doing things? Are there ways of reaching more clients that you haven't been exploiting? Are your prices in line with your competitors, or are you far too high or low? Do you even *know* who your competitors are, what exactly they do and how they do it, and how much they charge? If not, find out, find out, find out. That's working smart.

I'd like to make a confession here. I'm actually not that great a salesman. Seriously—I've listened to guys who could sell video games to Amish grandmothers. They have a gift of gab I may never achieve. My success has been built more upon innovation, imagination, motivation, reputation, and perspiration—and creating wealth from what I have earned. So I say to you, if you're witty, super-personable and great at sales, God bless. And if you're not, fret not; financial success can still be within your grasp. But in either case—even for you "super salesmen"—it always pays to be aware of what's going on around you; you should always be thinking to yourself, "Is there an innovative way that I can maximize my earnings? Is there something more that I can do? Am I missing an opportunity here?"

Work more hours. Sounds simple, and, frankly, it is. This one works whether you are self-employed or working for someone else. Maybe your employer has overtime available. Are you taking advantage of that opportunity? Perhaps you should. It's good both in the short run (more money today) as well as the long run (it demonstrates a good work ethic, which can lead to promotions and raises).

Personally, I can't abide people who moan and groan about their financial status and they ONLY work forty hours per week. It's ridiculous! Every financially successful person I know spent a huge portion of their life working seventy, eighty, and ninety-hour weeks. Forty hour work weeks are semi-retirement.

Can't pick up more hours where you work? **Get a side job. Get a second job.** Do what you have to do to get what you need and to get where you want to go. You're not entitled. If you want something, go out and get it!

Here's one of my favorite variations on this. It embodies "working smart" versus simply "working hard." **Start a side business.** Here's what I did:

When I was in the phone business, we would sell big and expensive new phone systems to businesses—mainly call centers. I started buying their old phone systems for cheap (they generally had no clue what to do with them) and would then advertise them in the paper and sell them as "used." It took three to four hours per week for me to do all of this, but I found a way to make extra spending money. Most people never would have thought of it, but I took advantage of an opportunity right in front of me.

People trip over opportunities like this every day. No matter what your occupation, I'll bet there's a way of making more money. Deliver pizzas for a living? Hand out business cards for some other enterprise with that large sausage and pepperoni—maybe your *own* business. For example, *anybody* can paint. If you handed out a card for "XYZ Painters" with your phone number on it, I'll bet within the first week somebody will call. *That's* being enterprising. Want to take it a step further? Maybe the florist next door to the pizza place would pay you to hand out *their* card, or a coupon, to all of your deliveries. Hey, you're going to those places anyway; think about ways you can maximize each trip. And you'll *still* be able to get that pizza there in thirty minutes or less!

If this sounds like small potatoes, bear in mind that this is the *mental foundation* upon which great fortunes are made. Wherever you are in your personal life cycle as you read this, I'll bet you could apply the pizza delivery or the used phone system concept. Don't look at my examples literally—think creatively. I can't think of everything for you, but I can help you to understand how successful entrepreneurs *think*.

Stop Trying to Keep Up With the Joneses
They're probably miserable and in debt

You may be thinking, "How does this materially differ from, "Spend wisely," and, "Live within your means"? I understand the confusion. Look at it this way: **Keeping up with the Joneses is an *emotional* issue, even more than it is a financial one.** It is based upon jealousy, which is one of the 7 Deadly Sins, meaning that it far supersedes "Generation E."

If there was a somewhat realistic American ideal of a fabulous residential property, it would probably be about four nicely manicured acres, a 5 bedroom, 5 bath home—all large rooms, professionally decorated, with a circular driveway, a 3-car garage, and an in-ground swimming pool. Does that sound about right? Now, how many of you have that house? Sorry, but I don't see many hands.

In most real estate markets, this is about a $1 million dollar house. In the more expensive neighborhoods of this country, it could cost you upwards of $5 or $6 million.

Now, let's look at an incredible conundrum. Who *needs* a really big house like this? Answer: A young couple with a few kids and some pets. Think about it. That's the perfect time to have that much land for the kids and the dogs to frolic, lots of rooms and bedrooms, and lots of toys (the swimming pool included). So we're talking about a couple in their thirties. How many couples in their thirties can afford such a mansion? Answer: Very, very few.

The conundrum continues: Who is more likely to be *able* to afford this dream house? Answer: A couple in their *fifties*. But do they need it? No; what for? Since when do two people need that much room and that many beds? It makes no sense.

So what we have are two scenarios both based upon wanting things we've been programmed to want. For the couple in their fifties, it's finally having the money to blow on something they really don't need. To me, that's dumb. I salute the fact that they had the fortitude to wait until they could afford it, but you have to admit, they are most likely doing it for purely emotional reasons, reasons that may still have a lot to do with jealousy of other people or concern for other people's perceptions of them. The money they might be spending on such an unnecessary luxury would be better utilized if placed into savings, disability policies, and all the sorts of things that would give their latter-year futures the stability to weather any storm. But if they've already done that and they still have money to blow, I suppose what to blow it on is a personal matter. Personally, I'd rather travel, but who am I to judge?

But the people I really have a problem with are the ones in their thirties. The percentage of families in America who can responsibly afford a house like this is less than 1%—and more of them are in their fifties than in their thirties. Despite that, it amazes me as to how many young couples—people my age—are trying to live this way—stretching on their tippy-toes to qualify for a designer mortgage that will choke them like a vice.

When it comes to keeping up with the Joneses, nothing says it more than the big purchases—homes, cars, and vacations. I won't even talk about designer coffees in this subchapter. There's an upscale coffee shop on almost every street corner in America today. That $5 coffee in your hand doesn't impress anyone—because everyone else has one, too. I doubt you are even thinking about impressions when you are buying it. Designer coffee is not about status. But homes—man, that's where the damage is done.

Think about someone who could easily afford that $1 million dollar plus mansion while still in their thirties. How about a top brain surgeon? Those guys probably make about $750,000 per year in salary alone, plus, if they're smart enough off of their investments, it could send them up around a million dollars a year—every year! Nice work if you can get it.

This brain surgeon, who may be your age and may send his kid to school with your kid, made a career choice early in life and went into a very lucrative field. Good for him! We need brain surgeons in this world.

Now look at yourself in the mirror. Maybe you're a policeman. What you do is of incredible value to society and I, for one, thank you for doing it. But let's face it; if you are doing it in your thirties, you are probably lucky to make around $60,000 a year. That's not bad; not bad at all. It is definitely above the American average. Perhaps you have a spouse. Maybe he or she is a social worker, a school teacher, a truck driver, or a nurse. All of these occupations are invaluable to the quality of life we all take for granted in this country. But these occupations also do not pay a lot of money. So together, you and your spouse make, perhaps, $100,000 a year. That's great! If you do everything I've told you to do in this book, you should be able to live a nice, comfortable, and secure life. That is, of course, *unless you start trying to live like the brain surgeon.*

This is the crucial failure, the disconnect so many people make and have. Jealousy, whether realized or not. So that $100,000 a year family, instead of doing all the right things as outlined in this book, "over houses" themselves in order for their kid to feel on par with the surgeon's kid. Maybe they figure it will give them a better chance at being invited over to the surgeon's home for dinner some time. And to what end?

All of these **emotional issues are completely counterproductive to your own financial success in life.** Life can be a lot like high school sometimes. If you have to buy breast implants in order to be accepted at the "popular girls' table" in the cafeteria, what does it say about them as well as you? Those people are *not* your friends, they're never going to *be* your friends, nor should you *want* them to be your friends. The relationship will always be as fake as those implants. If the brain surgeon is a good guy, he will want to be friends with you if he respects you and finds you interesting and fun to be with. If you possess all those qualities, but are socially shunned by certain people because you don't have a certain sized home or drive a certain type of car, don't bother. Those people are shallow creeps and any relationship you might have with them will be phony.

When you try to keep up with the Joneses, a number of scenarios can occur. For one thing, people aren't stupid. If you're the "cop and social worker family" and you try to move into or build a house like the brain surgeon owns, people will either figure that you are living way over your head or that you are doing something illegal. Neither of these are good. For this reason, so many "keeping up with the Joneses" people soon discover that their station in life has not risen—they still are not taken into the fold at the "popular girls' table" of life. There, I've just saved you a lot of money and therapy.

Take pride in who you are. Be a decent human being, work hard, and have solid values. As a policeman or a social worker, you had to have known from the start that you weren't going to live in a big mansion on what you earned at that job. Keep reminding yourself of that. Maybe you didn't quite have what it takes to be a brain surgeon, or more likely, you simply had no passion for that field. Fine then. You've heard the old joke: What do they call the person who finished last in medical school? Answer: Doctor. You may be every bit as smart as the brain surgeon, but you followed your own muse. Come to terms with that and hold your head up high. Accept what the field pays or make changes or adjustments to your vocation (re-read the "Make More Money" subchapter).

Live within the means of your chosen field. Better yet, live *below* your means. If you do, you'll have enough to fund all the wise expenditures I've outlined for you in this book. I can't say this enough: Wealth is what you keep, not what you make.

I can't tell you how many rich guys, ones who make a million dollars a year or more, spend 20% *more* than that. Do you know what that makes them, Mr. Policeman? Poorer than you! **Debt is a prison.** In my short time on earth, I have seen many mighty millionaires who have fallen. Can you imagine driving a Rolls Royce one day and a few years later working as a clerk in a store for a little over minimum wage? I've seen it happen.

Some of the worst emotional spenders are the "Suddenly Wealthy." These may be lottery winners, large inheritors, or professional athletes or entertainers. Emotionally, they try to buy their way into a certain social class. It matters not that they were driving a perfectly nice Volkswagen that they loved the day *before* they hit the jackpot. Now they feel they have to buy the Maserati because, well, you can't drive up to the entrance of a country club in a Volkswagen, now can you? And you *must* join the country club because…well, you can't hang out with poor people anymore, can you? This is why the aforementioned list of the Suddenly Wealthy (lottery winners, etc.) tend to hang onto their wealth for less time than almost any other demographic.

Sure, if you hit it rich, you want the types of things you never could afford before. But think it through first. Maybe you never felt you could adequately fund that 529 Plan for your kids or set up a good long-term savings vehicle for yourself. Maybe you never had long or short-term disability insurance. Take care of all that first. Once that's done, if you have money left over for a boat and you really, really always had a passion for boats, then buy yourself a darn boat! But do it for YOU. Don't do it to fit into some new social strata. Don't do it because you think it's expected of you.

Your net worth can go up and down. As an entrepreneur, I don't have all the advantages of the brain surgeon, either. Those guys make a pretty high and steady wage. Personally, I've had good years where I've out-earned them handily, and I've had some not-so-good years as well. Do you want to know the key to success? **Find a lifestyle and stick with it.** If you find you've had $1 million dollar years as well as $100,000 years, learn to live on $100,000 a year. That way, you can never lose. **The big years can provide a little extra gravy to get you through the leaner years.**

Lack of money can make people very insecure. It certainly makes one *financially* insecure. But deal with the emotional issues maturely. **Work hard to achieve financial security, *which has nothing at all to do with how big your house is or what kind of car you drive.*** While doing that, work hard on developing the emotional security. Be a good person, and do the right things. If you achieve that, you are a wealthy person no matter how much or how little you earn.

Always Pay Yourself First

There are a lot of people who feel they're doing all the right things. They've got a good job, they're aggressive and hard-working, they earn greater and greater amounts each year, they don't appear to overspend...and yet they never seem to have any real net worth. **Net worth is the liquidation value of your entirety. Net worth is your estate. The best form of net worth for you to have is *liquidity*, meaning, money you can lay you hands on relatively easily.**

For example, your home is not liquid...unless you want to move in with a friend and sleep on his floor. The same goes for your car ...how are you going to drive to work?

I find myself chirping a lot about homes and cars in this chapter, and it's because they can be such a trap. They are often the biggest measure of most people's self-worth. This is wrong. So take the person I'm describing in the first paragraph—the hard-worker who earns more and more each year. He or she has probably been programmed to think that this also mandates that he or she must also keep driving a better car and keep moving into a bigger and better house.

NO!

The irony of this is that this person may, in fact, be otherwise frugal with their spending—no big partying expenses, no large credit card bills, no closets full of junk they don't need or really want. But the house and car, well, isn't that what you're supposed to do as you move along life's highway? Keep moving up? Isn't that the reason you get up each morning and go to work?

NO!

Pay YOURSELF first! Paying yourself first means that the house and the car come *after* the IRA, the 401k, the money market, the investments, and the health and insurance plans. **Paying yourself first means creating enough wealth through automatic investment and savings that you could *literally retire and live off of only the interest of your investments.*** Paying yourself first means that, if you start early enough, working itself can literally be optional once you reach a relatively young age.

THIS IS DOABLE!

The house, the car, the big vacations; these are your enemies. THIS IS NOT A STARVATION DIET! It's not the ownership of a house or a car, or the going away for a week or two each year in and of itself that is the problem. It is the "movin' on up" mentality. As you earn more, these three big things do not have to grow each year as well. For when they do, it is almost always at the peril of the long range plan—the "paying yourself first."

Start early. If you do only one thing once you've laid this book down, have it be that no matter how young or old you are, you immediately take care of the basics I've outlined for you in the previous chapters. START NOW! **Time builds wealth.** Even if you never make more than $45,000 a year, if you make the largest possible contribution to your retirement programs, if you automatically and consistently set money aside for investment, if you become a saver, you will find yourself in a great position come retirement time. In fact, you will move *up* your retirement time. You will be able to set your *own* retirement time. You may even reach a point where you will be able to look at most of your present day earnings as icing on your financial cake. You will be able to spend that money on the things that make you happy. You will have financial freedom, and that, my friends is freedom, period.

Do it automatically. Don't even let that money hit your hand when payday comes. Every program I've suggested, you can set up to be automatically deducted every single pay cycle. If you are an employee, you already have taxes taken out every time you get paid. So just add a few more line items to those deductions.

Draw up a realistic budget. No matter how little you make, work within those constraints. Find a home or apartment you can afford. If you can't afford even a car, take public transportation. But even if you are making minimum wage, break it on down so that you are paying into these programs first. That prioritization is the key. Learn that and you've gotten more out of this book than you could ever imagine.

Most people have no concept of the compounding ability of money. I was sent a birth announcement from some dear friends. Instead of some baby clothes the kid would grow out of in a few months, or a toy that wouldn't last out the week, I gave them a check for the first payment into the kid's 529 College Savings Plan. I even gave the parents literature on how to open the account and keep it going. Now, as far as I'm concerned, this was a wonderful gift. The issue was not one of simply giving someone a check for a gift—we all do that from time to time. The idea was also to try to teach them how to use that check to start this college fund.

They took the check and cashed it. Months and months later, I asked them and they still hadn't started up their child's 529 Plan.

This is bad. It's not like I think they took the money and did something heinous with it. That's not the point. The point is, that first check I gave them is now gone. It should have been in that dedicated account and it would have been earning interest. Each subsequent month, they should have been depositing the same amount or greater and those checks would have been earning interest.

Had that been done, in the first year alone, they would have earned a few hundred dollars of interest toward their child's future education. Does that sound like a lot? Of course not. But now, stretch that principle and accruing interest out eighteen years, and suddenly, we're talking tens of thousands of dollars! Yes! THIS is how you grow wealth!

Those months and those payments are now gone forever. That interest will never be earned. When they finally begin that college fund, it will be a good thing, but it will still never get back that money that it should have had from the time the child was born.

Do NOT save for the big house. Do NOT save for the fancy car. Save for YOU! If you do, the other things will happen, I guarantee it. **Time is the key; automatic consistency is the key.**

Wake Up—Literally!

Get up early and get to work early. Most of the successful people I know (with the exception of the one who runs a night club) get into the office very early (5 to 6 am) and get more work done before other people start arriving (8 to 9 am).

There is a method to this madness. From 9 to 5, the workday is in full swing. Telephones are ringing, co-workers are running around, people are tugging you in a thousand directions. Ever feel like a gerbil on a fly wheel? There's such a thing as "being at work," but getting very little done. And it's not necessarily your fault. Many of us feel like air traffic controllers, putting out fires and reacting, reacting, reacting when we're on the job. Things may need to be done that way, but it makes it hard to move forward your long-range work agenda. The things that are not of greatest immediacy sometimes fall between the cracks.

That's what those first few hours are for. If you work for yourself, I deem them <u>mandatory</u>. I hate it, HATE IT, when people say, "Ah, now I own my own business. I work for myself. Now I can sleep in and take it easy." Those clowns are lucky to last a year.

Successful bosses are always the first in. They're often the last to leave as well, but there's something special about those early morning hours.

Employees can use this method as well. When I talked about asking for a raise in pay, I mentioned building a case for yourself. Well, coming in early is a great way to build such a case, although that's only scratching the surface. There are people who actually come in early just so they can put their feet up on their desk and contemplate their navel. That doesn't cut it. I'm talking about coming in early in order to spur productivity. It moves you out of that, "I only put out fires" mode. Accomplishing that, you can show your employer and clients significant gains in productivity and for that, you can build a case for greater personal financial reward.

Another great thing about getting in early is "The Breakfast Meeting." Smart businesspeople know the value of meeting with clients as often as possible. Business lunches are the norm. Once you're in business, before you take a bite of lunch, ask yourself why you're doing it alone. You should be doing it with someone else, every day, preferably with a client! Getting in early doubles those opportunities. Top people know that getting up and into work early is the key to success, so it is easier than you think to get a client to take a breakfast meeting with you. Face time is important. If you are seeing your client more often than does your competition, it often results in a higher volume of business for your company. Clients tend to be less interested in dinner meetings. Many people view that as family time, or else it becomes cocktail time. Also, if your client is, like you, an early riser in to work early, that is when they are fresh out of the shower and ready to conquer the world. If they get in early enough, they may be sort of burned out and groggy by the end of the day. So get them when they're spry and alert.

Also, breakfast and lunch meetings have the advantage of having natural "end times." You can't—or you shouldn't—stay out for a four-hour business lunch. That's rarely productive. The same goes for breakfast. But dinner can drag on and on and on, especially if cocktails are involved. Sure, in a few rare cases this elongated face time can help you solidify a big account, but I often find myself in these situations thinking, "Damn, there is so much other work I could be getting done while this guy keeps droning on about his kid's Little League team."

So if you notice, I've just advocated getting in to work early, taking as many breakfast business meetings as you can, taking as many lunch business meetings as you can, and doing a dinner business meeting as well, if possible. Holy cow; I just suggested that you work straight on through from 5 am to…whenever!

Yep.

That's what most successful people do. Sure, you get some sustenance during those meal meetings, but you're still working. And if you can't line up a business meal, consider brown bagging it at your desk so you can still keep on working. Is this suggestion obnoxious? Okay, throw stones at me if you like. But you wanted to know the tactics of highly successful people, and these are some of them. **Be productive!**

On the other hand, I know some people who are *so* productive that they can actually leave work *early*. A close friend of mine is a lawyer who is the top biller in his firm. He gets in at 5 am every day, works productively in solitude from 5 to 9, takes a one hour break to exercise and then continues working until 3 pm. And then he goes home. During that time, he is the "King of Productivity." He has done so much—particularly between 5 am and 9 am, that he can leave at 3 pm knowing that he has accomplished a lot—and his pay reflects that.

Bottom line: If you're asking me how to be successful, my recommendation is that you begin by ignoring what is generally considered to be normal "working hours." The person who is told that work is from 9 to 5 and who *only* works from 9 to 5, is rarely the person who gets ahead or makes a ton of money. **The person who gets ahead works far longer hours, and more often than not, those hours begin before the work day officially begins.**

Be Passionate About Whatever You Do

Life is a blank slate. Within reason, you can choose to do literally anything at all that you want. Sure, perhaps you'd love to be an NFL quarterback and that's probably not going to happen, but maybe you've got the skills to be a sportswriter or an athletic trainer. The point is, we've come a long way as a civilization from where people used to be born into an occupation that they could not avoid or rise above. So why the heck are there still so many people in this country who hate their jobs?

One reason, I believe, is that some people are told, "There's a lot of money to be made in this field." Now, I don't deny, that's a great business tip. But maybe some of those suggestions make for a better *investment* tip. Plumbers make a nice living, but not many people really want to fix toilets all day long. Doctors have always earned a nice living, but not everyone is cut out for blood and guts and death and disease on top of twelve years for school.

I've said throughout this book that wealth can be created by people in fields where they may not necessarily make a huge wage. Teachers, policemen, firemen, travel agents—these are not the fields people go into for the money. But people in those fields, and others who manage their money well, can still live a comfortable life.

But what about happiness? I'm not going to try to tackle the age old question, **"Does money buy happiness?" I say that the answer is that *financial security* HELPS buy happiness.** But your career should be your career—something of your own choosing that makes you want to get up in the morning. If you are doing it solely for the money, then no, you will probably not be a happy camper in the long run. The world is full of miserable doctors, lawyers, and engineers. Sure, they might make a great wage, but some of them feel no passion for or take joy in what they do.

Mercenaries—they're never to be trusted. A customer who only buys from you because you are a few pennies cheaper than the guy down the street will leave you the moment a guy *farther* down the street under-prices *you*. You can't build a business on that kind of customer. The same goes for workers. If you hire bus drivers and you get an applicant who says, "Yeah, I heard you pay $14 an hour. The place I'm at now only pays $13," that guy will leave you the moment a competitor offers him $15. And, frankly, he's said nothing to lead you to believe he even *likes* driving a bus.

On the other hand, there are people who truly enjoy driving for a living—bus drivers, truck drivers, what have you. There are actually lots of occupations out there where you get behind the wheel and just drive. Some people love it. If I'm hiring drivers, that's the applicant I want. And yes, they do exist, in most every field. Think about it. Think of the nastiest, crappiest job that you would *never* want to do. I'll bet you've dealt with people who do that job with a big, sincere smile on their face, as well as some who look as miserable as can be. It's all a matter of perspective. It's a big ol' world out there, and we're all a little different.

Your job will consume about half of your life. These days we spend on earth are precious. "Quality of life" is not just something to talk about when facing nursing home or hospice care. It's every day we're alive.

Sometimes it's the field we are in. Maybe you were forced into it somehow; maybe you took that tip about it being lucrative. But if you find it just isn't the right fit, take your head out of the sand, look around, and see what else would make you happier. I'll guarantee you, the happy dentist makes more money than the unhappy dentist. So how good a situation have you put yourself in, then, anyhow?

Some people take longer than others to mature. They goof off through high school, drop out of college, end up working in fast food, and are incredibly unhappy. But this is not where your story has to end. Maybe at age twenty-five you wake up and you realize that you have enough brain power and ambition to do better. So do it! You're not getting any younger. **Think about what you really want to do in life, and then figure out a path to get yourself there.** Okay, so maybe at twenty-five you don't have mom and dad anymore to pay your bills, but still, there are ways. Maybe you want to be that sports writer we talked about. Keep working at the burger joint while you take some writing and journalism classes at the local community college. It's not that expensive, and it's a great investment in yourself. Get on the school newspaper there. See if the Career Services office can hook you up with an internship with a local paper or radio station. Pretty soon, you might be able to ask your manager at work to reduce you to part-time because this writing thing is beginning to take off for you. Keep at it, keep your passion flowing, and within a few years you might be working for Sports Illustrated. Stranger things have happened.

Then there's the person who hates his boss. Honestly, I can't fathom this one. **If a work environment is toxic, then go elsewhere.** You're not an indentured slave. People change jobs all the time these days. But **if you like your job, you like your firm, then show some loyalty.** A lot of twenty and thirty-somethings today just jump from job to job every year or so, for wages alone. Again, this is mercenary. If you truly feel you are stuck in a situation where you cannot move ahead and another company values you more, then you have to do what you have to do. But I think some young people today are over-doing it.

Life is short. Time is precious. Don't waste it being miserable. If you have to work anyway, do something that makes you happy at a place that makes you happy. And if you want to be successful at it, be more than happy—be passionate. **Passion is what makes you not only want to *go* to work, but to be the best at what it is that you do.**

It's Not Who You Know— It's Who Knows YOU!

I almost feel like making the title of this subchapter serve as the body of it as well and leaving it at that. It's a profound statement, and one worth pondering. We've all heard the term, "It's who you know." I don't completely disagree with that. Social networking helps; it really does. I would rather do business with people I know than with total strangers. It's a trust issue, no doubt about it. If I don't know you, you can take my money and drop off the face of the earth. That makes me nervous. At least if I know you, or if I know someone who knows you, I have a greater confidence in our working together. If I've been put on to you by a friend or acquaintance and you burn me, among other things, I'm also going to put in a call to the person who recommended you.

Some people stumble with social networking. They go to a big event or function, but they don't talk to anybody. What's the point in that? That's where the title of this subchapter really comes from. If the local bank president speaks at some dinner I'm attending, *I* now know *him*, but *he* doesn't know *me*. He's done a great job for himself and his business because he got to speak, and if I was impressed by him and his presentation, I might now give him some of my business. But what about me? Will he be doing business with me? No. Why? Because I failed to go up to him and introduce myself. He doesn't know me!

Let's talk about that introduction stuff. First off, take advantage of business networking possibilities. Join the local and state Chambers of Commerce. Join other similar organizations. Join organizations within your chosen field. These are particularly good for continuing your education within your field as well as checking out new products. You also get a chance to develop a gut feeling for the types of people who run certain companies or vendors. Join other organizations that provide you with the opportunity to meet people who could either be potential customers or clients for your business.

Now, here's a pitfall I want you to avoid. Making pals is great. But if that's all you are doing once you join these sorts of organizations, don't con yourself into believing it is "for your business." It's not; it's no different than if you joined a bowling league or took a macramé class. Be honest with yourself. I join these organizations in order to make business contacts and make money. Anything else that comes along with it is gravy.

So let's get back to the introductions part. You've heard the bank president speak. Afterwards, go on up to him and shake his hand. Look him in the eye and tell him your name. And since this is a business networking event, your name is no longer "John Doe." Your name is "John Doe, Plumbing Contractor." In business, that is your "full name." **You must define yourself when you are in business.** Even if you are not the owner of a business, this is still important. Perhaps you're "John Doe, Business Management Software Consultant." You may work for a large national software company, but you're still not just "John Doe." You want this bank president to hear your "full name" and you want the people standing around within earshot to hear it, too.

Start a conversation. Sure, I know it's hard sometimes. It's practically like cruising a single's bar. But make that introduction, have a "full name," and have a little something to say, such as, "I really liked your talk. What kind of business management software does your bank use?" I'm not telling you to make a hard pitch. I'm telling you to make some sort of impression and, perhaps, open up the door to some future face time as well.

What comes next is a personal pet peeve of mine. I am astonished at how many people, even business owners, go around without business cards. **Business cards are the single most inexpensive form of marketing there is.** For a few dollars, you can have a simple card made up that says your name, your business, the business address, and the requisite phone, fax, and e-mail data. And yet time after time, I meet people, people I might have an interest in doing business with, and they have no cards with them. How will I remember them? Remembering them is *their* problem, not mine. They have *my* card (because I'm always packing), so they can do business with me. But the circle ends there.

A business card doesn't need to be fancy. I know, some people spend a lot on them. They're glossy with four color print. Some people even put their pictures on them. What's up with that? I know almost all real estate agents do that; why, I do not know. But you don't have to go that far overboard or that expensive to make them effective. Frankly, you don't have to provide even that much information on the card. Some people are in multiple businesses. You can choose to print up multiple cards, or you can simply have a white card with your name and contact data, like I do. The bottom line is, make sure you always carry a few. And if you're going to a networking event, bring a TON of them. Pass them out like candy on Halloween.

Make sure everyone you know knows what you do and what you are up to. So along with giving your full name when you first meet someone, realize that you may see that person again sometime. Have some more to tell about your recent business activities. Everyone always says, "What's new?" Have a good answer that can help your business. Don't start pulling out the pictures from your last vacation. How is that going to make you money? Instead say, "Yeah, we just got a big new contract installing some custom software into the candy factory at the edge of town." That's newsworthy. Maybe you've just introduced a new product. Think, think, think. This is not hard-selling or even pitching. You've been asked the classic banal question; now answer it in a way that could help you and your career. Let the people you meet come to know you as the Management Software Guy, rather than the Guy Who Just Went to Jamaica.

Now, I'm no social butterfly. I admit, I spend a lot of time at parties looking at my watch, thinking of things I'd rather be doing. So make it your priority to maximize these contact opportunities. And do a lot of them, if possible. Furthermore, follow-up is key. This brings me back to those breakfast and lunch meetings I talked about in a previous subchapter. Invite that bank president out for breakfast, particularly if you have a proposal or a need you wish to discuss. Those sorts of one-on-one meetings need not be just about business or your pitch. You're fleshing out the gray areas where he doesn't really know you. You're becoming a flesh and blood person to the person across from you eating toast and drinking coffee. This is good.

Where a lot of people drop the ball is in continued follow-up. They take me out to lunch when they want something, and then I never hear from them again until they want something again. If that's frequent, and what they want from me opens up a two-way street where I get something good out of the deal as well, then fine. But often, someone wants something from me, we do a deal, then I never hear from them again for another six years, when they feel they need me again. After that much time, I can barely recall who they are. They're not really someone I know that well. It's been six years, for crying out loud. I may have been wined and dined over twelve times in the past six years by someone else in their same field. I no longer need them, even though they feel that they need me. Game over; they blew it.

It's fine to take someone out to lunch just to keep the business contact alive. You'd be surprised at how much intelligence you can pick up from such an adventure. Again, this is why I tell people not to eat alone. You have to eat anyway; why not maximize the time spent chewing? It may stretch it out a few minutes longer, but you'll be doing something other than just feeding your face.

Eating is not your only networking option. Shoot an e-mail to a client or a business contact from time to time just to say hi. Drop by their office if you're in the neighborhood anyway. Keep it casual so that they know that's simply the kind of friendly guy you are. There's nothing worse than the guy who gets a reputation of, "Oh, here comes Larry again. What's he want this time?" while they roll their eyes and look for a place to hide. A few totally purposeless (on the surface) follow-ups with people help in establishing you as the person to be remembered and, frankly, liked.

This is also where activities such as golf and tennis come in. People do tons of business on the golf course or down at the marina, depending upon where you live. Try not to stay cooped up in your house when you're not working. Mix with people. Mix with people who are your clients, could be your clients, or could turn you on to the sorts of other people who could be your clients or customers. Playing tennis with your cousin Eddy who is in a field with no connection at all to yours is not clever networking.

Watch the Details

People tell me that I "micromanage," but that is okay with me. **Any time that I have let go of control, it has cost me money**—sometimes a LOT of money. Other people, no matter how good they are at what they do, generally do not have the same alignment of interest with you. Nobody will do the same job as you—not your attorney, not your CPA, not your best property manager. It is ultimately up to *you* to control your financial destiny. Accept responsibility!

Yes, this will take time from your day. But don't believe for a minute that this is counterproductive or unproductive. If I bring in a specialized repairman to fix a piece of my equipment, I watch what he does. Why?

Well, for one thing, there's always the possibility that I can learn to fix it myself the next time around and save a lot of money. For another thing, some repair people charge enormous amounts of money for "replacing parts" that they never really replaced or that never needed replacing. Watch the details! You don't have to get nasty about it; just watch what's going on and ask questions.

Question bills. Maybe you couldn't pull yourself away from a business crisis in order to watch the repairman. But when he hands you his bill, read it and ask intelligent and serious questions. If he says he replaced some part, ask him for the old one. That's made more than one crooked repairman sweat. Ask what a part does. Ask for a breakdown on exactly what it was that went wrong with the machine in the first place and how you can avoid having it happen again. Don't just write out checks so you can quickly go back to reading the newspaper!

Always remember the anecdote about John D. Rockefeller and the solder on his oil barrels. Transfer that story into how you should go about doing everything in your life. I call it a "healthy distrust," and I don't apologize for it. Again, the difference between me and someone with a reputation as a crazy man is that I don't do this sarcastically, nor do I lose my temper. In fact, let the *other guy* lose *his* temper. If that happens, it's often a good indication that you just caught the fox in the henhouse, stealing your eggs.

Ask questions, don't walk away until you've gotten answers that satisfy you, and don't be afraid to say what it is that you want and how you want it. These are the details. **Only settle for a compromise *willingly* and *knowingly*.** In life, you won't always get your way, but don't *not* get your way because you didn't even know what was going on until it was too late.

Follow Through

People often ask me how I have been so successful in business. There are obviously a number of variables that have helped make me successful, not the least of which has been some good luck. I have never had a problem getting customers or having enough business. Am I a great salesperson, in the typical stereotype? As I've said before, no. What I do, though, is I just make it easy for people to buy from me. **No matter what the business, I am knowledgeable, organized, focused on meeting the customer's needs, exceed expectations, and most importantly, I follow through on my commitments.** I do what I say that I am going to do, and people appreciate this.

Here's a mantra for you all: **Under-promise and over-deliver.** Some people get a lot of business by promising the earth, the moon, and the stars. Sure, that will get you a client—but can you deliver? Probably not. So what have you accomplished? You've gotten yourself a client...who will never do business with you again, and who will bad-mouth you to everyone he or she knows. That's the sort of thing that kills a businessman's reputation, and along with his reputation, his livelihood.

If you cannot be over to install a piece of equipment at someone's office on Tuesday, don't say that you can. Tell him when you *can* be there and DO IT! Does this mean you should be lazy and unambitious? Heck no! It's about being realistic. Yes, you certainly should knock yourself out in order to please a client; in order to get a contract or make a sale. But know your limitations. Some things simply cannot be done, or simply cannot be done by you for a certain price on a certain timetable. Always try your best, but remember—if you promise something for 3 pm and you can get it done by 2 pm, you're a hero. If you promise something for 3 pm and you get it done by 4 pm, you're a loser. Better to be a hero.

The follow-through also rolls down the hill to the lowest member of your team if you have one. I know some great salesmen who, after they make the sale, are quickly onto the next one. That's great, but only if the other people—the rest of the team that provides the actual service or delivers the product—also do their job correctly. Imagine what it feels like to be hung out to dry. That's what happens to the super-salesman who thinks that follow-through is "not his job." Technically, he may be correct. If his job is to make the sale and it's someone else's job to deliver the product, he's right—*and* he's wrong. It matters not to the customer which person dropped the ball. The customer relies on the person he first interacted with—or that person's boss—whether that person was the screw-up or not. And finger-pointing doesn't cut it. *Accepting responsibility* is what matters!

So yes, no matter where you are in the supply chain, your reputation is on the line and it is up to you to make sure the follow-through goes according to the promises *you made*.

There are many ways to do this. If you are the boss, then there are butts to kick and heads to make roll. You are empowered to fire and hire until you get a support team on board that can consistently make your company look good. This is not a time for being Mr. Nice Guy. This is how you make your living.

If, on the other hand, you are just a cog in a big machine, it is *still* your reputation that's being judged. You are still empowered to check and recheck that things are going well down the line. Maybe this does mean that you have to take a few minutes here and there out of your selling schedule to make a few phone calls to make sure everything is on track. And yes, if things are going awry, you may need to make some loud noises. If you find dead weight in your supply chain that is making you look bad, you may have to climb up the chain of command to make higher-ups understand where problems are occurring. **You have to be your customer's advocate.**

Will this make you popular with your co-workers or sub-contractors? Often times not. But you *will* earn people's respect. **When you do the right thing, the right people will notice and reward your behavior.**

Another tip, though: Don't forget to add the sugar with the medicine. If you become known to your co-workers or sub-contractors only as "the pushy guy" or "the demanding guy," they may start to dislike you so much that they begin to sabotage you on purpose. Balance things out. **Thank people when they do a good job for you and make you look good.** Little gifts can be a nice touch sometimes, too. Also, those business lunches and breakfasts I keep talking about—if you can't find a client to do them with, think about that co-worker or sub-contractor who you've been riding a lot lately. Maybe buy them a Happy Meal once in a while. Spend some non-work face-time with them. Let them see your likable side. Learn more about them. **The best way to *get* favors is to *trade* favors.** By learning more about what they do, maybe there are some things you could do to make *them* look good as well. And when that happens…you've got a good thing going on!

I learned the importance of follow-through from my father, who was in the construction business. He became so renowned for it that someone once made him a plaque that said: "We Do What We Say We Are Going to Do." It's simple, it's basic, but I can think of no greater goal for a business or a worker than this.

There's another twist to the phrase "follow through." I recently participated in a charity event where people were invited to test drive a particular brand of car. For every mile someone test drove, the car dealer contributed a dollar to charity. I thought this was a great idea. It raised money and awareness for a worthy cause, and it provided the car dealer with extra exposure—a win-win all around.

Well, I showed up, test drove a car—a brand of car, I might add, that I've driven and owned before and tend to like a lot and—came right back to the lot…and went home. *No one tried to sell me the car!* People, listen to me and understand where I'm coming from: I was IN THE CAR. I was DRIVING THE CAR. If you're a car salesman, isn't that the toughest obstacle right there? And lastly, I was easily pre-qualifiable as the kind of person who might want to buy that particular car. Yet no one even asked me if I was interested. No one asked me if I even liked the car. No one made a move to make a very substantial car sale to me. I even wandered around the lot another twenty minutes. Not a single human being so much as said "hello" to me. So I left.

Follow through. If I owned that car dealership, I would have had scalps on the wall of the salespeople who dropped the ball like that by not following through. **Lack of follow-through is when you are given an opportunity to make a sale, to get a client, and you don't even try.** What's that all about? What's the famous line: ABC— Always Be Closing? Every salesperson at that car dealership had been *handed* sales openings. Would they have closed them all? Of course not. But to not even try? That's just crazy and lazy. **Life gives us all opportunities and chances. When opportunity knocks, answer the darn door. Answering the door is the follow-through.**

Not a week goes by in my life when I am not looking to do business with some one or some entity. We all have needs. I'll need a person to provide a particular service, I'll get a recommendation from a friend to call a certain company, I'll place the call, I'll leave a message…and then I'll wait and wait days and days for someone to call me back. Are people so wealthy that they can just turn down business? If so, God bless 'em. I know I can't be that way. This never ceases to amaze me. If you're hungry, act like it. Look at every tip or lead you're given as a raw steak and you're a hungry mountain lion. Pounce on it; follow through.

Set Priorities

My life is full of "to-do" lists and yellow sticky notes. I first learned this technique from my father. Dad used to put sticky notes all over his desk. When something was of great importance or if it was of a more long-term nature, he actually took clear tape and pasted it on the loose bottom flap so that the entire piece of yellow 2-by-2-inch paper was sealed semi-permanently to his desk.

I was so impressed by my dad that when I was around eight years old, I mimicked his yellow sticky-note filled desk on my own desk at home. The problem was, my dad's desk had a plastic laminate top and mine was real wood. That tape did a number on the nice oak finish, and my mom was none too impressed. But both my parents knew my heart was in the right place.

It seems everyone today complains of varying degrees of ADD (Attention Deficit Disorder). Personally, my joke is that I have the self-diagnosed adult-onset version. True, some people actually have it and it is a nuisance, but even for the rest of us, it is very hard to remember everything we have to remember in this fast-paced world of ours. We need to be busy in order to be successful, and being busy makes it hard to keep everything in order inside our heads. We need reminder systems. Frankly, some of the best systems come fromprofessionals who actually *treat* people diagnosed with ADD.

Take the sticky notes. Now, I doubt that when my dad was using them so extensively he had even heard of ADD. But occupational therapists swear by them. Take those little sticky suckers and slap them all over your office. They come in lots of colors now, too, so don't be afraid of creating a color-coded system that works for you. Clocks—they're another great tool. Set alarms for important things. Have a phone appointment for a certain time? Don't just remember it; take your watch, the clock on your desk, or the clock on your computer or your cell phone and set it to go off when you're supposed to make that call. Use every trick in the book to keep yourself on task and on time.

The electronic age (and I've said before how much guys like me love gadgets) has given us tons of powerful tools to help us keep organized. PDA's, Blackberries, software programs—there's a treasure trove of stuff out there to try. Avail yourself. Never say, "I just can't get organized." *You have to get organized!* You have no choice in the matter. No successful person is truly disorganized.

Organization also means prioritization. What's the use in knowing you've got a dozen things to do if you don't know the order in which to do them? This is where "setting your priorities" is best manifested.

Knowing all of your specific deadlines is where you start. Write them or post them up somewhere. Put them in a little black book. Again, I won't go on listing the millions of ways in which this can be done. Go to your local office supply superstore and there's a different tool for organizing yourself with every step you take. Pick one up and use it. JUST DO IT!

Once you know your deadlines, figure out, realistically, how long each task takes. Over-estimate rather than under-estimate.

Look at the relative importance of various tasks. Don't just do what is most fun and easiest to do first. Look at what is most important; what is most critical; what is most potentially lucrative. Move that farther up the list than remembering to pass along that funny joke someone just e-mailed to you. **Prioritize your time!**

Be flexible with your prioritization. Be fluid. You are like an elite fighting force of the working world. You must be able to react to unforeseen obstacles. Have a 2:30 pm phone meeting but an important client has just walked through the door unexpectedly, and you don't want to keep him waiting? How quickly can you sew up that phone meeting? Is it with someone who is usually amicable enough to be cool with you rescheduling it for a little bit later? Is there someone else who can pinch-hit for you? **Think, react, prioritize.** Life—and especially business life—is like that circus act where the guy spins dozens of plates on sticks. Your job is to keep all those plates spinning, not allowing any to fall and crash to the ground. *You can do this!* But only if you know what's going on all around you and you stay on top of everything. And the way to do that is to write everything down, use organizational tools, and always, always be prioritizing and re-prioritizing.

Write down your goals. This is more esoteric than figuring out which engine to work on next or what client to call. Goal-setting is important, so important that it deserves being committed to paper from time to time. Write down your goals and check up on them as you would your business or family budget. How are you moving along with them? Are you hitting your marks? Are you making time for the long-range goals? That's what trips up so many of us. We get so engrossed in the daily grind that we forget what we're really doing it for.

If your dream is to open up a chain of brew pubs, along with making brew pub number one successful, you must remember to set aside time to move that "multi-location maven" ambition forward. It won't happen by itself. I know, working in that first pub keeps you hopping busy. That's good. That means you're doing something right. But it also means that you've developed a formula that you could, perhaps, replicate and thus double or triple your profits. Make time to make that happen! Brew pubs don't usually open until around 11:30 am, so use the morning hours to call some real estate agents, visit some new locations, meet with some local bankers— whatever is necessary to move toward your dream. **Successful people don't get buried under the minutia—they always keep their eyes on the prize.**

My world is all about automation and efficiency. **Always find ways to do things better than you are doing them currently.** Every area of our lives has room for improvement. The smoother that first brew pub runs, the more time you'll have to set up the next one. You are better off to build a solid infrastructure than to waste your time always fighting fires.

Know What You Spend

Keep a written record of what you spend. Personally, I use QuickBooks and Quicken and log in every bit of income and expense. Not only does it make things easier at tax time, but I can easily analyze my finances. These leading software programs, as well as others, can also interface directly with your bank as well as with your credit cards. Full integration helps make things run that much easier and smoother. Try it and see.

I know a guy who carries a "little black book" and writes down (to the penny) every bit of cash he spends each day (i.e., lunch, parking, etc.). I think this might be overkill, but you get the point. Do not trip over dollars to pickup nickels, most certainly keep track of those dollars.

I've touched a bit on this idea as we've gone along throughout this book and I've shared with you the John D. Rockefeller story about how he did, in fact, log in every single penny he acquired or spent from the time he was a relatively young boy. I believe that the Rockefeller tale was the beginning of this particular philosophy toward financial success here in America. There are ways to save everywhere in our lives, but it is a rag-tag non-system if one only does it sporadically and without comprehensive thought. You can decide to only order water when you go out to eat in a restaurant, but if you go out to eat far too often and without a clear purpose except epicurean pleasure, what have you really accomplished? You're only fooling yourself into believing you have been saving measurable amounts of money by choosing water over soda or alcohol. In order to really make fiscal progress, you need to look at *all* of your monthly spending and write up real budgets. You have to know what you spend!

I have some friends who never open or reconcile a bank statement—they just call the bank every couple of weeks to check their balance. Granted, what these guys do is better than nothing—but not by much. **You *have* to reconcile bank statements. You *have* to reconcile credit card statements.** These things are frequently wrong. It's not that someone is necessarily ripping you off; it's just that humans make errors. And don't tell me about computers. Humans make computers and put data into those computers. As they say, "Garbage in; garbage out."

It is amazing how often one digit can be mis-typed and it changes everything in one of your accounts. You write someone a check for $100, but your bank deducts $1,000. It happens. You have your banking set up to automatically deduct and pay a certain bill every single month. But in February, for some reason, it doesn't happen. Stay on top of things like this! Think about your credit rating. If you catch these errors as soon as they happen, you have a better chance of them not being reported and held against you. If you don't discover it until six months later, good luck.

Here's another common error: Did you ever write a check that was never cashed? It can pose a problem. Maybe it got lost in the mail. If it's to an important vendor that reports to the credit bureaus, again, knowing about it ASAP is critical.

But what about that check you wrote to your Nephew Normie for his birthday? Maybe he lost it. Maybe it got thrown out with the wrapping paper from all of his gifts. Without it, everyone will think that Uncle Braun was a cheapskate who stiffed him on a gift. Track this stuff! If it hasn't been cashed, phone him up and make sure he got it.

What if it's not a friend or relative, but a large vendor? Sometimes it's not a matter of something getting lost in the mail. Some businesses are simply so disorganized that money is lying all over the place. Don't let this be your business!

One of my businesses sent another company a refund check. It never got cashed. Now, some of you may think, "Heh, heh. Free money." That's not right. The company I sent that check to had been promised it. My good name was on the line. That's as important as my credit rating. So I called them up. This is the right thing to do.

What happens next can go a myriad of ways. Most banks charge about $25 to stop payment on a check. If I wrote someone a check for $15, I really don't want to spend $25 plus $15 to give them $15. That's stupid. On the other hand, I don't want the other company, in their mass of disorganization, to get a new check from me, find the old check as well, and then cash them both. This is also why I'm in love with electronic money transfer and automatic bank deductions. No checks to lose.

Sometimes the disorganization on the other end is so bad that even if you call the company, they never get their act together and your check never gets cashed. If so, always remember the rule of thumb is that most banks will not honor a check that is more than one year old. If after a year someone hasn't cashed a check from you, you should add it back in to your running balance.

All of this minutia, it's all part and parcel of knowing what you spend and tracking your financial affairs. It's imperative that you do it. Things can get out of hand so darn easily. Why let that happen when it is so easy to take charge and keep a good handle on things?

Know What Your Time is Worth

This subchapter may appear, on its surface, to be a bit of a contradiction of many of the things I've said thus far, but bear with me. It's all about the nuance.

I am a do-it-yourselfer. That's simply who I am and I love it. BUT…there's a point where this is a game of diminishing returns.

When you are first starting out in life, or if you simply don't make or possess very much money, doing things yourself is imperative. You can't *afford* to go out to dinner, so making your own meals saves you money, period. Everyone can learn to change the oil on their own car. If you're poor, this is another easy way to save some money. I could go on and on, but you get the point. **When you don't have money, but you do have time, your time is relatively "worthless." As a result, it is better to spend your time than to spend your money.**

But what happens farther on down the line? Is it practical to change your own oil when you have to take an hour out of productive work in order to do it? NO!

Know what your time is worth and exercise a division of labor. I know to the penny what my time is worth—it's several hundred dollars per hour. How do you calculate this? Simple. Take your yearly, monthly, or weekly income. Honestly divide it by the hours you actually work. Don't go by your salary and the hours you are actually *scheduled* to work; that's disingenuous. Count your commuting time, etc. So what is the answer to this math problem? That answer is what your time is worth.

Now, if you've got extra time and you were only going to sit on your butt and channel surf through bad television, then almost any task is worth your time. But it's when you start having to do chores and non-income producing tasks that actually cut into what could otherwise be productive work time that this becomes an issue worth exploring.

Generally, I pay people to do routine tasks when their cost is less than what my time is worth. If you can make $25 per hour practicing your trade, and it costs only $15 per hour to have somebody mow your lawn, why should you do this yourself? The only exception, obviously, is if you enjoy mowing your own yard and derive personal satisfaction from doing so (which I personally do, so I like to do this myself when my schedule allows). Otherwise, focus on what you do best and what brings you income. **Don't let banal chores and tasks keep you from earning to your full potential.** Work smarter, not harder.

Here's an example: I have a friend who's an attorney. He bills out at around $150 an hour. He owns a car where the closest authorized repair shop is an hour's drive away. So just for routine maintenance, he has to leave work during business hours, drive an hour, wait another hour, then drive back another hour. That's $450 down the drain (three hours times $150), and we haven't even factored in what it costs to work on the car itself.

I told him, "Why not check if the shop has a pick-up and delivery service?" This idea had never occurred to him. He called up and found out that, indeed, his shop did this sort of thing. The charge was $50. So for $50, two young guys would swing by his office, one would hop into his car, then drive it back to the shop, and once the work was done, they'd drive it back for him. Fifty dollars compared to $450. That's a net savings of $400.

See, the two young guys who worked at the repair shop's time was not worth what my friend's time was worth, so he was able to hire them at a great savings. These opportunities are out there, people. In America today, there is someone you can hire for literally every task you could possibly think of. I know people who have hired people to clean behind their refrigerators, pick them up from the airport, water their lawn, pull their weeds, watch their sick grandmother, walk their dog; you name it.

Some people feel that they must make choices between work and play. I say that there is another major time category, and that is "chore time." **When it comes to chores, look at the cost of your time, then look at the cost of hiring someone to do your chores.** From there, it's nothing more than a simple math problem that a fifth grader can do.

Life Is Not Fair

Schools today are sheltering kids. Every kid gets a trophy (no matter how badly they perform), everyone is equal regardless of outcome, and competition has been completely removed. News flash: The "real world" does not work this way—it can be a cold, hard place where only the strong survive.

Okay, so I'll tone down the rhetoric, but just a tiny bit. Perhaps five-year-olds shouldn't be taunted and called "Loser!" by some other kid who beats them at a board game. That's not good for either the loser or the winner, who may grow up to be an obnoxious jerk. And when little kids are just playing T-ball because their coordination is still developing (mine *still* is) and they can barely hold a baseball bat properly, perhaps it's alright to give them all an ice-cream party or a little statuette at the end of the season.

But there has to be a logical point after which the healthy, basic sense of self-esteem is developed and kids finally discover that *they will not always win*—or certainly not always win at *everything*.

Tiger Woods was probably the world's greatest golfer at every age that he has ever lived. But maybe he stinks at chess. I hear he's a pretty smart guy; but, perhaps, he could never quite master chemistry in high school. The point is, *everyone* has their weak points.

Speaking of chemistry, would you believe that there are some schools that don't even believe in grades? How the heck can you get an understanding of how well or poorly you are doing if you don't get graded at some point? And no, a long-winded "personal assessment" doesn't quite cut it, because yes, it also does pay to know how one compares with one's peers. If you got a D and almost everyone else in your class got an A or B, then it is probably safe to say that you have some deficiencies in this subject. Maybe you're not working hard enough, maybe you simply have no talent for it; who knows? But *no one* will know if there's no measurement of your production.

But this only speaks to the issues of getting what you have truly earned. All of us adults can attest to the fact that this does not hold true in real adult life. In fact, **adversity helps in personal growth.**

Back to Tiger Woods. He was so good at golf in high school that many thought he would simply go right into the pros. Instead, he took a scholarship to Stanford, one of the top colleges in the nation. There he, of course, flourished as a collegiate amateur golfer. But then there was a controversy. By this time, Tiger had won a ton of tournaments and was already a household name, despite still being a college student. Collegiate athletics have a lot of rules and regulations and regulatory agencies. It seems that Tiger was invited out to dinner with Arnold Palmer. Apparently, this was somehow misconstrued as some sort of collegiate athletics rules violation. Now, with so many college athletes receiving under-the-table money from boosters, or taking illegal steroids, why going out to dinner with Arnold would be a breaking of any rule is unfathomable to just about any thinking person. But Tiger had become a target. He was becoming bigger than the game. People were jealous.

Tiger was suddenly the subject of an NCAA witch hunt. And over what? A $25 dinner that Arnold had bought him. Was this an inducement to do something? To throw a college tournament? Did this make Tiger a professional? No, no, and no.

In response to this, Tiger's hand was forced and he left Stanford after only two years. The rest, as they say, is history. Right won out. But for a time, young Mr. Woods learned that *life is not fair*.

There will be jobs you apply for where you will be the most qualified candidate, but someone else will get the job instead; perhaps someone's relative. **Life is not fair.**

There will be business opportunities you will try to enter into, but someone will try to keep you out of the market, and not simply by out-performing you, but by trying to tilt the odds in their favor, illegally or semi-illegally. **Life is not fair.**

There will be times when someone will try to smear your good name for their own private purposes; perhaps to take business away from you or to get a promotion that you earned. **Life is not fair.**

I could drag this list out for page upon page. When someone is struck down by a crippling disease at far too young an age, it is not fair. When some innocent person is struck by a car or mugged and beaten by thugs, it is not fair.

But it IS life.

- **Life judges us on how we do when faced with adversity, rather than what advantages have been given to us.**
- **The sooner we learn about failure, the sooner we learn about resilience and recovery.**
- **Character is never truly tested until faced with significant adversity.**

- It is how quickly we get up after we've fallen that says more about us than how high we climb when unimpeded.
- Some people lead charmed lives, but when the first obstacle is thrown into their path, they crumble and never get back up. This is the definition of failure.

Many of us are sold a bill of goods early in life: If we stay in school and then go on to college, a great, lucrative dream job will be awaiting us on graduation day.

Not always.

Today, everybody has a bachelor's degree. So what? Perhaps decades ago when such a thing was a rarer commodity, a "C" student could waltz in and be "well taken care of" for the rest of his life, all due to his undergraduate degree.

No more.

When you step out of college, employers still want to see that spark behind your eyes, the fire that tells them you have the personal qualities that will make you a good, hard worker. Fresh out of school, the top employers will want to see good grades, not "gentleman's Cs". Work or interning experience is becoming more and more desirable as you try to prove your case for being hired. If you went to a state college instead of some Ivy League school, you may have an even harder time breaking in, good grades or not. But over time, it is not your educational pedigree that wins out; it will be your work ethic and your wits. But let me remind you—you do not "deserve" anything. What you get must be *earned*.

Be Flexible

Our future is always in front of us, but we have no idea where the winds of change will blow us. Imagine training and studying to be a zeppelin maker or driver. Where are those guys now? What about the people who used to make those big, flat, black discs with the little hole punched out in the middle? I think they used to call those things "records" and you played them on a "stereo." Where are those guys today?

It has been said many times that in fifteen years many of us will be employed or involved in industries that don't even exist today. It pays to be flexible. Look at your schooling as the foundation of your common sense and basic skills knowledge. But don't feel limited by your schooling.

So you studied to be a zeppelin maker (I'd imagine you'd be quite old by now). You're probably very handy. Perhaps you were an engineer. Well, there's no longer a need for anyone to engineer zeppelins, but there most certainly are needs for engineers and handy people. Be flexible. Use the basics that God gave you, not just the job-specific higher level skills. Most skills are easily transferable, if you're willing to think creatively and laterally.

Always be on the look-out for opportunity. Maybe you feel you're stuck in a particular job. No forward progress. Take your head out of the sand and see what else you could apply your skill set to. Sure, you may have to take a slight cut in pay in order to break into this new field. But if that field is growing and you got in at the right time, you could be exceeding your old salary in no time!

A healthy cynicism about the changing marketplace is another reason to always live below your means. Take the person we just talked about, the one who's feeling stuck in his job and sees the opportunity to make a lateral, morphing eventually into a forward move. If you've choked yourself with debt—with a house and a car and credit card bills you can ill afford—you cannot make that lateral move. You cannot change careers. You cannot take a temporary pay cut. You…are…stuck.

Learn From Mistakes

The only people who don't make mistakes are the people who don't do anything. I've learned more from my mistakes than from my successes. If you do a bad job, but no one notices, you will never really learn the true measure of your skills. In this sense, failure can sometimes be good.

An older guy I know told me a story of the first pizza place that moved into his little town. The pizza was lousy and the owner was rude, but the guy had the only game in town—if you like pizza, and who doesn't?—So he made a ton of money and retired early. He left the pizza parlor to his two sons, who made the same bad pizza and were just as rude as their father. But now that time had passed, other competitors had come into the local marketplace and this was no longer the only pizza place in town. The place closed its doors in no time. The original owner was lucky because he was the first to do something where it had never been done before, but he never learned what his mistakes were, nor did his sons. If they had, they would have improved the quality of their product as well as their customer service. I can imagine those two sons are just moping around today, wondering what the heck went wrong.

Some people keep making the same mistakes over and over again. In most of these cases, I'm sure that someone came along and tried to give them guidance and inform them what their error was. But some people are thick-headed. They will keep banging their heads against a wall, doing the same thing over and over, expecting a different result. Funny, but psychologists will tell you that that is the quintessential definition of insanity—doing the same thing over and over again and expecting a different outcome. **If you tried something one way and it didn't work, be open to trying it a different way the next time.** You can't do much worse!

Have a "Passive" Business Plan

I love this. A "passive" business plan is something that works for you even when you yourself aren't working.

Some investments are a passive business plan. You contribute to a mutual fund, it grows, and you spend no time on it. This is great. The same goes for 401ks, IRAs, stocks, etc. We've referred to it earlier as "saving for the future," but it is also income in and of itself, particularly the funds that are not restrictively dedicated to retirement (401ks and IRAs). If the day comes when you are out of work for one reason or another, this is something you can tap into if you have to. If you've started early and you're lucky enough not to be out of work until closer to mid-career, you might not even have to tap into the principal, but be able to live for a while off of the interest only, which is a beautiful thing.

I love real estate investment very much when it comes to passive income. I like to buy investment properties, rent them out to tenants who carry the mortgage and related expenses, and, if the market is right and I've set my rental rates correctly, I get some additional money in my pocket each month as well. Does real estate require some of my precious time? Usually. It's all a matter of how hands on or hands off you can afford to be. If your profit margin is tight, you may have to do most all your own repairs and bookkeeping in order to show a profit. This will take some hours per month. If your profit margin is greater, you may be able to farm more of that work out and simply collect your money at the end of the month. Either way, your investment will most always appreciate in value while your indebtedness (the mortgage) gradually goes down. Eventually, you will be in a position to sell that property at a nice lump sum profit— or else keep on renting it with very little monthly overhead, keeping almost all of the rental income yourself.

Businesses that throw off royalties or recurring commissions are another form of passive business income. My old telecom consulting business still pays me royalties each month. People in the insurance business continue to make commissions on policies they sold years and years ago. This book is another perfect example. With any luck, it will continue to provide me with an income for many, many years, although that is obviously not the primary reason I wrote it. Intellectual property (books, music, etc.) is a gift that keeps on giving.

Have Fun

I have to end this book with this one, final, and most important message: Life is what you make of it. Money is not everything, but being poor certainly stinks. **Wealth does not buy you happiness, but it gives you**

flexibility and options. Security is relative, but it is easier to *think* that you're secure if you have your financial house in order than if you don't. As much as a "control freak" as I am, I never forget the saying, "Man makes plans; God laughs." Alcoholics Anonymous always preaches the Serenity Prayer—"Grant me the serenity to accept the things I cannot change, the courage to change the things that I can, and the wisdom to know the difference." I like that a lot, and I'm not even an alcoholic.

Happiness comes from within. I know a lot of depressed millionaires, and even a billionaire. The happiest people I know are not necessarily the richest, but the ones who have attained their "center." They no longer care what anyone else thinks about them, they are not out to impress everybody, they don't care if the guy next door buys a bigger private jet than theirs; they're just doing what they like to do and they're creating their own challenges for themselves.

Life is a challenge. The nature of that challenge, though, is what you declare it to be. For a chef, it might be to keep creating new tastes and aromas, to open up a restaurant that will make everyone swoon, and once that is done, to simply keep on going—pushing the envelope into newer and more exotic cuisines. **Success is relative and if you are chasing someone else's idea of success, you may never be truly happy.** Be passionate about what you do, and if you take care of your finances, you will have the freedom to pursue your passion with verve and with little or no restrictions.

Surround yourself with people who you like and enjoy spending time with. I hate phony friends. Sure, I lecture that you should use socialization to move your career and financial goals forward. But know in your brain who your true friends are. I like to think I'm a pretty good judge of character. I know that some of the people who take me out to lunch or who invite me out on ski trips are not my best friends—they are hungry and ambitious people who want something from me. I can accept that up to a point. As long as things reach an even keel where we have a mutually beneficial relationship, I can share a steak or a joke with them from time to time. But I like to think I read people well. There's an old saying that states that your real friends are the ones you can call for bail money in the middle of the night; no questions asked. I've never needed to have anyone post bail for me, but I understand what they're saying: **Know the difference between friends and acquaintances. Avoid drama whenever possible.** I micromanage and I argue over principle sometimes, but once I turn my back and walk away, I try to leave the drama behind as well. There are things worth staying upset about and then there's everything else. Most of life is "everything else." **Be a positive person.** No one likes the perpetual victim. Believe me, we will all get screwed royally at least once or twenty times in our lives. Be reasonable in how much you should expect everyone else to come and comfort you when this happens. Instead, be like the bobbin that floats above the crashing waves. Yin and yang. Every bit of bad luck is usually followed by a bit of good luck. But speaking of luck, remember—successful people create their *own* luck. Luck is the product of good planning.

I once read about some big Hollywood mogul who was in the running to purchase a major studio, but got shut down by a competitor in the eleventh hour. Do you know what he said once it was apparent he had been beaten in that very public business arena? "Next!" He was ready for the next battle. He knew that in the end, it was only money and that nothing that had happened to him had put him in the poor house. Life would go on. He lost out on a deal and someone else won. "Next!" Bring on the next adventure.

Focus on giving 110% in whatever it is you do. This is easier to do when you are pursuing your passion. **Identify that passion and go for it.** But even if you get sidetracked though life; still give it all that you've got. Life is funny sometimes. People often take very circuitous routes to their final destination.

Teenage Mutant Ninja Turtles. It is said that this franchise, which has made *billions* of dollars since its inception, all started with a drawing two young guys made for a prototype of a stuffed animal. But they couldn't get anyone to finance the stuffed toy, nor did they have any money to put such a program together themselves.

So they ventured into turning the single drawing into one single-issue comic book. The black and white comic was cheap and easy to reproduce and sell on the underground comic book market. And sell it did. Eventually, investors came around and soon the two were financed to produce a comic book series. Still, no stuffed animal. The comic book series took off and suddenly, Saturday morning cartoons beckoned. From there it was feature films, toothpaste, breakfast cereal, Disney; you name it. And yes, eventually stuffed toys. These two guys were multimillionaires many times over before they finally achieved their original creative dream—a child's plush play toy.

Have fun. **If you hate your life, change it.** If you think the only way to have fun is to sail a yacht, but you can't afford one, buy a little sail boat and sail that. None of us knows how long we'll be here on earth. Too many people say, "I'll be happy tomorrow." Well, tomorrow is here. Be happy now. That doesn't mean go out and do something fiscally irresponsible. They say the best things in life are free, and a lot of them are. So while you have your long-range goals such as that big ol' yacht, work on being happy today as well. It can be done on almost any budget.